POWERSCORE
TEST PREPARATION

LSAT
LOGIC
GAMES
BIBLE

A Comprehensive System for Attacking the Logic Games Section of the LSAT

Published by
PowerScore Publishing, a division of PowerScore Incorporated
57 Hasell Street
Charleston, SC 29401

Author: David M. Killoran

Manufactured in Canada
January 2011

ISBN: 978-0-9801782-0-3

PowerScore Publications

PowerScore LSAT Logic Games Bible Workbook

The PowerScore LSAT Logic Games Bible Workbook™ is the ideal companion to the *PowerScore Logic Games Bible™*, providing the opportunity to apply the concepts and approaches presented in the renowned *Games Bible*. *The Logic Games Workbook* contains thirty logic games, reproduced in their entirety from actual released past LSATs, and multiple drills created to reinforce the skills you need to effectively attack the Logic Games section. Each game's answer key presents an ideal setup for the game, with every rule and important logical inference discussed and diagrammed, and all of the questions answered and explained.

Available on the PowerScore website for $29.99.
Website: www.powerscore.com/pubs.htm

PowerScore LSAT Game Type Training

LSAT Game Type Training provides you with the complete text of every LSAT Logic Game from LSAT PrepTests 1 through 20, sorted according to the games classification system used in the *PowerScore LSAT Logic Games Bible*.

Containing 80 different games, including hard-to-find games from the early PrepTests, this book is an ideal training tool to increase your LSAT Logic Games score.

Available on the PowerScore website for $29.99.
Website: www.powerscore.com/pubs.htm

PowerScore LSAT Game Type Training II

LSAT Game Type Training II provides you with the complete text of every LSAT Logic Game from LSAT PrepTests 21 through 40, sorted according to the games classification system used in the *PowerScore LSAT Logic Games Bible*. Containing 80 different games, this book is an ideal training tool to increase your LSAT Logic Games score.

Available on the PowerScore website for $44.99.
Website: www.powerscore.com/pubs.htm

PowerScore LSAT Logical Reasoning Bible

One of the most highly anticipated publications in LSAT history, the *PowerScore LSAT Logical Reasoning Bible™* is a comprehensive how-to manual for solving every type of Logical Reasoning question. Featuring over 100 real Logical Reasoning questions with detailed explanations, the Bible is the ultimate resource for improving your LSAT Logical Reasoning score.

Available on the PowerScore website for $49.99.
Website: www.powerscore.com/pubs.htm

PowerScore LSAT Logical Reasoning Bible Workbook

The PowerScore LSAT Logical Reasoning Bible Workbook™ is an ideal companion to the renowned *PowerScore Logical Reasoning Bible™*, designed specifically to test and reinforce *Logical Reasoning Bible™* concepts and strategies. The Workbook features a full chapter of reasoning drills, as well as six LSAT Logical Reasoning sections presented in their entirety (over 150 LSAC-released Logical Reasoning questions in all), followed by complete explanations of every stimulus, question, and answer choice.

Available on the PowerScore website for $34.99.
Website: www.powerscore.com/pubs.htm

PowerScore Flashcards

PowerScore Logic Games Bible Flashcards

The Logic Games Bible Flashcards relay and test foundational concepts such as games terminology, game-type recognition, and rule language, as well as advanced conceptual approaches including conditional reasoning, formal logic, and numerical distribution. Mini-challenges allow test takers to develop the skills necessary to create effective diagrams and draw sound logical inferences. Each set includes 140 cards that test the concepts and approaches to logic games taught in the *PowerScore LSAT Logic Games Bible* and in PowerScore LSAT courses.

Available on the PowerScore website for $24.99.
Website: www.powerscore.com/pubs.htm

PowerScore Logical Reasoning Bible Flashcards

The Logical Reasoning Bible Flashcards introduce and test concepts taught in our courses and in PowerScore's LSAT Logical Reasoning Bible. The flashcards cover everything from foundational definitions and question type recognition to more advanced Logical Reasoning skills, including causal reasoning, conditional reasoning, and understanding formal logic. *The Logical Reasoning Bible Flashcards* can be used as a stand-alone study aid, or as an ideal complement to the renowned *Logical Reasoning Bible*.

Available on the PowerScore website for $29.99.
Website: www.powerscore.com/pubs.htm

Tutoring and Admissions Counseling

PowerScore LSAT Private, Virtual, and Telephone Tutoring

PowerScore Private Tutoring gives students the opportunity to work one-on-one with a PowerScore tutor for the most specialized learning experience. Whether you need personalized lesson plans or you want a review on a few concepts, PowerScore can create a tutoring experience that will address all of your LSAT difficulties.

Our tutors have all scored in the 99th percentile on an actual LSAT. Aside from mastering the test themselves, every PowerScore tutor can clearly explain the underlying principles of the LSAT to any student.

PowerScore offers individual tutoring hours or tutoring packages. Please visit www.powerscore.com, or call 1-800-545-1750 for more information.

PowerScore Law School Admissions Counseling

While your LSAT score and GPA will undeniably be major factors during your admissions cycle, to truly separate yourself from the rest of the applicant pool you must assemble the most powerful application folder possible. To do this you must have an outstanding personal statement, top-notch letters of recommendation, and flawless overall presentation.

PowerScore has gathered a team of admissions experts—including former law school admissions board members, top lawyers, and students from top-twenty law schools—to address your admissions counseling and personal statement needs and help you get to where you want to be.

Please visit www.powerscore.com, or call 1-800-545-1750 for more information.

CONTENTS

CHAPTER ONE: INTRODUCTION

CHAPTER TWO: LINEAR GAMES

CHAPTER THREE: ADVANCED LINEAR GAMES

CHAPTER FOUR: GROUPING GAMES

CHAPTER FIVE: GROUPING/LINEAR COMBINATION GAMES

CHAPTER SIX: PURE SEQUENCING GAMES

CHAPTER SEVEN: THE FORGOTTEN FEW

CHAPTER EIGHT: ADVANCED FEATURES AND TECHNIQUES

CHAPTER NINE: SECTION STRATEGY AND MANAGEMENT

APPENDIXES

ENDNOTES

About PowerScore

PowerScore is one of the nation's fastest growing test preparation companies. Founded in 1997, PowerScore offers LSAT, GMAT, GRE, and SAT preparation classes in over 125 locations in the U.S. and abroad. Preparation options include Full-length courses, Weekend courses, Virtual courses, and private tutoring. For more information, please visit our website at www.powerscore.com or call us at (800) 545-1750.

For supplemental information about this book, please visit the Logic Games Bible website at www.powerscore.com/gamesbible. The website contains additions to the text and answers to questions submitted by students.

CHAPTER ONE: INTRODUCTION

Introduction

Welcome to the *PowerScore LSAT Logic Games Bible*. The purpose of this book is to provide you with a complete and cohesive system for attacking the Analytical Reasoning section of the Law School Admission Test (LSAT). By carefully studying and correctly applying the techniques we employ, we are certain that you will increase your Analytical Reasoning score.

In an effort to clearly explain the fundamental principles of the Analytical Reasoning section (also known as *Logic Games*), each chapter of this book contains a variety of drills, explanations, and Logic Games. The explanations and drills have been created by the staff at PowerScore, makers of the world's best LSAT preparation courses. The techniques in this book have been tested in live classes, through individual tutoring, and on the LSAT itself. Each Logic Game comes from an actual LSAT and is used with the permission of Law Services, the producers of the LSAT. We feel the use of real Logic Games is essential to your success on the LSAT, and no game in this book has been modified from its original form on the LSAT.

Each part of this book has been designed to reinforce your understanding of the concepts behind the Logic Games section. In order to effectively and efficiently apply our methods, we strongly recommend that you carefully read and then reread each of the discussions regarding game recognition, rule diagramming, and inference production. Also, we suggest that as you finish each question you look not only at the correct answer choice, but also at the incorrect answer choices. Look again at the problem and determine which elements led to the correct answer. Study the explanations and setups provided in the book and check them against your own work. By doing so you will greatly increase your chances of scoring high on the Logic Games section.

Finally, in our LSAT courses, our admissions counseling programs, and in our publications, we always strive to present the most accurate and up-to-date information available. Consequently, we have devoted a section of our website to *Logic Games Bible* students. This free online resource area offers supplements to the book material, answers questions posed by students, offers study plans, and provides updates as needed. There is also an official book evaluation form that we strongly encourage you to use. The exclusive *LSAT Logic Games Bible* online area can be accessed at:

www.powerscore.com/gamesbible

> If you are looking to further improve your LSAT score, we also recommend that you pick up a copy of the renowned PowerScore LSAT Logical Reasoning Bible. The Logical Reasoning Bible contains our system for attacking the Logical Reasoning section of the LSAT. When combined with the Logic Games Bible, you will have a formidable methodology for attacking the test. The LSAT Logical Reasoning Bible is available through our website at www.powerscore.com and at fine retailers everywhere.

If we can assist you in your LSAT preparation in any way, or if you have any questions or comments, please do not hesitate to email us at lgbible@powerscore.com. Additional contact information is provided at the end of this book. We look forward to hearing from you!

A Brief Overview of the LSAT

The Law School Admission Test is administered four times a year: in February, June, September/October, and December. This standardized test is required for admission to any American Bar Association-approved law school. According to Law Services, the producers of the test, the LSAT is designed "to measure skills that are considered essential for success in law school: the reading and comprehension of complex texts with accuracy and insight; the organization and management of information and the ability to draw reasonable inferences from it; the ability to think critically; and the analysis and evaluation of the reasoning and arguments of others." The LSAT consists of the following five sections:

- •2 Sections of Logical Reasoning (short arguments, 24-26 questions each)
- •1 Section of Reading Comprehension (3 long reading passages, 2 short comparative reading passages, 26-28 total questions)
- •1 Section of Analytical Reasoning (4 logic games, 22-24 total questions)
- •1 Experimental Section of one of the above three section types.

You are given 35 minutes to complete each section. The experimental section is unscored and is not returned to the test taker. A break of 10 to 15 minutes is given between the 3rd and 4th sections.

The five-section test is followed by a 35 minute writing sample.

When you take an actual LSAT, they take your thumbprint at the testing site. This is done in case of test security problems.

The Logical Reasoning Section

Each Logical Reasoning Section is composed of approximately 24 to 26 short arguments. Every short argument is followed by a question such as: "Which one of the following weakens the argument?" "Which one of the following parallels the argument?" or "Which one of the following must be true according to the argument?" The key to this section is time management and an understanding of the reasoning types and question types that frequently appear.

Since there are two scored sections of Logical Reasoning on every LSAT, this section accounts for approximately 50% of your score.

At the conclusion of the LSAT, and for five business days after the LSAT, you have the option to cancel your score. Unfortunately, there is no way to determine exactly what your score would be before cancelling.

The Analytical Reasoning Section

This section, also known as Logic Games, is probably the most difficult for students taking the LSAT for the first time. The section consists of four games or puzzles, each followed by a series of five to eight questions. The questions are designed to test your ability to evaluate a set of relationships and to make inferences about those relationships. To perform well on this section you must understand the types of games that frequently appear and develop the ability to properly diagram the rules and make inferences.

The Reading Comprehension Section

This section is composed of three long reading passages, each approximately 450 words in length, and two shorter comparative reading passages. The passage topics are drawn from a variety of subjects, and each passage is followed by a series of five to eight questions that ask you to determine viewpoints in the passage, analyze organizational traits, evaluate specific sections of the passage, or compare facets of two different passages.

The Experimental Section

Each LSAT contains one undesignated experimental section, and it does not count towards your score. The experimental can be any of the three section types described above, and the purpose of the section is to test and evaluate questions that will be used on *future* LSATs. By pretesting questions before their use in a scored section, the experimental helps the makers of the test determine the test scale.

The Writing Sample

For many years the Writing Sample was administered before the LSAT.

A 35-minute Writing Sample is given at the conclusion of the LSAT. The Writing Sample is not scored, but a copy is sent to each of the law schools to which you apply. In the Writing Sample you are asked to write a short essay that defends one of two possible courses of action.

You must attempt the Writing Sample! If you do not, Law Services reserves the right not to score your test.

Do not agonize over the Writing Sample; in law school admissions, the Writing Sample is not a major determining element for three reasons: the admissions committee is aware that the essay is given after a grueling three hour test and is about a subject you have no personal interest in; they already have a better sample of your writing ability in the personal statement; and the committee has a limited amount of time to evaluate applications.

The LSAT Scoring Scale

Each administered LSAT contains approximately 101 questions, and each LSAT score is based on the total number of questions a test taker correctly answers, a total known as the raw score. After the raw score is determined, a unique Score Conversion Chart is used for each LSAT to convert the raw score into a scaled LSAT score. Since June 1991, the LSAT has utilized a 120 to 180 scoring scale, with 120 being the lowest possible score and 180 being the highest possible score. Notably, this 120 to 180 scale is just a renumbered version of the 200 to 800 scale most test takers are familiar with from the SAT and GMAT. Just drop the "1" and add a "0" to the 120 and 180.

Although the number of questions per test has remained relatively constant over the last eight years, the overall logical difficulty of each test has varied. This is not surprising since the test is made by humans and there is no precise way to completely predetermine logical difficulty. To account for these variances in test "toughness," the test makers adjust the Scoring Conversion Chart for each LSAT in order to make similar LSAT scores from different tests mean the same thing. For example, the LSAT given in June may be logically more difficult than the LSAT given in December, but by making the June LSAT scale "looser" than the December scale, a 160 on each test would represent the same level of performance. This scale adjustment, known as equating, is extremely important to law school admissions offices around the country. Imagine the difficulties that would be posed by unequated tests: admissions officers would have to not only examine individual LSAT scores, but also take into account which LSAT each score came from. This would present an information nightmare.

The LSAT Percentile Table

It is important not to lose sight of what LSAT scaled scores actually represent. The 120 to 180 test scale contains 61 different possible scores. Each score places a student in a certain relative position compared to other test takers. These relative positions are represented through a percentile that correlates to each score. The percentile indicates where the test taker ranks in the overall pool of test takers. For example, a score of 165 represents the 93rd percentile, meaning a student with a score of 165 scored better than 93 percent of the people who have taken the test in the last three years. The percentile is critical since it is a true indicator of your positioning relative to other test takers, and thus law school applicants.

Charting out the entire percentage table yields a rough "bell curve." The number of test takers in the 120s and 170s is very low (only 1.6% of all test takers receive a score in the 170s), and most test takers are bunched in the middle, comprising the "top" of the bell. In fact, approximately 40% of all test takers score between 145 and 155 inclusive, and about 70% of all test takers score between 140 and 160 inclusive.

The median score on the LSAT scale is approximately 151. The median, or middle, score is the score at which approximately 50% of test takers have a lower score and 50% of test takers have a higher score. Typically, to achieve a score of 151, you must answer between 56 and 61 questions correctly from a total of 101 questions. In other words, to achieve a score that is perfectly average, you can miss between 40 and 45 questions. Thus, it is important to remember that you don't have to answer every question correctly in order to receive an excellent LSAT score. There is room for error, and accordingly you should never let any single question occupy an inordinate amount of your time.

Since the LSAT has 61 possible scores, why didn't the test makers change the scale to 0 to 60? Probably for merciful reasons. How would you tell your friends that you scored a 3 on the LSAT? 123 sounds so much better.

There is no penalty for answering incorrectly on the LSAT. Therefore, you should guess on any questions you cannot complete.

The Law School Admission Council uses a variety of names that all refer to one or more portions of the entire operation that administers the LSAT and attendant services. These names include Law Services, LSAC, and LSAS, and you will see various references to those names throughout this book. There is no need for you to know the meaning of each specific name.

The use of the LSAT in law school admissions is not without controversy. It is largely taken for granted that your LSAT score is one of the most important determinants of the type of school you can attend. At many law schools a multiplier made up of your LSAT score and your undergraduate grade point average is used to help determine the relative standing of applicants, and at some schools a sufficiently high multiplier guarantees your admission.

For all the importance of the LSAT, it is not without flaws. As a standardized test currently given in the paper-and-pencil format, there are a number of skills that the LSAT cannot measure, such as listening skills, note-taking ability, perseverance, etc. Law Services is aware of these limitations and as a matter of course they warn all law schools about overemphasizing LSAT results. Still, since the test ultimately returns a number for each student, it is hard to escape the tendency to rank applicants accordingly. Fortunately, once you get to law school the LSAT is forgotten. For the time being consider the test a temporary hurdle you must leap in order to reach the ultimate goal.

For more information on the LSAT, or to register for the test, contact Law Services at (215) 968-1001 or at their website at www.lsat.com.

The Analytical Reasoning Section

As you know, the focus of this book is on the Analytical Reasoning section. Each Analytical Reasoning section contains four games and a total of 22-24 questions. Since you have thirty-five minutes to complete the section, you have an average of eight minutes and forty-five seconds to complete each game. Of course, the amount of time you spend on each game will vary with the difficulty and the number of questions per game. For many students, the time constraint is what makes Logic Games the most difficult section on the LSAT, and as we progress through this book, we will discuss time management techniques as well as timesaving techniques that you can employ within the section.

Each logic game contains three separate parts: the scenario, the rules, and the questions.

The Scenario

The game scenario introduces sets of variables—people, places, things, or events—involved in an easy to understand activity such as sitting in seats or singing songs. Here is an example of a game scenario:

> Seven comics—Janet, Khan, Leticia, Ming, Neville, Olivia, and Paul—
> will be scheduled to perform in the finals of a comedy competition.
> During the evening of the competition, each comic, performing alone,
> will give exactly one performance.

In the above scenario there are two variable sets: the comics J, K, L, M, N, O, and P, and the seven performance positions, which would be numbered 1 through 7.

In basic terms, the scenario "sets the table" for the game and provides you with a quick picture of the situation to be analyzed. Although many game scenarios simply introduce the variables, on occasion the test makers place numerical information in the scenario, and this information is critical to understanding the possibilities inherent in the game.

Because you cannot afford to misunderstand any of the basics of the game, you must read the game scenario very closely.

On average, you have 8 minutes and 45 seconds to complete each game.

The last chapter of this book contains an extensive discussion of overall section time management.

Always write down and keep track of each variable set.

The Rules

The second part of every game is the rules—a set of statements that describe and control the relationships between the variables. Here are the rules that accompany the above game scenario:

> Neville performs either second or sixth.
> Paul performs at some time after Leticia performs.
> Janet performs at some time after Khan performs.
> There is exactly one performance between Neville's
>   performance and Olivia's performance, whether or
>   not Neville performs before Olivia performs.

The initial rules apply to every question unless otherwise indicated.

Each of the initial rules in a game applies to each and every question; however, on occasion a question will explicitly suspend one or more rules for the purposes of that question only. These "suspension" questions always occur at the end of the game.

The third and final part of each logic game is a set of approximately five to eight questions that test your knowledge of the relationships between the variables, the structural features of the game, and the way those relationships and features change as conditions in the game change. More on the questions in a moment.

Approaching the Games

Always read through the entire scenario and each rule before you begin diagramming.

As you begin each game you should carefully and completely read through the entire game scenario and all of the rules *before* you begin writing. This initial reading will help you determine the type of game you are facing, as well as what variable sets exist and what relationships govern their actions. This advice will save you time by allowing you to formulate an exact plan of action, and it will save you from diagramming a rule and then re-diagramming if you find a later rule that alters the situation. At this point in the game you must also fix the rules in your memory. Students who fail to identify strongly with the rules inevitably struggle with the questions. It is also important to identify the most powerful rules in a game and to consider how the rules interact with one another. Of course, we will discuss how to do this throughout our analysis.

In general, these are the initial steps you must take to efficiently move through each game:

1. Read through and fix the rules in your mind.
2. Diagram the scenario and the rules.
3. Make inferences.
4. Use the rules and inferences to attack the questions.

Your initial reading of the game will also indicate what setup to use to attack the game. Many students are not aware of the best ways to set up logic games, and waste far too much time during the actual exam wondering what approach to take. Because you must read the rules and set up a diagram quickly and efficiently, the key to succeeding on the Logic Games section is to know the ideal approach to every game type before walking into the exam.

One of the goals of this book is to teach you how to create the ideal setup for any game you encounter.

You should use the space at the bottom of each game page to diagram your initial setup. This setup should include:

Make a main diagram at the bottom of the page.

1. A list of the variables and their number. For example: J K L M N O P [7]
2. An identification of any randoms in the game (randoms are variables that do not appear in any rules).
3. A diagrammatic representation of the variable sets.
4. A diagrammatic representation of the rules.
5. A list of inferences. Making inferences involves deducing hidden rules or facts from the given relationships between variables. Inferences almost always follow from a combination of the rules or limiting structural factors within the game.

By following the above list and using the scenario and rules from the previous pages, we can produce the setup on the following page:

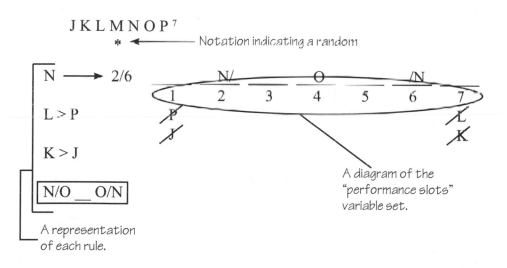

The above setup is linear in nature, and in the next chapter, we will further discuss this type of game, as well as how to create this type of diagram.

Once you have completed your game setup, you should *not* draw or otherwise write on your main diagram again. As you do each question, use the space *next* to the question to reproduce a miniature diagram with the basic structural features of your main diagram. You should *not* use your main diagram for the work of individual questions. For example, if

After making the initial setup, do not write on your main diagram.

a question introduces the condition that L sits in the third of seven chairs, draw the seven chair spaces next to the question, place L in the third space, make inferences, and then proceed with the question. Refer to your main setup for the details of the relationship between the variables. There are several important benefits that you receive from working next to the question: First, should you need to return to the question later, your work will be readily available and accessible; second, keeping the individual conditions of each question separate from the main setup reduces the possibility that you will mistake a local condition for a global rule; and third, you will be able to more clearly see which conditions produced which results.

Do the work for each question next to that question.

As you complete each question, it is absolutely essential that you *not* erase your previous work. Each question that you complete adds to your repository of game knowledge, and that knowledge can be invaluable when answering other questions. For example, suppose the first question in a game produces a scenario where A is in the first position. Then, the second question asks for a complete and accurate listing of the positions A can occupy. Based on the first question, A can clearly be in the first position, and therefore you can eliminate any answer in the second question which does not contain the first position as a possibility. Thus, the work you do in *some* questions can be used to help answer other questions. This is true as long as the work you are referencing conforms to the conditions in the question you are currently answering. For example, if the third question in the same game states, "If A is in the third position, which of the following can be true?" then you cannot use the information from the first question to help answer the third question because A was in the first position in the first question, and thus does not fit the condition imposed in the third question.

Do not erase unless you make a mistake.

The work done on some questions can be used to help solve other questions.

For students who ignore the above recommendations, the results are often quite negative: confusion, disorganization, constant rereading of the rules, and missed questions. Some students say that they save time by using their main diagram for each question. While they may save a short amount of time, the overall costs always outweigh the benefits, particularly since those same students have a tendency to erase during the game. As we proceed with our analysis of the games section, we will revisit this topic from time to time and ultimately prove the efficacy of our recommendations.

The Questions

Once you have completed your diagram and made inferences, you will be ready to answer the questions. Keep in mind that each question has exactly the same value and that there is no penalty for guessing. Thus, if you cannot complete the section you should guess on the questions that remain. If you cannot complete an individual question, do not spend an undue amount of time on the question. Instead, move on and complete the other questions.

Games questions are either global or local. Global questions ask about information derived only from the initial rules, such as "Who can finish first?" or "Which one of the following must be true?" Use the rules and your main diagram to answer global questions. Local questions generally begin with the words "if," "when," or "suppose," and occur when the question imposes a new condition in addition to the initial rules, such as "If Laura sits in the third chair, which one of the following must be true?" The additional conditions imposed by local questions apply to that question only and do not apply to any of the other questions. It is essential that you focus on the implications of the new conditions. Ask yourself how this condition affects the variables and the existing rules. For local questions, reproduce a mini-setup next to the question, apply the local condition, and proceed. We will discuss how to do this in our games discussion in the next chapter.

Within the global/local designation all questions ultimately ask for one of four things: what must be true, what is not necessarily true, what could be true, and what cannot be true. All questions are a variation of one of these four basic ideas, which we will discuss in greater detail in Chapter Two. At all times, you must be aware of the exact nature of the question you are being asked, especially when "except" questions appear. If you find that you are missing questions because you miss words such as "false" or "except" when reading, then take a moment at the beginning of the game to circle the key words in each question, words such as "must," "could," etc.

The key to quickly answering questions is to identify with the rules and inferences in a game. This involves both properly diagramming the rules and simple memorization. If you often find yourself rereading the rules during a game, you are failing to identify with the rules. And do not forget to constantly apply your inferences to each question!

Guessing strategy is discussed in the last chapter of this book.

Local questions almost always require you to produce a "mini-setup" next to the question.

If you frequently misread questions, circle the key part of each question before you begin the game. You will not forget about a word like "except" if you have it underlined!

Attacking the Section

The key to optimal performance on Logic Games is to be focused and organized. This involves a number of factors:

1. Play to your strengths and away from your weaknesses

You are not required to do the games in the order presented on the test, and you should not expect that the test makers will present the games in the best order for you. Students who expect to have difficulty on the games section should attack the games in order of their personal preferences and strengths and weaknesses. You can implement this strategy by quickly previewing each of the four games as you start the section. By doing so you can then select a game that you feel is the best fit for your strengths.

2. Create a strong setup for the game

Often, the key to powerful games performance is to create a good setup. At least 80% of the games on the LSAT are "setup games" wherein the quality of your setup dictates whether or not you are successful in answering the questions. In the following chapters, make sure to focus on the guidelines given for diagramming and inference-making. Mastering those elements will help you become an expert in handling any type of game.

3. Look to make inferences

There are always inferences in a game, and the test makers expect you to make at least a few of them. Always check the rules and your setup with an eye towards finding inferences, and then use those inferences relentlessly to attack the questions.

4. Be smart during the game

If necessary, skip over time consuming questions and return to them later. Remember that it is sometimes advisable to do the questions out of order. For example, if the first question in a game asks you for a complete and accurate list of the positions "C" could occupy, because of time considerations it would be advisable to skip that question and complete the remaining questions. Then you could return to the first question and use the knowledge you gained from the other questions to quickly and easily answer the first question.

Although test takers have found the first game on many LSATs to be the easiest, there is no set order of difficulty, and you cannot predict where the easiest or hardest game will appear. On some tests the first game has been the hardest and the last game has been the easiest. That said, for the majority of LSATs, the hardest game usually appears second or third, and the easiest game usually appears first.

5. Do not be intimidated by size

A lengthy game scenario and a large number of initial rules do not necessarily equal greater difficulty. Some of the longest games are easy because they contain so many restrictions and limitations.

6. Keep an awareness of time

As stated previously, you have approximately eight minutes and forty-five seconds to complete each game and bubble in your answers. Use a timer during the LSAT so you always know how much time remains, and do not let one game or question consume so much time that you suffer later on.

7. Maintain a positive attitude and concentrate

Above all, you must attack each game with a positive and energetic attitude. The games themselves are often challenging yet fun, and students who actively involve themselves in the games generally perform better overall.

Chapter One is a basic overview of the Logic Games section; subsequent chapters will explain and expand on the ideas presented in this chapter.

Memorize these points! They are basic principles you must know in order to perform powerfully.

If you do all four games, you have 8 minutes and 45 seconds to complete each game, inclusive of answer transferring. If you do only three games, you have 11 minutes and 40 seconds to complete each game. If you do just two games, you have 17 minutes and 30 seconds to complete each game.

You can do the games out of order and according to your strengths and weaknesses.

There are three parts to every Logic Game: the scenario, the rules, and the questions.

Always read the scenario and rules once through before you begin diagramming.

Fix the rules in your mind.

Make a main diagram for each game. Include the following:
    List the variables and their exact total number
    Identify randoms
    Diagram the variable sets
    Diagram the rules
    Make inferences
    Identify the powerful rules and variables

Write neatly.

You can do the questions out of order if it saves time or is more efficient.

For local questions, do your work next to the question.

Always look to use your inferences when answering questions.

Do not erase unless you have made a mistake.

Do not forget that work from one question might be useful on other questions.

Maintain a positive attitude, concentrate, and try to enjoy yourself.

CHAPTER TWO: LINEAR GAMES

The Concept of Linearity

Linearity involves the fixed positioning and ordering of variables. In every Linear game, one of the variable sets is chosen as the "base" and is diagrammed in a straight line, either horizontally or vertically, and the remaining variable sets are placed into slots above or next to the base. For example, consider this game scenario:

> A tutor is planning a daily schedule of individual tutoring sessions for each of six students—S, T, W, X, Y, and Z. The tutor will meet with exactly one student at a time, for exactly one hour each session. The tutor will meet with students starting at 1 P. M., for six consecutive hours.

In this game, the hours would be chosen as the base because they have an inherent sense of order (2 P. M. comes immediately after 1 P. M., and immediately before 3 P. M., etc.). The six students would then be placed into individual slots above the six hours, as follows:

S T W X Y Z ⟶ 　 $\underline{\hphantom{x}}$ 　 $\underline{\hphantom{x}}$ 　 $\underline{\hphantom{x}}$ 　 $\underline{\hphantom{x}}$ 　 $\underline{\hphantom{x}}$ 　 $\underline{\hphantom{x}}$
　　　　　　　　　　　1　　2　　3　　4　　5　　6

The game could also be set up vertically, and the six students would be placed into individual slots next to the hours:

Variable sets with the greatest sense of inherent order are always chosen as the base because they provide a logical framework within which to place all other variable sets. Certain types of variable sets are always chosen as the base—days of the week, for example. In the above game, if you decide to choose the six students as the base, throughout the questions you will have to keep in mind an extra fact: the order of the hours. Since choosing the days as the base eliminates this problem, it is a superior choice.

Linearity and Grouping are the two core concepts that appear in the Games section. Grouping will be discussed in Chapter Four.

Most of the examples in this chapter will assume the use of a horizontal diagram with six slots like the one to the left.

Always choose a base which has an inherent sense of order.

It is your choice whether to diagram the game horizontally or vertically, although some games demand a vertical setup, such as a game about floors of an office building, and some games demand a horizontal setup, such as a game about houses on a street.

The diagrams above reflect what is known as a one-to-one variable set relationship. In a one-to-one relationship, each variable fills exactly one slot and there are the same number of slots as variables to be placed. For example, there are six hours and six students, and one student will be tutored each hour. Thus, there is one student for each hour, and a total of six students for six hours (a numerical distribution of 1-1-1-1-1-1). The numerical relationship of the variable sets is one of the key indicators of the difficulty of a game, and we will discuss this concept again later in this chapter.

Rule Representation

Your representation of the rules is critical to your success on a game. Many students inefficiently diagram the rules and pay a heavy price when attempting to answer the questions. In representing the rules, there are two primary considerations: how to diagram the rule itself and how to show the implications of the rule on your main diagram. The following section will discuss many of the rule types that commonly appear in Linear games.

Not Laws™

Not Laws physically notate where a variable cannot be placed. For example, if a rule states, "T cannot go first," then this can be represented with a Not Law underneath the first slot:

By crossing out (also known as "negating") T under the first slot, you can easily see that T cannot be placed in that slot. Not Laws are very useful since it is essential that you establish the events that cannot be true in a game. In fact, in representing the rules, you should always search for what must be true and what cannot be true. These two characteristics represent the "endpoints" of the spectrum of possibilities within a game, and by defining the endpoints you define the range of possibilities within a game. Additionally, Global questions often appear in order to test your knowledge of what must and what cannot be true, such as "Which one of the following must be true?" (Answer: T cannot be in the first slot). Interestingly, with the above rule, the Not Law is the representation of the rule itself. In many other cases, however, Not Laws will follow after the rule has been separately represented. One such case is with blocks.

Blocks

In Linear games, blocks reflect the idea of a fixed spatial relationship between variables. Blocks represent variables that are next to one another, not next to one another, or separated by a fixed number of spaces. The basic block indicates that two variables are adjoining, as shown by the following rule:

> Y is tutored during the hour immediately before Z is tutored.

This rule should be diagrammed using the block notation $\boxed{\text{Y Z}}$. Furthermore, since Y is always ahead of Z, Z can never be first and therefore an Z Not Law should be placed under the first slot as indicated below. And, since Z is always behind Y, Y can never be last and a Y Not Law should be placed under the last slot (using the example on page 15, it is the sixth slot):

Split-Blocks

A split-block indicates that the variables are separated by a fixed number of spaces, as shown by this rule:

> D is inspected two days before E is inspected.

The rule should be diagrammed as $\boxed{\text{D \_\_\_ E}}$ (Even though D is inspected two days before E, that means that there is exactly one day between D and E). As in the previous rule, Not Laws can again be drawn based on the restrictions created by the rule:

The language used by the test makers to indicate the presence of a split-block can be confusing, and you must pay close attention to wording used. Here are three of the most frequently used language constructions in split-block rules:

CHAPTER TWO: LINEAR GAMES

In horizontal Linear games, "before" typically means "to the left of," and "after" means "to the right of."

Within the Logic Games Bible we often use proprietary terms (e.g. "Not Law") to represent concepts and techniques. The terms are used as a simple shorthand to represent complex ideas (for example, imagine how much more work you would have to do if every time you wanted to reference the idea of a "car" you had to describe exactly what a car does and how it works).

You are not required to memorize the terms we use, but a working knowledge of their meaning will allow you to gain more value from this book. What is most important, however, is that you understand the concept that underlies each term because these concepts appear on many of the LSAT games you will encounter.

Spaces Ahead or Spaces Before

When the phrase "spaces ahead" or one of its synonyms appears, count the spaces *from* one variable to the other. Consider again the rule from the prior example:

D is inspected exactly two days before E is inspected.

The phrase "two days before" indicates the presence of a split-block. In this instance, D is established as being ahead of E, by exactly two days. Starting from E, count forward:

Then:

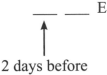

Resulting in the final block representation:

$$\boxed{\text{D \underline{\quad} E}}$$

Note that during the test you would not physically draw out each step; we do this simply to illustrate the mental process you would go through.

Spaces Behind or Spaces After

With this wording, simply reverse the process given above. For example, consider the following rule:

F marches exactly three groups behind G.

The phrase "three groups behind" indicates the presence of a split-block. In this instance, F is established as being behind G, by exactly three groups. Starting from G, count backward:

G ___

1 group behind

Then:

G ___ ___

↑

2 groups behind

Note that "spaces ahead" and "spaces behind" can be attacked in the same way. For example, in the "spaces behind" example to the left, the rule could have been viewed as stating that G was 3 groups ahead of F. In both cases the diagram is identical.

And finally:

G ___ ___ ___

↑

3 groups behind

Resulting in the final block representation:

| G ___ ___ F |

The diagrams here are presented horizontally, but they could just have easily been presented vertically.

Spaces Between or Spaces Separated By

With the phrase "spaces between" or any synonymous phrase, simply put that exact number of spaces between the two variables. Consider the following rule:

There are exactly three spaces between L and M, and M is examined before L.

The phrase "three spaces between" indicates the presence of a split-block. In this instance, M is established as being ahead of L, with exactly three examinations between them. Diagram as follows:

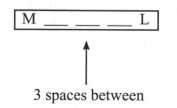

| M ___ ___ ___ L |

↑

3 spaces between

Always read carefully—the test makers will place wrong answers that will check to see if you correctly interpreted the wording of a split-block rule (for example, did you see the "between," or did you misinterpret it as "before" or "after"?).

Rotating Blocks

The previous blocks all addressed fixed relationships wherein the order of the variables was known. Rotating blocks present an extra consideration: the order of the variables is not given. For example, consider the following rule:

> S and T are displayed on consecutive days.

This rule establishes two possibilities:

and

Rotating blocks require special attention because the two options are easy to forget during the time pressure of the test.

For the sake of absolute clarity, we prefer to write out both possibilities when diagramming this rule, as follows:

$$\begin{array}{|c|} \hline S\ T \\ \hline T\ S \\ \hline \end{array}$$

We use this representation because during the time pressure of the test it is easy to forget the exact meaning of the rule or get confused if you do not have it diagrammed in an easy-to-read fashion. If you are striving for the fastest rule representation possible, diagram rotating blocks with a circle:

$$(\ S\ T\ )$$

The circle is meant to convey the idea that the two variables can "go back and forth." Throughout this book, however, we will typically diagram rotating blocks by showing both options in block form in order to reinforce the idea of multiple possibilities.

If you would like more help in memorizing the rule representations and diagram elements discussed in this book, we offer the PowerScore LSAT Logic Game Bible Flashcards, available for sale through our website.

Rotating Split-blocks

Rotating split-blocks can typically be diagrammed in more compact form than regular rotating blocks. Consider the following split-block rule:

> There are two days between the day Q is inspected and the day R is inspected.

In this case, the rule specifies that there must be two days between Q and R, but it does not specify whether Q or R is inspected first. Thus, there are two possible configurations for Q and R:

and

However, we can diagram this rule in more compact form:

The "/" notation indicates that there are two options for that space of the block. And, it is no mistake that the first option is Q/R and that the second option is R/Q. This notation allows for an efficient representation of both possibilities:

The option represented by the variables before the slash, which is:

and

The option represented by the variables after the slash, which is:

| R _ _ Q |

Not-blocks

Not-blocks, or negative blocks, indicate that variables cannot be next to one another, or cannot be separated by a fixed amount of space. Consider the following rule:

Q is not inspected the day before R is inspected.

This rule should be diagrammed with a slash over the block, as in Q/R , which means that Q can never appear in the slot before R. Interestingly, no Not Laws can be drawn from this rule until either Q or R is placed into the setup by another rule or by one of the questions.

Not-blocks can also appear with split-blocks. For example:

D is not inspected exactly two days before E is inspected.

This rule would be diagrammed as:

D / E

In Linear games, blocks tend to be much more useful than not-blocks since the placement of blocks is always a concern, whereas not-blocks only come into play once one of the variables has been placed.

Always read the rules carefully to make sure you do not miss the word "not." The presence of the word "not" typically produces an opposite diagram from rules that do not contain the word "not."

Verticality and Horizontality in Blocks

Once you decide to diagram a game horizontally or vertically, make sure your blocks properly reflect the orientation of the setup. As we have seen, in horizontal setups a block such as $\boxed{QR}$ indicates adjacency. But in a vertical setup, a block diagrammed the same way would indicate similarity or overlap, that is, the variables would both be placed in the same slot:

$\boxed{QR}$

1 ___
2 ___
3 ___
4 ___
5 ___
6 ___

In the diagram above, the QR block indicates that Q and R will be inspected on the same day, not adjoining days. To indicate that Q is inspected the day before R in the above diagram, the block should be diagrammed as:

This block is known as a vertical block. Again, Not Laws (R not in 1, Q not in 6) would follow as before.

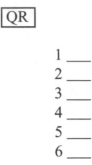

In games with vertical setups, vertical blocks indicate adjacency. In games with horizontal setups, vertical blocks indicate similarity or overlap.

In a horizontal setup, vertical blocks indicate identicalness or similarity:

$\begin{array}{|c|}\hline Q \\ R \\ \hline\end{array}$

___ ___ ___ ___ ___ ___
1   2   3   4   5   6

In the diagram above, the QR block indicates that Q and R will be inspected on the same day, not adjoining days. No Not Laws would follow from this block.

Sequencing Rules

Sequencing rules establish the relative positioning of variables. The key to differentiating a sequencing rule from a block rule is that block rules precisely fix the variables in relationship to each other (for example, one space ahead or two spaces in between) and sequencing rules do not. For example, a rule might state that

> Q is inspected before R is inspected.

To represent sequential relationships, we use ">" or "<" symbols, and thus we can diagram this rule as Q > R.

When we use the ">" symbol, we consider it to be a relative positioning indicator, not an absolute numerical value indicator. Thus, "A > B" indicates that A is to the left of B in a horizontal diagram, no more and no less. Diagramming the relationship as "A < B" would mean the same thing, and thus you can choose which representation you prefer. In this book, however, we will diagram all sequential relationships with a ">" symbol, and in each case we will take that ">" symbol to mean that the variable in front of the sign is to the left of the other variable (if this is confusing to you, simply make your diagrams with the "<" sign).

Returning to the Q > R rule, we only know that Q is inspected before R, but not by how many days. However, since Q is always inspected before R, in a diagram with six variables for six spaces, R can never be inspected first, and because R is always inspected after Q, Q can never be inspected last, and the following Not Laws result:

If the rule stated that

> Q is inspected before R is inspected but after H is inspected.

The diagram for the rule would be H > Q > R, and the following Not Laws would result:

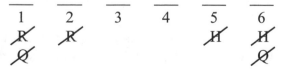

This section is only a short introduction to sequencing rules. Chapter Seven will address games based entirely on sequencing rules, and therein we will discuss the diagramming of sequencing rules in greater detail.

Three variables linked in a sequence such as the one to the left always yield six Not Laws.

On occasion, a rule such as the following will appear:

H and Q are both inspected before R is inspected.

This rule should be diagrammed as

```
    H
 - - - - > R
    Q
```

This representation is known as a Double-branched Sequence. The dotted line before the ">" sign indicates that H and Q do not have a direct relationship with each other. Visually, the dotted line creates two "branches," one above the dotted line involving H, and one below the line involving Q. The line serves as a reminder that the relationship between H and Q is uncertain: H may be inspected before Q, Q may be inspected before H (or, if more than one variable can be placed in a space, that H and Q could be inspected at exactly the same time). The only known relationship is that both H and Q must be inspected before R. From this sequence several Not Laws result in a one-to-one relationship game:

In the above diagram, R cannot be placed either first or second because there must be room for H and Q, and H and Q cannot be placed sixth since there must be room for R.

The following rule also produces a Branched Sequence:

A is inspected before B, C, and D are inspected.

This Triple-branched Sequence should be diagrammed as:

In this representation, the two dotted lines create three separate branches, one for B, one for C, and one for D. Again, we cannot ascertain the exact relationship between B, C, and D other than to say that all three are inspected after A is inspected.

From this sequential rule several Not Laws result in a one-to-one relationship game:

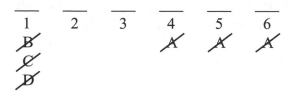

Although this short section only addresses sequential rules, do not forget that the test makers can combine rules. For example, a block can be combined with sequential rule:

F is displayed immediately prior to G, and G is displayed at some point before I.

This rule should be diagrammed as:

$$\boxed{F\ G} > I$$

The following Not Laws would result from the rule:

In Chapter Six, we will discuss sequencing rules in more depth.

Dual Options

When only two
variables can
occupy a slot,
this is known as
a dual-option.

Certain variables or slots have a limited number of possibilities. When there are only two variables that can occupy a single slot, this can be shown with a Dual Option. Consider the following rule:

Either H or J must be inspected on the third day.

In this case, since it must be true that H or J is inspected on the third day, H/J is placed on the third day. As you can see, what must be true is represented by placing the variables above the slots, and what cannot be true is represented by Not Laws below the numbers:

In the case of the dual-option above, it is also true that no other variable besides H or J can appear third, so it might seem appropriate to show Not Laws on that slot for all other variables. This representation would be correct, but since H and J are already placed on the third day, it is obvious that no other variable can be inspected on that day, and therefore showing Not Laws on the third day would be redundant. However, if you find it helpful to show the Not Laws, by all means do what works best for you.

Split Dual-Options

When a single
variable can
occupy only two
slots, this is
known as a split
dual-option, or
sometimes as a
split-option.

Occasionally, a single variable will have only two possible positions. This is known as a Split Dual-Option. Consider the following rule:

H must be inspected on the third day or the fifth day.

Of course, if H can only be inspected on the third or fifth day, H cannot be inspected on the first, second, fourth, or sixth days. Since the positioning of H is still a bit uncertain, in this case it makes sense to show H Not Laws on the other days:

Triple Options

Sometimes a rule or an inference will lead you to determine that a single space can contain only one of three variables. This is known as a Triple Option. Consider the following rule:

> A, B, or C must be displayed on the first day.

This rule would be represented directly on the diagram as follows:

$$\frac{\text{A/B/C}}{1} \quad \frac{}{2} \quad \frac{}{3} \quad \frac{}{4} \quad \frac{}{5} \quad \frac{}{6}$$

Split triple-options can also occur, but they are extremely tricky to work with, and we do not recommend that you use them as part of your rule representation arsenal.

Conditional Rules

The final type of Linear game rule is the most complex. Conditional reasoning is a fundamental component of both the Logical Reasoning and Logic Games sections of the LSAT. In the Logic Games section, conditional rules appear most often in Grouping games, and thus we will also discuss conditional reasoning in the Grouping chapter. However, since basic conditional rules appear frequently in Linear games, we will begin our discussion here.

Conditional reasoning involves sufficient and necessary conditions. A sufficient condition can be defined as an event or circumstance whose occurrence indicates that a necessary condition must also occur. A necessary condition can be defined as an event or circumstance whose occurrence is required in order for a sufficient condition to occur. In other words, if a sufficient condition occurs, you automatically know that the necessary condition also occurs. If a necessary condition occurs, then it is possible that the sufficient condition will occur, but not certain. In English, conditional statements are often brought up using the "if...then" construction. Consider the following statement:

> If you get an A+, then you must have studied.

If the above statement is true, then anyone who receives an A+ must have studied. Since getting an A+ automatically indicates that studying must have occurred, "get an A+" is the sufficient condition and it follows that "must have studied" is the necessary condition. We represent this statement as follows:

Sufficient	Necessary
A+ $\longrightarrow$	Study

The PowerScore LSAT Logical Reasoning Bible has an extensive discussion of conditional reasoning as it applies to the Logical Reasoning section of the LSAT.

In a diagram of a conditional statement, the sufficient condition always comes at the "beginning" of the arrow, and the necessary condition always comes at the "end" of the arrow. Although the above example may seem relatively easy, the makers of the LSAT often use conditional reasoning to ensnare unwary test takers, especially in the Logical Reasoning section.

Taking the above statement as true, consider the following three statements:

1. John studied for the test, so he must have received an A+ on the test.

2. John did not receive an A+ on the test, so he must not have studied on the test.

3. John did not study for the test, so he must not have received an A+ on the test.

Two of the three statements above are invalid, and one of the three statements is valid. Can you tell which one is valid?

Statement 1 is invalid. Just because John studied for the test does not mean he actually received an A+. He may have only received a B, or perhaps he even failed. This error is referred to as a Mistaken Reversal™.

Statement 2 is also invalid. Just because John did not receive an A+ does not mean he did not study. He may have studied but did not happen to receive an A+. Perhaps he received a B instead. This error is referred to as a Mistaken Negation™.

Statement 3 is valid. If studying is the necessary condition for getting an A+, and John did not study, then according to the original statement there is no way John could have received an A+. This inference is known as the contrapositive, and you can see that when the necessary condition fails to occur, then the sufficient condition cannot occur.

The form here reverses *and* negates the Study and A+ elements. When you are looking to find the contrapositive, do not think about the elements and what they represent. Instead, simply reverse and negate the two terms.

There is a contrapositive for every conditional statement, and if the initial statement is true, then the contrapositive is also true. The contrapositive is simply a different way of expressing the initial statement. To analogize, it is like examining a penny: both sides look different but intrinsically the value is the same.

One of the confusing elements in recognizing conditional statements is that so many different terms can be used to introduce sufficient or necessary conditions. Consider the following statements:

> To get an A+ you must study.
>
> Studying is necessary to get an A+.
>
> When someone gets an A+, it shows they must have studied.
>
> Only someone who studies can get an A+.
>
> Unless you study, you cannot get an A+.
>
> You will get an A+ only if you study.

Take a moment to examine the above statements. Interestingly, each of the statements would be diagrammed exactly the same way:

A contrapositive denies the necessary condition, thereby making it impossible for the sufficient condition to occur. Contrapositives can often yield important insights into a game.

Because the contrapositive both reverses and negates, it is a combination of a Mistaken Reversal and Mistaken Negation. Since the contrapositive is valid, it is as if two wrongs do make a right.

	Sufficient	Necessary
	A+ $\longrightarrow$	Study

In Logical Reasoning it is essential that you be able to recognize the many terms that identify and precede sufficient and necessary conditions. In Logic Games, the test makers typically use the following terms:

To introduce a sufficient condition: To introduce a necessary condition:

If	Then
When	Only
	Only if
	Unless

In the case of "unless," "except," "until," and "without," a special two-step process called the Unless Equation is applied to the diagram:

1. Whatever term is modified by "unless," "except," "until," or "without" becomes the necessary condition.

2. The remaining term is negated and becomes the sufficient condition.

For example, consider the following:

> Unless a person studies, he or she will not receive an A+.

Since "unless" modifies "a person studies," "Study" becomes the necessary condition. The remainder, "he or she will not receive an A+," is negated by dropping the "not" and becomes "he or she will receive an A+." Thus, the sufficient condition is "A+," and the diagram is as follows:

	Sufficient	Necessary
	A+ $\longrightarrow$	Study

Conditional Rules in Linear Games

When conditional reasoning is applied to Linear Logic Games, the rules often specify exact place assignments for the variables. For example:

> Laron performs second only if Nancy performs sixth.

In this rule, the phrase "only if" introduces a necessary condition. Rewording the sentence may help to make the relationship clearer, "If

To diagram a statement containing "unless," convert the variable modified by "unless" into the necessary condition. Take the remainder, negate it, and convert it into the sufficient condition. The same technique applies to statements containing "until," "except," and "without."

Another way to handle terms like "unless" is to substitute the phrase "if not" for "unless." The only drawback to this method is that it tends to produce diagrams containing negatives.

Laron performs second then Nancy performs sixth." This rule should be diagrammed as:

$$L_2 \longrightarrow N_6$$

Thus, any game situation where Laron performed second would force Nancy to perform sixth. However, do not make the error of mistakenly reversing the relationship. That is, if Nancy performs sixth, that does not automatically mean that Laron performs second. He *could* perform second, but he does not have to perform second. The test makers will have attractive wrong answer choices ready for you if you make a Mistaken Reversal.

Of course, via the contrapositive, if Nancy does *not* perform sixth, then Laron cannot perform second:

$$\cancel{N}_6 \longrightarrow \cancel{L}_2$$

Therefore, any situation where Nancy did not perform sixth would then preclude Laron from performing second.

Conditional rules can also involve some of the other rule representations that we have encountered thus far, for example:

Conditionality and Blocks

Examine the following rule:

> If V is displayed immediately before W, then S must be displayed third.

This rule would be diagrammed as:

$$\boxed{V\ W} \longrightarrow S_3$$

Conditionality and Sequencing

Consider the following rule:

> If Kahlil performs first, then Martin performs at some time before Paulo.

This rule would be diagrammed as:

$$K_1 \longrightarrow M > P$$

Now that you are familiar with some rule basics, try your hand at some rule representation drills.

Conditional Reasoning Mini-Diagramming Drill

Each of the following statements contains a sufficient condition and a necessary condition; therefore, each of the following statements can be described as a "conditional statement." In the spaces provided write the proper arrow diagram for each of the following conditional statements. Then write the proper arrow diagram for the contrapositive of each of the following conditional statements. *Answers on next page*

Example: If R is delivered first, then X is delivered fourth.

original diagram: R1 ——————→ X4

contrapositive: X̸4̸ ——————→ R̸1̸

1. If R is inspected on the third day, S is not inspected on the fifth day.

original diagram:

contrapositive:

2. G does not speak fourth unless Q speaks second.

original diagram:

contrapositive:

3. If F's delivery is earlier than M's, then L's delivery is earlier than H's.

original diagram:

contrapositive:

4. T dances sixth only if P dances third.

original diagram:

contrapositive:

5. B swims immediately before C only if D does not swim immediately before E.

original diagram:

contrapositive:

Conditional Reasoning Mini-Diagramming Drill Answer Key

1.   original: R3 $\longrightarrow$ S̸5̸
        (If R is inspected third then S is not inspected fifth.)

        contrapositive: S5 $\longrightarrow$ R̸3̸
        (If S is inspected fifth then R is not inspected third.)

2.   original: G4 $\longrightarrow$ Q2
        (If G speaks fourth then Q speaks second.)

        contrapositive: Q̸2̸ $\longrightarrow$ G̸4̸
        (If Q does not speak second then G does not speak fourth.)

        Note: "Unless" again determines the necessary condition.

3.   original: F > M $\longrightarrow$ L > H
        (If F > M then L > H.)

        contrapositive: L̸≯H $\longrightarrow$ F̸≯M
        (If not L > H then not F > M.)

4.   original: T6 $\longrightarrow$ P3
        (If T dances sixth then P dances third.)

        contrapositive: P̸3̸ $\longrightarrow$ T̸6̸
        (If P does not dance third then T does not dance sixth.)

        Note: "Only if" introduces a necessary condition.

5.   original: | B C | $\longrightarrow$ | D̸/̸E |
        (If BC then not DE.)

        contrapositive: | D E | $\longrightarrow$ | B̸/̸C |
        (If DE then not BC.)

        Note: "Only if" introduces a necessary condition.

As you may have noticed in the mini-drill, the contrapositive can yield some interesting insights into the relationship between the variables. You should always be on the lookout for conditional statements in Logic Games, and when you identify them, be sure to consider the implications of the contrapositive. We will discuss conditional reasoning and the contrapositive in further detail in the chapter on Grouping games.

Linear Games Rule Diagramming Drill

In the space provided, supply the best symbolic representation (if any) of each of the following rules. If applicable, show any corresponding implications (Not Laws, dual-options, etc.) on the linear diagram provided. Assume a one-to-one relationship for each item, with no ties possible. *Answers on Page 36*

1. G is recorded earlier than H.

recording positions = $\overline{\underset{1}{}}$ $\overline{\underset{2}{}}$ $\overline{\underset{3}{}}$ $\overline{\underset{4}{}}$ $\overline{\underset{5}{}}$ $\overline{\underset{6}{}}$

2. Z is selected during one of the first two days.

days = $\overline{\underset{1}{}}$ $\overline{\underset{2}{}}$ $\overline{\underset{3}{}}$ $\overline{\underset{4}{}}$ $\overline{\underset{5}{}}$ $\overline{\underset{6}{}}$

3. C must sit 4 chairs behind D, and E must sit 3 chairs before C.

chairs = $\overline{\underset{1}{}}$ $\overline{\underset{2}{}}$ $\overline{\underset{3}{}}$ $\overline{\underset{4}{}}$ $\overline{\underset{5}{}}$ $\overline{\underset{6}{}}$

4. Either S or T must speak on the third day.

days = $\overline{\underset{1}{}}$ $\overline{\underset{2}{}}$ $\overline{\underset{3}{}}$ $\overline{\underset{4}{}}$ $\overline{\underset{5}{}}$ $\overline{\underset{6}{}}$

5. Tom can sit neither immediately before nor immediately after Pat.

seats = $\overline{\underset{1}{}}$ $\overline{\underset{2}{}}$ $\overline{\underset{3}{}}$ $\overline{\underset{4}{}}$ $\overline{\underset{5}{}}$ $\overline{\underset{6}{}}$

Drill continued on the next page.

Linear Games Rule Diagramming Drill

6. If J is performed fourth, K is performed sixth.

performances =	1	2	3	4	5	6

$$J4 \rightarrow K6$$
$$\cancel{K6 \rightarrow J4}$$

7. A is not shorter than B.

$$A \doteq B$$

height (tallest first) =	1	2	3	4	5	6

8. If A sits next to B, then B does not sit next to C.

seats =	1	2	3	4	5	6

9. Y is inspected before both X and Z are inspected.

$$Y \rightarrow \boxed{XZ}$$

$$Y \rightarrow \frac{X}{Z}$$

inspections =	1	2	3	4	5	6

$$Y \rightarrow \frac{X}{Z}$$

10. M and T must be performed on consecutive days.

$$\boxed{MT}$$
$$\boxed{TM}$$

days =	1	2	3	4	5	6

1.   G > H

recording positions = 1   2   3   4   5   6
                     H̶   6̶

2.   Z ———→ 1 or 2

days =   Z/   /Z
          1   2   3   4   5   6
                    Z̶   Z̶   Z̶   Z̶

3. | D E __ __ C |

Due to the size of the block, it can only be placed in two different positions: 1-5 or 2-6. The best strategy from here would be to show those two possibilities:

Poss #2:   D   E   C
Poss #1:   D   E   C
chairs =   1   2   3   4   5   6
                 C̶   C̶   C̶   C̶   E̶   E̶
                 E̶   D̶   E̶   D̶   D̶
                                D̶

4.   3 ———→ S/T

                           S/T
days =   ___ ___ ___ ___ ___ ___
           1   2   3   4   5   6

5. | T/P | No Not Laws can be drawn from this rule.

      | P/T |

seats =   ___ ___ ___ ___ ___ ___
           1   2   3   4   5   6

6.   J4 ———→ K6   No Not Laws can be drawn from this rule.
      K̶6̶ ———→ J̶4̶

performances =   ___ ___ ___ ___ ___ ___
                  1   2   3   4   5   6

7.   A > B

If this was not a one-to-one relationship, this would be a trick question with no Not Laws, and a diagram of A ≥ B. However, according to the rule, A is not shorter than B, which means A is either taller than B, or A is the same height as B. In a one-to-one relationship where each variable completely fills a single space, A and B cannot be the same height, and thus you can infer that B is not first and A is not last, and the proper diagram for this rule is A > B.

8.

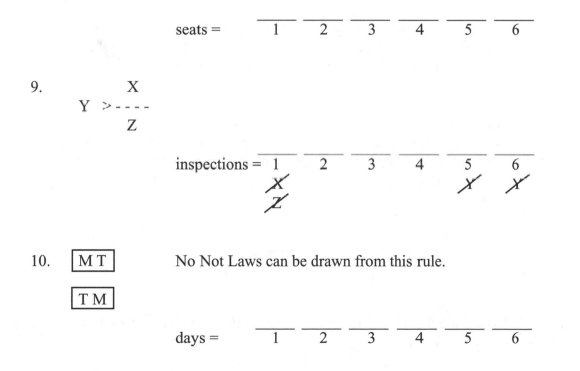

Most students diagram this rule as: AB ⟶ BC. However, the application of the rule reveals that you can *never* have ABC or CBA in a row, and thus this rule is properly represented by the not-blocks. Note, however, that ACB and BCA are still possible. Again, no Not Laws can be drawn.

9.

10.   No Not Laws can be drawn from this rule.

Final Note: In most cases not-blocks and rotating blocks do not allow you to make initial inferences. However, once other rules are added to the blocks, inferences often follow.

Internal versus External Diagramming

Up to this point we have focused on creating efficient and useful representations of the rules. Before moving on to a discussion of making inferences, let's examine one additional rule diagramming consideration.

Many rules are automatically diagrammed in "external" fashion, that is, away from or off to the side of the part of the diagram that contains the slots or spaces. Certain rules are diagrammed "internally," that is, directly on the part of the diagram that contains the slots or spaces. For example, consider the following rule:

> R cannot be inspected first.

This rule is best represented with a Not Law underneath the first slot:

This is considered an internally diagrammed rule because the representation is immediately next to or within the slots. Other rules, such as dual-options, are also best represented directly on the diagram.

Some rules, of course, cannot be diagrammed internally. A rule stating that, "When X is third then Y is sixth" must be separated from the slots and diagrammed off to the side because this rule only comes into play in certain instances.

The general rule is that if you can represent a rule efficiently within in the slotted part of the diagram, then do so. Diagramming the rule internally gives you a powerful visual reminder of the presence of the rule and lowers the chances that you will forget that rule. Consider the following situation:

> Three speakers—F, G, and H—give six consecutive one-hour speeches, two speeches per speaker. Exactly one speaker speaks during each hour.
> > The speaker that gives the first speech must also give the second speech.

Most students, when faced with this scenario, would create a setup similar to the following:

F F G G H H [6]

This external rule representation, while perfectly reasonable, does not have the same visual power as an internally diagrammed representation. At the least, the rule should also be represented directly on the diagram:

F G H ³

1 ——→ 2   ___ ___ ___ ___ ___ ___
                 1 —→ 2   3   4   5   6

This "internal" representation assures that you will never forget that rule, and it will make your analysis process during the questions faster and more compact.

Of course, if you further consider the nature of this game, since all six spaces must be filled and the speaker that gives the first speech must also give the second speech, you can infer that the first and second speakers must always be the same. This could be shown on the diagram in even more powerful fashion as a block:

F G H ³

1 ——→ 2 | 1   2 | ___ ___ ___ ___
                            3   4   5   6

This representation would assure that any time you assigned the first or second speech you would automatically assign the other speech as well.

As we move forward, you will see other instances where rules are diagrammed internally. Keep in mind that although not all rules can be diagrammed in this manner, you will gain speed and accuracy advantages when you recognize the correct situations to diagram this way.

Note that this is an unusual but valid reversal of the conditional rule given in the scenario. Conditional rules do not normally reverse in this manner, but the circumstances in this scenario allow you to infer that the first two speakers must be the same. If you are wondering why this works, think about the contrapositive and the limited number of speakers available, as well as the fact that all speech slots must be assigned.

Making Inferences

Inferences are relationships that must be true in a game but are not explicitly stated by the rules or game scenario. One of the keys to powerful games performance is making inferences after you have diagrammed all of the rules. In some games, a single inference can be the difference between the game seeming easy or difficult. For some people inference making is intuitive, and for others it is very difficult. Here are three basic but time-tested strategies for making inferences:

Linkage

Linkage should always be the first step you take to make inferences.

Linkage is the simplest and most basic way to make inferences. Linkage involves finding a variable that appears in at least two rules and then combining those two rules. Often that combination will produce an inference of value. Consider the following two rules:

> K must be played before L.
> L must be played before M.

Individually the two rules would be diagrammed as follows:

K > L
L > M

If we represented Not Laws from each rule, we would have the following:

Clearly, "L" is common to both rules. By combining the rules we come up with the following relationship:

K > L > M

Three variables in a sequence similar to the one to the right always yield 6 Not Laws.

We can now infer that K must be played before M, and this information helps us to establish all of the applicable Not Laws:

Linkage between the rules should always be the first place you look to discover inferences. Incidentally, the above example again proves the

value of reading all of the rules before you begin diagramming. If you
had diagrammed each rule individually, then later discovered the linkage,
you would then have to return to the two rules and diagram the additional
implications of the linkage. That would be an inefficient approach and thus
detract from your performance.

Here is another example featuring linkage:

These examples
of linkage all
relate to Linear
games. Other
linkage examples
will appear in the
chapters devoted
to other game
types.

> If Q is displayed fourth, then R must be displayed first.
> R and S are displayed consecutively.

Individually the two rules would be diagrammed as follows:

Q4 ⟶ R1

| R S |
| S R |

    __   __   __   __   __   __
     1   2   3   4   5   6

However, if R is first, then according to the second rule S must be second,
which should be written as:

Q4 ⟶ R1, S2

Thus, combining the two rules leads to the further inference that S must be
second when Q is fourth. Although this cannot be represented directly on
the diagram, this relationship can and should be displayed as above, as an
addition to the original representation of the first rule.

Here is final example featuring linkage:

> W and X cannot speak consecutively.
> X must speak third or fifth.

Individually the two rules would be diagrammed as follows:

Although these
three examples
each feature
linkage between
two rules, there
are situations
that arise where
three rules are
linked.

| W/X |
| X/W |

    __   __   X/   __   /X   __
     1   2   3   4   5   6

At first, it may appear that linking the two rules yields no inference, but
if X is always third or fifth, then W can never be placed fourth (to do so
would cause a violation regardless of whether X was third or fifth). This
leads to a W Not Law on 4:

    __   __   X/   __   /X   __
     1   2   3   4   5   6
                  W̷

Rule Combinations

As we study more and more game types, your arsenal of rule recognition skills will increase. In certain games, there are classic combinations which always yield certain inferences. In contrast to linkage, however, making inference from rule combinations does not rely upon the connection of a variable common to two or more rules. For example, consider this scenario:

> Six lawyers—H, J, K, L, M, and O—must speak at a convention. The six speeches are delivered one at a time, consecutively, according to the following restrictions:
>> K and L must speak consecutively.
>> O must speak fifth.

From the scenario and rules above, we can draw the following diagram:

Because of the interaction of the two rules, we can infer that K and L can never speak sixth (there is not enough room for K and L to be next to each other). In addition, because O must speak fifth, only H, J, and M remain as possible candidates to speak sixth. This could be shown as a triple-option (H/J/M):

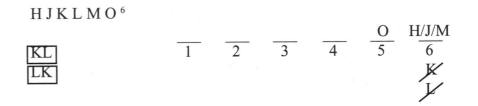

This type of rule combination is one of many we will discuss in this book.

Restrictions

In Logic Games always look to the restricted points for inferences. Restricted points are the areas in the game where only a few options exist—for example, a limited number of variables to fill in a slot, a block with a limited number of placement options, or a slot with a large number of Not Laws. If you can identify a restriction, generally there are inferences that will follow from your examination of that point. The trick is to determine exactly where the restrictions in a game actually occur.

Note that rule combination inferences are normally produced by a restriction that results from combining the two rules.

Consider the following example:

> A salesman must visit five families—the Browns, the Chans, the Duartes, the Egohs, and the Feinsteins—one after another, not necessarily in that order. The visits must conform to the following restrictions:
>> The Browns must be visited first or fifth.
>> The Feinsteins cannot be visited third.
>> The Chans must be visited fourth.

Using the scenario and rules above, we can produce the following diagram:

B C D E F⁵

$$\frac{B/}{1} \quad \frac{}{2} \quad \frac{}{3} \quad \frac{C}{4} \quad \frac{/B}{5}$$

The easiest way to find restrictions in a game is to examine the Not Laws for each slot. The slot with the most Not Laws may be so restricted that it has a limited number of possibilities. In this case, the third slot is the most restricted active slot since it has two Not Laws. Technically, the fourth slot is the most restricted since it has only one option, the Chans. But, since the fourth slot has already been filled by the Chans, it is no longer "active" and we can disregard it from further consideration. However, since the Chans have been placed, they cannot go in any other slot, and so it is now true that neither B, C, nor F can be visited third. Since there are only five families to visit and B, C, and F have been eliminated from contention, it follows that either D or E must be visited third. That inference should be shown with a D/E dual-option on the third slot:

B C D E F⁵

Restrictions also frequently occur with blocks, especially split-blocks. Consider the following scenario:

A child must play five games—P, Q, R, S, and T—one after another, not necessarily in that order. The games must be played according to the following conditions:

The child plays exactly two games between playing S and playing T, whether or not S is played before T.

P is played immediately before Q is played.

Once again, using the scenario and rules, we can produce the following initial setup:

P Q R S T [5]

| S/T __ __ T/S |
| P Q |

1	2	3	4	5
Q̸		S̸/T̸		P̸

Blocks have a
reduced number
of spacing
options and
as such they
can play a very
powerful role in
games.

As usual, P cannot be played fifth since Q must be played behind it, and Q cannot be played first since P must always be played ahead of it. However, the S and T split-block is more interesting because it has a limited number of spacing options. In fact, the ST split-block can only be placed into positions 1-4 or 2-5. Thus, S and T cannot be played third. At this point it appears that we have our inferences and that we are ready to continue on. But consider the interaction of the two blocks. If S and T are in the 1-4 position, then P and Q must be in 2-3. If S and T are in the 2-5 position, then P and Q must be in the 3-4 position. That means that either P or Q must always be played third. Additionally, we can infer that R must always be played first or fifth:

P Q R S T [5]

| S/T __ __ T/S |
| P Q |

R/		P/Q		/R
1	2	3	4	5
Q̸		S̸/T̸		P̸

Given these inferences, there are only two possible "templates" to the game based on the placement of the two blocks:

Template #2:	R	S/T	P	Q	T/S
Template #1:	S/T	P	Q	T/S	R
	1	2	3	4	5

These two templates encompass four solution sets to the game and make it abundantly clear how the interaction of some rules and game restrictions can set off a series of powerful inferences. In a later chapter we will discuss templates in detail, but you will see references to this approach throughout the book. Templates result from restrictions within the game, and in many games the best setup is one that shows these possibility blueprints.

Consider one more example:

> A doctor must see six patients—C, D, E, F, G and H—one after another, not necessarily in that order. The patients must be seen according to the following conditions:
> > E is seen exactly three patients after C.
> > D is seen immediately before F is seen.

Using the scenario and rules, we can produce the following initial setup:

C D E F G H[6]

Although this game has restrictions—the placement of the block is limited to 1-4, 2-5, or 3-6—there are still many different solutions. However, suppose for a moment that the test makers asked a question that contained a specific condition, such as:

> If G is seen third, which one of the following must be true?

The addition of this new condition affects the restrictions in the basic diagram to such an extent that only one solution is possible:

Step One: G is seen third

$$\frac{\quad}{1} \quad \frac{\quad}{2} \quad \frac{G}{3} \quad \frac{\quad}{4} \quad \frac{\quad}{5} \quad \frac{\quad}{6}$$

Step Two: The CE split-block must be placed into slots 1-4 because if it is placed in slots 2-5 there will be no room for the DF block

$$\frac{C}{1} \quad \frac{\quad}{2} \quad \frac{G}{3} \quad \frac{E}{4} \quad \frac{\quad}{5} \quad \frac{\quad}{6}$$

Step Three: The DF block must be placed into 5-6

$$\frac{C}{1} \quad \frac{}{2} \quad \frac{G}{3} \quad \frac{E}{4} \quad \frac{D}{5} \quad \frac{F}{6}$$

Step Four: H must be placed into 2

$$\frac{C}{1} \quad \frac{H}{2} \quad \frac{G}{3} \quad \frac{E}{4} \quad \frac{D}{5} \quad \frac{F}{6}$$

Randoms are weaker variables that typically are placed after more powerful variables have been placed.

Note that the random H, a variable with little power, is placed last.

After completing these steps in response to the question, you could then use the single solution to easily select the correct answer choice.

The point is that restrictions, when present in a game, never go away. You must always track them and be prepared for questions that will force you to address the restriction.

Avoiding False Inferences

The test makers always check to see if you have interpreted the rules correctly, and some rules are easier to misinterpret than others. Here are four mistakes that students often make:

Conditional Rule Reversal

As previously discussed, a conditional rule is triggered when the sufficient condition occurs. For example, consider the following rule:

> When M is shown first, then O is shown sixth.

This rule would be diagrammed as:

$$M_1 \longrightarrow O_6$$

When M appears in the first slot, then O *must* appear in the sixth slot. However, many test takers make the mistake of reversing the relationship, and when faced with O in the sixth slot, they assume that M must be in the first slot. This is not a valid inference, and this mistake is known as a Mistaken Reversal.

Misinterpreting Block Language

As discussed on pages 18 and 19, the test makers will use different language to denote different blocks. "Before" and "after" are used in one manner, whereas "between" has an entirely different meaning. Many students make the mistake of misreading this language, and then they draw inferences based on a relationship that is actually incorrect. You must always read each rule very carefully because making a mistake in the rules will almost always cause a high number of missed questions.

False Blocks

The test makers are savvy, and they know that the average student does not carefully read the language of the rules. Consider the following rule from a recent Linear game:

> Each rock classic is immediately preceded on the CD by a new composition.

In this game, songs were being selected for a demo CD, and each song was classified as either a rock classic (R) or a new composition (N). Most students, upon reading the rule above, immediately diagrammed the rule as follows:

However, this representation is incorrect. The diagram above implies that R and N are always in a block formation, that is, every time N appears then R immediately follows, and every time R appears then N immediately precedes. Take a moment to re-read the rule. Does the rule state that the two variables are in block formation? No, what the rules states is that every rock classic is preceded by a new composition. There is no statement that every new composition is followed by a rock classic. So, this rule is only triggered when a rock classic is present. Thus, the rule is conditional, and should be diagrammed as follows:

This representation correctly indicates that the relationship in the rule occurs when a rock classic is present. Under this representation, it becomes possible for two or more new compositions to appear in a row (NN, NNN, etc.).

False Not-Block Inferences

As discussed on page 21, not-blocks indicate that variables cannot be next to one another, or cannot be separated by a fixed amount of space. Some students make the mistake of combining not-blocks with Not Laws to arrive at false inferences. Consider the following two rules:

> B is not inspected the day before C is inspected.
> C cannot be inspected second.

The diagram for these two rules would be:

Many students, after reviewing these two rules, make one of the following two errors:

1. They mistakenly conclude that B cannot be inspected first, and then place a B Not Law under slot 1. These students erroneously act as if the BC relationship is a positive block (in a positive block, if C could not be inspected second, then B could not be inspected first).

2. They mistakenly conclude that B must be inspected second, and then place B into slot 2. The error here is to act as if the C Not Law on slot 2 then forces B into slot 2. That outcome does not have to occur, although, of course, B could be inspected second.

Remember, not-blocks only come in to play when one of the variables in the not-block is placed on the diagram.

Balanced versus Unbalanced Games

Up to this point we have been discussing "Balanced" games, where the number of supplied variables equals the number of available slots, resulting in a one-to-one numerical relationship of variables to slots. As you might expect, not every Linear game features a Balanced scenario, and since Unbalanced games are generally more difficult than Balanced games, it is to your advantage to be able to recognize what type of numerical situation you are facing.

There are two types of Unbalanced Linear games: Underfunded and Overloaded. Underfunded games feature a fewer number of variables than available slots, for example, seven passengers assigned to nine seats on a plane. Overloaded games feature a greater number of variables than available slots, for example, eight piano lessons to be taught over five days. Overloaded scenarios often produce the most difficult Linear games.

Inherent in the discussion of Balanced and Unbalanced games is the idea of numerical distributions. A numerical distribution allocates one set of variables among another set of variables. For example, consider the game scenario from the first page of this chapter:

> A tutor is planning a daily schedule of individual tutoring sessions for each of six students—S, T, W, X, Y, and Z. The tutor will meet with exactly one student at a time, for exactly one hour each session. The tutor will meet with students starting at 1 P. M., for six consecutive hours.

As mentioned previously, this sets up a 1-1-1-1-1-1 numerical distribution where there is a single factory to be inspected on a single day and there are exactly enough factories to fill in all of the days. Most Linear games have a numerical distribution that can be represented along similar lines. However, Overloaded games must be represented a bit differently. Consider the following game scenario:

> Dr. Saitawa schedules six patients—G, H, L, M, O, and P—for surgery during a single week on Monday through Friday. Dr. Saitawa will operate on exactly one patient each day, except for one of the days when Dr. Saitawa will operate on two patients in separate, non-simultaneous sessions.

In this game there are six patients to be placed into five days. So instead of having a 1-1-1-1-1 numerical relationship (5 into 5), we have a 2-1-1-1-1 relationship (6 into 5), and it is uncertain which day receives two patients. This uncertainty is very important and has a tremendous impact on the game. For example, once a patient has been assigned to a day, it is still possible that another patient could be assigned to that day and thus the day is not "closed off" from further consideration. This makes the game more difficult because there are more options to consider.

Given the numerical distribution for Overloaded games, you might wonder how Underfunded games can be represented. Actually, it depends on the nature of the game. For our earlier example of seven passengers being assigned to nine seats, the deficit of variables can be countered by creating two "E" placeholder variables to represent the two empty seats. Thus, in our example you would write down the seven passengers and then two additional "E's," bringing the total number of variables to account for to nine, and the numerical distribution would be 1-1-1-1-1-1-1-1-1, just like in a normal one-to-one game. In other Underfunded games the rules make it clear you should double at least some of the variables, and by doing so there are enough variables to fill all of the spaces (for a sample of a game like this, see the example at the bottom of page 38. In that game, F, G, and H are doubled, and in that way there are six variables for six spaces.). We will see more of these games later when we further discuss numerical distributions.

Now that we have discussed some of the basic concepts of Linear Games, here is a Linear Games setup drill that will test your understanding of the concepts and help develop your diagramming skills. The purpose of this drill is to gain a clear understanding of the principles we have discussed, so speed is not a consideration. Your speed will naturally develop as your ability to analyze the components of each game increases.

Linear Setup Practice Drill

Each of the following items presents a scenario and corresponding rules similar to those found in actual Logic Games. Using the space provided, diagram the setup and include a representation of all sequences, blocks, not-blocks, and Not Laws™. Occasionally, a problem will contain a corresponding question. Use your knowledge of the rules and the setup to answer the question. After you complete *each* item, check your work against the diagram in the answer key, and carefully read the comments concerning each diagram. *Answers begin on Page 58*

1. Six swimmers—H, J, K, L, N, and P—are assigned to six swimming lanes numbered 1 though 6. Exactly one swimmer is assigned to each lane. The lane assignments conform to the following conditions:

    Swimmer K is assigned a lower-numbered lane than is swimmer J.
    Swimmer P is assigned a lower-numbered lane than is swimmer K.

2. Five dogs—an Akita, a Bulldog, a Cocker Spaniel, a Doberman, and an English Setter—compete in the final round of a dog show. Each dog will be shown alone to the judges exactly once in accordance with the following conditions:

    The Doberman can be shown neither immediately before nor immediately after the English Setter.
    The Akita must be shown two places before the Doberman.

    Question 2.1. Which one of the following must be true?

    (A) If the Akita is shown third, the English Setter must be shown second.
    (B) If the Bulldog is shown fourth, the Akita must be shown third.
    (C) If the Cocker Spaniel is shown third, the English Setter must be shown first.
    (D) If the Doberman is shown third, the Bulldog must be shown second.
    (E) If the English Setter is shown second, the Cocker Spaniel must be shown fourth.

3. A manager must schedule five meetings—Accounting, Finance, Management, Resources, and Training—during a single workweek, Monday through Friday. Each meeting will be scheduled for exactly one day, and exactly one meeting is held per day. The meeting schedule must observe the following constraints:

    The Management meeting is held the day before the Finance meeting.

    The Resources meeting is held at some time after the Finance meeting.

    The Accounting meeting is held second.

4. Six students—T, V, W, X, Y, and Z—are scheduled to speak in a debate contest. Each student will speak exactly once, and no two speakers will speak at the same time. The schedule must satisfy the following requirements:

    T speaks at some time before W.

    X must be the fourth speaker.

    V speaks immediately after T.

5. A jazz band director is selecting the songs for an evening's performance. Seven songs—F, G, H, J, Q, R, and S—will be played one after another, not necessarily in that order. Each song will be played exactly once, according to the following conditions:

F must be played immediately before or immediately after G.

H must be played immediately before or immediately after J.

S must be played fourth.

G must be played after F.

H must be played before J.

Question 5.1. Which one of the following cannot be true?

(A) F and R are played consecutively.
(B) G and Q are played consecutively.
(C) H and R are played consecutively.
(D) J and Q are played consecutively.
(E) Q and R are played consecutively.

6. A college dormitory manager must assign five students—P, Q, R, S, and T—to five different floors of the dormitory—floors 1, 2, 3, 5, and 6. The assignments must comply with the following restrictions:

P must be assigned to the floor directly above Q.

R must be assigned to floor 6.

7. Seven attorneys—C, D, F, G, H, J, and K—are scheduled to interview for a position with a local law firm. The seven interviews are conducted on six different days, Monday through Saturday. On one of the days two attorneys will be interviewed and on all other days exactly one attorney will be interviewed. The interview schedule must conform to the following conditions:

    F and K must be interviewed on the same day.

    J must be interviewed on Thursday.

    F must be interviewed after C but before G.

    D and H cannot be interviewed on consecutive days.

    K must be interviewed on either Tuesday or Friday.

    Question 7.1. Which one of the following could be true?

    (A) C is interviewed on Wednesday.
    (B) C is interviewed on Friday.
    (C) D is interviewed on Tuesday.
    (D) G is interviewed on Wednesday.
    (E) G is interviewed on Friday.

8. Each of six patrons—L, M, N, O, P, and Q—will be assigned to exactly one of seven tables. The tables stand consecutively and are numbered 1 through 7, and each table is assigned no more than one patron. Table assignments must meet the following requirements:

    N cannot be assigned to table 3, 5, or 7.

    P and Q must sit at lower-numbered tables than M.

    Tables 5, 6, and 7 must be occupied by a patron.

    O sits at a higher-numbered table than M.

9. There are exactly seven office buildings numbered 1 through 7 on a street. Each building is occupied by exactly one of seven companies: A, B, C, D, E, F, and G. All of the buildings are on the same side of the street, which runs from west to east. Building 1 is the westernmost building. The following restrictions apply:

Company A does not occupy building 1, 3, 5, or 7.
Company C occupies the building immediately to the west of Company D.
Company B occupies one of the three westernmost buildings.
Company F is the third building to the east of Company E.
The easternmost building is not occupied by Company G.

10. A dance academy instructor must schedule eight dance classes—a charleston class, a foxtrot class, a jitterbug class, a limbo class, a polka class, a rumba class, a tango class, and a waltz class—for a single day. Exactly two classes will be scheduled at a time, and the scheduling must be made according to the following conditions:

The limbo class and the rumba class are not scheduled for the same time.
The charleston class and the polka class must be scheduled for the same time.
The tango class and the rumba class are not scheduled for the same time.
The limbo class is scheduled at some time after the polka class.
The rumba class and the waltz class are not scheduled for the same time.

Question 10.1. If the tango class is scheduled for the same time as the foxtrot class, which one of the following must be true?

(A) The jitterbug class and the limbo class must be scheduled for the same time.
(B) The jitterbug class and the rumba class must be scheduled for the same time.
(C) The jitterbug class and the waltz class must be scheduled for the same time.
(D) The limbo class and the rumba class must be scheduled for the same time.
(E) The rumba class and the waltz class must be scheduled for the same time.

11. A driver must pick up exactly eight passengers—P, R, S, T, V, X, Y, and Z—one at a time, not necessarily in that order. The pickups must be made in accordance with the following conditions:

Either T or V must be picked up fifth.

Either Y or Z must be picked up third.

The driver picks up exactly one passenger between picking up T and picking up Z.

S is picked up eighth when Y is picked up third.

Z must be picked up ahead of T.

Question 11.1. If V is picked up fifth, which one of the following must be true?

(A) P is picked up first.
(B) R is picked up sixth.
(C) S is picked up eighth.
(D) X is picked up seventh.
(E) Z is picked up sixth.

12. A doctor must schedule nine patients—L, M, O, P, R, S, T, V, and X—during a given week, Monday through Sunday. At least one patient must be scheduled for each day, and the schedule must observe the following constraints:

> M and S must be scheduled for the same day.
> On the day P is scheduled, P must be the only patient scheduled to see the doctor.
> Exactly one patient is scheduled for Wednesday.
> T cannot be scheduled for Thursday.
> If P is scheduled for Monday, then V and X must be scheduled for Saturday.
> R is not scheduled for Thursday unless L is scheduled for Monday.

Question 12.1. If L is scheduled for Monday, which one of the following must be true?

(A) R is scheduled for Thursday.
(B) V is scheduled for Saturday.
(C) S is scheduled for Saturday.
(D) P is not scheduled for Monday.
(E) V is not scheduled for Monday.

Question 12.2. Which one of the following statements about the doctor's schedule must be true?

(A) The maximum number of patients scheduled for Monday is one.
(B) The maximum number of patients scheduled for Tuesday is two.
(C) The maximum number of patients scheduled for Friday is three.
(D) The minimum number of patients scheduled for Saturday is two.
(E) The minimum number of patients scheduled for Sunday is two.

Linear Setup Practice Drill Answer Key

Note: Most of the problems in this drill are diagrammed with horizontal setups. In many cases these problems could be diagrammed with vertical setups, although some games should be shown horizontally, such as one about houses on a street. Also, if you encounter a Not Law in the answer key that appears incorrectly placed, put that variable into that position and observe the consequences. This will allow you to better understand the interaction taking place between the variables and the rules.

Drill #1. There are two variable sets in this problem: the six swimmers and the six swimming lanes. Because the swimming lanes have an inherent sense of order, they are chosen as the base. Since each lane will be filled by exactly one swimmer, a single slot is drawn above each lane number, and the swimmers are connected to the lanes in a one-to-one relationship (In this case 1-1-1-1-1-1).

H J K L N P [6]

P > K > J

The two sequencing rules can be linked together to form one "super" rule. The A > B > C format of the super rule appears frequently on the LSAT and always yields exactly six Not Laws.

Drill #2. There are two variable sets in this problem: the five dogs and the five positions in which they are shown. Since the positions in which the dogs are shown has an inherent sense of order, they are chosen as the base. Again, the two variable sets are in a one-to-one relationship (1-1-1-1-1).

A B C D E [5]

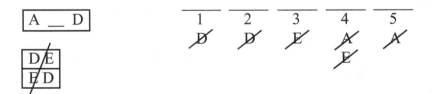

E can never appear in slot 3 or 4 because E and D cannot be consecutive, and when this rule is combined with the $\boxed{A \_ D}$ rule, we run into the following problems:

> When $\boxed{A \_ D}$ is in the first and third slots, then the third slot is occupied, and since D is third, E can't be fourth.
> When $\boxed{A \_ D}$ is in the second and fourth slots, then the fourth slot is occupied, and since D is fourth then E can't be third.
> When $\boxed{A \_ D}$ is in the third and fifth slots, then the third slot is occupied by A, and since D is fifth then E can't be fourth.

Thus, since $\boxed{A \_ D}$ must be in one of the three positions outlined above, and in none of those scenarios can E be third or fourth, we can eliminate E from those two slots. The best way to understand an inference of this nature is to reverse-engineer it; that is, put E in third slot and see what problems occur, then put E in the fourth slot see what happens. You will quickly see why placing E in either position causes difficulty.

From a visual standpoint, the unwieldy block has only three spacing options: 1-3, 2-4, and 3-5. The following diagram shows each option drawn out:

	1	2	3	4	5	
Option #3:	E/	/E	A		D	Block in 3-5
Option #2:	E	A		D		Block in 2-4
Option #1:	A		D		E	Block in 1-3

Although this problem is too simple to appear as an entire Logic Game, it is indicative of the type of "endgame" situations that occur after several variables have already been placed in a question.

In Options #1 and #3, the third position is occupied by D and A, respectively. In Option #2, D is shown fourth and from the rules it follows that E cannot be shown third or fifth. Thus, in each of the three options, the third position is either occupied or otherwise off-limits to E. Since these are the only three templates for the game, it follows that E can never be shown third.

In Option #2, the fourth position is occupied by D. In Option #1, D is shown third and thus E cannot be shown fourth. In Option #3, D is shown fifth and so E cannot be shown fourth. Thus, in each option the fourth position is either occupied or otherwise unavailable to E. It therefore follows that E can never be shown fourth.

The inference that E cannot be shown third or fourth would certainly be tested during the game. To find such an inference in the future, be on the lookout for split-blocks (which have limited placement options) and not-blocks that link to one of the variables in the split-block.

Question 2.1. The correct answer is (C). If C is shown third, then A must be shown second and D must be shown fourth. Since D and E cannot be shown consecutively, it must be true that E is shown first.

Answer choice (A) is incorrect since E could be shown first instead of second.
Answer choice (B) is incorrect since A could be shown first instead of third.
Answer choice (D) is incorrect since B could be shown fourth instead of second.
Answer choice (E) is incorrect since C could be shown first instead of fourth.

Drill #3. Whenever a game introduces the days of a week as a variable set, always use the days of the week as the base. As in the first two problems, the two variable sets are in a one-to-one relationship (1-1-1-1-1).

A F M R T [5]

This problem provides an excellent example of why you should always read each rule before beginning your diagram. Because A must be held on Tuesday, it follows that F, M, and R cannot be held on Monday. Accordingly, T must be held on Monday, and the MFR sequence must fill in Wednesday, Thursday, and Friday.

Drill #4. In this problem the speaking order should be chosen as the base, and the variables are in a one-to-one relationship (1-1-1-1-1-1).

T V W X Y Z [6]

The first point of interest in this problem is in the representation of X. Since X must speak fourth, it automatically follows that X cannot speak first, second, third, fifth, or sixth. As mentioned previously, an argument could thus be made that X Not Laws should be shown on those slots. This representation would be correct, but since X is already placed, and, therefore, out of consideration, this would be redundant. However, if you find yourself continually missing these types of inferences, you can certainly show the X Not Laws.

The second point of interest is in the placement of the TV block. Since T and V cannot speak fifth or sixth, it follows that the TV block must be either 1-2 or 2-3. Accordingly, either T or V must always speak second and no other student can speak second. This "dual option" is represented by T/V in the second slot. It is interesting to note that in both problem #3 and this problem the limited placement options of the block ultimately yield the key inferences. In any logic game that contains a block, always make sure to account for the possibilities presented by that block.

The final piece of relevant information in this problem concerns W, Y, and Z. Although we cannot be sure of the exact placement of these three variables, we can deduce that they will never stand consecutively. In fact, one of the group must always occupy the first or third slot, and the remaining two variables must occupy the fifth and sixth slots. In logic games it is almost always fruitful to examine the possibilities among those variables that have yet to be placed by a question.

Linear Setup Practice Drill Answer Key

<u>Drill #5.</u> In this problem the order of performance is chosen as the base, and the variable sets are in a one-to-one relationship (1-1-1-1-1-1-1).

F G H J Q R S[7]

Again, this problem proves that you must thoroughly read all of the rules before starting your diagram. The first and fourth rules set up an FG block, and the second and fifth rules set up an HJ block. The two blocks ultimately prove to be the key to the problem. Since S effectively splits the diagram into two equal parts, one of the blocks must be placed into the first three slots and the other block must be placed into the last three slots. Since one block always appears in slots 1-2 or 2-3, slot 2 must always be occupied by one of the four block variables and therefore can never be occupied by Q or R. Additionally, since the other block must always appear in slots 5-6 or 6-7, slot 6 also cannot be occupied by Q or R. Finally, since S is already in slot 4, F and H cannot be played third, and G and J cannot be played fifth. Regarding the third and fifth slots, whenever a variable (such as S) is placed into the middle of a one-to-one linear diagram, any fixed blocks will yield Not Laws before and after that variable.

Question 5.1. The correct answer is (E). If Q and R are played consecutively, there would not be enough room to place the FG and HJ blocks.

Answer choice (A) is incorrect because R could be first and F could be second. There is another possibility (R could be fifth and F could be sixth) but one hypothetical is sufficient to disprove the answer choice and the same is true for the other incorrect answer choices.

Answer choice (B) is incorrect because G could be second and Q could be third.

Answer choice (C) is incorrect because R could be first and H could be second.

Answer choice (D) is incorrect because J could be second and Q could be third.

Note that this game would probably contain some question or answer choice that would test your knowledge of the fact that the two blocks can never stand consecutively. Since there is not enough room to place the blocks side-by-side, the following inferences can be made:

Linear Setup Practice Drill Answer Key

Drill #6. Of the two variable sets, the floors should be chosen as the base because they have the greatest sense of inherent order. When displaying the floors, even though the listed floors do not include floor 4, the fourth floor should be shown anyway. The value of this decision will prove itself in a moment. The variable sets are in a one-to-one relationship (1-1-1-1-1), and in this case the best representation is vertical since that is the way the floors of buildings exist in the real world.

P Q R S T [5]

P
Q

```
6    R
5    S/T   P̶ Q̶
4    XXX
3    ___   Q̶
2    P/Q   S̶ T̶
1    ___   P̶
```

By showing floor 4, it becomes apparent that neither P nor Q can be assigned to floor 5 (in addition, Q cannot be assigned to floor 3). It then follows that the PQ block must be on either floors 3-2 or floors 2-1. Thus, either P or Q must be assigned to floor 2 and S and T cannot be assigned there.

In any game where one of the internal spaces is skipped, still show that space on your diagram, but mark it through with an "X." The test makers *always* test you to see if you understand the implications of the missing space.

Linear Setup Practice Drill Answer Key

<u>Drill #7.</u> As discussed in problem #3, the days of the week should always be chosen as the base. Interestingly, in this problem there are only six days but seven attorneys to be scheduled. Thus, this is an Unbalanced game that is Overloaded. Ordinarily this would be a cause for concern because Linear games are easier when each space is filled by just one variable (e.g. Balanced games). In problems such as this one where the number of variables is Unbalanced (7 into 6), the extra uncertainty often increases the overall difficulty. Here that uncertainty is somewhat alleviated since the first rule schedules F and K to be interviewed together. With F and K as a block, there are just six separate "variables" to assign (FK, C, D, G, H, and J). Thus, the distribution could be characterized as a 1-1-1-1-1-1 relationship of attorneys to days of the week, where it just happens that one of the "1's" is the FK block.

Most students set this game up as follows:

$C D F G H J K^7$

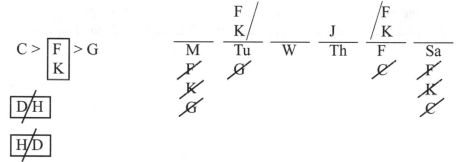

While this partial representation is accurate, it does not characterize the full scope of the possibilities. Since the FK block is limited to Tuesday or Friday, and the FK block is involved in a sequence with other variables, why not draw out two separate templates that show the possibilities when the FK block is placed? This technique, known as Identifying the Templates™, occasionally produces startling inferences and usually provides you with a greater understanding of the game. Identifying the Templates should generally be used when certain variables or blocks have a limited number of placement options (usually two or three) and their placement correspondingly affects other variables. Here are the two templates in this problem:

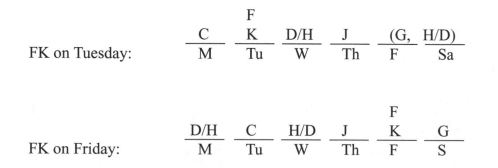

With F and K on Tuesday, C must be interviewed on Monday. This leaves D, G, and H to be interviewed on Wednesday, Friday, and Saturday. Since D and H cannot be interviewed on consecutive days, either D or H must be interviewed on Wednesday, and the remainder interviewed on Friday or Saturday. Since Friday and Saturday are limited to G and D or H, this option is shown

---

in parentheses. Thus, the (G, H/D) notation helps to represent four possibilities: G on Friday and H on Saturday; G on Friday and D on Saturday; G on Saturday and D on Friday; and G on Saturday and H on Friday.

With F and K on Friday, G must be interviewed on Saturday. This leaves C, D, and H to be interviewed on Monday, Tuesday, and Wednesday. Since D and H cannot be interviewed consecutively, C must be interviewed on Tuesday. Since D and H can be interviewed on either Monday or Wednesday, this template therefore represents two possibilities. By combining both templates, we find that this problem contains only six unique solutions and we have identified each one.

Question 7.1. Answer choice (E) is correct and is proven by the first of the two templates.

Answer choice (A) cannot be true since only D or H can be interviewed on Wednesday.
Answer choice (B) cannot be true since C can be interviewed only on Monday or Tuesday.
Answer choice (C) cannot be true since only K, F, and C can be interviewed on Tuesday.
Answer choice (D) cannot be true since only D or H can be interviewed on Wednesday.

<u>Drill #8</u>. Of the two variable sets, the tables should be chosen as the base since they are numbered and stand consecutively. At first it appears that this problem is Unbalanced in the same way as problem #7, but in this case the game is Underfunded with only six patrons for the seven tables (6 into 7). However, this shortage can be alleviated by representing the "missing" patron with an "E" for empty. Whenever there is a shortage of variables (in this case, the patrons) available to fill a set number of spaces (in this case, the tables), you can always combat this problem by representing the missing variable with an E (or if the given variables already include E, use another letter, such as X). With the shortage of variables eliminated, the variable set relationship can be seen as a one-to-one (1-1-1-1-1-1-1).

As discussed earlier, in all game types, one of the basic methods for identifying inferences is to examine the points of restriction in the game. In games with Not Laws, that involves looking closely at the slots with the greatest number of Not Laws. In this case, it becomes apparent that table 7 is the most restricted table in the problem. In fact, since five of the seven variables cannot sit at table 7 (E is counted as a variable for this purpose), only two patrons—L and O—are available to sit at table 7. This inference would most likely be tested in a game by a question such as, "If L is assigned to table 3, which one of the following must be true?" The correct answer would be "O must be assigned to table 7." In one-to-one Linear games, always examine any space that has a large number of Not Laws, and do not forget that any variable that is already placed is automatically eliminated from all other slots!

In addition, the "O" Not Law on table 4 is correct because placing O on 4 causes a violation of the third rule:

> When O is placed at table 4, then tables 1, 2, and 3 must be occupied by patrons P, Q, and M (not necessarily in that order). This forces the Empty table (variable "E") to be assigned to table 5, 6, or 7. Unfortunately, that assignment is a violation of the third rule that states that tables 5, 6, and 7 must be occupied by a patron.

Drill #9. The buildings should be chosen as the base since they are numbered and stand on the same side of the street. The two variables sets are in a one-to-one relationship (1-1-1-1-1-1-1), and the game should be set up horizontally since that is the way streets exist in the real world.

A B C D E F G [7]

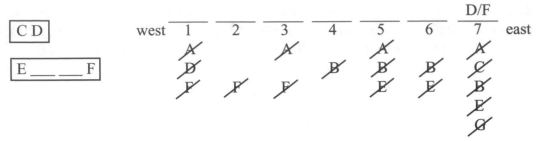

As in the previous problem, the abundance of Not Laws on the seventh building leads to the inference that only companies D and F can occupy building 7. Since D and F are both involved in block rules, it makes sense to apply the Identify the Templates technique used previously in problem #7:

	B/G	E	G/B	A	F	C	D
D in 7:	E	A	B	F	G	C	D
	1	2	3	4	5	6	7

	B/G	A	G/B	E	C	D	F
	B	C	D	E	G	A	F
F in 7:	C	D	B	E	G	A	F
	1	2	3	4	5	6	7

As you can see, the two major templates have themselves been split into smaller sub-templates. This method is the most efficient since the placement of each of the two blocks then limits the placement of the other block. It is interesting to note that, although the Identify the Templates method of attack often consumes more time than the average setup, it also allows you to answer the questions more quickly. In this problem there are only seven different solutions, and identifying each one would allow you to answer any question quickly and easily.

As a note of warning, the majority of Linear games cannot be attacked with the Identify method since their rules simply do not combine to produce enough restrictions. However, part of the purpose of this drill is to challenge you to identify the dominant features of any linear setup and concomitantly employ the correct techniques to attack the game most effectively. There will be times when your ability to employ certain techniques at the right moment is critical, and this drill helps prepare you for those moments.

Linear Setup Practice Drill Answer Key

<u>Drill #10</u>. The dance class times should be selected as the base since they have a consecutive nature. There are eight dance classes and eight time slots, and therefore the two variable sets are in a one-to-one relationship (1-1-1-1-1-1-1-1). However, since two dance classes are scheduled for each time slot the distribution could also be seen as 2-2-2-2. The two representations essentially mean the same thing.

C F J L P R T W [8]

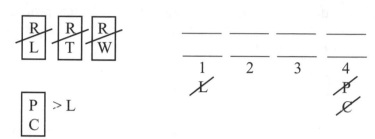

Since there are two classes in each time slot, we can represent the second class in each time period with another "stack" of slots. Blocks that represent the same time period can be drawn vertically, and blocks that represent consecutive time periods can be drawn horizontally. Thus, because L and R cannot be scheduled for the same time period, that not-block must be drawn vertically (whether R or L is on top is irrelevant for this problem).

Some students attempt to use the following representation for the time slots:

The above representation is flawed and will lead to problems in the future. Do not use it! The primary problem is that blocks cannot be meaningfully represented. A block that shows the same time period would be drawn horizontally, and a block that shows consecutive time periods would also be drawn horizontally. Thus, there would be no way to determine the exact meaning of a block during a game other than through memory or a rereading of the rule. This is obviously inefficient, and therefore a weak representation.

The key feature of the problem is the three not-blocks. In games with a large number of not-blocks, powerful inferences can often be made regarding which variables can and cannot go together. In this case, R appears in each of the not-blocks, and that eliminates R from being paired with L, T, or W. Since P and C must be scheduled together, it follows that R cannot be scheduled with C, L, P, T, or W. Therefore, R can only be paired with F or J:

This inference is tested in the accompanying question:

Question 10.1. Answer choice (B) is correct. If F is scheduled with T, then only J remains to be paired with R.

> Answer choice (A) is incorrect since if J and L are scheduled for the same time, there would be no class to schedule with R.
>
> Answer choice (C) is incorrect since if J and W are scheduled for the same time, there would be no class to schedule with R.
>
> Answer choice (D) is incorrect since according to the first rule L and R can never be scheduled together.
>
> Answer choice (E) is incorrect since according to the fifth rule R and W can never be scheduled together.

<u>Drill #11</u>. The order of pickup should be chosen as the base in this problem, and the variable sets are in a one-to-one relationship (1-1-1-1-1-1-1-1).

P R S T V X Y Z ^{8}

The interaction of the first, second, third, and fifth rules establishes that there are only two possibilities for the third and fifth pickups: Z in three and T in five, or Y in three and V in five. Using this information the best attack is to Identify the Templates:

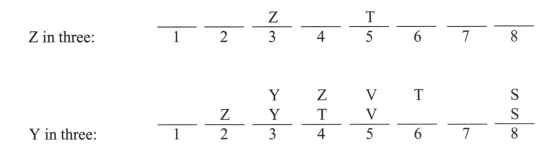

This form of Identify the Templates, where only some of the variables are placed, is more likely to occur on a Linear game than the form seen in problems #7 and #9, where all of the variables are placed.

Note also that the fourth rule is conditional, and uses the conditional indicator "when." We did not show the contrapositive because over time you should begin to understand that the contrapositive inherently follows from any conditional relationship. The rule of thumb is to write out the contrapositive when you feel that doing so will make the game easier for you.

Linear Setup Practice Drill Answer Key

Question 11.1. Answer choice (C) is correct. If V is picked up fifth, Y must be picked up third, and when Y is picked up third then S must be picked up eighth.

Answer choice (A) is incorrect since it could be true, but it does not have to be true.
Answer choice (B) is incorrect since it could be true, but it does not have to be true.
Answer choice (D) is incorrect since it could be true, but it does not have to be true.
Answer choice (E) is incorrect since it cannot be true.

Linear Setup Practice Drill Answer Key

<u>Drill #12</u>. As discussed in previous problems, the days of the week should be chosen as the base. The patients should be distributed across the days, and similar to problem #7, there is an unbalanced relationship between the patients and the days of the week (9 to 7). Whenever an unbalanced relationship such as this one occurs in a game, it should always be examined closely. In this case there are two numerical distributions possible for spreading the nine patients across the seven days:

Distribution #1:
```
3 - 1 - 1 - 1 - 1 - 1 - 1
M                   P
S
```

Distribution #2:
```
2 - 2 - 1 - 1 - 1 - 1 - 1
M                   P
S
```

In distribution #1, one of the seven days receives three scheduled patients, and each of the other six days receives one patient. In distribution #2, two of the seven days receives two patients each, and each of the other five days receives one patient. Numerical distributions will be discussed in more detail later in the course, but for the time being the following is a quick analysis of this numerical distribution.

There are seven days, and each day must have at least one scheduled patient. Thus, the minimum requirements for each day use up seven of the patients:

This arrangement leaves two patients as "free agents" that can be scheduled for any day. If both free agents are scheduled together, say on Monday, the following arrangement would appear:

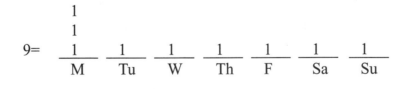

Thus, we arrive at the 3-1-1-1-1-1-1 distribution. Note that the "3" does not have to be on Monday. It is just easier to represent the distribution with the 3 at the beginning, and so technically this is called an unfixed distribution. The distinction will be further explained later in this book.

To arrive at distribution #2, simply split up the two free agents and schedule them for different days:

```
      1   1
9=    1   1   1   1   1   1   1
     ___ ___ ___ ___ ___ ___ ___
      M   Tu  W   Th  F   Sa  Su
```

Thus, we arrive at the 2-2-1-1-1-1-1 distribution. As before, the groups of "2" do not have to appear on Monday and Tuesday.

Some students object that the 3-1-1-1-1-1-1 distribution cannot occur since the first rule establishes that M and S must be scheduled together. However, the rule does not state that M and S are the *only* two patients scheduled for the same time and thus it is possible that another patient could be scheduled along with M and S. Of course, in the 3-1-1-1-1-1-1 distribution M and S must be part of the group of 3 and in the 2-2-1-1-1-1-1 M and S must form one of the groups of 2.

Now that we have discussed the numbers (which are always primary in Logic Games), let's diagram the rules:

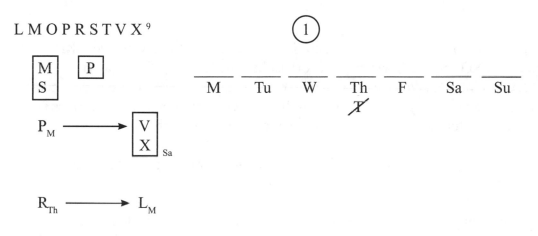

Question 12.1. Answer choice (D) is the correct answer. If L is scheduled for Monday, then according to the second rule P cannot be scheduled for Monday.

> Answer choice (A) is incorrect because it reverses the last rule and is therefore not necessarily true.
> Answer choice (B) is incorrect because it is not necessarily true.
> Answer choice (C) is incorrect because it is not necessarily true.
> Answer choice (E) is incorrect because it is not necessarily true.

This question can be confusing, and many students mistakenly select answer choice (A). Although answer choice (A) could occur, it does not have to occur, and because this is a Must Be True question, answer choice (A) is thus incorrect. Let's take a moment to analyze the last rule:

> "R is not scheduled for Thursday unless L is scheduled for Monday."

The critical part of the sentence is the word "unless," and when "unless" appears it introduces the necessary condition, and then the rest is negated and becomes the sufficient condition. Hence, the proper diagram for the rule is:

$$R_{Th} \longrightarrow L_M$$

Linear Setup Practice Drill Answer Key

Let's review that again. To diagram a statement involving "unless" (or its analogues "except," "until," or "without"), take the following two steps:

> 1. The clause modified by "unless" becomes the necessary condition.
>
> 2. The remainder is negated—which normally involves removing or adding a "not"—and becomes the sufficient condition.

Thus, in the rule under consideration, "unless" modifies "L is scheduled for Monday" and that becomes the necessary condition; the remainder, "R is not scheduled for Thursday," is negated to "R is scheduled for Thursday" and becomes the sufficient condition. Hence the diagram

$$R_{Th} \longrightarrow L_M.$$

So, with this diagram in mind for question 12.1, when L is scheduled for Monday, the necessary condition is met. This does NOT mean, however, that R must be scheduled for Thursday (it is possible but not certain). To infer R is on Thursday would be a Mistaken Reversal of the statement and erroneous (this error is covered in the Avoiding False Inferences section on page 46). Since (A) tries to say that it must be true that R is on Thursday, answer choice (A) is therefore wrong.

Question 12.2. Answer choice (C) is correct since the maximum number of patients that can ever be scheduled for a single day is three (3-1-1-1-1-1-1).

> Answer choice (A) is incorrect since three is the maximum number of patients that could be scheduled for Monday.
> Answer choice (B) is incorrect since three is the maximum number of patients that could be scheduled for Tuesday.
> Answer choice (D) is incorrect since one is the minimum number of patients that could be scheduled for Saturday.
> Answer choice (E) is incorrect since one is the minimum number of patients that could be scheduled for Sunday.

Most games that feature a Numerical Distribution have at least one question that tests to see if you identified the distribution.

The Questions

Now that you have had an opportunity to hone your setup and inference making skills, it is time to discuss the questions in more detail. As mentioned in the first chapter, questions are either Global or Local. Global questions ask about information that can be derived from the initial rules whereas Local questions impose a new condition in addition to the initial rules.

If you have a strong setup, many of the Global questions should be relatively easy. Global questions are easily identifiable because they ask broad questions without adding any new conditions. For example, a Global question might ask, "Which one of the following cannot be true?" or "Which one of the following is a pair of songs that must occupy consecutive tracks?" Local questions generally can be identified by the "if" (or "when" or "suppose") at the beginning of the question stem. The "if" clause provides a new rule for you to consider *for that question only*. Most Local questions will require you to make a mini-diagram next to the question itself (we will discuss this point later). The Global and Local designations broadly categorize every question on the games section.

Logical Opposition

In addition to being Global or Local, each question can be specifically categorized by its logical characteristics. Although this may sound formidable, it simply refers to whether a question asks for what cannot be true, what could be true, what is not necessarily true, or what must be true. Those four questions cover the range of logical possibilities when discussing the truth, and *every* Logic Game question has one of those four characteristics.

As you know, each problem on the LSAT has only one correct answer. The other four answer choices are incorrect, which is the logical opposite of correct. Thus, it can be said that each incorrect answer choice has the exact logical opposite characteristic of the correct answer choice. So, if we can identify the logical characteristic of the correct answer choice, we can immediately determine the characteristic of the four incorrect answers as well. For example, if a question asks for the answer choice that could be true, the correct answer choice obviously has the characteristic of "could be true," and the four wrong answer choices have the exact opposite characteristic, which is "cannot be true." This idea of logical opposition functions as a guide to the exact characteristic of every answer choice on the games section. Here are the pairs of logical opposites:

Always read to the end of the "if" clause in a question and then stop to consider the implications of the new information.

	Characteristic	Opposite
1.	Cannot Be True	Could Be True

If a question asks for what cannot be true:
    One correct answer: Cannot Be True
    Four incorrect answers: Could Be True

	Characteristic	Opposite
2.	Could Be True	Cannot Be True

If a question asks for what could be true:
    One correct answer: Could Be True
    Four incorrect answers: Cannot Be True

	Characteristic	Opposite
3.	Not Necessarily True	Must Be True

If a question asks for what is not necessarily true:
    One correct answer: Not Necessarily True
    Four incorrect answers: Must Be True

	Characteristic	Opposite
4.	Must Be True	Not Necessarily True

If a question asks for what must be true:
    One correct answer: Must Be True
    Four incorrect answers: Not Necessarily True

Logical opposition underlies all Logic Game questions.

Since the range of truth only extends from cannot be true to must be true, the four characteristics above represent all of the possible questions you can be asked.

Note that the four items above naturally divide into two pairs: Could Be True vs. Cannot Be True, and Must Be True vs. Not Necessarily True. Each item in a pair is the logical opposite of the other item in the pair. For example, Could Be True is the logical opposite of Cannot Be True, and Cannot Be True is the logical opposite of Could Be True. When you are analyzing questions, the correct and incorrect answer choices will all be classified into one of these two pairs.

Although many students intuitively understand the concept above, let's take a moment to further analyze this important idea. Imagine for a moment that "truth" can be measured on a scale of 0 to 100. According to our discussion, there are two separate pairs that represent every possibility:

<u>Truth</u>

First pair:

     Must Be True   = 100 (if something Must Be True then it
                                        is 100% of the truth, so to speak)

     Not Necessarily True   = 0 to 99 (everything but Must Be True)

Second pair:

     Could Be True   = 1 to 100 (everything but Cannot Be
                                       True)

     Cannot Be True   = 0   (None of the truth, so to speak)

Cannot Be True and Could Be True are logical opposites that encompass all possibilities. Since Cannot Be True is so specific, that means that Could Be True encompasses every other possibility (probably, must, etc).

The same holds true for Must Be True and Not Necessarily True. Since Must Be True is so specific, that means that Not Necessarily True encompasses every other possibility (maybe, cannot, etc).

By looking closely at the quantities each possibility represents, we can see that Could Be True (1 to 100) actually includes Must Be True (100). This makes sense because Could Be True, if it is to be the exact logical opposite of Cannot Be True, should include every other possibility besides Cannot Be True. The same relationship also holds true for Not Necessarily True (0 to 99) and Cannot Be True (0). The operational effect of this fact is that wrong answer choices can have characteristics that "go beyond" the simple logical opposite of the correct answer. For example, if a question asks for what Cannot Be True, then all four of the incorrect answer choices must have the characteristic of Could Be True. However, within those four Could Be True answers, some may go even further and have the characteristic of Must Be True. The same holds true for a question that asks for what Must Be True. The four incorrect answers choices will have the characteristic of Not Necessarily True, and within those four Not Necessarily True answers some may go further and have the characteristic of Cannot Be True.

Some students ask if Could Be True and Not Necessarily True mean the same thing. Could Be True (1 to 100) and Not Necessarily True (0 to 99) are largely the same (between 1 and 99 they are identical), but they differ significantly at the extremes (0 and 100). Could Be True actually includes

Must Be True, the opposite of Not Necessarily True, and Not Necessarily True includes Cannot Be True, the opposite of Could Be True. So, despite being similar in many respects, each term actually includes the exact opposite of the other term.

Using the following examples let's consider how the truth characteristic applies to actual questions, which have been additionally categorized as Global or Local:

> If G is seated second, which one of the following could be true?
> > Categorization: Local, Could Be True
> > > (the 4 incorrect answers Cannot Be True)

> Which one of the following cannot be true?
> > Categorization: Global, Cannot Be True
> > > (the 4 incorrect answers Could Be True)

> If R is selected fifth, which one of the following must be true?
> > Categorization: Local, Must Be True
> > > (the 4 incorrect answers are Not Necessarily True)

Always be on the lookout for the word "except."

For the most part, understanding the questions above should not be too difficult. However, the test makers often append the word "except" to questions similar to those above in order to confuse test takers. In these cases, "except" functions to logically turn the question upside down. Consider the following two examples:

> Which one of the following must be true?
> > Categorization: Global, Must Be True
> > > (the 4 incorrect answers are Not Necessarily True)

> Each of the following must be true EXCEPT:
> > Categorization: Global, Not Necessarily True
> > > (the 4 incorrect answers Must Be True)

As a rule, the LSAT makers always capitalize "except" when it appears in a question stem. They do so because they are aware of how dramatically it changes the meaning of a question.

Another confusing ploy the test makers use is to pose questions in terms of falsity, such as "Which one of the following cannot be false?" Most students are unaccustomed to thinking in terms of false, and thus lose valuable time trying to understand the exact meaning of the question. Since false and true are opposites, whenever you are faced with a question posed in terms of falsity, convert it into one of the four "true" questions we have already reviewed. Here is the conversion table:

Question in False		True Equivalent
1. Must Be False	$\longrightarrow$	Cannot Be True
2. Not Necessarily False	$\longrightarrow$	Could Be True
3. Could Be False	$\longrightarrow$	Not Necessarily True
4. Cannot Be False	$\longrightarrow$	Must Be True

When a question is posed in terms of falsity, convert it to true. When a question is posed in terms of truth, use it that way.

In using this table, **always convert from False to True**. Never convert from true into false. If the question asks, "Which one of the following could be false?" immediately convert that question to "Which one of the following is not necessarily true?" and then proceed, knowing that the four incorrect answers Must Be True.

Once again, here are some categorized examples:

Which one of the following could be false?
>Categorization: Global, Not Necessarily True
>>(the 4 incorrect answers Must Be True)

If J speaks third, which one of the following must be false?
>Categorization: Local, Cannot Be True
>>(the 4 incorrect answers Could Be True)

Each of the following cannot be false EXCEPT:
>Categorization: Global, Not Necessarily True (remember, convert false to true and then apply the "except")
>>(the 4 incorrect answer Must Be True)

We know what you are thinking: why should I really care about these global/local, cannot/could/not necessarily/must be true/false designations? The answer is simple: if you do not know what you are being asked, you cannot answer the question. The LSAT is a precision exam, and to excel you must know as much as possible about the test before you walk in. There are students out there who will see a question such as, "Each one of the following could be false EXCEPT" and they will freeze while trying to determine exactly what the question means (the correct answer "must be true"). By memorizing the tables above, you will save time and gain confidence.

Every second counts on the LSAT.

Question Stem Classification Drill

For each of the following items, classify the question stem as Global or Local, and then identify the truth characteristic of the correct answer and then the truth characteristic of the four incorrect answers. Remember, always convert false into true. *Answers on the next page*

Example: "Which one of the following must be true?"

Classification: Global, Must Be True
Four Incorrect Answers: Not Necessarily True

1. Question: "If G is the second most expensive suite, then which one of the following could be true?"

Classification: _____

Four Incorrect Answers: _____

2. Question: "If K is displayed third, then each of the following could be true EXCEPT:"

Classification: _____

Four Incorrect Answers: _____

3. Question: "Which one of the following could be false?"

Classification: _____

Four Incorrect Answers: _____

4. Question: "If R is delivered earlier than S, then which one of the following cannot be false?"

Classification: _____

Four Incorrect Answers: _____

5. Question: "Each of the following must be false EXCEPT:"

Classification: _____

Four Incorrect Answers: _____

Question Stem Classification Drill Answer Key

1.   Classification: Local, Could Be True
                Four Incorrect Answers: Cannot Be True

2.   Classification: Local, Cannot Be True
                Four Incorrect Answers: Could Be True

3.   Classification: Global, Not Necessarily True
                Four Incorrect Answers: Must Be True

                Remember, "could be false" is the equivalent to "not necessarily true."

4.   Classification: Local, Must Be True
                Four Incorrect Answers: Not Necessarily True

                Remember, "cannot be false" is the equivalent to "must be true."

5.   Classification: Global, Could Be True
                Four Incorrect Answers: Cannot Be True

                Remember, "must be false" is the equivalent to "cannot be true."

Four Specific Question Types

Now that we have discussed the general characteristics of Logic Games questions, let us further discuss four very specific question types:

List Questions

The first question in a game is often a List question.

List questions present a list of variables that can either fill a slot or possibly solve the game. Here is an example:

> Which one of the following could be a list of the students in the order of their tutoring sessions, from 1 P.M. to 6 P.M.?
>
> (A) S, T, Z, W, X, Y
> (B) T, W, X, Y, Z, S
> (C) T, X, W, Y, S, Z
> (D) W, X, Y, S, Z, T
> (E) X, T, W, Y, Z, S

Games featuring numerical distributions often test the distribution in a List question.

This type of List question asks you to select the answer choice that contains a solution to the game that does not violate any of the rules. The best technique for attacking this type of List question is to take a *single* rule and apply it to each of the five answer choices, one at a time. Eliminate any answer choice that violates the rule. Then, choose another rule and apply the same procedure to the remaining answer choices. Do this until you have only one answer choice left. If you run out of rules and there is still more than one answer choice remaining, look to see if the game scenario contains some limiting feature that you overlooked, such as that one variable is used multiple times. When choosing a rule to apply, do not choose randomly. First, choose rules that are simple and thus visually easy to apply. For example, a rule that states that "S cannot be at 6 P.M." involves only one variable and would be very easy to apply, whereas a rule such as "X must be placed ahead of Y and Z" involves three variables and would be more time-consuming to apply. List questions are usually Global but can be Local. The above question would be designated as a Global, Could be True, List question.

Another type of List question supplies a list of all of the variables that could be placed in a single slot, as in the following:

> Which one of the following is a complete and accurate list of the singers any of which could be the first to perform?
>
> (A) P, S
> (B) P, Q, R, S
> (C) P, Q, R, V
> (D) Q, R, S, V
> (E) Q, R, S, T, V

The question above is not suggesting that each list of variables starts at the first space and goes out from there; rather, the question asks you to identify every variable that could be first in some scenario in the game. Thus, if in one scenario P could be first, then P must appear in the correct answer choice. If in another scenario Q could be first, then Q must also appear in the correct answer choice, and so on.

The initial approach to this question is the same as in the first example above. First, check the rules to see if any of the variables cause a violation when placed in the slot. Second, check all Not Laws for that slot and scan all the answer choices to see if any answers can be eliminated on that basis.

Maximum/Minimum Questions

Maximum/minimum questions generally ask you to identify the greatest or least number of possibilities in a certain scenario, and these questions typically fall into one of two types:

- Questions that ask for the maximum or minimum number of possible variables that can fill a position, or the maximum or minimum number of positions a variable can fill.

- Questions that asked for the maximum or minimum number of variables that can be placed between two other variables, or from one variable to another.

In answering maximum/minimum questions, you must control the variables in order to produce the optimal situation to either maximize the situation or minimize the situation. Essentially, you get to play LSAT god for the purposes of the question, altering and adjusting each situation to produce the desired results.

Consider the following examples from different games:

> What is the maximum possible number of speeches any one of which could be the one given on the third day?

> What is the minimum number of different procedures used by the six surgeons?

> What is the minimum possible number of houses between the Tanners and the Carrolls, counting from east to west?

Maximum/minimum questions are usually Global but can be Local. For the above examples, the first question is a Global, Must Be True, Maximum question (this is the case in spite of the "could be the one" language—since there is only one possible figure that can represent the maximum number of speeches, the correct answer *must be* the maximum number). The second and third questions are Global, Must Be True, Minimum questions.

"5 If" Questions

"5 if" questions are identifiable not by an element in the question stem, but by the language in the five answer choices. Here is an example from an actual game that appears later in the book:

"5 if" problems are dangerous because they are quite time-consuming.

In this question, each of the five answer choices begins with the word "if," hence the "5 if" designation. The "if" adds a new condition to the scenario that must be taken into account, and thus each answer choice is essentially a whole new question. Consequently, test takers are forced to work out a new scenario or solution for each (or most) of the five answer choices. Because these questions are basically five questions in one, they can be incredibly time consuming. If you are a slow test taker or struggling with time issues, you would be well advised to skip these questions or do them after you have completed the other questions in a game.

Suspension Questions

Suspension questions always appear at the end of the game, and they either suspend one of the rules from the game, or they suspend a rule from the game and replace it with a different condition. These questions, although rare, are also very time consuming because usually you must redraw most of the diagram and re-evaluate the relationship of the rules.

Here is an example:

Suppose that the condition that the Marketing conference is scheduled immediately after the Finance conference is replaced with the condition that the Marketing conference is scheduled immediately after the Operations conference and sometime before the Design conference. If all the other conditions remain the same, then which of the conferences could be the Sales conference?

(A)   the first
(B)   the second
(C)   the third
(D)   the fifth
(E)   the seventh

Again, if you are struggling with time, this is a question that you might want to skip, or return to at the end of the section.

Attacking the Questions

One of the critical elements in attacking the questions is the ability to classify the questions as Global or Local, and then to designate each question as one of the "true" characteristics discussed on pages 73-77. Classifying each question will tell you exactly what you are being asked, thereby making your task easier.

The fastest way of finding the correct answer is to read the question stem, process the implications mentally, and then identify the correct answer from among the five answer choices. Of course, this does not happen all that often! Usually, much more work is involved.

In the likely scenario that you do not immediately see the correct answer, keep in mind that there are several simple methods of attacking the questions, as outlined below.

Solve for the Truth

The first step in any Local question is to consider the effects of the condition posed in the question stem. This usually involves drawing out a skeletal version of the main diagram (more on this in the next section) and then working out the problem. Although this may take a few moments, this approach, which is both obvious and intuitive, is often the most effective.

Process of Elimination

As you encounter questions on the LSAT, keep in mind that you do not always have to prove that the right answer is indisputably correct. At times you will be able to easily find the correct answer, especially when using Not Laws or inferences. But it can be equally useful to eliminate each of the incorrect answers and then be left with the correct answer. This process of elimination is extremely useful and can be the most efficient technique for finding the correct answer, especially if you are having difficulty with solving a problem. Even if you cannot prove that answer choice (B) is correct, if you can disprove answer choices (A), (C), (D), and (E), you will know that (B) is correct.

Use process of elimination when applicable.

Hypotheticals

Whenever you find yourself stumped by a problem, instead of just aimlessly pondering what the right answer might be, try to solve the question with a hypothetical. A hypothetical is a possible solution to the question that *you quickly create* to gain insight into the answers. Some questions can be entirely solved with hypotheticals, and in other questions hypotheticals can eliminate several incorrect answer choices. Consider the following question:

Hypotheticals can be a powerful tool for attacking some questions, and although they have an element of creative randomness to them, they are based on the rules and the specific conditions present in individual questions. For example, let's say that a question asks for what must be true when L is in the second position. To create a hypothetical for this question, one would place L in 2, and then attempt to fit the other variables around L in accordance with the rules. The process of performing this operation typically will reveal certain truths about the scenario; that is, what could be true, what cannot be true, etc. Literally, the process of creating hypotheticals is one that forces you to work with the specific scenario, and that typically leads to insights that eliminate certain answers or confirm others.

Which one of the following must be true?

(A)   C speaks third.
(B)   D speaks fourth.
(C)   E speaks fifth.
(D)   F speaks sixth.
(E)   G speaks seventh.

Suppose you were not sure which one of the answers had to be true, and you saw no easy way to solve the problem. Instead of skipping the problem or wasting valuable time, you could quickly create a hypothetical solution to help eliminate some of the incorrect answer choices. Let us say you came up with the following hypothetical:

$$\frac{C}{1} \quad \frac{E}{2} \quad \frac{D}{3} \quad \frac{A}{4} \quad \frac{B}{5} \quad \frac{F}{6} \quad \frac{G}{7}$$

Using this hypothetical, you could eliminate answer choice (A), (B), and (C), leaving only answer choices (D) and (E). If necessary, you could produce another hypothetical to determine whether answer choice (D) or (E) is correct. Although this method will take a bit of time, it is worth it if you can get the question correct. Plus, each hypothetical you create adds to your arsenal of game information, and makes you more comfortable with the way the rules interact. Often, one of the hypotheticals you make can later be used to answer another question.

Let us look at another example. Consider the following question:

Which one of the following could be true?

(A)   P speaks first.
(B)   Q speaks second.
(C)   R speaks third.
(D)   S speaks fourth.
(E)   T speaks fifth.

Again, assume that you do not see an obvious answer and you have already checked your inferences, Not Laws, etc. In this problem, a single hypothetical could prove the correct answer choice. Let us say you came up with the following hypothetical:

$$\frac{T}{1} \quad \frac{P}{2} \quad \frac{R}{3} \quad \frac{Q}{4} \quad \frac{S}{5} \quad \frac{V}{6} \quad \frac{W}{7}$$

This hypothetical alone proves answer choice (C) correct. If you find yourself spending a lot of time thinking about a question, a better approach would probably be to try a few hypotheticals. By coming up with hypotheticals, you are at least making some progress in answering the question.

Placing Diagrams

When you make your main diagram to represent all of the rules, you should create that diagram at the bottom of the page in the empty space beneath the questions, as indicated in the example below:

The process of creating hypotheticals is easier in practice than it sounds in theory, and this book often refers to hypothetical scenarios to explain why certain answers are right or wrong.

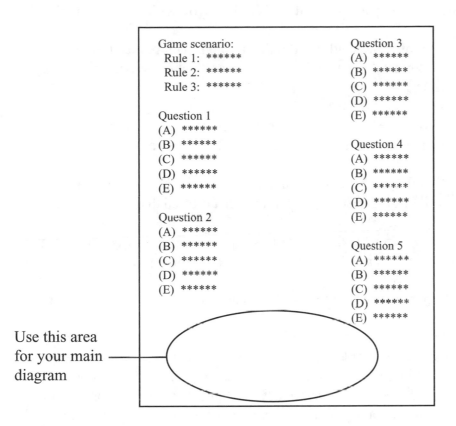

Use this area for your main diagram

The sole exception to this rule is when the test makers supply a diagram within the game scenario and you decide to use that diagram.

When creating your main diagram, do not write too small or too large, do not crowd the rules together, and do not orient your diagram too far to the left or right. In some instances you may find that you need more room on one side than you previously thought, and it is helpful if you still have some room on each side of the diagram to work with. And, of course, you must write neatly.

Remember, you cannot use scratch paper during the scored portions of the LSAT, and so the space at the bottom of each game is the only space you will be able to use to make your main diagram. Yes, we know that there is not much space to work with on some games, but this is one of the challenges set by the test makers.

Diagramming Local Questions

Always do the work for Local questions next to the question itself.

For many Global questions, the work you do in creating your main setup and making inferences will be sufficient to answer the question. Local questions, which supply you with a new piece of information specific to that question only, generally require additional work. You should do this work next to the question itself. This affords you with several benefits:

1. By doing the work next to the problem, you reduce the visual disconnection between your work and the question. This saves you time.

2. If you need to come back to a question, when you return you will be able to see the work you did up to that point.

3. Should you be able to reuse the work you did for the question, you will be able to see the conditions that created that work more easily.

There are two alternate theories to this approach that are widely propagated and we believe each is flawed. Let us take a moment to examine why:

Flawed Approach #1: Do the work for each question on the main diagram

Do not erase any of your work unless you have made a mistake.

This approach suggests that the work for each question should be done on the main diagram. In order to use this method, you must erase your previous work before beginning each question. Erasing your work has a number of negative effects: you could accidentally erase important information that applies to all questions, you could accidentally leave information that applies only to one question, and most importantly, every time you erase your work you lose some of the knowledge that you created about the game. This method also destroys your ability to reuse your work, an approach discussed below. As a rule, *never* erase any of your work unless you have made a mistake.

Flawed Approach #2: Create a "grid" and do the work for each question in rows within the grid

This approach requires that you create a grid near the main setup. The work for each question is then done within rows of the grid, as follows:

	1	2	3	4	5	6
Question #1	T	V	W	Z	X	S
Question #2	V	W		Z		
Question #3		S	X	Z	T	

Although this method is superior to using the first flawed approach above, it too has several negative effects:

1. Drawing the grid and a main setup requires a large amount of space—space that the test makers do not always provide. In contrast, doing the work next to the question is space-efficient.

2. Using the grid creates a three-step visual disconnect: Your eye must travel between the question, the main setup, and the grid. This takes time and can cause confusion. In contrast, doing the work next to the question requires only a two-step visual disconnect: Your eye travels between the question and the corresponding work to the main setup. This saves time and eliminates confusion.

3. Using the grid tends to train students to use horizontal setups that do not contain a vertical component. As will be discussed in the Advanced Linear games section, this is particularly troublesome because the most complex Linear games have both vertical and horizontal components. For example, consider the following game. In this game music classes, three teachers, and three students were each assigned to one of four consecutive days. This produced a setup akin to the following:

    | Student: | __ | __ | __ | __ | (R, S, T) |
    | Teacher: | __ | __ | __ | __ | (G, H, J) |
    | Class: | __ | __ | __ | __ | (B, C, D, E) |
    | | 1 | 2 | 3 | 4 | |

    Trying to reproduce a similar diagram within a grid is a nightmare as each question requires three rows, something the grid is ill-equipped to handle. Any technique you use should work equally well for the hard questions and the easy questions. This is not the case for the grid.

4. As Linear games become more complex, the grid tends to work less and less efficiently. In contrast, working next to the question is always efficient since it allows you to draw the most appropriate diagram for the conditions.

By the way, it seems that many proponents of the grid also use notations such as "X," "O,", and "✓." This type of notation is relatively useless because it abstracts the representation process. Variables are always better represented by directly placing them on the diagram and using Not Laws, etc.

Any setup that use an X, O, or check is weak. See Appendix Three for more information.

Now that we have discussed some flawed methods of diagramming the questions, let us return to the discussion of working next to the question itself. Working next to the question often requires you to re-create the basics of the main setup. This re-creation will be in skeletal form only; there is no need to redraw the entire diagram or all of the rules. Consider the following example:

Main diagram from a Logic game:

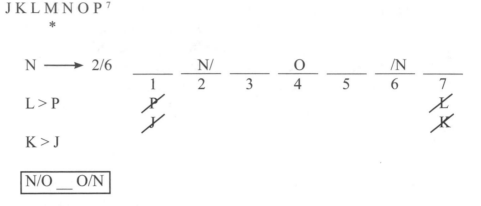

Question #8 from the same game. Do the work next to the question!

11. If P performs second and K performs fifth, the third performer must be

(A) J
(B) L
(C) M
(D) N
(E) O

Note that the work is done on a diagram that reflects just the simple base of the game—none of the rules are redrawn and you can even skip numbering the spaces if you feel comfortable.

Reusing Information

As you work with each question, your knowledge of the game naturally increases. As you approach each question, do not forget that you may have already gained information in a previous question that might apply to the question you are working on. Some students, upon hearing this advice, respond by saying, "But isn't the information in each question relevant to that question only?" Yes, the conditions in the question stem are relevant to that question only, but the work done for that question *may* apply elsewhere. Consider the following scenario:

The first question of the game is a Global, Could Be True, List question, such as this one:

1. Which one of the following is an acceptable schedule for the six speakers?

	Mon.	Tues.	Wed.	Thurs.	Fri.
(A)	B	C	D	E, G	H
(B)	E	B	D	C	G
(C)	C	G	D	B	E, H
(D)	B	C	D	G	E, H
(E)	G	B	D	E	C, H

The correct answer to this question is (E), and this question is considered "easy." Note that once you have established (E) as the correct answer (and it is likely that you would be extremely confident in selecting answer choice (E)), you know that the sequence of G—B—D—E—C, H is a workable solution to the game. In other words, the solution in answer choice (E) is a valid hypothetical given to you for free by the test makers.

Continuing on in the game, question #2 states:

2. Which one of the following is a complete and accurate list of those speakers each of which CANNOT speak on Tuesday?

(A)   C, G
(B)   D, H
(C)   B, C
(D)   B, D
(E)   D, G, H

Since this Global, Cannot Be True, List question asks about Tuesday, the information we derived in question #1 is applicable. In fact, since we know from question #1 answer choice (E) that B can speak on Tuesday, any answer in question #2 that contains B is automatically incorrect. Since both answer choices (C) and (D) contain B, they are both incorrect. Thus, the answer choice to question #1 can be used to eliminate two of the answers in question #2. This certainly reduces the amount of work you have to do in question #2 and it has the added benefit of increasing your speed and confidence as you work through the question.

And, the benefits of using work from question #1 in this game do not stop there. Consider question #3 from the same game:

3. If E speaks on Thursday, B could speak on

(A)   Monday, but on no other day
(B)   Thursday, but on no other day
(C)   Monday or else on Tuesday, but on no other day
(D)   Tuesday or else on Wednesday, but on no other day
(E)   Wednesday or else on Thursday, but on no other day

Only reuse previous answers and work in which you have complete confidence. For instance, if you answer a List question and you are not sure you have the correct answer, do not use the information from that question!

The question to the left is a Local, Could Be True question.

Because E is scheduled for Thursday in question #1 answer choice (E), the solution to question #1 again meets the criteria given in question #3. Thus, we know from question #1 that when E speaks on Thursday, it is possible that B speaks on Tuesday. We can now use this information to attack some of the answer choices in question #3. Specifically, we can eliminate answer choices (A), (B), and (E) since they do not allow for the possibility that B can speak on Tuesday. We are now left with only answer choice (C) and (D) to consider, and it will not take very long to determine which one is correct.

Remember, to reuse work it must meet the criteria given in the question stem of the question on which you are working.

To summarize, it is possible to reuse information from previous questions on subsequent questions, *as long as the work you use meets the criteria in the question you are working on.* The application of this technique to the actual LSAT game under discussion eliminates 5 of the 10 answer choices in questions #2 and #3 without requiring any other work besides referring back to question #1. This technique can be immensely powerful and you should always look to apply it when doing Logic Games. In our discussion of the games in this book, you will see a number of references to this approach.

Final Pregame Note

In our explanations we often include points of interest outside the game, as well as general strategy tips. Therefore, even if you answered the question correctly, you should still read the explanation.

At this point we have covered many of the basic concepts that appear in Linear games, and more importantly, we have defined much of the terminology that we will use in our analysis of the games to come. On the next page is the first of six Linear game challenges. Each game comes from an actual LSAT and has been reproduced exactly as it first appeared, down to the original question numbering. Thus, if a game appeared last in the Analytical Reasoning section, we have numbered it appropriately, perhaps as questions #18-24. The date the game appeared is also given in the header. On the pages immediately following each game, there is a comprehensive explanation of the setup, the inferences, and each question, along with strategy and technical notes. Please be sure to read the explanations carefully, as they will give you a true sense of how to best attack each game.

Write neatly! Sometimes there is not much room to fit in the main diagram on the page or the mini-diagram next to a question.

If you would like to test yourself under timed conditions, you should give yourself 8 minutes and 45 seconds for each game. However, with the first few games we would prefer that you worry less about time and focus more on properly diagramming and analyzing the game. In that vein, before continuing on, we recommend that you go back and review or reread this chapter. Regardless, good luck on the games!

During a period of six consecutive days—day 1 through day 6—each of exactly six factories—F, G, H, J, Q, and R—will be inspected. During this period, each of the factories will be inspected exactly once, one factory per day. The schedule for the inspections must conform to the following conditions:

F is inspected on either day 1 or day 6.
J is inspected on an earlier day than Q is inspected.
Q is inspected on the day immediately before R is inspected.
If G is inspected on day 3, Q is inspected on day 5.

1. Which one of the following could be a list of the factories in the order of their scheduled inspections, from day 1 through day 6?

   (A)   F, Q, R, H, J, G
   (B)   G, H, J, Q, R, F
   (C)   G, J, Q, H, R, F
   (D)   G, J, Q, R, F, H
   (E)   J, H, G, Q, R, F

2. Which one of the following must be false?

   (A)   The inspection of G is scheduled for day 4.
   (B)   The inspection of H is scheduled for day 6.
   (C)   The inspection of J is scheduled for day 4.
   (D)   The inspection of Q is scheduled for day 3.
   (E)   The inspection of R is scheduled for day 2.

3. The inspection of which one of the following CANNOT be scheduled for day 5?

   (A)   G
   (B)   H
   (C)   J
   (D)   Q
   (E)   R

4. The inspections scheduled for day 3 and day 5, respectively, could be those of

   (A)   G and H
   (B)   G and R
   (C)   H and G
   (D)   R and J
   (E)   R and H

5. If the inspection of R is scheduled for the day immediately before the inspection of F, which one of the following must be true about the schedule?

   (A)   The inspection of either G or H is scheduled for day 1.
   (B)   The inspection of either G or J is scheduled for day 1.
   (C)   The inspection of either G or J is scheduled for day 2.
   (D)   The inspection of either H or J is scheduled for day 3.
   (E)   The inspection of either H or J is scheduled for day 4.

6. If the inspections of G and of H are scheduled, not necessarily in that order, for days as far apart as possible, which one of the following is a complete and accurate list of the factories any one of which could be scheduled for inspection for day 1?

   (A)   F, J
   (B)   G, H
   (C)   G, H, J
   (D)   F, G, H
   (E)   F, G, H, J

7. If the inspection of G is scheduled for the day immediately before the inspection of Q, which one of the following could be true?

   (A)   The inspection of G is scheduled for day 5.
   (B)   The inspection of H is scheduled for day 6.
   (C)   The inspection of J is scheduled for day 2.
   (D)   The inspection of Q is scheduled for day 4.
   (E)   The inspection of R is scheduled for day 3.

Analysis of Linear Game #1: June 1996 Questions 1-7

This was the first game on the June 1996 LSAT, and for most students it was a perfect game to begin the section. Previously in this chapter we used the scenario for some of our discussions. The game should be set up as follows:

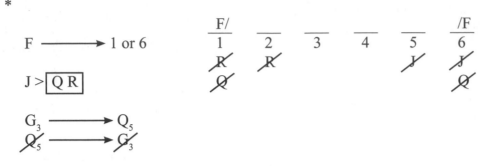

This game is perfectly Balanced, with 6 variables each filling one of 6 slots. The great benefit of doing Balanced games is that as you use a variable, that variable is eliminated from the list and can no longer be used; when you fill a space, that space is unavailable to all other variables. In contrast, Unbalanced games have variables that can sometimes be used again (as in the sixth game in this set), and sometimes a space can contain two or more variables. This tends to make things much more confusing as all of the variables could be used again even if already placed once, and spaces that contain a single variable might still be able to accommodate another.

An analysis of the variables reveals that H is a random, and this is indicated by the "*" notation. The first thing that jumps out regarding the rules is the linkage that can be made between second and third rule. This allows us to make a JQR super rule that yields six Not Laws (if you are unsure why a particular Not Law is given, attempt to place the variable in that space and observe the consequences. This should help you better understand why certain Not Laws appear). Furthermore, since Q appears in both the super rule and the last rule, we can make the following inference:

> If G is inspected on day 3, then Q is inspected on day 5 and R is inspected on day 6. Since R is inspected on day 6, F must be inspected on day 1. This inference leads to the further inference that only two possible scenarios exist when G is inspected on day 3: F-H-G-J-Q-R or F-J-G-H-Q-R.

The other issue to consider is the interaction between F and the Not Laws. If F is inspected first, then the Not Laws shift over one space, and R and Q cannot be inspected second, and R cannot be inspected third. The same logic in reverse can be applied to F in 6.

Rule Diagramming Note: The rule that states, "If G is inspected on day 3, Q is inspected on day 5" is conditional in nature and is represented with an arrow. The second diagram, with the slashes, is the contrapositive of the first diagram, and indicates that if Q is not inspected on day 5, then G is not inspected on day 3. Remember, the contrapositive of a statement is simply another way of expressing the original statement. The famous analogy we use is one that involves a penny: the two sides of a penny look different, but each side refers to the same intrinsic value. The same is true for a statement and its contrapositive.

Also remember, as with all condition rules, to avoid making a Mistaken Reversal: when Q is inspected on day 5, G can be, but does not have to be, inspected on day 3.

With the above analysis, you should be ready to attack the questions.

Question #1: Global, Could Be True, List. The correct answer choice is (B)

This is a Global List question, so apply the proper technique! Generally, the first rule to apply is one that can be seen easily from a visual perspective. In this case you have the choice of several rules that fit that criterion. Let us start with the rule that states F is inspected on either day 1 or day 6. Applying this rule eliminates answer choice (D). Next, apply the rule that states that Q must be inspected the day before R is inspected. This eliminates answer choice (C). Now apply the rules that states that J is inspected on an earlier day than Q is inspected. This eliminates answer choice (A). Now we are down to answer choices (B) and (E). By applying the last rule about G in 3, we can eliminate answer choice (E), and thus answer choice (B) must be the correct answer.

Notice how easy this technique makes this question. There is no stress involved and very little mental energy has been expended. In other words, a perfect way to start the game. Fortunately, many games begin with List questions. One of the further benefits of this type of question is that you have now produced one workable hypothetical, G-H-J-Q-R-F, that you know is valid. Always do List questions first if possible because they are generally easy and always provide you with helpful information.

Question #2: Global, Cannot Be True. The correct answer choice is (E)

This question has been phrased in terms of falsity. Remember, always convert "false" questions into terms of "true." As discussed earlier in this chapter, "must be false" is identical to "cannot be true," and so this question simply asks which one of the following cannot be true. In Global Cannot Be True questions, always look to your Not Laws first for an answer since Not Laws reflect which variables have global restrictions. In this case, our initial Not Laws tell us that answer choice (E) must be correct since R can never be inspected on day 2. Again, Global Cannot Be True questions and Global Must Be True questions lend themselves very well to the use of Not Laws. You did the work for the setup, so why not enjoy the results?

Question #3: Global, Cannot Be True. The correct answer choice is (C)

This question is almost the same as #2, except now the focus is specifically on day 5. According to our Not Laws, J cannot be inspected on day 5, and so it must be that answer choice (C) is correct. This is an excellent example of what "attacking the question" means. By using the Not Laws, you should already know what the answer is before looking at the answer choices. Instead of slowly looking at answer choice (A), then (B), and so on, why not immediately look for "J" as one of the choices? This saves time, and more importantly, builds your confidence as you find the answer that you are looking for.

An interesting aside: the worst answer choice for a student to select in this question is answer choice (E). Why? Because from the hypothetical we produced in question #1 we know that R *can* be scheduled for day 5. Even if you cannot figure out which answer was definitely correct in this problem, you could use that hypothetical to kill answer choice (E) and improve your odds of answering correctly. And, although this information is not of very great value on this question, in future games this technique will prove to be very helpful indeed.

Question #4: Global, Could Be True. The correct answer choice is (E)

Since this question focuses specifically on days 3 and 5, again apply the Not Laws from day 3 and day 5. There are none for day 3, but we see that J cannot be inspected on day 5, and so we can kill off answer choice (D), which attempts to place J in day 5. Now, apply linkage to help eliminate more answer choices: Day 3 appears in the question and it also appears in the last rule. Thus, as you should recall, if G is inspected on day 3, then Q must be inspected on day 5. This information is sufficient to eliminate answer choices (A) and (B) since both have G on day 3 but another variable besides Q on day 5. Now we are down to only two remaining answer choices, yet we have only had to do a minimal amount of work. At this point, quickly scan the two remaining answer choices to see if you can identify the correct answer without doing further work. If you cannot, why not use one of the answer choices to help make a hypothetical that will solve the problem? To prove a "Could Be True" answer, all that is needed is one hypothetical that shows that one of the scenarios is possible, or alternately, a hypothetical that shows that one of the scenarios is impossible. Let us try answer choice (C) first. Make the following notation *right beside the problem*:

$$\underline{\quad} \quad \underline{\quad} \quad \underline{\text{H}} \quad \underline{\quad} \quad \underline{\text{G}} \quad \underline{\quad}$$

Diagramming note: We did not write out the numbers since most people do not need the numbers when they work next to the question. Had this been the main diagram you would most certainly have wanted to write out the number for each space.

As you might see, this scenario presents a problem because there is no room for the QR block. If F is inspected on day 1, there are not two consecutive spaces available for the QR block. If F is inspected on day 6, the only two spaces available for Q and R are days 1 and 2, but that leaves no room for J and so answer choice (C) cannot be correct. By process of elimination this means answer choice (E) must be correct. Notice that we do not need to prove that (E) is possible since we have already eliminated each of the other answer choices. Since the other four are incorrect, answer choice (E) must be correct. Mark it and continue. For those of you wondering if answer choice (E) can fit in a valid solution, here is a hypothetical that fits (E) and fits all of the rules of the game: J-Q-R-G-H-F.

Question #5: Local, Must Be True. The correct answer choice is (D)

The local condition specifies that R is inspected the day before F, which creates this block sequence:

$$J > \boxed{Q\ R\ F}$$

Of course, you should draw out that block sequence right next to the problem. At this point, there are several different ways to proceed with this question. One approach is to check any previous hypothetical to see if it conforms to the requirements in this question. Fortuitously, the only hypothetical we have—from question #1 answer choice (B)—actually conforms to the local condition imposed in this question. Thus, we can use that hypothetical, G-H-J-Q-R-F, to help answer this question. Accordingly, we can eliminate answer choices (C) and (E) since the hypothetical proves that neither *must* be true. Note how the hypothetical partially agrees with answer choices (A), (B), and (D), but it does not prove that they *must* be true.

The other method of attack is to use the linkage involving F. Since F must be in day 1 or day 6, and in this question F is scheduled behind R, we can infer that F must be inspected on day 6. Accordingly, we can make the following hypothetical right next to the problem:

$$\underline{\hspace{1.2em}}\quad\underline{\hspace{1.2em}}\quad\underline{\hspace{1.2em}}\quad\underline{\text{Q}}\quad\underline{\text{R}}\quad\underline{\text{F}}$$
$$1\qquad 2\qquad 3\qquad 4\qquad 5\qquad 6$$
$$\qquad\qquad\cancel{G}$$

Although you may not realize it, this hypothetical solves the problem. If Q, R, and F are already placed, and G cannot be inspected third (that would violate the G3 then Q5 rule), that leaves only H or J to fill day 3. That inference is reflected in the wording of answer choice (D) and thus (D) is correct.

Question #6: Local, Must Be True, List. The correct answer choice is (D)

Note that the question stem asks for a complete and accurate list, and the correct answer must list *all* of the factories that could appear on day 1. So, the correct answer must contain each and every factory that is possible for day 1. As strange as it may sound, the question asks for what must be true about what is possible.

If G and H are to be scheduled as far apart as possible, this would likely place G and H in days 1 and 5 or days 2 and 6 (do not forget that F must be in either day 1 or day 6). Again, there are several ways to approach this question depending on your level of game understanding. At the most advanced level, answer choices (A), (C), and (E) can likely be eliminated since each contains J. If J is inspected on day 1, then F would be inspected on day 6 and G and H would not be as far apart as possible—a violation of the "if" clause in the question. Only F differentiates answer choice (B) from answer choice (D), and since F is a day 1 or day 6 player, it seems likely that answer choice (D) is correct, and in fact it *is* the correct answer. If that type of theoretical analysis makes you a bit nervous, you can always resort to the other form of attack on this question: make a few quick hypotheticals. Here is one that eliminates answer choices (B) and (C): F-G-J-Q-R-H. Another that eliminates answer choice (A) is: G-J-Q-R-H-F. And again, the inclusion of J in answer choice (E) should be a tip-off that answer choice (E) is likely incorrect.

Question #7: Local, Could Be True. The correct answer choice is (C)

The last question in a game is often the most difficult, and that general rule holds true here. Let us take a moment to examine why Law Services so often makes the last question difficult. The key to understanding this phenomenon is to look at it from a psychological perspective. As you near the end of a game, your mind naturally begins to focus on quickly finishing the game at hand and preparing for the next game. At just this point, when you want to go more quickly, Law Services throws in a difficult question. This tends to have the effect of slowing you down considerably, and that usually leads to a degree of frustration. Once you become frustrated, your chances of missing the question increase. And when you go to the next game, you may still be thinking about what happened on the last question, and that can contribute to a poor start on the new game, causing further trouble. In a nutshell, do not forget about the importance of psychology on the test. You must remain positive, focused, and calm throughout each section. If you become upset or frustrated, take a moment to relax and regain your equilibrium.

The local condition in the question stem sets up the following relationship:

$$J > \boxed{G\ Q\ R}$$

This sequential relationship automatically produces several Not Laws:

In addition, the interaction of the last rule and the sequence further establishes that G cannot be inspected on day 3 since it would then be impossible for Q to be inspected on day 5 (in this question if G is inspected on day 3 then R would be inspected on day 5). Also, because of the block produced by the question stem, if G cannot be inspected on day 3, then Q cannot be inspected on day 4 and R cannot be inspected on day 5. Using these inferences and the Not Laws above, we can eliminate answer choices (A), (D), and (E) from consideration. At this point, unless you see what distinguishes answer choice (B) from answer choice (C), the best strategy would probably be to try a quick hypothetical using either answer choice. As it turns out, answer choice (B) is incorrect, since if H is inspected on day 6 the following impossible scenario results:

$$\frac{F}{1} \quad \frac{J}{2} \quad \frac{G}{3} \quad \frac{Q}{4} \quad \frac{R}{5} \quad \frac{H}{6}$$

As shown above, G is inspected on day 3, but Q is not inspected on day 5—a violation of the last rule. By process of elimination, answer choice (C) is proven correct.

Some students question whether answer choice (C) can be valid since it leads to a solution (F-J-H-G-Q-R) where Q is inspected on day 5 but G is not inspected on day 3. Remember, the conditional rule only activates if G is inspected on day 3. If Q is inspected on day 5, nothing necessarily happens (to think otherwise would be a Mistaken Reversal).

A messenger will deliver exactly seven packages—L, M, N, O, P, S, and T—one at a time, not necessarily in that order. The seven deliveries must be made according to the following conditions:

P is delivered either first or seventh.

The messenger delivers N at some time after delivering L.

The messenger delivers T at some time after delivering M.

The messenger delivers exactly one package between delivering L and delivering O, whether or not L is delivered before O.

The messenger delivers exactly one package between delivering M and delivering P, whether or not M is delivered before P.

8. Which one of the following is an order in which the messenger could make the deliveries, from first to seventh?

   (A) L, N, S, O, M, T, P
   (B) M, T, P, S, L, N, O
   (C) O, S, L, N, M, T, P
   (D) P, N, M, S, O, T, L
   (E) P, T, M, S, L, N, O

9. Which one of the following could be true?

   (A) N is delivered first.
   (B) T is delivered first.
   (C) T is delivered second.
   (D) M is delivered fourth.
   (E) S is delivered seventh.

10. If N is delivered fourth, which one of the following could be true?

    (A) L is delivered first.
    (B) L is delivered second.
    (C) M is delivered third.
    (D) O is delivered fifth.
    (E) S is delivered first.

11. If T is delivered fourth, the seventh package delivered must be

    (A) L
    (B) N
    (C) O
    (D) P
    (E) S

12. If the messenger delivers M at some time after delivering O, the fifth package delivered could be any one of the following EXCEPT:

    (A) L
    (B) M
    (C) N
    (D) S
    (E) T

This was the second game on the September 1998 LSAT, and many of our students were able to score a perfect 5-0 on the questions. The game should be set up as follows:

L M N O P S T ^{7}
       *

This game is perfectly Balanced, with 7 variables each filling one of 7 slots. An analysis of the variables reveals that S is a random, and this is indicated by the "*" notation. The first inference that can be made comes from the linkage of M and P. Since P must be delivered first or seventh, and exactly one package is delivered between P and M, it follows that M must be delivered third or fifth. Therefore, M cannot be delivered first, second, fourth, sixth or seventh. Since the earliest M can be delivered is third, that affects the delivery of T, and it can be inferred that T cannot be delivered first, second, or third.

Two other Not Laws also bear further examination. First, S cannot be delivered third because it sets off a the following chain: M would be delivered fifth and P would be delivered seventh; in turn L and O have to be delivered second and fourth, with L being delivered second; this causes a problem since there is no room for N, which must be delivered after L. Second, O cannot be delivered fifth because of the problems it causes: M would have to be delivered third and P would have to be delivered first; since O and L must be separated by one package, L would have to be delivered seventh, and that is impossible since L must be delivered ahead of N.

Additionally, since the MP split-block is reduced to exactly two spacing options, one approach to setting up the game involves drawing out the two options (Identify the Templates™—to be discussed in a later chapter), which are labeled #1 and #2 below:

	#1:						M	T	P
	#2:	P		M					
		1	2	3	4	5	6	7

In option #1, we can link rules and apply the M > T rule, which yields the inference that T must be sixth when P is seventh and M is fifth. At this point, it should be apparent that you will have to keep an eye on L, N, and O since they are linked together. In general, the variables L, M, and P are the most powerful since each appears in two separate rules.

Question #8: Global, Could Be True, List. The correct answer choice is (C)

This type of question is your best friend when it comes to Games questions. Always make sure to apply the proper List question technique. The best rule to start with is the rule that states that P is delivered either first or seventh. Applying this rule eliminates answer choice (B). Next apply the rule that states that L > N. This eliminates answer choice (D). Now apply the M > T rule, and you can eliminate answer choice (E). Of course, so far we have applied the rules in order, but that also happens to be the preferred order from a visual standpoint. The last two rules are less desirable, because they force you to deal with variables that can switch back and forth, and so they are harder to see within the answer choices. That is why we have held them until the end, not because they are the last two rules. The order in which you apply the rules to a List question should not be determined by the order of the presentation of the rules. Finally, by applying the LO split-block rule, we can eliminate answer choice (A), and it follows that answer choice (C) is correct by process of elimination. This question is very easy and you should have had no trouble with it.

Question #9: Global, Could Be True. The correct answer choice is (E)

This question can easily be attacked by applying the Not Laws deduced in the setup. The Not Laws eliminate answer choices (A), (B), (C), and (D), and thus answer choice (E) is correct.

Question #10: Local, Could Be True. The correct answer choice is (A)

This is a Local question, and thus you should reproduce a mini-setup next to the question. Since this is a Could Be True question, and we have two major templates produced by the MP split-block (one template with P delivered first, and another template with P delivered last), why not reproduce both templates, and show each with N delivered fourth, as follows:

#1:	L/O	S	O/L	N	M	T	P
~~#2:~~	~~P~~	~~L~~	~~M~~	~~N~~			
	1	2	3	4	5	6	7

Note that the "#1" and "#2" designations are for our discussion purposes only; during the game you would not want to waste the time writing these designations out. An analysis of the two templates reveals that template #2 can never occur, and thus, that template is crossed out. If N is delivered fourth, then L would have to be delivered second (remember, we are only discussing template #2), but if L is delivered second, then the LO split-block dictates that O must be delivered fourth, and O cannot be delivered fourth in template #2 because N is already delivered there. Thus, in checking the answers, we should only refer to template #1.

In template #1 the only uncertainty involves L and O, and because this is a Could Be True question, you should immediately look at any answer that references L or O. Answer choice (A) references L, and since (A) could be true, it is the correct answer. Answer choice (B) also references L, but (B) cannot be true, and so it is incorrect. Answer choice (D) references O, but (D) cannot be true, and so it is also incorrect. Remember, once you make your mini-diagram in a Could Be True question, attack the answers by ignoring the variables that are placed. Instead, you can gain time by looking only at those answers that contain unplaced or moving variables (such as L and O in this problem).

Question #11: Local, Must Be True. The correct answer choice is (C)

Again, this is a Local question, and we can make a mini-setup in the space next to the question. Start with the condition given in the question stem:

$$\frac{}{1} \quad \frac{}{2} \quad \frac{}{3} \quad \frac{T}{4} \quad \frac{}{5} \quad \frac{}{6} \quad \frac{}{7}$$

Since M > T, we can infer that P must be delivered first, and M must be delivered third:

$$\frac{P}{1} \quad \frac{}{2} \quad \frac{M}{3} \quad \frac{T}{4} \quad \frac{}{5} \quad \frac{}{6} \quad \frac{}{7}$$

And, since L and O are in a split-block, we can continue to add inferences:

$$\frac{P}{1} \quad \frac{}{2} \quad \frac{M}{3} \quad \frac{T}{4} \quad \frac{L/O}{5} \quad \frac{}{6} \quad \frac{O/L}{7}$$

However, since L > N, we can infer that L must be delivered fifth, N must be delivered sixth, and O must be delivered seventh. And since six variables have been placed, it follows that S must be delivered second:

$$\frac{P}{1} \quad \frac{S}{2} \quad \frac{M}{3} \quad \frac{T}{4} \quad \frac{L}{5} \quad \frac{N}{6} \quad \frac{O}{7}$$

Accordingly, the correct answer choice must be (C).

Note how S, the random variable, is the last variable to be placed. Randoms are typically the least powerful variables in a game because they are not involved in any rules and therefore when they are placed they do not affect other variables directly. Randoms do take up space and so they have some power, but a variable such as L or M is much more powerful in this game because each of those variables directly affects two variables. Consider this point a bit more closely by comparing variables S and L:

Variable Placed	Effect
S	1. Takes up the assigned space, thereby prohibiting other variables from occupying that space.
L	1. Takes up the assigned space, thereby prohibiting other variables from occupying that space. 2. Limits the placement of N. 3. Limits the placement of O.

Aside from the fact that L has fewer placement options due to its relationships with other variables, once L is placed it has powerful effects on those variables. S, on the other hand, has no direct effect on other variables. So, when solving a problem, S would not be one of the first variables you should look at. Instead, you should look to the power variables within a game to help you solve the questions. One side effect of the lesser power of randoms is that you often see them placed last within individual solutions. Since they are largely "free," they can often float until the end before they need to be placed.

Question #12: Local, Could Be True, Except. The correct answer choice is (A)

The inclusion of "Except" in the question stem turns the meaning of the question "upside down," and so the four incorrect answer choices have the characteristic of Could Be True, and the one correct answer choice has the characteristic of Cannot Be True. In this way, the question can be analyzed as a simple Cannot Be True question, and in doing so we have negated the confusing effect of the word "except."

By adding the "if" statement in the question stem to our original rules, we arrive at the following chain sequence:

$$O > M > T$$

Once again, this is a Local question and the best approach is to make a mini-diagram next to the question, again accounting for the two basic templates created by the MP split-block:

#1:	(L,	N,	O,	S)	M	T	P
#2:	P	O	M	L	(N,	S,	T)
	1	2	3	4	5	6	7

In the first template, P is delivered last and M is delivered fifth. According to the third rule, T must then be delivered sixth. The remaining four variables—L, N, O, and S—must then be delivered in the first four positions, in accordance with the remaining rules. The parentheses around L, N, O, and S are an efficient notation that indicates the enclosed variables are to be placed in the consecutive spaces in some order.

In the second template, P is delivered first and M is delivered third. According to the condition in the question stem, O must then be delivered second. And, because O is delivered second, L must then be delivered fourth as dictated by the fourth rule. The remaining three variables—N, S, and T—must then be delivered in the final three spaces in some order.

Since the question stem specifically focuses on the fifth package delivered, we can use our mini-diagram to quickly deduce which packages can be delivered fifth and then use that information to eliminate answer choices. From the first template it is proven that package M can be delivered fifth, and thus answer choice (B) can be eliminated. From the second template, it can be determined that packages N, S, and T can be delivered fifth, and this information eliminates answer choices (C), (D), and (E). At this point, the only remaining answer choice is (A), and it follows that response (A) is correct.

An alternate way to use the two templates is to say that the list of variables that could possibly appear fifth includes M from the first template, and N, S, and T from the second template. An examination of the answer choices reveals that only L in answer choice (A) does not appear as a possibility, and thus answer choice (A) must be correct.

Charlie makes a soup by adding exactly six kinds of foods—kale, lentils, mushrooms, onions, tomatoes, and zucchini—to a broth, one food at a time. No food is added more than once. The order in which Charlie adds the foods to the broth must be consistent with the following:

> If the mushrooms are added third, then the lentils are added last.
>
> If the zucchini is added first, then the lentils are added at some time before the onions.
>
> Neither the tomatoes nor the kale is added fifth.
>
> The mushrooms are added at some time before the tomatoes or the kale, but not before both.

1. Which one of the following could be the order in which the foods are added to the broth?

   (A) kale, mushrooms, onions, lentils, tomatoes, zucchini

   (B) kale, zucchini, mushrooms, tomatoes, lentils, onions

   (C) lentils, mushrooms, zucchini, kale, onions, tomatoes

   (D) zucchini, lentils, kale, mushrooms, onions, tomatoes

   (E) zucchini, tomatoes, onions, mushrooms, lentils, kale

2. Which one of the following foods CANNOT be added first?

   (A) kale
   (B) lentils
   (C) mushrooms
   (D) onions
   (E) tomatoes

3. If the lentils are added last, then which one of the following must be true?

   (A) At least one of the foods is added at some time before the zucchini.
   (B) At least two of the foods are added at some time before the kale.
   (C) The mushrooms are added third.
   (D) The zucchini is added third.
   (E) The tomatoes are added fourth.

4. Which one of the following could be an accurate partial ordering of the foods added to the broth?

   (A) lentils: second; mushrooms: third
   (B) mushrooms: fourth; lentils: last
   (C) onions: second; mushrooms: fifth
   (D) zucchini: first; lentils: last
   (E) zucchini: first; mushrooms: second

5. If the zucchini is added first, then which one of the following CANNOT be true?

   (A) The kale is added second.
   (B) The tomatoes are added second.
   (C) The lentils are added third.
   (D) The lentils are added fourth.
   (E) The onions are added fourth.

K L M O T Z⁶

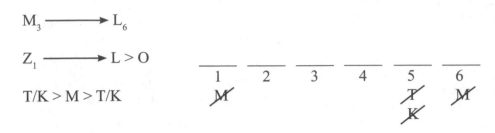

This game—a balanced basic linear game—provides a great start to the June 2003 LSAT. The game features six foods added one at a time, and thus we have created a diagram with six spaces. Because no food can be added more than once, the variables are in a one-to-one relationship with the spaces.

The first two rules of this game are conditional, and Linear games that feature conditional rules often are slightly harder than games that feature only Not Law, block, and sequencing rules. A close examination of the first two rules yields some useful inferences:

> When Z is added first, L must be added before O. Thus, when Z is added first, L cannot be added sixth and O cannot be added second:

$$Z_1 \longleftarrow\!\!\!\!|\longrightarrow L_6$$

$$Z_1 \longleftarrow\!\!\!\!|\longrightarrow O_2$$

> From the first rule, we know that when M is added third, L must be added sixth. Thus, if M is added third, then L could not come before O, and therefore when M is third, Z cannot be first:

$$Z_1 \longleftarrow\!\!\!\!|\longrightarrow M_3$$

> Clearly, when Z is added first, the number of solutions to the game is limited. These scenarios are tested in question #5 and will be discussed in more detail then.

The last rule also bears examination. The rule is sequential, but contains an element of uncertainty because you cannot determine the exact relative order of the variables. There are only two possible orders that result from the rule:

$$T > M > K$$
or
$$K > M > T$$

Regardless of the exact order, we can infer that M is never added first or last (this is shown on our diagram with Not Laws). Additionally, if M is added second, either T or K must be added first; if M is added fifth, either T or K must be added sixth.

Combining the third and fourth rules, we can infer that if M is added fourth, then T or K must be added sixth.

If we combine the first and last rule, we can infer that if M is added third, then either T or K must be added fourth.

The above discussion should help you focus on M and Z as key variables in this game. Of additional note is the fact that there are no randoms in this game.

Question #1: Global, Could Be True, List. The correct answer choice is (D)

Answer choice (A) is incorrect because T cannot be added fifth.
Answer choice (B) is incorrect because if M is added third then L must be added sixth.
Answer choice (C) is incorrect because either K or T must be added before M.
Answer choice (D) is the correct answer.
Answer choice (E) is incorrect because if Z is added first then L must be added before O.

Question #2: Global, Cannot Be True. The correct answer choice is (C)

From our Not Laws we know that M cannot be added first, and thus answer choice (C) is correct.

Question #3: Local, Must Be True. The correct answer choice is (A)

If L is added last, from our first inference we know that Z cannot be added first. Thus, as stated in answer choice (A), at least one of the foods is added at some time before Z.

Question #4: Global, Could Be True. The correct answer choice is (C)

This is an unusual partial List question.

Answer choice (A) is incorrect because when M is added third then L must be added sixth.
Answer choice (B) is incorrect because the proposed scenario would force K or T to be added fifth, and that would be a violation of the third rule.
Answer choice (C) is the correct answer.
Answer choice (D) is incorrect because if Z is added first then L cannot be added last.
Answer choice (E) is incorrect because if Z is added first then M cannot be added second.

Note that answer choices (B), (D), and (E) are all violations of the inferences discussed above.

Question #5: Local, Cannot Be True. The correct answer choice is (D)

This question tests the limited scenarios that result when Z is added first. When Z is added first, M cannot be second, third, or last. Hence, we can create two hypotheticals based on the position of M:

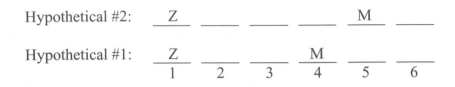

Because the position of M is restricted, we should first apply the last rule (and the third rule because it affects K and T) :

Hypothetical #2: Z (K/T, ____ ____) M T/K

Hypothetical #1: Z (K/T, ___) M ___ T/K
 1   2   3   4   5   6

Finally, by applying the second rule, we can fill in each hypothetical:

Hypothetical #2: Z (K/T, L > O) M T/K

Hypothetical #1: Z (K/T, L) M O T/K
 1   2   3   4   5   6

When applying the second rule, in Hypothetical #1 we can infer that O must be added fifth by taking the following steps:

1. There are only three open spaces.
2. Since K/T > M, we know that K/T must be added second or third.
3. Since L > O, L must then be second or third.
4. The only remaining space for O is the fifth.

Both hypotheticals must be considered when answering the question. Answer choice (D) is correct: in Hypothetical #1 we know M is fourth, and in Hypothetical #2 we know L cannot be fourth because L > O. Thus, L cannot be added fourth when Z is added first.

Question #5 is probably the most difficult question, and the only effective way to attack the question is to use hypotheticals. Hopefully, by quickly answering questions #1 through #4 you will build enough time to comfortably work through question #5.

In the course of one month Garibaldi has exactly seven different meetings. Each of her meetings is with exactly one of five foreign dignitaries: Fuentes, Matsuba, Rhee, Soleimani, or Tbahi. The following constraints govern Garibaldi's meetings:

She has exactly three meetings with Fuentes, and exactly one with each of the other dignitaries.

She does not have any meetings in a row with Fuentes.

Her meeting with Soleimani is the very next one after her meeting with Tbahi.

Neither the first nor last of her meetings is with Matsuba.

1. Which one of the following could be the sequence of the meetings Garibaldi has with the dignitaries?

   (A) Fuentes, Rhee, Tbahi, Soleimani, Fuentes, Matsuba, Rhee
   (B) Fuentes, Tbahi, Soleimani, Matsuba, Fuentes, Fuentes, Rhee
   (C) Fuentes, Rhee, Fuentes, Matsuba, Fuentes, Tbahi, Soleimani
   (D) Fuentes, Tbahi, Matsuba, Fuentes, Soleimani, Rhee, Fuentes
   (E) Fuentes, Tbahi, Soleimani, Fuentes, Rhee, Fuentes, Matsuba

2. If Garibaldi's last meeting is with Rhee, then which one of the following could be true?

   (A) Garibaldi's second meeting is with Soleimani.
   (B) Garibaldi's third meeting is with Matsuba.
   (C) Garibaldi's fourth meeting is with Soleimani
   (D) Garibaldi's fifth meeting is with Matsuba.
   (E) Garibaldi's sixth meeting is with Soleimani.

3. If Garibaldi's second meeting is with Fuentes, then which one of the following is a complete and accurate list of the dignitaries with any one of whom Garibaldi's fourth meeting could be?

   (A) Fuentes, Soleimani, Rhee
   (B) Matsuba, Rhee, Tbahi
   (C) Matsuba, Soleimani
   (D) Rhee, Tbahi
   (E) Fuentes, Soleimani

4. If Garibaldi's meeting with Rhee is the very next one after Garibaldi's meeting with Soleimani, then which one of the following must be true?

   (A) Garibaldi's third meeting is with Fuentes.
   (B) Garibaldi's fourth meeting is with Rhee.
   (C) Garibaldi's fifth meeting is with Fuentes.
   (D) Garibaldi's sixth meeting is with Rhee.
   (E) Garibaldi's seventh meeting is with Fuentes.

5. If Garibaldi's first meeting is with Tbahi, then Garibaldi's meeting with Rhee could be the

   (A) second meeting
   (B) third meeting
   (C) fifth meeting
   (D) sixth meeting
   (E) seventh meeting

6. If Garibaldi's meeting with Matsuba is the very next meeting after Garibaldi's meeting with Rhee, then with which one of the following dignitaries must Garibaldi's fourth meeting be?

   (A) Fuentes
   (B) Matsuba
   (C) Rhee
   (D) Soleimani
   (E) Tbahi

Analysis of Linear Game #4: October 2004 Questions 1-6

This is a basic linear game featuring five dignitaries placed in seven meetings. Because there are only five dignitaries, this game is underfunded, but the very first rule establishes that F must meet with Garibaldi three times, and so the composition of the group of dignitaries is precisely defined and balanced.

After reviewing the game scenario and the rules, you should make the following basic setup for this game:

F F F M R S T [7]

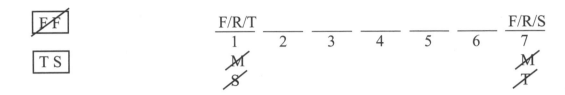

Note that the fourth rule involving M is represented by Not Laws on meetings 1 and 7. Let's take a moment to discuss the second and third rules.

Rule #2. This rule establishes that none of the three meetings with F can be consecutive. At a minimum, then, the three meetings with F require five spaces (meaning that among other things that if the TS block created by rule #3 is placed at the beginning or end of the meeting schedule then the placement of the three F's will automatically be determined). Given the open-ended nature of this rule, and the fact that it addresses three of the seven meetings, this rule will play a major role in the game.

Rule #3. This rule creates a fixed block involving T and S. Because S is always the next meeting after T, S can never be Garibaldi's first meeting; because T is always the meeting before S, T can never be Garibaldi's last meeting. These two inferences are shown as Not Laws on the diagram above.

This game does not present a large amount of information in the scenario and rules, and you should expect to see a high number of Local questions, which will supply the additional information needed to place some of the variables. Given the dearth of information generated in the setup, we have elected to show the triple-options present for the first and last meetings. Since there are only five dignitaries, and the Not Laws eliminate two of those dignitaries from attending the first or last meeting, only three possible dignitaries could attend either meeting.

One other point of note is that R is a random in this game, and R can attend the first or last meeting.

Question #1: Global, Could Be True, List. The correct answer choice is (C)

As with any List question, simply apply the rules to the answer choices. Remember to apply the rules in order of the easiest to "see" within the answers. In this game, that order would be rule #4, rule #3, rule #2, and then rule #1 (rule #2 and rule #3 are equally easy to see, but we chose to apply rule #3 first since that allows rules #2 and #1—both of which involve F— to be applied together).

Answer choice (A): This answer is eliminated by the first rule. In this instance, there are only two meetings with F, instead of three.

Answer choice (B): This answer choice is incorrect because two of the meetings with F are consecutive, a violation of the second rule.

Answer choice (C): This is the correct answer choice.

Answer choice (D): Because T and S are not a block, this answer choice violates the third rule, and is therefore incorrect.

Answer choice (E): Because M is last, this answer choice violates the fourth rule and is incorrect.

Question #2: Local, Could Be True. The correct answer choice is (D)

This question is best attacked with hypotheticals. The question stem establishes that R is Garibaldi's seventh meeting:

From our discussion of the first and last meetings, we know that either F or T must now be Garibaldi's first meeting. However, the placement of R has limited the options for F, and if T is placed first then from the third rule S must be the second meeting, and there would not be sufficient room to separate the three meetings with F (meetings 1, 2, and 7 would be occupied, leaving only meetings 3-6 for the three F's). Consequently, we can infer that F must be Garibaldi's first meeting:

At this point, the placement of the TS block and the two remaining F's must be considered. The TS block cannot occupy meetings #3-4 or #5-6 because that would force two of the three F's to be consecutive (if this does not appear logical, try placing the TS block in either of those positions and observe the results). Consequently, there are only two possible scenarios:

1. TS occupies the second and third meetings and the remaining two F's occupy the meetings fourth and sixth meetings. M is then forced into the fifth meeting.

2. TS occupies the fourth and fifth meetings and the remaining two F's occupy the third and sixth meetings. M is then forced into the second meeting.

The two scenarios can be diagrammed as follows:

Scenario #2:	F	M	F	T	S	F	R
Scenario #1:	F	T	S	F	M	F	R
	1	2	3	4	5	6	7

Answer choices (A), (C), and (E): According to the two solutions to this question, Garibaldi's meets with S in either the third or fifth meetings. Consequently, each of these answer choices is incorrect.

Answer choice (B): As shown by the two diagrams, Garibaldi's third meeting must either be with F or S, and thus this answer choice is incorrect.

Answer choice (D): This is the correct answer choice.

Question #3: Local, Could Be True, List. The correct answer choice is (E)

The assignment of F to the second meeting has an immediate impact on the choices for the *first* meeting. We know that only F, R or T could be Garibaldi's first meeting. With F as the second meeting, the first meeting cannot be with F as that would violate the second rule. The first meeting also cannot be with T as there is no room to place S immediately after T. Consequently, when F is Garibaldi's second meeting, R *must* be Garibaldi's first meeting:

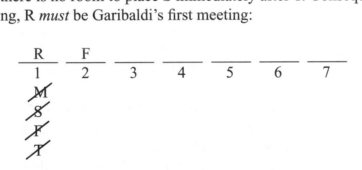

This powerful deduction immediately eliminates answer choices (A), (B), and (D), each of which contain R. A very insightful test maker might realize at this point which variables could be Garibaldi's fourth meeting, but let's continue analyzing this problem as if we did not have that insight.

Comparing the remaining two answer choices, (C) and (E), both contain S, so the comparison should focus on M and F, the unique variables in each of the remaining answer choices.

Answer choice (C): A quick test of this answer would be to create a hypothetical that places M into the fourth meeting:

R	F		M			
1	2	3	4	5	6	7

Placing M fourth immediately forces the two remaining F's into the fifth and seventh meetings:

R	F		M	F		F
1	2	3	4	5	6	7

At this point there is no room for the TS block, and so we can eliminate this answer choice since placing M fourth does not allow us to create a viable solution.

Answer choice (E): This is the correct answer choice. The following hypothetical proves that F can be Garibaldi's fourth meeting:

R	F	M	F	T	S	F
1	2	3	4	5	6	7

Question #4: Local, Must Be True. The correct answer choice is (E)

The condition in the question stem creates an SR block. Adding this to the third rule, we arrive at the following super-block:

$$\boxed{T \ S \ R}$$

The size of this block presents immediate problems for the three F's, and you must consider the placement options of the block prior to attacking the answer choices. First, the block cannot be placed at the beginning or the end of the series of meetings because that would not leave sufficient room to separate the three meetings with F (if meetings 1-3 are occupied by the block, then only meetings 4-7 are available for the three F's; if meetings 5-7 are occupied by the block, then only meetings 1-4 are available for the three F's). Consequently, the TSR block must be placed in either meetings 2-4, 3-5, or 4-6. We can also deduce that F must be Garibaldi's first meeting because only F, R, or T could be Garibaldi's first meeting, and with T and R involved in the block neither can be first. With this fact in hand, you should quickly create hypotheticals reflecting each placement option:

Option #1: TSR as the second, third, and fourth meetings

When the TSR block is placed as the second, third, and fourth meetings, the remaining two F's must be placed as the fifth and seventh meetings, leaving M as the sixth meeting.

F	T	S	R	F	M	F
1	2	3	4	5	6	7

Option #2: TSR as the third, fourth, and fifth meetings

Hopefully you realized that this placement option would be unworkable prior to drawing out the diagram. When the TSR block is placed as the third, fourth, and fifth meetings, there is no way to place the other two F's so that they do not violate the second rule. Consequently, TSR cannot be placed in this position and a viable hypothetical cannot be created.

F		T	S	R		
1	2	3	4	5	6	7

Option #3: TSR as the fourth, fifth, and sixth meetings

When the TSR block is placed as the fourth, fifth, and sixth meetings, the remaining two F's must be placed as the third and seventh meetings, leaving M as the second meeting.

F	M	F	T	S	R	F
1	2	3	4	5	6	7

Thus, the condition in the question stem only allows for two solutions to the question:

TSR in 4-5-6:

F	M	F	T	S	R	F

TSR in 2-3-4:

F	T	S	R	F	M	F
1	2	3	4	5	6	7

Answer choices (A), (B), (C), and (D): Each of these answer choices could be true. However, this is a Must be true question, and thus each of these answers is incorrect.

Answer choice (E): This is the correct answer choice. As proven by the two solutions above, F is always the last meeting.

Question #5: Local, Could Be True. The correct answer choice is (D)

This is one of the easier questions in the game. If Garibaldi's first meeting is with T, then according to the third rule, Garibaldi's second meeting must be with S:

T	S					
1	2	3	4	5	6	7

At this juncture, the three F's must be placed in such a way that they are not consecutive. There is only one way that this can occur, by placing F in the third, fifth, and seventh meetings :

T	S	F		F		F
1	2	3	4	5	6	7

The remaining two variables—M and R—form a dual-option in the fourth and sixth meetings:

T	S	F	M/R	F	R/M	F
1	2	3	4	5	6	7

Consequently, Garibaldi's meeting with R could be either the fourth or sixth meeting, and answer choice (D) is correct.

Answer choices (A), (B), (C), and (E): Each of these answer choices is proven incorrect by the diagram above.

Question #6: Local, Must Be True. The correct answer choice is (A)

The condition in this question stem creates an RM block. Initially, it may seem as though this block has a wide number of placement options, but take a moment to consider the five variable groups created by this rule:

The interaction of the RM block, the TS block, and the second rule limits the placement options of each variable (creating a classic Separation Principle scenario, a concept that will be discussed in more detail in the next chapter). For example, because the F's cannot be consecutive, they must be separated by the two blocks. Consider this for a moment—if you have to separate the three F's with just two blocks, where must the F's be placed? One of the blocks has to separate the first two F's, and the other block has to separate the last two F's, like so:

If the two blocks are not placed as they are above, at least two of the F's will be consecutive, violating the second rule. Consequently, the F's are forced into the first, fourth, and seventh meetings. The two blocks are interchangeable, and either TS or RM could be in either position 2-3 or 5-6.

Answer choice (A): This is the correct answer choice. If you are still uncertain about this answer choice, try placing a variable other than F into the fourth meeting. You will quickly see that any variable other than F in the fourth meeting will not allow for a workable solution.

Answer choices (B), (C), (D), and (E): Each of these answer choices is incorrect because they would not yield a viable solution for the question.

In order to separate the game from its answer key and explanations,
the fifth game is on the next page.

An apartment building has five floors. Each floor has either one or two apartments. There are exactly eight apartments in the building. The residents of the building are J, K, L, M, N, O, P, and Q, who each live in a different apartment.

J lives on a floor with two apartments.
K lives on the floor directly above P.
The second floor is made up of only one apartment.
M and N live on the same floor.
O does not live on the same floor as Q.
L lives in the only apartment on her floor.
Q does not live on the first or second floor.

6. Which one of the following must be true?

    (A)   Q lives on the third floor.
    (B)   Q lives on the fifth floor.
    (C)   L does not live on the fourth floor.
    (D)   N does not live on the second floor.
    (E)   J lives on the first floor.

7. Which one of the following CANNOT be true?

    (A)   K lives on the second floor.
    (B)   M lives on the first floor.
    (C)   N lives on the fourth floor.
    (D)   O lives on the third floor.
    (E)   P lives on the fifth floor.

8. If J lives on the fourth floor and K lives on the fifth floor, which one of the following can be true?

    (A)   O lives on the first floor.
    (B)   Q lives on the fourth floor.
    (C)   N lives on the fifth floor.
    (D)   L lives on the fourth floor.
    (E)   P lives on the third floor.

9. If O lives on the second floor, which one of the following CANNOT be true?

    (A)   K lives on the fourth floor.
    (B)   K lives on the fifth floor.
    (C)   L lives on the first floor.
    (D)   L lives on the third floor.
    (E)   L lives on the fourth floor.

10. If M lives on the fourth floor, which one of the following must be false?

    (A)   O lives on the fifth floor.
    (B)   J lives on the first floor.
    (C)   L lives on the second floor.
    (D)   Q lives on the third floor.
    (E)   P lives on the first floor.

11. Which one of the following must be true?

    (A)   If J lives on the fourth floor, then Q does not live on the fifth floor.
    (B)   If O lives on the second floor, then L does not live on the fourth floor.
    (C)   If N lives on the fourth floor, then K does not live on the second floor.
    (D)   If K lives on the third floor, then O does not live on the fifth floor.
    (E)   If P lives on the fourth floor, then M does not live on the third floor.

12. If O lives on the fourth floor and P lives on the second floor, which one of the following must be true?

    (A)   L lives on the first floor.
    (B)   M lives on the third floor.
    (C)   Q lives on the third floor.
    (D)   N lives on the fifth floor.
    (E)   Q lives on the fifth floor.

Analysis of Linear Game #5: October 1991 Questions 6-12

This game comes from the second LSAT of the modern era, the October 1991 LSAT. The Logic Games section on the October 1991 exam was interesting because for the typical student, the games were presented in order of difficulty. On a related note, you will sometimes hear that older LSATs from the early 1990s are no longer relevant and that they need not be studied. The main proponents of this ridiculous view are certain test preparation companies that do not want to incur the expense of providing these LSATs to their students. Because Law Services charges a licensing fee for every question used, it is far cheaper for most companies to offer simulated questions in place of real questions. At PowerScore we are dedicated to the use of real questions, and students in our Full-length LSAT course receive a personal copy of every official LSAT question currently in release. Now that you have completed this game from 1991, we are sure you can see that these older tests still have great value.

In the context of our overall discussion of Linear games, this game differs from the first two because this game is not Balanced. Instead, this is an Unbalanced game that is Overloaded, since we have eight apartments that must be distributed over five floors. The given rules and restrictions can then be used to create a 2-2-2-1-1 unfixed numerical distribution. Unfortunately, this distribution proves to be of little value in the game. This occurrence should not deter you from seeking numerical distributions in the future. There are many examples of games where the numerical distribution proved to be the key to answering one or more questions.

The game should be set up as follows:

J K L M N O P Q [8]

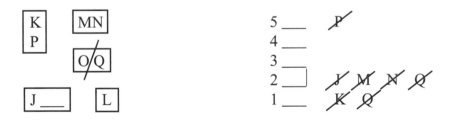

One difficult aspect of this game is the uncertainty over which floors contain two apartments. Since it is certain that there is at least one apartment per floor, we have placed slots on each of the five floors of our diagram. In the case of the second floor, which is known to have only one apartment, a short vertical line has been placed at the end of the slot. This vertical line serves as a visual reminder that the second floor contains one and only one apartment. Also of note in this game is the importance of correctly diagramming each rule. In the case of K, who lives one floor above P, the block must be shown vertically since the main diagram is vertical. On the other hand, the rule involving M and N must be shown horizontally because they live on the same floor. By diagramming these rules correctly, you gain a powerful advantage over the game, and you also eliminate a possible source of confusion. Also note that if this game were set up horizontally, then the diagramming of each rule would shift accordingly. For example, the KP block would be horizontal, whereas the MN block would be vertical. In essence you align the blocks with the diagram in order to make the most visual sense. On a vertical diagram a vertical block suggests one variable on top of another, but on a horizontal diagram a vertical block suggests that the two variables share the same space.

Let us take a moment to examine the Not Laws in the game:

> The occupancy limitation on the second floor produces Not Laws for J, M, and N, each of which is involved in a block rule.

> Because K must live on the floor *directly* above P, P cannot live on the fifth floor and K cannot live on the first floor.

> The last rule creates Q Not Laws on the first two floors. Also note that although Q cannot live on the first and second floors, this does not affect the placement of O. In Linear games, not-blocks tend to be relatively weak rules (this will not be the case when discussing grouping games), because the not-block cannot be applied until one of the variables in the block is placed. Since Q has not been placed, it has not yet had an effect on O. This type of relationship was discussed in the Avoiding False Inferences section earlier in the chapter.

One of the keys to doing well on the questions is to remember all of the different rules, each of which is unique in form (this is, of course, why we represent rules visually—doing so makes them easier to remember).

Question #6: Global, Must Be True. The correct answer choice is (D)

This question is tailor-made for a Not Law attack. Since M and N must live on the same floor, and the second floor contains only one apartment, answer choice (D) must be correct.

Question #7: Global, Cannot Be True. The correct answer choice is (E)

This question is also suited for a Not Law attack. Since P must live one floor below K, it follows that P cannot live on the fifth floor, and therefore answer choice (E) must be correct. As you may have noticed, with many Global questions, especially the ones that appear early in a game, the first avenue of attack is to check the existing Not Laws. Make sure you always follow this guideline!

Question #8: Local, Could Be True. The correct answer choice is (A)

After completing the first two questions with relative ease, you should arrive at this question feeling confident. Since this is a Local question, you should as always make a mini-diagram next to the question. The "if" statement in the question, in combination with the second rule, produces the following setup:

Several of the answer choices can be eliminated by using the rule that states that each floor has either one or two apartments. Since both J and P live on the fourth floor, no other residents can live on the fourth floor, and answer choices (B) and (D) can be eliminated. Since K lives on the fifth floor, the M and N block cannot live on the fifth floor, and answer choice (C) can be eliminated. Answer choice (E) can be eliminated since P must live on the fourth floor. Accordingly, answer choice (A) is correct.

Question #9: Local, Cannot Be True. The correct answer choice is (E)

This question is more difficult than any of the first three questions in this game, and it is based upon one of the test maker's favorite modes of attack, the use of uncertainty.

If O lives on the second floor, then the second floor is completely occupied, and no other resident can live on the second floor. For some variables, such as the MN block or the J block, this has no effect. For the KP block, however, the placement options are significantly reduced. Since the second floor is now "closed off," the KP block must be placed on the third and fourth floors (3-4) or on the fourth and fifth floors (4-5). At this point, many test takers stop their analysis under the mistaken impression that since the exact position of the block cannot be determined, further examination is worthless. In fact, to get past this situation you must Hurdle the Uncertainties™: in games situations with limited solutions, it is often possible to make inferences in spite of the uncertainty. In this case, since the KP block is always on 3-4 or 4-5, it can be concluded that K or P is *always* on the fourth floor. *So, even though we cannot be certain of the KP block placement, we can deduce that in this question K or P must be on the fourth floor, and we must account for the space taken up by the K/P dual option:*

```
5  ___
4  K/P  ___|
3  ___
2  O|
1  ___
```

Thus, since K or P must always live on the fourth floor, L cannot live on the fourth floor since L must live in the only apartment on her floor. Therefore, answer choice (E) is correct. Note that an answer that attempted to place either M or N on the fourth floor would also have been correct as the presence of K or P on the fourth floor would have eliminated the MN block from the fourth floor.

Essentially, the placement of O builds a "wall" on the second floor. This wall affects the placement of any block which takes up adjoining spaces, such as the KP block. In Linear games where blocks are present, always closely examine the placement of a variable (such as O) into an interior space (such as the second floor). There may be inferences that follow from the reduced placement options of a block (such as either K or P must live on the fourth floor). Opportunities to Hurdle the Uncertainty™ will appear in a number of games (including questions #10, #11, and #12 in this game), and we will discuss the concept again in the Grouping section.

Question #10: Local, Cannot Be True. The correct answer choice is (C)

Do not forget to convert Must Be False into Cannot Be True! This question uses the same Hurdle the Uncertainties™ principle seen in question #9. If M lives on the fourth floor, then the MN block completely occupies the fourth floor, again creating a wall in the interior of the game. This affects the placement of the KP block, which is now limited to floors one and two (1-2) or floors two and three (2-3). Accordingly, either K or P must live on the second floor:

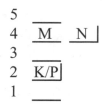

Thus, no other variable can live on the second floor, and answer choice (C) must be correct.

Question #11: Global, Must Be True. The correct answer choice is (B)

If you have difficulty finishing the Logic Games section, or if you find yourself in trouble on a game, this "5 if" question format is one you should avoid. Observe the construction of the question: a Global Must Be True question stem where each of the five answer choices begins with an "if" statement. Essentially, each of the answer choices is a new scenario, and for the most part information cannot be shared among the answer choices in this question. This type of question is designed to consume time! Avoid it if you have time problems in the Logic Games section.

In a possible oversight by the test makers, this question contains an Achilles heel which allows the observant test taker to answer the question quickly. Whenever you encounter a Logic Games question where each answer choice begins with the word "if," always make sure to check your previous work in case some of the information can be reused. In this case, the information from question #9 is duplicated in answer choice (B). Since question #9 proves that, when O lives on the second floor, L cannot live on the fourth floor, and that is what answer choice (B) states in question #11, it must be true that answer choice (B) is correct.

Honestly, it is a stroke of good fortune that the information from question #9 solves this question. Generally, on questions where each answer choice begins with "if," using the information from previous questions would perhaps eliminate one or two answer choices at most. Of course, that would still provide a great advantage. Here, that technique answers a very time-consuming question quite quickly. Always remember to check your previous work to see if it applies to the question you are working on, especially when you know the question is specifically designed to consume time. Should you wish to complete this question, and you fail to refer to previous work, your only choice is to work through each answer until you come to one you can prove correct.

Question #12: Local, Must Be True. The correct answer choice is (C)

The Local conditions in the question stem establish the following partial setup:

```
5  __
4  O        L̸  Ø  M  N̸
3  K        L̸  M  N̸
2  P|       L̸  M  N̸  Ø
1  __
```

Because L, M, and N cannot live on the second, third, or fourth floors, they must live on either the first or fifth floors, and because the MN block and L each require a floor of its own, it can be inferred that L, M, and N will completely occupy the first and fifth floors, creating a L/MN dual split-option:

```
5  MN / L
4  O
3  K
2  P|
1  L / MN
```

Given this information, you can Hurdle the Uncertainties™ and come to the realization that only floor three and floor four are available for J and Q, and since Q cannot live on the same floor as O, Q must live on the third floor and thus J must live on the fourth floor, resulting in the following setup:

```
5  MN / L
4  O      J
3  K      Q
2  P|
1  L / MN
```

It follows that answer choice (C) is correct. Also of interest is the fact that this is the first question in the game to directly address the OQ not-block. The test makers probably left this rule out of the game until the end in an effort to see whether careless test takers would forget about the rule and then miss the question. You must fix the rules in your mind at the beginning of the game and never forget them!

During a four-week period, each of seven previously unadvertised products—G, H, J, K, L, M, and O—will be advertised. A different pair of these products will be advertised each week. Exactly one of the products will be a member of two of these four pairs. The following constraints must be observed:

> J is not advertised during a given week unless H is advertised during the immediately preceding week.
>
> The product that is advertised during two of the weeks is advertised during week 4 but is not advertised during week 3.
>
> G is not advertised during a given week unless either J or else O is also advertised that week.
>
> K is advertised during one of the first two weeks.
>
> O is one of the products advertised during week 3.

18. Which one of the following could be the schedule of advertisements?

    (A) week 1: G, J; week 2: K, L; week 3: O, M; week 4: H, L
    (B) week 1: H, K; week 2: J, G; week 3: O, L; week 4: M, K
    (C) week 1: H, K; week 2: J, M; week 3: O, L; week 4: G, M
    (D) week 1: H, L; week 2: J, M; week 3: O, G; week 4: K, L
    (E) week 1: K, M; week 2: H, J; week 3: O, G; week 4: L, M

19. Which one of the following is a pair of products that CANNOT be advertised during the same week as each other?

    (A) H and K
    (B) H and M
    (C) J and O
    (D) K and L
    (E) L and M

20. Which one of the following must be advertised during week 2 ?

    (A) G
    (B) J
    (C) K
    (D) L
    (E) M

21. Which one of the following CANNOT be the product that is advertised during two of the weeks?

    (A) G
    (B) H
    (C) K
    (D) L
    (E) M

22. If L is the product that is advertised during two of the weeks, which one of the following is a product that must be advertised during one of the weeks in which L is advertised?

    (A) G
    (B) H
    (C) J
    (D) K
    (E) M

23. Which one of the following is a product that could be advertised in any of the four weeks?

    (A) H
    (B) J
    (C) K
    (D) L
    (E) O

24. Which one of the following is a pair of products that could be advertised during the same week as each other?

    (A) G and H
    (B) H and J
    (C) H and O
    (D) K and O
    (E) M and O

Analysis of Linear Game #6: December 1996 Questions 18-24

This game is certainly the most difficult of the six games in this section, so do not be upset if you struggled. Like game #5, this game is Unbalanced, but in this case the game is Underfunded, not Overloaded. As mentioned previously in this chapter, Unbalanced Linear games are almost always more difficult than Balanced Linear games. It is incumbent upon you to always keep track of whether or not a game is Balanced, and then use that information to your advantage. For example, if this were the first game in a Logic Games section, the best strategy might be to skip this game and return to it later in the section. There would surely be easier games in the section; you could attack them first, then return to this more difficult game having already answered a number of questions correctly. For those students who took the December 1996 LSAT, it was fortunate that the most difficult game of the test appeared last in the section. Thus, most students had already successfully completed many of the easier questions in the section when they arrived at this game.

Let us take a moment to examine the Underfunded aspect of the game. There are seven products that must fill eight advertising periods (7 into 8). In order to compensate for this shortfall, exactly one of the products is advertised twice. This doubling produces a 2-1-1-1-1-1 numerical distribution. Regrettably, we cannot ascertain exactly which product is doubled, and this greatly contributes to the difficulty of the game.

Since the products are advertised over a four-week period, and two products are advertised each week, our linear setup will feature two slots per week, diagrammed in stacks:

Note that you do not want to draw out the 8 spaces on one horizontal line. Having two stacks creates a vertical component and that allows for better representation of the different types of blocks (e.g. the HJ block versus the blocks involving G).

Using this structure, most students diagram the game in a manner similar to the following:

G H J K L M O [7]
     * *

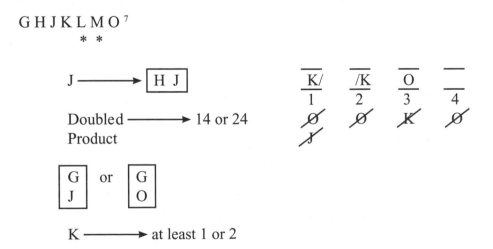

Several of the rules are quite tricky. The first rule, which states that "J is not advertised during a given week unless H is advertised during the immediately preceding week," can be partially represented as a block because of the "immediately preceding" qualifier. However, because of the "unless" portion of the rule (see the discussion of conditional reasoning starting on page 28), the block only occurs when J is present. Hence, the rule is diagrammed as a conditional statement with an arrow. When J is advertised, H must be advertised in the preceding week. This rule automatically means that J cannot be doubled because this would cause H to be doubled as well (and only one variable can be doubled).

However, the normal Not Laws that follow from a block do not occur in this case because of the fact that one of the products is doubled (and thus the problems created by the Underfunded aspect of the game begin). While it is true that J cannot be advertised during week 1, it is *not* true that H cannot be advertised during week 4. Since H could be the doubled product, H could be advertised during week 1 and week 4, for example (J would be advertised during week 2).

The second rule also produces two notable inferences. The rule states that the product that is advertised twice is advertised during week 4, but not during week 3. Thus, the only two options would be to advertise that doubled product on weeks 1 and 4 (1-4) or weeks 2 and 4 (2-4). Because the major point of uncertainty in this game is the doubled product, this information is very valuable. Since the doubled product must be advertised during weeks 1 and 4 or weeks 2 and 4, any variable that appears in week 3 cannot be the doubled product and therefore cannot appear in any week except week 3. By combining this inference with the last rule, we can infer that O cannot be advertised during weeks 1, 2, or 4. The second rule also allows us to infer that any product advertised during weeks 1, 2, or 4 cannot be advertised during week 3, since the doubling does not allow for week 3 to be used. By combining this inference with the rule involving K, we can infer that since K must be advertised during week 1 or 2 at the least, K cannot be advertised during week 3. K could still be advertised during week 4 since K could be the doubled product. Thus, a K Not Law cannot be placed on week 4.

There is still one critical inference yet to be uncovered, but because very few students discover this inference during the setup, we will continue on to the questions now, and then discuss the inference when it arises in question #20. The game diagram above is therefore only partially complete. We will fill in the rest of the diagram as we analyze the questions. We take this approach in an effort to more realistically deconstruct the way most students attack this game, and thereby provide more insightful and useful analysis. Of course it would be preferable for you to discover all inferences in a game before proceeding to the questions, but there will be times when this does not occur. How you react to that situation is just as important as your ability to make initial inferences.

Question #18: Global, Could Be True, List. The correct answer choice is (B)

The most obvious rule to check first, O in week 3, does not eliminate any of the five answer choices. Either the third or fourth rule should be used next because they are the easiest to apply visually. Answer choice (C) can be eliminated because G is not advertised with J or O, and answer choice (D) can be eliminated because K is not advertised during week 1 or 2. Next, apply the first rule, because the application of the first rule requires less work visually than the second rule. Answer choice (A) can be eliminated since J cannot be advertised during week 1, and answer choice (E) can be eliminated because J is advertised during week 2 but H is not advertised during week 1. Thus, answer choice (B) is proven correct by process of elimination. Note also that by applying the rules "out of order," you save time because it is not necessary to apply the second rule, and the second rule would probably have required more processing time than the other rules because it forces variables to be counted.

Question #19: Global, Cannot Be True. The correct answer choice is (C)

This is a question that separates students. Some students recognize the importance of the doubled product during the setup and then apply that knowledge to the rule stating that G must be advertised with either J or O. From this they are able to infer that J and O can never be advertised together: if J and O are advertised together, the pairing of J and O must occur in week 3, but then neither J nor O could be doubled, and one of J and O would have to be doubled in order to go with G. That line of reasoning indicates that answer choice (C) is correct.

For students who did not make that inference during their setup, there were still several steps available to help direct them to the correct answer. First, the correct answer in question #18 proves that H and K can be advertised during the same week, and so answer choice (A) can be eliminated with no work. Always remember to use the hypotheticals produced by earlier questions, especially List questions! Now, assume that none of the remaining answer choices appears noteworthy. The variables that cannot go together are probably prohibited from doing so because of their involvement with other variables. This makes it likely that any answer choice containing a random variable (a variable not cited in any rule) is less likely to be correct. L and M are the two randoms in the game, and answer choices (B), (D), and (E) each contain at least one random. Thus, answer choice (C) appears to be the most likely answer choice to initially analyze. This does not mean that you automatically choose answer choice (C) as the correct answer. It means that you can now closely examine (C) knowing that it has some characteristics that make it more likely to be correct than the other answer choices. Proceed by attempting to make a hypothetical with the two variables in (C). When a workable hypothetical cannot be produced, you will know that answer choice (C) is correct.

Question #20: Global, Must Be True. The correct answer choice is (B)

This is the defining question of the game. From the language in the question, it is clear that one of the five variables listed in the answer choices *must* be advertised during the second week, yet prior to this question very few students realize that any of the products must be advertised during week 2. Answering this question correctly is crucial since this information will definitely impact your ability to answer the subsequent questions both quickly and accurately.

The easiest way to attack this question is to again use the information from the hypothetical created in question #18. From answer choice (B) in that question, it is certain that either J or G must be the product advertised in week 2. Let us stop and take a moment to analyze this critical insight. First, as indicated by the question stem to #20, you now know that one of the products will *always* be advertised on week 2. If you did not discover this inference previously (and most people do not), you know you are missing a key piece of information that will undoubtedly help you solve not only question #20, but other questions as well.

When you know that one of the products must be advertised on week 2, then you can deduce that every single solution to the game will contain that product on week 2. This is a vital point since you can then look at any other hypothetical and immediately know that one of the two products listed on week 2 will be the one that is always on week 2. So, in question #18, when we determine that (B) is the correct answer, we know that either J or G must be the product that is always on week 2, and we can then look at only J or G in question #20. If there were other hypotheticals we could look at those also, and we would see that either J or G would always be present. For example, if another question produced J and K on week 2, this would show G does not have to be on week 2, and G would be eliminated from consideration; since J would be the only common variable between the two hypotheticals, then J would be proven correct. Thus, even though question #18 lists just one possible schedule of ads ("could be" a schedule of ads) it will still contain the product that we know from the wording of question #20 must always be on week 2.

Another way of thinking about questions #18 and #20 would be to say that if a product must always be advertised on week 2, and then if it does not appear on week 2 in one of the solutions, then how can that particular product be the one that is always on week 2? Therefore, any product not on week 2 in the solution to question #18 is immediately eliminated as the product that must be advertised on week 2 (for example, if (D) was the answer to #20, then L would be in *every* solution to the game. But L is not in the solution to #18, so how could it be L?).

In applying this thinking to similar questions in other games, whenever you encounter a question that indicates that a variable must be in a certain group or position, then every other solution to the game will contain that variable in that position. So, if a question asks, "Which one of the following people must always be in the first group of runners?" and the correct answer to another question indicates that W, X, and Y are the only runners in the first group, then you would automatically know that one of W, X, and Y would have to be the runner that is always in the first group. Similarly, if a question asks, "Which one of the following must always be the third factory inspected?" and the correct answer to another question indicates that P is the third factory inspected, then you would automatically know that P is always the third factory inspected.

Returning to our consideration of G and J from question #18, the fact that one of those two must be the correct answer eliminates answer choices (C), (D), and (E) in question #20, once again demonstrating how important it is for you to answer List questions correctly and then use their information when applicable. Now that the contenders have been narrowed to two, you can easily make a hypothetical that proves or disproves one of the answers. Let us begin by attempting to prove that G does not have to be advertised in week 2 (it is almost always easier to disprove a Must Be True statement than prove it). The following hypothetical proves that answer choice (A) is incorrect:

$$\frac{\underline{K}}{\underline{H}} \quad \frac{\underline{L}}{\underline{J}} \quad \frac{\underline{G}}{\underline{O}} \quad \frac{\underline{M}}{\underline{H}}$$
$$1 \qquad 2 \qquad 3 \qquad 4$$

Since answer choice (A) can be disproved, it follows that answer choice (B) is correct and J must be advertised during week 2. We can then infer that H must be advertised during week 1 (Why must H be advertised during week 1? Because in this question we discover that J must be advertised during week 2. Adding that piece of information to the first rule of the game then leads us to the inference that H must be advertised during week 1).

Adding these new inferences and Not Laws, we arrive at the following optimal setup for the game:

$$
\begin{array}{cccc}
\text{K/} & \text{/K} & & \\
\text{H} & \text{J} & \text{O} & \underline{} \\
\overline{1} & \overline{2} & \overline{3} & 4 \\
\cancel{G} & \cancel{G} & \cancel{K} & \cancel{G} \\
\cancel{J} & \cancel{H} & \cancel{J} & \cancel{J} \\
\cancel{O} & & \cancel{H} & \cancel{O}
\end{array}
$$

Note that H cannot be advertised in weeks 2 or 3 due to the second rule (that is, if H is the doubled variable it would have to be in 1-4). J cannot be doubled since that would also require H to be doubled—a violation of the rules. Therefore, J can be eliminated from weeks 1, 3, and 4. Since G must be advertised with either J or O, and J and O cannot be doubled, G must be advertised during week 2 or 3, and thus G cannot be advertised during weeks 1 or 4.

The above setup is optimal and should be used for all subsequent questions. Of course, you would want to check the previous questions to make sure you have not made any errors.

Perceptive students may have noticed another way to disprove answer choice (A) in this question. If G is advertised during week 2, then automatically J must also be advertised during week 2, since G must be advertised with either J or O, and O cannot be advertised during week 2. Since selecting answer choice (A) would automatically make answer choice (B) correct, answer choice (A) must be incorrect since there can be only one correct answer.

An additional note on the difficulty of this game: the importance of the inference contained in this question is reflected in the very nature of the questions themselves. Six of the seven questions in this game are Global, which means that most of the questions are based on information derived from the initial setup. If you miss this one key inference or never answer this question, you are automatically at a disadvantage in answering the rest of the questions. In other words, if you skip this question, you are passing on a chance to discover a major inference that applies to every other question.

Question #21: Global, Cannot Be True. The correct answer choice is (A)

If a product is advertised during two weeks, then, according to the second rule, that product must be advertised during week 4. In the optimal setup created in question #20, it was established that neither G, J, or O could be advertised in week 4. Consequently, answer choice (A) must be correct.

Question #22: Local, Must Be True. The correct answer choice is (E)

This is the only Local question of the game. Given the information in the question stem, according to the second rule L must be advertised during week 4:

$$
\begin{array}{cccc}
\text{G K L M} & & & \\
\underline{\text{H}} & \underline{\text{J}} & \underline{\text{O}} & \underline{\text{L}} \\
1 & 2 & 3 & 4
\end{array}
$$

Since only G, K, and M are available to fill the second advertising slot in week 4, it can be inferred that either G, K, or M must be advertised with L. It follows that either answer choice (A), (D), or (E) is correct. Since G must be advertised along with J or O, G must be advertised in week 2 or 3, and thus G cannot be advertised with L. Consequently, answer choice (A) can be eliminated. Since L is the doubled product and K must then be advertised in week 1 or 2 only, it follows that K cannot be advertised with L, and answer choice (D) can be eliminated. Answer choice (E) is thereby proven correct by process of elimination.

Note how much easier this question is to solve with the knowledge that J must be advertised during week 2.

Question #23: Global, Could Be True. The correct answer choice is (D)

This question can effectively be attacked by applying the Not Laws from the optimal setup. The Not Laws show that there are restrictions on the placement of G, H, J, K, and O, eliminating answer choices (A), (B), (C), and (E). Accordingly, answer choice (D) is correct.

Question #24: Global, Could Be True. The correct answer choice is (E)

Answer choice (A) can be eliminated since G must be paired with either J or O. Answer choice (B) can be eliminated because if J and H were paired, then H would appear in both weeks 1 and 2, a violation of the rules. Answer choices (C) and (D) can be eliminated since neither H nor K can be advertised during week 3. Thus, answer choice (E) is proven correct by process of elimination.

Note that only answer choice (E) contains one of the randoms of the game. As briefly mentioned in question #19, randoms are more likely to be able to be paired with other variables, and you can use that information to select likely contenders for the correct answer choice. Do not use randoms to automatically choose an answer, just use them to help determine which answer choices to look at first.

Final Chapter Note

We strongly urge you to look at this entire chapter again before moving on to the next chapter. In particular, make sure you feel comfortable with the discussions of rule diagramming, sufficient and necessary conditions, numerical distributions, and especially the game explanations. There are many subtle Games points spread throughout this chapter, and we will encounter them again as we move deeper into our discussion.

CHAPTER THREE: ADVANCED LINEAR GAMES

Multiple Stacks

The previous chapter discussed games that involved just two variable sets: one variable set classified as the base and another variable set controlled by the base. This chapter examines Linear games that feature three or more variable sets. As before, one of the variable sets will be classified as the base, and the other variable sets will generally be "stacked" in rows above the base. In this sense, Advanced Linear games are identical to the games in the last chapter. However, the presence of three or more variable sets creates a far greater degree of complexity in the game. For example, there are 5040 different solutions to a basic Linear game featuring seven variables placed into seven ordered positions (for you math majors, the combinations are represented by 7 factorial (7!)). Of course, the 5040 solutions are only possible *prior* to the consideration of the rules of the game. As soon as the rules are considered, the number of possible solutions decreases significantly. Now examine an Advanced Linear game featuring two variable sets of seven being placed into a base created by a third variable set (in other words, a single variable set has been added to the previous example): there are now 25,401,600 possible solutions to the game. In other words, the addition of just one variable set exponentially increases the number of possible solutions to the game. Again, the rules will decrease the number of possible solutions, but the fact remains that Advanced Linear games inherently have more solutions and thus greater complexity.

> Advanced Linear games are the same as the games in the last chapter, but there are now more variable sets with which to contend.

> An Advanced Linear game with four separate variable sets of seven elements each will have over 128 billion solutions before the rules are applied. No wonder everyone thinks Games are challenging!

When working with this increased complexity, you must organize your information as efficiently as possible. When you diagram multiple variable sets, choose a base and then "stack" each variable set on top of one another, as follows:

Three variable sets:

> Create a new stack for each additional variable set.

Variable set #3: __   __   __   __

Variable set #2: __   __   __   __
Variable set #1 (base): 1   2   3   4

Four variable sets:

Variable set #4: ___ ___ ___ ___

Variable set #3: ___ ___ ___ ___

Variable set #2: ___

Variable set #1 (base): 1   2   3   4

Of course, there will be times when one (or more) of the variable sets naturally fills in the spaces and does not need its own row, as in the following game scenario:

> During three days—Monday through Wednesday—a compliance officer will inspect exactly six companies—three banks: Amity, Bonded, and Community; and three brokerages: Xenon, Yarra, and Zenith. Each day, exactly two companies are inspected: one in the morning and one in the afternoon.

Accordingly, there are five variable sets:

> Set #1: the three days Monday, Tuesday, and Wednesday
> Set #2: the three banks A, B, and C
> Set #3: the three brokerages X, Y, and Z
> Set #4: the three morning inspections
> Set #5: the three afternoon inspections

Since the days of the week have the greatest sense of inherent order, they should be chosen as the base, and since the morning and afternoon inspections naturally correspond to the days, they should be shown as stacks:

In multi-stack games one variable set is often used to "fill in" the spaces in the diagram created by another variable set.

Afternoon Inspections: ___ ___ ___

Morning Inspections: ___ ___ ___
                       M   T   W

The remaining two variable sets—the banks and the brokerages—can now be placed into the six spaces representing the days and times. In this way all five variable sets are displayed, and the diagram is orderly and logical.

Repeated Variable Sets

Most games use each variable set just a single time. However, some games repeat variable sets. Consider the following game scenario:

> At a small newspaper, over a period of six consecutive weeks, six restaurants—A, B, C, D, E, and F—will each be reviewed once by the editor, Gomez, and once by the head writer, Hughes. Each reviewer reviews exactly one restaurant per week.

In this game, the restaurant variable set will be assigned once to Gomez, and then assigned again to Hughes:

Hughes:	___	___	___	___	___	___	(A, B, C, D, E, F)
Gomez:	___	___	___	___	___	___	(A, B, C, D, E, F)
Weeks:	1	2	3	4	5	6	

The one disadvantage to a variable set being repeated is that the variables in the set will appear more than once, and that repetition must be tracked. For example, in the game above, you must track "A" when it is assigned to Gomez and also when it is assigned to Hughes, and so you must be able to differentiate between those assignments. When diagramming the rules, the best technique to track individual assignments with repeated variable sets is to use subscripts. More on this in a bit.

Diagramming with Multiple Stacks

Linked Variable Set Rules

In addition to rules addressing individual variable sets, the test makers will also include rules that interrelate different variable sets. Consider the following partial game:

> Exactly six runners—P, Q, R, S, T, and U—compete in a marathon. Each runner finishes the race, and no two runners finish at the same time. The information that follows is all that is known about the six runners:
> > Each runner is either an amateur or a professional, but not both.
> > Four of the runners are female and two are male.

In this game there are four variable sets: the six finishing places (which are chosen as the base due to their inherent natural order), the set of runners, the amateur/professional set, and the male/female set.

With the base chosen, "stack" each variable set on top of one another, as follows:

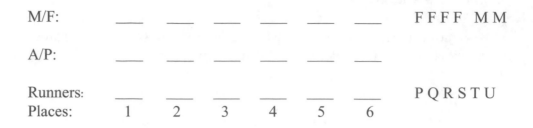

M/F: ___ ___ ___ ___ ___ ___   F F F F M M

A/P: ___ ___ ___ ___ ___ ___

Runners: ___ ___ ___ ___ ___ ___   P Q R S T U

Places: 1   2   3   4   5   6

Now that the variable sets have been established, let us continue on and examine the next rule that was presented:

> The two male runners are professionals.

As would be expected, this rule connects two of the variable sets: the male/female variable set and the amateur/professional set. Rules that connect different variable sets are extremely common in Advanced Linear games, and you should always be prepared for them. In this case, the rule above creates two linked vertical blocks where M (male) connects to P (professional):

In games with more than two variable sets, always be prepared for rules that link the variable sets together.

Not all the blocks will be simple vertical or horizontal blocks. The test makers like to challenge test takers to handle more complex blocks that have both vertical and horizontal components. Consider a game about five cars coming off an assembly line, where each car has a different exterior color, a different interior color, and a different type of transmission. Let us say that the basic setup for the game appears as follows:

Trans: ___ ___ ___ ___ ___

Int Color: ___ ___ ___ ___ ___

Ext Color: ___ ___ ___ ___ ___

Cars: 1   2   3   4   5

Now, suppose that a rule is presented that states:

> The car with the blue exterior is assembled immediately before the car with the
> red interior but immediately after a car with a manual transmission.

Some students might be tempted to diagram this rule as a horizontal block
with subscripts, as follows:

$$\boxed{M_T \; B_E \; R_I}$$

This approach would be a mistake because it does not take into account
the multi-stacked aspect of the game. A better representation is a block
that also takes into account the vertical aspect of the game:

$$
\boxed{
\begin{array}{ccc}
\underline{M} & \underline{} & \underline{} \\
\underline{} & \underline{} & \underline{R} \\
\underline{} & \underline{B} & \underline{}
\end{array}
}
$$

This second representation is far superior to the first because it displays
both the horizontal separation and the vertical separation of the individual
elements. Visually, this representation is more powerful.

The rules that link variable sets are not always block-oriented—the test
makers also like to insert sequencing rules that link multiple variable sets.
For example, the following rule from a different game sequentially links
two different variable sets:

> Exactly two of the taxis that arrive before D are yellow.

This rule links a variable set about color to a variable set about taxis.
Because each variable set is placed in a different row, tracking a rule
such as this one can be challenging. Some students use subscripts to
track each variable set in Advanced Linear sequencing rules, but that is a
decision that should be made based upon the complexity of the game and
how confident you feel. For example, with this rule, most students feel
comfortable with this representation:

$$\begin{array}{c} Y \\ ----{>}D \\ Y \end{array}$$

The following sequencing rule, however, requires the use of subscripts:

Ronald receives a better grade in chemistry than in french.

In this game, chemistry and french were each different variable sets, and Ronald (and six other students) was assigned a grade for *each* class. The best representation of the rule is as follows:

$$R_C > R_F$$

Because the students are a repeated variable set, "R" appears multiple times in the game, and the only way to track the different appearances of R is to use a subscript for each variable set (in this case, "C" for chemistry and "F" for french).

Internal Diagram Spacing

When creating diagrams for games that have two or more stacks, you *must* leave extra vertical space between the rows in case there is a need to place individual Not Laws under a space within a variable set. For example, consider the following diagram:

Trans:	___	___	___	___	___
Int Color:	___	___	___	___	___
Ext Color:	___	___	___	___	___
Cars:	1	2	3	4	5

Now consider the problem presented by a rule such as the following:

The third car cannot have a red interior.

This rule can only be diagrammed as a Not Law, yet there is no space under the interior color row to place that Not Law. Thus, the Not Law would have to appear under the diagram, along with every other Not Law in the game. This would quickly become confusing because every Not Law for every variable set would appear under the diagram, and they would all be mixed together. However, if you provide sufficient vertical space, this rule can be diagrammed immediately under the interior color row:

The rule to the right does not allow for an easy way to show the vertical separation between the chemistry and french variable sets, hence the use of subscripts.

If you have diagrammed your variable sets vertically in columns, then leave extra horizontal space between each column.

Trans: ___   ___   ___   ___   ___

Int Color: ___   ___   ___   ___   ___
                          ~~R~~

Ext Color: ___   ___   ___   ___   ___
Cars: 1   2   3   4   5

Leave extra space between each stack in case Not Laws need to be placed on one of the spaces.

With this diagram, each Not Law can be efficiently connected to the proper variable set (any Not Laws that appear underneath the diagram would be connected to the exterior color variable set).

Side Not Laws

In certain situations Not Laws can be placed to the side of the setup to indicate that a variable cannot be placed in the row. For example, after referring to the setup for the game in the middle of page 130, imagine that a rule was added to that game that stated the following:

>   Amity cannot be inspected in the morning.

This rule could be represented on the diagram as follows:

Afternoon Inspections: ___   ___   ___

Morning Inspections: ___   ___   ___   ~~A~~
                             M   T   W

Not Laws do not always have to go directly underneath the space—they can be represented on the side of the diagram where appropriate.

This representation can save time and avoid confusion. Time is saved because the Not Law is written only once, not three times. Confusion is avoided since placing the Not Law under each space might give the false impression that A could not appear on either the morning or afternoon of that day (and under the pressure of the test, this confusion could occur).

Note that Side Not Laws typically only appear when one or more of the variable sets is used to fill in spaces created by other variable sets (as the banks and brokerages are in this game).

This type of rule diagramming also applies to vertical setups, although appropriate adjustments must be made for the change in perspective.

Each of the following items presents an Advanced Linear game scenario. Using the space provided, diagram the game. Occasionally, a problem will contain a corresponding rule. Use your knowledge of rule representation to properly display each rule. *Answers begin on Page 138*

1. Seven doctors—F, G, H, J, K, L, and M—are scheduled to interview for a position with a local hospital. The seven interviews are conducted on seven different days, Monday through Sunday. Each doctor is assigned to one of seven different interviewers—P, Q, R, S, T, V, and W.

2. Six runners—R, S, T, V, X, and Z—are assigned to six lanes on a track numbered 1 though 6. Exactly one runner is assigned to each lane, and each runner wears one of six letters—A, B, C, D, E, and F.

3. Three apartment buildings—the Highlander, the Ivy, and the Jacaranda—each have exactly five floors, numbered 1 through 5. Each floor of each building is decorated in exactly one of three styles—Colonial, Federal, or Georgian. Each style is used at least once in each building.
    In the Jacaranda, the only floor decorated in the Colonial style is immediately above the only floor decorated in the Georgian style.
    The fourth floor of the Highlander is not decorated in the Federal style.

4. Eight librarians—C, D, E, F, G, H, J, and K—are assigned to eight work shifts at the local library. Each librarian is assigned exactly one shift, and only one librarian is assigned to each shift. The shifts are on Monday, Tuesday, Wednesday, and Friday, with one shift in the morning and one shift in the afternoon of each day. The assignments must be made according to the following conditions:

>   Librarian C does not work in the morning of any day.
>   Librarian F works an earlier shift than librarian G.
>   Librarians D and E work in the morning on consecutive calendar days.

5. There are exactly ten houses and no others on Magnolia Street. On the west side of the street, from north to south, are houses 1, 3, 5, 7, and 9; on the east side of the street, from north to south, are houses 2, 4, 6, 8, and 10. The houses on the west side are located directly across the street from the houses on the east side, and the following pairs of houses face each other: 1 and 2; 3 and 4; 5 and 6; 7 and 8; 9 and 10. Each house is painted in exactly one of the following colors: blue, green, white, and yellow. The houses are painted according to the following rules:

>   No house is painted in the same color as the house directly across the street.
>   House 4 is green.
>   No house on the west side of the street is white.

Advanced Linear Setup Practice Drill Answer Key

<u>Drill #1</u>. There are three variable sets in this problem: the seven interview positions (days), the seven doctors, and the seven interviewers. Because the days of the week have the greatest sense of inherent order, they should be chosen as the base. Consequently, the diagram should appear as follows:

Doc: F G H J K L M [7]
Int: P Q R S T V W [7]

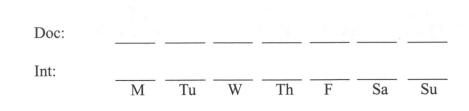

<u>Drill #2</u>. There are three variable sets in this problem: the six lanes, the six runners, and the six letters. Choosing the base in this problem requires a bit more thought because two variable sets—the lanes and the letters— appear to have inherent order. However, the letters do not have a fixed order; instead they are just assigned randomly to any runner. On the other hand, the lanes do have a fixed order, and they should be chosen as the base, leading to the following setup:

Run: R S T V X Z [6]
Lett: A B C D E F [6]

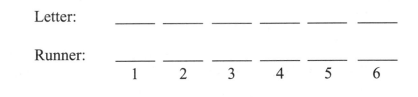

<u>Drill #3</u>. There are three variable sets in this problem: the three apartment buildings, the five floors, and the three styles. The best setup for buildings with floors is vertical, and thus the buildings should be the base, and the floors should number 1-5 from the bottom to the top, as in the real world:

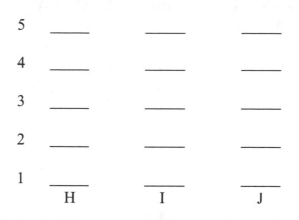

The styles are a repeating variable set, and thus all three styles will appear in each building. However, if any given floor cannot be decorated in one of the styles, that will leave a dual-option of the other two styles.

The first rule establishes a vertical block:

$$\boxed{\begin{array}{c} C \\ G \end{array}}_{\,J}$$

Further, this rule indicates that C and G are each used exactly once in the Jacaranda, and thus we can infer that F must appear three times in the Jacaranda. We also know that in the Jacaranda, C cannot be on the first floor, and G cannot be on the fifth floor. These two Not Laws are written off to the side of the J column, and lead to dual-options. The second rule creates an F Not Law on floor 4 of the Highlander. This Not Law is written off to the side of the H column next to floor 4. and also creates a dual-option. Combining the information above leads to the following setup:

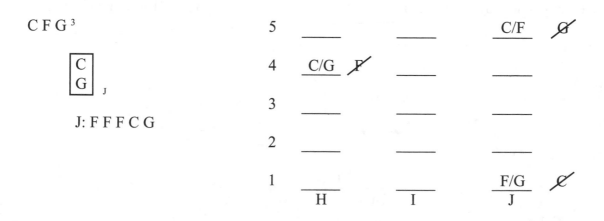

Advanced Linear Setup Practice Drill Answer Key

<u>Drill #4</u>. There are four variable sets in this problem: the four days, the four morning shifts, the four afternoon shifts, and the eight librarians. However, the librarians should be used to fill the morning and afternoon shifts, and thus only two stacks are necessary. The days of the week should, as usual, be chosen as the base. Also, note that although Thursday has been skipped in the list of days, you should still show Thursday but then "X" it out, as follows:

C D E F G H J K [8]

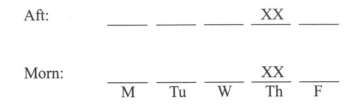

The first rule, "Librarian C does not work in the morning of any day," should be shown as a Side Not Law on the morning shift, thus relegating C to one of the four afternoon shifts.

The second rule, "Librarian F works an earlier shift than librarian G," can be very tricky. This rule, which is diagrammed as F > G, does not automatically create Not Laws for G on Monday and for F on Friday. This is because "earlier" allows for F to work the morning shift and G to work the afternoon shift of the same day. Thus, G can be assigned to work on Monday and F can be assigned to work on Friday. However, G cannot work on Monday morning, and F cannot work on Friday afternoon, and hence Not Laws must be placed on those positions.

The last rule, "Librarians D and E work in the morning on consecutive calendar days," creates a rotating block:

$$\boxed{\begin{array}{c} DE \\ ED \end{array}}$$

Because the rule references consecutive calendar days, this block must be assigned to Monday-Tuesday or Tuesday-Wednesday (remember, since Thursday is unavailable, Friday will not be consecutive with any other day). Accordingly, either D or E must be assigned to Tuesday morning.

Combining the information above leads to the following diagram:

C D E F G H J K [8]

Advanced Linear Setup Practice Drill Answer Key

There are further inferences to be made, such as the chain reaction that occurs when G is assigned to Monday afternoon: F must be assigned to Monday morning, and then the DE block must be assigned in some order to Tuesday and Wednesday mornings.

Drill #5. There are three variable sets in this problem: the five houses on the west side, the five houses on the east side, and the four house colors. Because of the geographic specifications of the problems, the houses should be used as the base, and the game should be diagrammed vertically.

The first rule creates a horizontal not-block. In order to save time, instead of writing out a not-block for each individual color, we will simply use the following designation:

"C" stands for color, and thus block means that the same color cannot appear at houses that are across from each other.

The second rule is diagrammed directly on the diagram, and the application of the first rule leads to the inference that house 3 is not green, and this inference is shown by a G Not Law.

The last rule is shown by a W Not Law at the bottom of the west side of houses. This is technically a Side Not Law, but since the diagram is presented vertically, it appears to be another basic Not Law. However, in vertical diagrams the "Side" is actually at the bottom.

Note that the combination of Not Laws on house 3 leads to a B/Y dual option.

Combining the information above, the diagram appears as follows:

B G W Y [4]

1	___		2	___
3	B/Y ~~G~~		4	G
5	___		6	___
7	___		8	___
9	___		10	___

~~W~~

The Separation Principle™

The Separation Principle appears in both Basic Linear and Advanced Linear games. The Separation Principle applies when variables involved in not-blocks are placed into a limited number of spaces. For example, suppose that two boys are being seated in three chairs, with the rule that the two boys cannot sit next to one another. The minimum amount of room needed to accommodate the not-block rule is:

Since the minimum requirement happens to be the same as the number of available spaces, the boys are forced into spaces 1 and 3:

$$\frac{B}{1} \quad \frac{}{2} \quad \frac{B}{3}$$

Now suppose we expand the scenario to three boys being seated in five chairs, still with the rule that no boy can sit next to another boy. The minimum space required when the not-block rule is applied to the three boys is:

Again, the minimum requirement happens to be identical to the number of available spaces, and the boys are forced into spaces 1, 3, and 5:

$$\frac{B}{1} \quad \frac{}{2} \quad \frac{B}{3} \quad \frac{}{4} \quad \frac{B}{5}$$

Now suppose we expand the scenario to four boys being seated into seven chairs, still with the rule that no boys can sit next to each other. The minimum space required by the not-block rule is:

Again, the minimum space requirement happens to be identical to the number of available spaces, and the boys are forced into spaces 1, 3, 5, and 7:

$$\frac{B}{1} \quad \frac{}{2} \quad \frac{B}{3} \quad \frac{}{4} \quad \frac{B}{5} \quad \frac{}{6} \quad \frac{B}{7}$$

Now, consider the following sample game scenario:

> The Metro Zoo exhibits exactly seven animals—one bear, two lions, two tigers, and two zebras—in seven consecutive cages according to the following restrictions:
>> Each animal is exhibited exactly once, in one cage only. No cage is reused.
>> Two animals of the same type are never exhibited consecutively.
>> A lion is never exhibited immediately before or immediately after a tiger.

The second rule creates three not-blocks:

The third rule creates two more not-blocks:

In a game with so many not-blocks, there are enormous restrictions facing the variables. Most games contain only one or two not-blocks, and those not-blocks typically do not place any variables by their own power and they usually come into play only after the other rules have been applied. Not-block rules are also easy to forget, and thus you often see questions where the last inferential step involves a not-block. In some cases, games have contained not-block rules that were only used once, in the last question, with the test makers theorizing that some students will have forgotten that the not-block rule exists by that point.

In the next chapter we will examine Grouping games, which tend to feature a greater number of "negative" rules, like not-blocks.

The most important not-blocks in this game involve the lions and tigers. Essentially, the two lions and the two tigers form a group of four variables, none of which can be placed next to any other. This means that these four variables must be spread out over the seven spaces, with at least one space separating each variable. Because of the Separation Principle, this can only be accomplished by placing the four variables in spaces 1, 3, 5, and 7 (just like our example with four boys spread over seven spaces). Obviously the arrangement in this game is a bit harder to discern because the group of four variables contains two subgroups, the lions and tigers.

Because the lions and tigers represent four variables involved in not-blocks being placed into seven spaces, the following inference is made:

The bear and the two zebras would then be exhibited in cages 2, 4, and 6 in some order. Obviously, a setup containing this much information would make answering the questions quite easy.

The point to derive from this discussion is that not-blocks can be quite powerful, especially when there are several of them and they are inter-related.

The Overlap Principle

The Overlap Principle states:

> When members of two separate variable sets are both assigned into a fixed number of spaces, there will be an overlap between the groups if the sum of the two groups is greater than the total of the spaces.

If this Principle sounds a bit daunting, do not worry! To help make the definition make sense, we will use a simple example. Consider the following scenario:

> There are three chairs in a classroom. Two of the chairs are green and two boys sit in the chairs.
>
> Given the above information, what can be inferred?

The variable sets can be represented as follows:

Boys:	B B	
Chair Color:	G G	
Chairs:	1 2 3	

In this case the three chairs would be the base and the other two variable sets would be stacked on top of the chairs in the usual fashion:

Boys: ___   ___   ___

Chair Color: ___   ___   ___
Chairs: 1   2   3

No matter how you place the two boys and the two green chairs, *at least one of the boys must sit in a green chair*. For example, if the boys sit in chairs 1 and 2, you could make chair 3 green, but then either chair 1 or 2 would have to be green. In this case the sum of boys (2) plus the sum of the green chairs (2) equals 4, but there are only 3 spaces available to hold all those elements. Thus, there must be an overlap between the boys and the chair color. This is not a principle that the test makers use frequently, but it is useful to be acquainted with the idea because the test makers will test to see if you recognize it when it appears.

The Overlap Principle can apply to a wide variety of group sizes, e.g., two groups of three being placed into a group of five, or a group of three and a group of two being placed into four spaces. Consider the following scenario:

> A mechanic repairs seven cars in consecutive order. Four of the cars are red, two of the cars are blue, and one car is green. Each car is also a convertible or hardtop, and four of the cars are convertible and three are hardtops.

From this scenario alone, prior to the introduction of any rules, you should be able to see that at least one of the red cars is a convertible car. Why? Because of the Overlap Principle:

> The total number of red cars (4) plus the total number of convertibles (4) equals 8, which is greater than the total number of total spaces (7).

In other words, imagine that the red cars are the first four cars that the mechanic repairs. At least one of those cars must have been a convertible, because at this point there are only three cars left to repair but we know there are four total convertibles.

From an occurrence standpoint, unlike the Separation Principle, which can occur in any Linear game, the Overlap Principle occurs only in Advanced Linear games. This is because the Overlap Principle appears with multiple variable sets. Like the Separation Principle, however, when the Overlap Principle is in play the test makers always check to see if you recognized its occurrence.

Final Pregame Note

Remember, Advanced Linear games are an extension of the Basic Linear games discussed in the previous chapter, and thus all of the rule representations and inference-making patterns discussed in that chapter still apply. The concept of linearity is a critical one on the LSAT, and so in addition to the games in Chapters Two and Three, you will also see linearity in the games in Chapters Five, Six, and Seven.

As always, please read the explanations to each game carefully, as they will give you a true sense of how to best attack each game. Plus, the explanations always include points that expand the discussion given above.

If you would like to test yourself under timed conditions, you should give yourself 8 minutes and 45 seconds for each game. Good luck on the games!

Eight physics students—four majors: Frank, Gwen, Henry, and Joan; and four nonmajors: Victor, Wanda, Xavier, and Yvette—are being assigned to four laboratory benches, numbered 1 through 4. Each student is assigned to exactly one bench, and exactly two students are assigned to each bench. Assignments of students to benches must conform to the following conditions:

Exactly one major is assigned to each bench.
Frank and Joan are assigned to consecutively numbered benches, with Frank assigned to the lower-numbered bench.
Frank is assigned to the same bench as Victor.
Gwen is not assigned to the same bench as Wanda.

1. Which one of the following could be the assignment of students to benches?

   (A)   1: Frank, Victor; 2: Joan, Gwen; 3: Henry, Wanda; 4: Xavier, Yvette
   (B)   1: Gwen, Yvette; 2: Frank, Xavier; 3: Joan, Wanda; 4: Henry, Victor
   (C)   1: Henry, Wanda; 2: Gwen, Xavier; 3: Frank, Victor; 4: Joan, Yvette
   (D)   1: Henry, Xavier; 2: Joan, Wanda; 3: Frank, Victor; 4: Gwen, Yvette
   (E)   1: Henry, Yvette; 2: Gwen, Wanda; 3: Frank, Victor; 4: Joan, Xavier

2. If Victor is assigned to bench 2 and Wanda is assigned to bench 4, which one of the following must be true?

   (A)   Frank is assigned to bench 1.
   (B)   Gwen is assigned to bench 1.
   (C)   Henry is assigned to bench 3.
   (D)   Xavier is assigned to bench 1.
   (E)   Yvette is assigned to bench 3.

3. If Gwen and Henry are not assigned to consecutively numbered benches, which one of the following must be true?

   (A)   Victor is assigned to bench 2.
   (B)   Victor is assigned to bench 3.
   (C)   Wanda is assigned to bench 1.
   (D)   Wanda is assigned to bench 3.
   (E)   Wanda is assigned to bench 4.

4. If Henry and Yvette are both assigned to bench 1, which one of the following could be true?

   (A)   Gwen is assigned to bench 3.
   (B)   Joan is assigned to bench 2.
   (C)   Wanda is assigned to bench 2.
   (D)   Wanda is assigned to bench 3.
   (E)   Xavier is assigned to bench 3.

5. If Gwen is assigned to bench 4 and Xavier is assigned to bench 3, then any one of the following could be true EXCEPT:

   (A)   Gwen is assigned to the same bench as Yvette.
   (B)   Henry is assigned to the same bench as Wanda.
   (C)   Henry is assigned to the same bench as Xavier.
   (D)   Joan is assigned to the same bench as Xavier.
   (E)   Joan is assigned to the same bench as Yvette.

6. If Wanda is assigned to a lower-numbered bench than is Joan, then Henry must be assigned to a

   (A)   lower-numbered bench than is Frank
   (B)   lower-numbered bench than is Gwen
   (C)   lower-numbered bench than is Xavier
   (D)   higher-numbered bench than is Victor
   (E)   higher-numbered bench than is Yvette

7. Which one of the following could be the assignments for bench 2 and bench 4 ?

   (A)   2: Gwen, Xavier
         4: Henry, Yvette
   (B)   2: Henry, Yvette
         4: Joan, Xavier
   (C)   2: Joan, Victor
         4: Gwen, Xavier
   (D)   2: Joan, Wanda
         4: Gwen, Xavier
   (E)   2: Joan, Xavier
         4: Henry, Yvette

Analysis of Advanced Linear Game #1: September 1998 Questions 1-7

In this Defined, Balanced game there are three variable sets: the four majors, the four nonmajors, and the four laboratory benches. Since the laboratory benches have a sense of order, they should be selected as the base. A diagram similar to the following should be created:

Majors: F G H J [4]
Nonmajors: V W X Y [4]

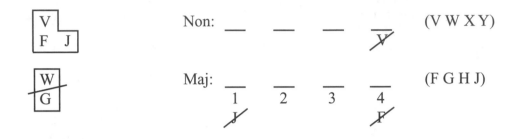

The second rule can be somewhat confusing. "Lower-numbered" mean one number is less than another; for example, 2 is less than 3. Do not confuse the meaning of this rule with ranking-type games where 1 is ranked higher than 2, etc. (games like this *do* occur on the LSAT). When the rule discusses "lower-numbered" or "higher-numbered" elements, it means actual numerical value and 1 is always lower than 2, 2 is always lower than 3, 3 is always lower than 4, and so on. Thus the rule is properly diagrammed as an FJ block. Applying the basic principle of linkage to the second and third rules produces the VFJ super-block. This super block is clearly one of the keys to the game since it has a limited number of placement options. In fact, the game is made somewhat easier by the fact that there are only two "active" rules to track: the VFJ super-block and the GW not-block. The first rule is essentially dead since it is incorporated into the main setup. With only two active rules to consider, you should always be looking to apply them as you attack the questions.

Question #1: Global, Could Be True, List. The correct answer choice is (C)

As usual, apply the List question technique. Answer choice (A) can be eliminated since bench 2 contains two majors, a violation of the rules (and, of course, bench 4 contains two nonmajors). This question is rather irritating because of the layout chosen by the test makers. It would have been much easier had they separated the benches with some space instead of lining them up. Answer choice (C) is correct.

Question #2: Local, Must Be True. The correct answer choice is (B)

If V is assigned to bench 2, then, by application of the super-block, F must be assigned to bench 2, and J must be assigned to bench 3. Then, when W is assigned to bench 4, this affects G, who can no longer be assigned to bench 4, or benches 2 and 3 since they are taken by F and J. Therefore, G must be assigned to bench 1:

```
Non:  __    V    __    W

Maj:  G     F     J     H
      ─     ─     ─     ─
      1     2     3     4
                        ∅
```

Since G must be assigned to bench 1, answer choice (B) is proven correct. Additionally, when G is assigned to bench 1, H is forced into bench 4. The last two variables, X and Y, create a dual option that rotates between benches 1 and 3.

Question #3: Local, Must Be True. The correct answer choice is (A)

The question stem contains the unusual condition that majors G and H cannot be consecutive, creating a GH not-block. The key to the question is realizing that since G and H are majors, their placement will have a direct effect on the other two majors, F and J, who happen to be in a block configuration. Since the VFJ super-block can only be assigned to three positions—benches 1 and 2, benches 2 and 3, or benches 3 and 4—it makes sense to quickly examine the effect these placements have on G and H. If F and J are assigned to benches 1 and 2, this would force G and H to be consecutive, and if F and J are assigned to benches 3 and 4, this would also force G and H to be consecutive, so the VFJ super-block must be assigned to benches 2 and 3:

```
Non:  __    V    __    __

Maj:  G/H   F     J    H/G
      ─     ─     ─     ─
      1     2     3     4
```

Consequently answer choice (A) is proven correct.

Should you find yourself having difficulty with this question, it is interesting to note that the hypothetical produced in question #2 (where G and H were not consecutive) can be used to eliminate answer choices (B), (C), and (D), leaving just answer choices (A) and (E) to attack. This a great example of how using applicable prior work can get you out of difficulty.

Question #4: Local, Could Be True. The correct answer choice is (D)

When H and Y are assigned to bench 1, the VFJ super block has only two options: benches 2 and 3 or benches 3 and 4. Since that much information could be tough to juggle in your mind, why not make two quick hypotheticals showing both possibilities?

Possibility #1: VFJ assigned to benches 2 and 3

```
Non:  Y     V     W     X
      ─     ─     ─     ─
                        W

Maj:  H     F     J     G
      ─     ─     ─     ─
      1     2     3     4
```

Possibility #2: VFJ assigned to benches 3 and 4

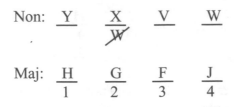

Non: Y   X̶/W̶   V   W

Maj: H   G   F   J
      1   2   3   4

In both possibilities the key to assigning the remaining variables is in the GW not-block. In possibility #1, when G is assigned to bench 4, W cannot be assigned to bench 4 and must instead be assigned to bench 3. In possibility #2, when G is assigned to bench 2, W cannot be assigned to bench 2 and must instead be assigned to bench 4. Possibility #1 proves that answer choice (D) is correct.

Question #5: Local, Could Be True, Except. The correct answer choice is (E)

Since this is an Except question, four of the answer choices Could Be True, and the one correct answer choice Cannot be true. The question states that G is assigned to bench 4, and X to bench 3. From the global conditions, we know that W cannot be at the same bench as G, so she cannot be at bench 4. From the super-block, we know that V cannot be at bench 4. Since X is at bench 3, he cannot be at bench 4. This leaves Y as the only possible non-major to sit at bench 4, so she must be seated there, and we now know that bench 4 seats only G and Y. Thus, answer choice (E) is correct because J cannot be assigned to the same bench as Y.

If you do not see the inference pattern above, remember that you can make hypotheticals based on the limited positions of the VFJ super-block. In this case, the VFJ super-block has only two possible assignments: benches 1 and 2 or benches 2 and 3:

Possibility #1: VFJ assigned to benches 1 and 2

Non: V   W   X   Y/W̶

Maj: F   J   H   G
      1   2   3   4

Possibility #2: VFJ assigned to benches 2 and 3

Non: W   V   X   Y/W̶

Maj: H   F   J   G
      1   2   3   4

Again, after the VFJ super-block is placed, the application of the GW not-block allows all the variables to be assigned. By comparing each answer choice against the two hypotheticals, you could still determine that answer choice (E) is correct.

Question #6: Local, Must Be True. The correct answer choice is (A)

The question stem sets up the following sequence:

$$W > J$$

Although this rule interrelates the majors and nonmajors, more importantly it ties in the VFJ super-block. If W is assigned to a lower-number bench than J, it follows that W is assigned to a lower-numbered bench than V and F as well:

$$W > \boxed{\begin{matrix} V & \\ F & J \end{matrix}}$$

Consequently, the VFJ super-block is again forced into only two possible positions: benches 2 and 3 or benches 3 and 4. As in the previous two questions, the best attack is to quickly make the two applicable hypotheticals:

Possibility #1: VFJ assigned to benches 2 and 3

Non:	W	V	X/Y	Y/X

Maj:	H	F	J	G
	1	2	3	4
	∅			

Possibility #2: VFJ assigned to benches 3 and 4

Non:	W/	/W	V	__

Maj:	H/G	G/H	F	J
	1	2	3	4

When the above hypotheticals are applied to the answer choices, it is apparent that answer choice (A) is correct. Answer choices (B), (C), and (E) could be true but do not have to be true. Answer choice (D) can never be true.

Question #7: Global, Could Be True, List. The correct answer choice is (D)

This is an unusual List question since it addresses only two of the four benches, and those benches are not sequential. An application of the VFJ super-block and the WG not-block eliminates only answer choice (C) (V is with J instead of F). That is a frustrating result since in normal List questions the application of the rules knocks off several, if not all, of the incorrect answers. Since the rule application only eliminated one answer choice, the key must be in the two benches that are not listed, benches 1 and 3. And this general way of thinking is a powerful tool in many other games as well: if the variables that you are working with do not seem to solve the problem, consider the other variables yet to be placed, or as in this situation, the other spaces that are unlisted and yet to be considered.

Answer choice (A) can be eliminated because the assignment of the given variables leaves no room for the VFJ super-block. If you are uncertain of this, take a moment to make a hypothetical with G and X assigned to bench 2 and H and Y assigned to bench 4. It immediately becomes apparent that F and J will have to be assigned to benches 1 and 3, a violation of the rules.

Answer choices (B) and (E) can both be eliminated for the same reason: the assignment of the respective variables ultimately forces W and G together on one of the benches, a violation of the rules. For answer choice (B), W and G would be assigned together on bench 1, and for answer choice (E), W and G would be assigned together on bench 3.

Since answer choices (A), (B), (C), and (E) have been eliminated, answer choice (D) must be correct.

Overall, this is a tough question to face at the end of the game. Unless you focus on mentally placing the VFJ block and WG not-block into benches 1 and 3, none of the remaining answers appears incorrect. For many students the only solution is to try each answer choice and work out a hypothetical that proves or disproves the answer. Of course this is very time consuming. If you are having time difficulties with the games section, it might be useful to skip this question once you realize how long it is going to take. You could simply guess among answer choices (A), (B), (D), and (E).

Parts of this game—especially questions #4, #6, and #7—can take a considerable amount of work. But by focusing on the two active and powerful rules, you should be able to do this work at a fairly high rate of speed. Plus, the two rules are so potent that their application consistently yields the placement of other variables, and this tends to give most test takers a high degree of confidence with their answer choices. Even if it takes a little extra time to work with the hypotheticals, knowing you have definitively reached the correct answer is a worthwhile reward.

A tour group plans to visit exactly five archaeological sites. Each site was discovered by exactly one of the following archaeologists—Ferrara, Gallagher, Oliphant—and each dates from the eighth, ninth, or tenth century (A.D.). The tour must satisfy the following conditions:

The site visited second dates from the ninth century.

Neither the site visited fourth nor the site visited fifth was discovered by Oliphant.

Exactly one of the sites was discovered by Gallagher, and it dates from the tenth century.

If a site dates from the eighth century, it was discovered by Oliphant.

The site visited third dates from a more recent century than does either the site visited first or that visited fourth.

13. Which one of the following could be an accurate list of the discoverers of the five sites, listed in the order in which the sites are visited?

   (A)   Oliphant, Oliphant, Gallagher, Oliphant, Ferrara
   (B)   Gallagher, Oliphant, Ferrara, Ferrara, Ferrara
   (C)   Oliphant, Gallagher, Oliphant, Ferrara, Ferrara
   (D)   Oliphant, Oliphant, Gallagher, Ferrara, Gallagher
   (E)   Ferrara, Oliphant, Gallagher, Ferrara, Ferrara

14. If exactly one of the five sites the tour group visits dates from the tenth century, then which one of the following CANNOT be a site that was discovered by Ferrara?

   (A)   the site visited first
   (B)   the site visited second
   (C)   the site visited third
   (D)   the site visited fourth
   (E)   the site visited fifth

15. Which one of the following could be a site that dates from the eighth century?

   (A)   the site visited first
   (B)   the site visited second
   (C)   the site visited third
   (D)   the site visited fourth
   (E)   the site visited fifth

16. Which one of the following is a complete and accurate list of the sites each of which CANNOT be the site discovered by Gallagher?

   (A)   third, fourth, fifth
   (B)   second, third, fourth
   (C)   first, fourth, fifth
   (D)   first, second, fifth
   (E)   first, second, fourth

17. The tour group could visit at most how many sites that were discovered by Ferrara?

   (A)   one
   (B)   two
   (C)   three
   (D)   four
   (E)   five

The setup to this Advanced Linear game is more challenging than the setup of the first game of this section, primarily because although this game appears to have only a few initial inferences, the relationship of the rules is such that most of the diagram can be filled in. With the proper diagram, the questions are relatively easy.

From the game scenario, we know that there are three variable sets: the five archaeological sites, the three archaeologists, and the three centuries. The five archaeological sites and the three centuries each have numerical order, but the archaeological sites are the better choice for the base since each site has a single archaeologist and a single date. This choice creates a linear setup with two stacks, one for the archaeologists and one for the centuries (remember to leave ample vertical space between the two stacks since each row will likely have its own Not Laws):

Centuries: 8 9 10 [3]
Archaeologists: F G O [3]

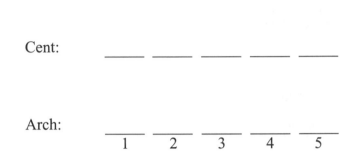

Because the rules have so many consequences, let's examine each rule individually.

Rule #1. This rule is the most straightforward rule of the game, and it can be represented by placing a "9" in second site space of the Century row:

Rule #2. If neither the fourth or fifth site was discovered by O, we can place O Not Laws on each space. And, because there are only three archaeologists, with O eliminated from discovering the fourth and fifth sites we can infer that either F or G discovered those sites. This fact can be represented by individual F/G dual-options on each site:

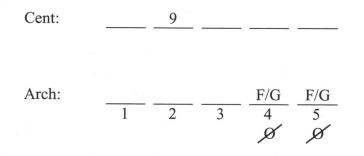

Rule #3. While the first two rules can be represented directly on the diagram, this rule must be diagrammed separately. The rule is a bit challenging to represent because it contains two separate pieces of information. The first piece of information is that G discovered exactly one site, and the second piece of information is that the site discovered by G dates from the 10th century. There are different ways to represent this rule, but we will use the following diagram:

$$G_{Once} \longrightarrow 10$$

From the contrapositive of this rule we can infer that any site that dates from the 8th or 9th century was not discovered by G, and must therefore have been discovered by F or O. Also, be careful not to make a Mistaken Reversal and assume that any site that dates from the 10th century was discovered by G; that is not necessarily the case.

Using the information above, we can infer that since the second site dates from the 9th century it was not discovered by G, and must therefore have been discovered by F or O:

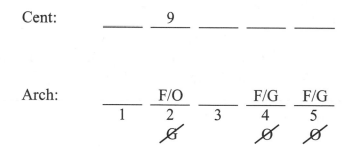

Rule #4. This is another important conditional rule, which can be diagrammed as follows:

$$8 \longrightarrow O$$

Operationally, this rule indicates that every time a site dates from the 8th century, it must have been discovered by O. The contrapositive of this rule reveals that if a site was not discovered by O, then it cannot date from the 8th century and must instead date from the 9th or 10th century. Thus, the fourth and fifth sites, which were not discovered by O, cannot date from the 8th century, and they must date from the 9th or 10th century. We can add this to our diagram with dual-options:

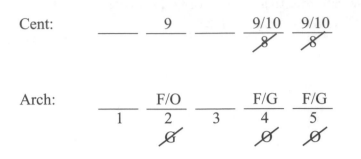

Rule #5. Although we have already gained a fair amount of information from the first four rules, the final rule will allow us to fill in most of the remaining spaces in the diagram.

The last rule states that the third site dates from a *more recent* century than either the first or fourth site. Thus, the third site cannot date from the 8th century, and the first and fourth sites cannot date from the 10th century. By itself, this information only seems to result in a series of dual-options for the dates of these sites. However, because we have already concluded that the fourth site must date from the 9th or 10th century (this inference was produced by combining the second and fourth rules), and this rule indicates that the fourth site cannot date from the 10th century, we can conclude that the fourth site dates from the 9th century. And, because the fourth site must date from the 9th century, we can use this rule to determine that the third site must date from the 10th century. Consequently, we can fill in the entire century row with either the exact site dates or with dual-options:

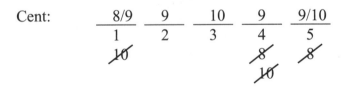

Further, because the fourth site cannot date from the 10th century, from the third rule we can infer G cannot discover the fourth site, and so the fourth site must be discovered by F. We can also use the third rule to determine that the first site was not discovered by G, and must have been discovered by F or O. These inferences allow us to arrive at our final diagram:

Cent:

8/9	9	10	9	9/10
1̸0̸			8̸	8̸
			1̸0̸	

Arch:

F/O	F/O		F	F/G
1	2	3	4	5
G̸	G̸		G̸	G̸
			O̸	

Note that all of the dual-options are not independent. For example, if the first site dates from the 8th century, then according to the fourth rule it must have been discovered by O. The third rule is also active, and during the game you must keep track of the placement of G. Regardless, you now have a powerful setup with which to attack the game.

Question #13: Global, Could Be True, List. The correct answer choice is (E)

In this List question, if you use just the given rules, only rules #2 and #3 provide useful information. Thus, the easiest approach is to use the archaeologist row from the diagram to attack the answer choices.

Answer choice (A): According to the second rule, O cannot have discovered the fourth site, and thus this answer choice is incorrect.

Answer choice (B): From our discussion of the setup to this game, we know that G cannot discover the first site, and hence this answer choice is incorrect.

Answer choice (C): From the combination of the first and third rules of the game, we know that G cannot have discovered the second site, and so this answer choice is incorrect.

Answer choice (D): The second rule stipulates that G discovered exactly one of the sites. Because this answer choice shows G discovering two of the sites, it is incorrect.

With the first four answer choices eliminated, answer choice (E) is proven correct.

Question #14: Local, Cannot Be True. The correct answer choice is (C)

The question stem asserts that only one of the five sites dates from the 10th century, and because we have already established that the third site dates from the 10th century, we know that the third site is the only site from the 10th century. In addition, from the third rule we know that G must discover a site from the 10th century, and so we can conclude that G must discover the third site. In this Cannot be true question, then, F cannot discover the third site and answer choice (C) is correct.

Note that although other deductions could be made (such as that the fifth site dates from the 9th century), and an entire diagram could be drawn out for this question, there is no point in doing so since our initial diagram already determined that the third site was from the 10th century and that provides the starting point for a fast and clear path to the correct answer.

Answer choices (A), (B), (D), and (E) are each incorrect because F could discover any of the sites listed in these answer choices.

Question #15: Global, Could Be True. The correct answer choice is (A)

Although creating the setup to this game takes a fair amount of time, Global questions such as this one allow us to make up time. Our setup indicates that only one site—the first—could date from the 8th century, and thus answer choice (A) is correct.

Answer choices (B), (C), (D), and (E): Each of these sites must be from either the 9th or 10th century.

Question #16: Global, Cannot Be True, List. The correct answer choice is (E)

Again, our initial setup easily answers this question. The setup indicates that G cannot discover the first, second, and fourth sites. The only answer choice that contains these three sites is answer choice (E).

Answer choices (A), (B), (C), and (D): Because G could have discovered the third or fifth site, any answer choice that contains the third or fifth site is incorrect.

Question #17: Global, Must Be True, Maximum. The correct answer choice is (D)

From the diagram, we know that F discovered the fourth site, and the dual-options and Not Laws indicate that F could have discovered each of the other sites as well. Thus, it might appear that F could have discovered all five sites. However, this would be an incorrect conclusion because the third rule states that G must have discovered exactly one site. Thus, F cannot have discovered all five sites and answer choice (E) can be eliminated from contention.

Because F is a random in this game, four appears to be a very likely correct answer. Before simply choosing four as the correct answer, however, the rules regarding O should be examined to ensure that O does not have to discover one or more of the sites. A quick review of the rules and the diagram indicates that O does not have to discover any of the sites, and thus answer choice (D) is correct.

Answer choices (A), (B), and (C): Because the question stem asks for the *maximum* number of sites discovered by F, and each one of these answer choices is less than the maximum, these answers are incorrect.

Answer choice (E): Because G must have discovered exactly one site, F cannot discover all five sites and this answer choice is incorrect.

A locally known guitarist's demo CD contains exactly seven different songs—S, T, V, W, X, Y, and Z. Each song occupies exactly one of the CD's seven tracks. Some of the songs are rock classics; the others are new compositions. The following conditions must hold:

> S occupies the fourth track of the CD. Both W and Y precede S on the CD. T precedes W on the CD. A rock classic occupies the sixth track of the CD. Each rock classic is immediately preceded on the CD by a new composition.
> Z is a rock classic.

11. Which one of the following could be the order of the songs on the CD, from the first track through the seventh?

    (A)　T, W, V, S, Y, X, Z
    (B)　V, Y, T, S, W, Z, X
    (C)　X, Y, W, S, T, Z, S
    (D)　Y, T, W, S, X, Z, V
    (E)　Z, T, X, W, V, Y, S

12. Which one of the following is a pair of songs that must occupy consecutive tracks on the CD?

    (A)　S and V
    (B)　S and W
    (C)　T and Z
    (D)　T and Y
    (E)　V and Z

13. Which one of the following songs must be a new composition?

    (A)　S
    (B)　T
    (C)　W
    (D)　X
    (E)　Y

14. If W precedes Y on the CD, then which one of the following must be true?

    (A)　S is a rock classic.
    (B)　V is a rock classic.
    (C)　Y is a rock classic.
    (D)　T is a new composition.
    (E)　W is a new composition.

15. If there are exactly two songs on the CD that both precede V and are preceded by Y, then which one of the following could be true?

    (Λ)　V occupies the seventh track of the CD.
    (B)　X occupies the fifth track of the CD.
    (C)　Y occupies the third track of the CD.
    (D)　T is a rock classic.
    (E)　W is a rock classic.

The diagram to this game is quite powerful since most of the spaces can be filled in.

From the game scenario, we know that there are three variable sets: the seven tracks, the seven songs, and the two types (new or rock classic). Because the seven tracks have a numerical order, they are the better choice for the base. This choice creates a linear setup with two stacks, one for the songs and one for the types (remember to leave ample vertical space between the two stacks since each row will likely have its own Not Laws):

Types: N R ^{2}
Songs: S T V W X Y Z ^{7}

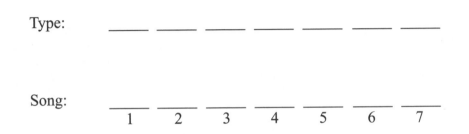

Because the rules have so many consequences, let's examine each rule:

Rule #1. This rule is the most straightforward rule of the game, and it can be represented by placing an "S" in fourth space of the Song row:

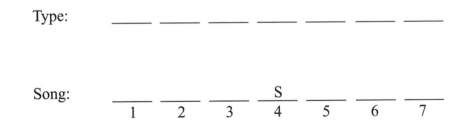

Rule #2. This rule states that both W and Y precede S on the CD, and this rule can be diagrammed as:

```
    W
---- > S
    Y
```

By itself, this rule means that W and Y cannot be tracks 5, 6, or 7 on the CD (because the first rule establishes that S is 4th)

<u>Rule #3</u>. This rule can be diagrammed as:

$$T > W$$

When combined with rule #2, we can create the following sequence:

$$T > W$$
$$\text{-------} > S$$
$$Y$$

This sequence indicates that T, W, and Y must all precede S on the CD. Of course, if T, W, and Y precede S, they occupy the first three spaces, and that leaves only spaces 5, 6, and 7 for V, X, and Z:

Type: ___ ___ ___ ___ ___ ___ ___

Song: (T > W,   Y)   S   (V,   X,   Z)
           1   2   3   4   5   6   7
          W̶   X̶

Thus, although all songs have not been specifically placed, we do know how they are divided on either side of S. Also, because T must precede W, we can ascertain that W cannot be first and T cannot be third.

<u>Rule #4</u>. This rule specifies that the sixth track is a rock classic. This information can be added directly to the diagram:

Type: ___ ___ ___ ___ ___ R ___

Song: (T > W,   Y)   S   (V,   X,   Z)
           1   2   3   4   5   6   7
          W̶   X̶

<u>Rule #5</u>. This rule can be diagrammed as:

R ⟶ [N R]

Note that this rule only applies to rock classics. A new song does not have to be followed by a rock classic.

The appearance of this rule creates several inferences. First, because a rock classic must be preceded by a new song, the first song on the CD must be a new song (a rock classic cannot be first because then it would not be preceded by a new song). Second, because the sixth song is a rock classic, we can automatically determine that the fifth song must be a new song. Third, because the sixth song is a rock classic, the seventh song must be a new song (if it were a rock classic then the sixth song would have to be a new song). Adding this information creates the following setup:

Rule #6. This rule states that Z is a rock classic. When considered with the fifth rule, this rule can be diagrammed as follows:

However, we already know from the analysis in rule #3 that Z must be the fifth, sixth, or seventh song on the CD. And, since the analysis in rule #5 indicated that, of those three tracks, only the sixth could be a rock track, we can determine that Z must be the sixth track on the CD. Accordingly, V and X must occupy the fifth and seventh tracks, not necessarily in that order:

Type: N _____ _____ _____ N R N

Song: (T > W, Y) S V/X Z X/V
      1   2   3   4   5   6   7

Compiling all of the information above, we arrive at the final setup for this game:

Types: N R [2]
Songs: S T V W X Y Z [7]

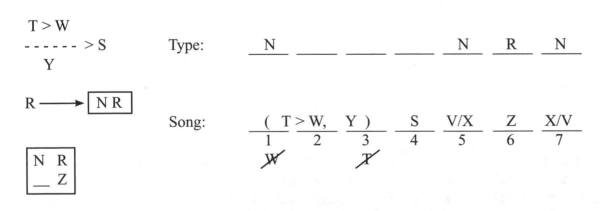

Question #11: Global, Could Be True, List. The correct answer choice is (D)

To attack this List question in a foolproof manner, simply apply the first three rules. For an even faster approach, apply the rules and inferences together (for example, first apply the rule that states that S is fourth, then apply the inference that indicates that Z is sixth, etc).

Answer choice (A): This answer choice is incorrect because Y does not precede S, and Z is not sixth.

Answer choice (B): This answer choice can be eliminated because W does not precede S.

Answer choice (C): This answer choice is incorrect because V does not appear (and therefore S appears twice), and T does not precede W.

Answer choice (D): This is the correct answer choice.

Answer choice (E): This answer choice can be eliminated because S is not fourth and Z is not sixth.

Question #12: Global, Must Be True. The correct answer choice is (E)

Use the final diagram to quickly and easily solve this question. Examine each answer choice and determine whether the two songs must be consecutive, or whether they can be separated in a valid hypothetical.

Answer choice (A): This answer choice is incorrect because S and V can be the fourth and seventh tracks, respectively.

Answer choice (B): This answer choice can be eliminated because S and W can be the second and fourth tracks, respectively.

Answer choice (C): This answer choice is incorrect because T is always first or second, and Z is always sixth.

Answer choice (D): This answer choice can be eliminated because T and Y can be the first and third tracks, respectively.

Answer choice (E): This is the correct answer choice. V must be fifth or seventh, and Z must be sixth, so V and Z are always consecutive whether it is VZ or ZV.

Question #13: Global, Must Be True. The correct answer choice is (D)

With Global questions in this game, simply refer to the main diagram. In this case, we know that the first, fifth and seventh songs must be new songs. With the first song, either T or Y must be first, but there is no way to determine which must be first. With the fifth and seventh songs, those to tracks are occupied by V and X, so both V and X must be new songs. A quick scan of the answer choices reveals that X is present, and thus answer choice (D) is correct.

Answer choices (A), (B), (C), and (E): These answer choices are incorrect because each of the listed songs could be rock classics.

Answer choice (D): This is the correct answer choice. X must be fifth or seventh, and both the fifth and seventh songs are new songs.

Question #14: Local, Must Be True. The correct answer choice is (D)

The question stem indicates that W precedes Y on the CD. That sets up the following chain relationship:

$$T > W > Y > S$$

Since S must be the fourth track on the CD, the diagram appears as follows:

Type:	N				N	R	N

Song:	T	W	Y	S	V/X	Z	X/V
	1	2	3	4	5	6	7

Answer choice (A): This answer is incorrect because S could be a new song or a rock classic.

Answer choice (B): This answer choice is incorrect because V is a new song.

Answer choice (C): This answer is incorrect because Y could be a new song or a rock classic.

Answer choice (D): This is the correct answer choice. T must be first, and the first track is a new song as discussed in the setup to the game.

Answer choice (E): This answer choice is incorrect because W could be a new song or a rock classic.

Question #15: Local, Could Be True. The correct answer choice is (E)

The condition in the question stem is worded in a clumsy fashion. Let's examine the statement piece by piece to derive what the test makers meant to say.

The question stem states that "there are exactly two songs on the CD that both precede V and are preceded by Y." The portion that states that "there are exactly two songs on the CD that both precede V," means that there are exactly two tracks in front of V, which would be diagrammed as follows:

The portion that states that "there are exactly two songs on the CD that...are preceded by Y," means that there are exactly two tracks behind Y, which would be diagrammed as follows:

Combing those two statements (they are combined by the "and" in the question stem) yields the following diagram:

The challenge is now to place that split-block on the main diagram. Because V is restricted to fifth or seventh, V is a logical starting point. If V is seventh, then Y would have to be fourth, which is impossible since S must be fourth. Thus, V must be fifth, and therefore Y must be second under the conditions in this question:

Type:	N				N	R	N

Song:	T	Y	W	S	V	Z	X
	1	2	3	4	5	6	7

Of course, when Y is second, then T must be first and W must be third (because T > W). Also, when V is fifth, then X must be seventh, and thus the entire song order is established.

Answer choice (A): This answer choice is incorrect because V must be fifth.

Answer choice (B): This answer choice is incorrect because X must be seventh.

Answer choice (C): This answer choice is incorrect because Y must be second.

Answer choice (D): This answer choice is incorrect because T must be a new song.

Answer choice (E): This is the correct answer choice. W could be either a new song or a rock classic.

In order to separate the game from its answer key and explanations,
the fourth game is on the next page.

Game #4: February 1993 Questions 8-12

Doctor Yamata works only on Mondays, Tuesdays, Wednesdays, Fridays, and Saturdays. She performs four different activities—lecturing, operating, treating patients, and conducting research. Each working day she performs exactly one activity in the morning and exactly one activity in the afternoon. During each week her work schedule must satisfy the following restrictions:

> She performs operations on exactly three mornings.
> If she operates on Monday, she does not operate on Tuesday.
> She lectures in the afternoon on exactly two consecutive calendar days.
> She treats patients on exactly one morning and exactly three afternoons.
> She conducts research on exactly one morning.
> On Saturday she neither lectures nor performs operations.

8. Which one of the following must be a day on which Doctor Yamata lectures?

   (A) Monday
   (B) Tuesday
   (C) Wednesday
   (D) Friday
   (E) Saturday

9. On Wednesday Doctor Yamata could be scheduled to

   (A) conduct research in the morning and operate in the afternoon
   (B) lecture in the morning and treat patients in the afternoon
   (C) operate in the morning and lecture in the afternoon
   (D) operate in the morning and conduct research in the afternoon
   (E) treat patients in the morning and treat patients in the afternoon

10. Which one of the following statements must be true?

    (A) There is one day on which the doctor treats patients both in the morning and in the afternoon.
    (B) The doctor conducts research on one of the days on which she lectures.
    (C) The doctor conducts research on one of the days on which she treats patients.
    (D) The doctor lectures on one of the days on which she treats patients.
    (E) The doctor lectures on one of the days on which she operates.

11. If Doctor Yamata operates on Tuesday, then her schedule for treating patients could be

    (A) Monday morning, Monday afternoon, Friday morning, Friday afternoon
    (B) Monday morning, Friday afternoon, Saturday morning, Saturday afternoon
    (C) Monday afternoon, Wednesday morning, Wednesday afternoon, Saturday afternoon
    (D) Wednesday morning, Wednesday afternoon, Friday afternoon, Saturday afternoon
    (E) Wednesday afternoon, Friday afternoon, Saturday morning, Saturday afternoon

12. Which one of the following is a pair of days on both of which Doctor Yamata must treat patients?

    (A) Monday and Tuesday
    (B) Monday and Saturday
    (C) Tuesday and Friday
    (D) Tuesday and Saturday
    (E) Friday and Saturday

This Defined, Balanced game is one of our favorites of all time. The game contains four variable sets: days of the week, morning activities, afternoon activities, and the four different activities. In setting up the game most students make a crucial mistake: they fail to show Thursday on the diagram. At first, this would not seem to be a big issue since the game scenario does not identify Thursday as a day on which Doctor Yamata works. But, because of the rule that states that "she lectures on exactly *two consecutive calendar days*," the issue of consecutive days is critical, and a diagram without Thursday gives the false impression that Wednesday and Friday are consecutive. Once this mistake is made, the options for the LL block appear greater than they actually are, and making inferences becomes difficult. Fortunately, the first question of the game reveals that there is a major inference involving one of the lectures. Answering this question is critical to your success on the game (just as with question #20 of game #6 of the last chapter). Remember, if you are faced with a Global question that indicates that one (or more) of the variables *must* be placed in a certain position (as with questions #8 and #12 of this game), you must answer the question. If you do not, you will miss a critical piece of information that will likely affect your performance on all other questions. In the case of question #8, if you do not have the answer when you arrive at the question, it is a fairly clear signal that you have missed something big in the setup.

When representing Thursday, mark each slot with an "X" in order to indicate that no work is done:

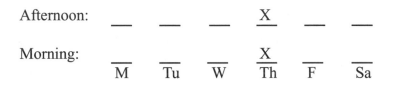

Note that you could show Sunday but it too would have an X in both slots. With this basic diagram the rules can now be applied:

L O T R [4]

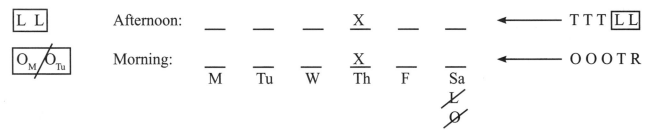

Listing which activities occur in the morning and afternoon takes a considerable amount of time, and these activities have been placed on the right side of the diagram. The rules indicate that in the afternoon there will be three T's and two L's, and in the morning there will be three O's, one R, and one T. This is extremely valuable information since it defines the composition of each row. Now that the rules have been added, we can begin to make inferences.

The first inference involves Saturday afternoon. According to the rules, Doctor Yamata can only lecture or treat patients in the afternoon. But on Saturday she cannot lecture, so it follows that she must treat patients, and a "T" can be placed on Saturday afternoon:

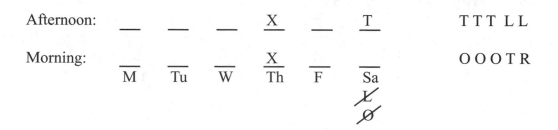

Afternoon: __   __   __   X   __   T   T T T L L

Morning: __   __   __   X   __   __   O O O T R

    M   Tu   W   Th   F   Sa

Once T is established on Saturday afternoon, it becomes apparent that the LL block can only be placed on Monday-Tuesday or Tuesday-Wednesday:

Afternoon: L/   L   /L   X   __   T   T T T L L

Morning: __   __   __   X   __   __   O O O T R

    M   Tu   W   Th   F   Sa

Note that Tuesday must always have a lecture and the other lecture will be placed on Monday or Wednesday, as shown by the split-option. Thus, in the afternoon, only two treatments remain to be assigned. One treatment will be placed on Friday afternoon (since it cannot be a lecture it must be a treatment), and the other treatment will fill in the Monday-Wednesday option:

Afternoon: L/T   L   T/L   X   T   T   T T T L L

Morning: __   __   __   X   __   __   O O O T R

    M   Tu   W   Th   F   Sa

Consequently the afternoon spaces are filled, and it is revealed that only two solutions to the afternoon set exist:

Afternoon option #1:   L   L   T   X   T   T

Afternoon option #2:   T   L   L   X   T   T

    M   Tu   W   Th   F   Sa

When seen in this light, it becomes obvious that the answer to question #8 is (B).

With the afternoon completed, we can now turn to an analysis of the morning row. Since Doctor Yamata cannot operate on Saturdays, on Saturday morning she is left with the choice of treating patients or conducting research. This is shown with a dual-option on Saturday morning:

Afternoon:	L/T	L	T/L	X	T	T			T T T L L
Morning:				X		R/T			O O O T R
	M	Tu	W	Th	F	Sa			

(Sa crossed out with ø)

This leaves four morning spaces to be filled by three O's and the remainder of the T/R dual-option. At first glance it may seem that no inferences can be drawn regarding the placement of these variables. However, the rule involving operations on Monday and Tuesday has a powerful effect on the possible placement of the three O's: because only one operation can be performed on the Monday-Tuesday pair, this forces the other two operations to be performed on Wednesday and Friday:

Afternoon:	L/T	L	T/L	X	T	T			T T T L L
Morning:			O	X	O	R/T			O O O T R
	M	Tu	W	Th	F	Sa			

(Sa crossed out with ø)

In summary, when an operation is performed on Monday, the operations rule prevents Doctor Yamata from operating on Tuesday; therefore, the remaining two operations must be performed on Wednesday and Friday. When an operation is performed on Tuesday, Doctor Yamata cannot operate on Monday, and the remaining two operations must again be performed on Wednesday and Friday. Hence, we can infer that operations are always performed on Wednesday and Friday.

The diagram is not yet complete. The final operation must be performed on Monday or Tuesday morning, next to the remainder of the T/R dual-option. This can be somewhat difficult to diagram, and we use a special parenthetical notation:

Morning:	(O , T/R)	
	M	Tu

The parentheses indicate that one of the two enclosed spaces must be an operation and the other space must be a treatment or research; it also indicates that the order is unknown. In this way the notation efficiently captures the four possibilities for Monday and Tuesday morning: OT, OR, TO, and RO. With this final piece the diagram for the game is complete:

LOTP[4]

L L	Afternoon:	T/L	L	L/T	X	T	T	◄——— T T T L L
O_M / O_Tu	Morning:	(O , T/R)	O	X	O	R/T	◄——— O O O T R
		M	Tu	W	Th	F	Sa	

(Sa crossed out with ø)

Question #8: Global, Must Be True. The correct answer choice is (B)

As discussed in the setup to the game, the inference regarding the placement of the LL block in the afternoons proves answer choice (B) correct.

Question #9: Global, Could Be True. The correct answer choice is (C)

According to the final diagram, on Wednesday morning Doctor Yamata can only be scheduled to perform an operation. Thus, answer choices (A), (B), and (E) can be eliminated. On Wednesday afternoon she can only treat patients or lecture, and so answer choice (D) can be eliminated. Thus, answer choice (C) must be correct.

Question #10: Global, Must Be True. The correct answer choice is (E)

This is the most difficult question of the game. Each of the answers seem vague—in direct contrast to the final diagram, which is quite specific. The correct answer choice, (E), uses the Overlap Principle.

In answer choice (E) the Overlap Principle applies to the lectures and operations on Monday, Tuesday and Wednesday. Two operations and two lectures must be assigned within this three day period and consequently there must be an overlap between the two groups. Consider all the possible permutations of the lectures and operations for those days:

	M	Tu	W			M	Tu	W
Afternoon:	L	L	_		Afternoon:	_	L	L
Morning:	_	O	O		Morning:	_	O	O

	M	Tu	W			M	Tu	W
Afternoon:	L	L	_		Afternoon:	_	L	L
Morning:	O	_	O		Morning:	O	_	O

In each case at least one lecture is given on a day the doctor operates, and sometimes it occurs twice.

Question #11: Local, Could Be True. The correct answer choice is (E)

According to the rules, Doctor Yamata must treat patients once in the mornings and three times in the afternoons. Answer choices (A) and (B) are both incorrect because they feature two mornings and two afternoons. We have also determined that Doctor Yamata must operate on Wednesday morning, and therefore she cannot treat patients in that slot. Since answer choices (C) and (D) both include Wednesday morning, they are incorrect. Accordingly, answer choice (E) is correct. Note that there are a number of ways to attack this question. For example, it is known that Doctor Yamata must treat patients on both Friday and Saturday afternoon. That fact eliminates answer choices (A) and (C).

Question #12: Global, Must Be True. The correct answer choice is (E)

The first set of inferences proved that Doctor Yamata must treat patients on both Friday afternoon and Saturday afternoon. It follows that answer choice (E) is correct. In a sense, both question #8 and #12 are part of a pair: if you get one correct, you will likely get the other correct. That shows the powerful nature of the inferences, and the necessity of identifying those inferences.

It is also interesting to note that in this game four of the five questions are Global. When a game has a majority of Global questions, that often indicates that the game contains deep and challenging inferences. That is certainly the case here.

CHAPTER FOUR: GROUPING GAMES

The Principle of Grouping

Grouping games require you to analyze the variables in terms of which ones can and cannot be together. The emphasis on ordering—the basis of Linear games—is usually not present in Grouping games. Consider the following example:

> A four-member panel is selected from seven applicants—G, H, J, P, Q, R, and S. The panel is selected according to the following restrictions:
> If J is selected, then R is selected.
> If R is selected, then H is not selected.

In this game, the concept of order or linearity does not appear; instead, the focus is on placing the variables into a workable group.

Grouping games involve a fundamentally different principle than Linear games.

Unified Grouping Theory™

When analyzing Grouping games, we use a system similar to the one for Linear games discussed on page 49. This system can be used to classify every type of Grouping game that appears on the LSAT, and understanding the proper classification for a game increases your ability to attack the game.

Group Size

Every Grouping game references a group or groups to be selected, and these groups are always used as the base for the game. We use the term "Definition" to describe the number of variables being selected, and the first step in classifying a Grouping game is to identify whether the game is Defined, Undefined, or Partially Defined.

Correctly classifying each Grouping game will assist you in setting up the game.

One way to view this principle is to realize that to fully understand something, you must be able to identify and classify its component parts.

Defined™: In these games the exact number of variables to be selected is fixed in the scenario or the rules. For example, "exactly six people will be selected to attend a dinner party" or "there are three subcommittees, each having three members." Because the total number of variables to be selected is always constant, and thus the number of places remaining to be filled is always known, many students find these games preferable to Undefined or Partially Defined games.

Undefined games
are generally the
most difficult
type of Grouping
game.

<u>Undefined</u>™: The number of variables to be selected in an Undefined game is not fixed, and is only limited by the total number of variables. For example, "a clothing store carries exactly ten clothing lines. The store is having a sale on some of these clothing lines." The lack of definition in these games makes them more difficult because you never know with certainty how many variables are being selected until you process all of the rules and take into account any conditions in the question stem.

<u>Partially Defined</u>™: There is a minimum and/or maximum number of variables to be selected in these games, but the *exact* number of variables selected in the game cannot be determined. For example, a game might state, "a committee of at least four members is formed from among nine candidates." Or, as stated in another game, "each manager oversees at least two but no more than four employees."

Partially Defined grouping games are generally preferable to Undefined games because although the exact numbers in each group are not specified, there is a more narrow range of possibilities. When these games appear, you are typically forced to juggle several structural solutions, but this is not necessarily as difficult as it sounds. The key to handling these games is to make sure you account for the "loose" nature of the numbers when you create the setup. That accounting could involve something as simple as noting that there can be more members in a group, or it could be as complex as creating extra diagrams. The nature of the game will dictate the proper approach to use.

Regardless of the type of Grouping game you encounter, you *must* always be aware of the group size. There is no chance of success in a game if you do not focus on the group to be selected.

Multiple Group Characteristics

There is an additional subclassification that applies to Defined games only. This classification relates to the composition of a Defined grouping game with multiple groups (for example, the groups might be two groups of lawmakers or children assigned to three different canoes). The categories are:

Moving™: In some games the test makers will indicate that an exact number of variables are to be selected (the Defined component) but there are still sub-groups within that set that are undefined, or "Moving." For example, consider this partial game scenario from a game that appears later in this chapter:

> At a benefit dinner, a community theater's seven sponsors will be seated at three tables—1, 2, and 3. Each table has at least two sponsors seated at it, and each sponsor is seated at exactly one table.

In this case there are seven seats—this is the Defined aspect—but the exact assignment of seats to tables is uncertain, or "moving" inside the Defined group. Two of the tables will have two sponsors and one of the tables will have three sponsors (a 3-2-2 numerical distribution) but it cannot be ascertained exactly which table has the three sponsors. Thus this game would be classified as Defined-Moving.

The Moving vs. Fixed classification does not apply to Undefined games because by definition they are always Moving.

Here is another example:

> Each of six people—C, D, F, G, H and K—plays exactly one of two sports—basketball or football.

Again, the game is defined as having six slots, but the spread of the slots can vary from three in basketball and three in football (3-3 numerical distribution), to five in basketball and one in football (5-1 numerical distribution), etc. The number of people playing each sport "moves" depending on the constraints imposed by each question.

Note also that the "moving" designation is often associated with a numerical distribution, which is a concept we will discuss in more detail in a later chapter.

Fixed™: Games of this type are more straightforward. The selection group is set (or "fixed") and there is no movement within the group or any existing sub-group. Here is an example from a game that will appear at the end of this section:

> A university library budget committee must reduce exactly five of eight areas of expenditure—G, L, M, N, P, R, S, and W.

In this game the five selections are Fixed and there is no uncertainty about the size of the groups. The game would be classified as Defined-Fixed.

The Selection Pool

Another trackable grouping element involves the variables available to be placed (also known as the "selection pool"). Virtually all games have an exactly-defined number of available variables, but those variables do not always have the same characteristics.

Uniform Variables™: If the variables all are equal members of the same basic group, the selection pool is known as Uniform. Here is an example of a Uniform selection group:

> There are exactly five instruments in storage: a clarinet, a flute, a saxophone, a trumpet, and a violin. Each instrument can be played by exactly one of three band members: Edwin, Jorge, or Marshall.

In this example, the five instruments are distributed to the three band members. Within this grouping and without respect to the rules, the five instruments are functionally identical and no one instrument has any special distinguishing marks aside from the name of each instrument.

Subdivided Variables™: If the selection pool is divided into specific sub-groups and each sub-group has a unique characteristic, the selection pool is called Subdivided. Here is an example:

> The members of a six-person school honor board will be selected from among three parents—A, B, and C—three students—F, G, and H—and four teachers—R, S, T, and V.

In this game, you must track the differences between variables because, for example, B, a parent, has a differentiating characteristic from G, a student. As you might expect, the test makers then use these different groups in the rules and the questions. To track these groups, often the best approach is the use of subscripts, such as:

$$B_P \qquad\qquad G_S \qquad\qquad R_T$$

Subdivided selection pools make a game more difficult because there are more elements to track.

The Relationship of the Selection Pool to the Group Size

Identifying the relationship of the number of available variables to the number of available spaces is critical. This relationship is known as Balance. Just as with Linear games, understanding the element of Balance will help you spot problems in a game and suggest certain areas that require your attention.

Balance applies to all Defined games (and some Partially Defined games). Undefined games, because of their lack of certainty, do not have a Balance element. Balance, as it relates to Grouping, can be analyzed as follows:

Balanced™: The number of variables to be selected is equal to the overall number of available spaces. For example, "eight students are divided into two four-person study groups."

Unbalanced™: The number of variables to be selected is *not* equal to the overall number of available spaces. Unbalanced games are either Overloaded or Underfunded:

> **Overloaded**™: There are extra candidates for the available spaces. For example, "nine candidates for a five-person research panel." In Overloaded games, each valid solution contains some unused or unselected variables.

> **Underfunded**™: There are not enough candidates for the available spaces. This lack is almost always solved by reusing one or more of the candidates. For example, "seven television advertisements must be aired during two weeks, five advertisements per week." In this example, some of the advertisements would be repeated until all ten slots are filled.

As a technical aside, please note that the issue of Balance is one that relates only to the number of variables available for the number of selections to be made. If a game has 9 candidates for 5 spaces, it could be viewed as 9 variables being placed into 2 groups: a group of 5 "selected" variables and a group of 4 "unselected" variables. From this perspective the game could be called Balanced (9 into 9). But in the classification above, we have chosen to use Balance as an indicator of the relative number of variables to selected positions. If there are fewer or greater variables than selected positions, the game will be classified as Unbalanced. Thus, a game of 9 candidates for 5 spaces will be classified as Defined (exactly 5 spaces are available), Unbalanced (there are 9 candidates for the 5 spaces), and Overloaded (there are a greater number

The issue of Balance involves the number of variables available to fill the given spaces.

Grouping games will be classified in different ways according to the game. For example, an Undefined game cannot have a Balance component, since there is not a set number of spaces to be filled. On the other hand, Defined games always have a Balance component.

of candidates than selection spaces).

This classification decision can also affect the way certain Grouping games are diagrammed. For example, when diagramming an Overloaded game, we will not diagram the "unselected" variable group. Note that this is a decision based on preference and efficiency. For most students it is easier to work with just the spaces for the selected variables and then mentally consider the remaining variables. However, it may be that for some students, it helps to show the "unselected" group. There is no right or wrong here—just what works best for you. In our diagrams, when a game has 9 candidates for 5 spaces, we will show just the 5 spaces for the selected candidates, and we will *not* show the 4 spaces for the unselected candidates.

Some games have complex classifications, such as Defined-Moving, Unbalanced: Overloaded. Some have very simple classifications such as Undefined. The classification depends on the elements presented by the test makers.

Now that the entire Unified Grouping Theory has been delineated, you may wonder why there are so many classifications and subclassifications for the games. The Theory is complex because the LSAT is complex; to accurately characterize the variety of Grouping game elements used by the test makers requires a system that is comprehensive and detailed. Fortunately, in the discussion of each game at the end of a chapter, there will be an opportunity to revisit the classification system and observe its application and utility. In the meantime, review the discussion to make certain that you understand the kind of elements that must be tracked when you encounter a Grouping game, and then try the drill on the next page.

Grouping Games—Unified Grouping Theory Classification Drill

Each of the following items provides a Grouping game scenario. In the space provided, supply the most accurate classification of the game using the categories defined by the Unified Grouping Theory (Defined/Partially Defined/Undefined, Fixed/Moving, Balanced/Unbalanced, Overloaded/Underfunded). *Answers on the next page*

1. Nine realtors are divided among exactly three offices—office 1, office 2, and office 3. Each office will be assigned exactly three realtors, and each realtor will be assigned to only one office.

   Classification: _____

2. Exactly eight of ten rowers are each assigned to two rowing teams of four persons each.

   Classification: _____

3. Ten candidates are being considered for some positions at a law firm. Only applicants who are interviewed will be hired.

   Classification: _____

4. A dinner reservation for at least five people will be made at a local restaurant. The diners will be selected from a group of eleven friends.

   Classification: _____

5. Exactly six of nine book editors are selected to edit exactly four books, with each selected editor editing exactly one book and each book being edited by at least one editor.

   Classification: _____

6. Exactly eight students are assigned to two buses, bus 1 and bus 2. Each student is assigned to exactly one bus.

   Classification: _____

7. The members of three committees will be selected from among seven applicants. Each committee must have exactly three members. Each applicant must be assigned to at least one committee, and applicants can be assigned to more than one committee.

   Classification: _____

1. Classification: Defined-Fixed, Balanced

   Since each office contains exactly three realtors, the game is Defined-Fixed. Since there are nine realtors for exactly nine positions, the game is Balanced.

2. Classification: Defined-Fixed, Unbalanced: Overloaded

   Since each rowing team contains exactly four rowers, the game is Defined-Fixed. Since there are ten rowers for exactly eight positions, the game is Unbalanced: Overloaded.

3. Classification: Undefined

   Since the number of candidates to be hired at the law firm is unknown, the game is Undefined. Since the game is Undefined there is no Moving/Fixed element, nor is there a Balance element.

4. Classification: Partially Defined

   Since the number of diners is at least five, but it is uncertain exactly how many diners there will be, the game is Partially Defined. Since the game is Partially Defined, there is no Moving/Fixed element, nor is there a Balance element.

5. Classification: Defined-Moving, Unbalanced: Overloaded

   Since exactly six editors will be assigned to the four books, but it is unknown how many editors will edit each book (it is either a 3-1-1-1 numerical distribution or a 2-2-1-1 numerical distribution), the game is Defined-Moving. Since there are nine editors for the six positions, the game is Unbalanced: Overloaded.

6. Classification: Defined-Moving, Balanced

   Since each of the eight students is assigned to a bus, but it is unknown exactly how many students are assigned to each bus, the game is Defined-Moving. Since all eight students are assigned to the two buses, the game is Balanced.

7. Classification: Defined-Fixed, Unbalanced: Underfunded

   Since each committee contains exactly three members, the game is Defined-Fixed. Since there are only seven applicants for the nine positions, the game is Unbalanced: Underfunded. The seven-into-nine scenario creates a numerical distribution of 3-1-1-1-1-1-1 or 2-2-1-1-1-1-1. Remember, each of the seven applicants must be assigned to at least one committee. That means that seven of the nine committee spaces are automatically filled. The remaining two spaces go to either one applicant who is then assigned to all three committees—the 3-1-1-1-1-1-1 distribution—or to two applicants who are each assigned to two committees—the 2-2-1-1-1-1-1 distribution. Numerical distributions will be revisited in a later chapter.

In a diagram, the number of groups being created affects how the groups are shown. For example, if there is only one group to be diagrammed, as in "There are nine candidates for a five-person group," the group will be displayed horizontally as follows:

— — — — —
5-person group

Please note that the spaces are *not* numbered because being "first" or "second" in the group has no meaning.

In contrast, when there are two or more groups, the diagram will contain both horizontal and vertical elements. If the game states, "There are two groups—group 1 and group 2—of four children each," the two groups will be displayed as follows:

The numbering represents the group identifiers. We will *not* display the game in entirely horizontal fashion, as follows:

— — — — —   — — — —
    1   2

This diagram takes up more space and is less efficient than the previous diagram. Vertical stacking allows for a more compact representation of the two groups, and it also allows you to see all of the available spaces in closer spatial relationship.

The use of the vertical component will also affect the representation of certain rules, especially negative grouping rules.

Many grouping rules can be displayed using the "arrows" from the conditional reasoning section in Chapter Two.

Many of the rules in Grouping games can be diagrammed in the same way as those in Linear games. Nevertheless, since the emphasis in Grouping games is on the assemblage of the variables, more of the rules involve conditional reasoning. Fortunately, you can use the same symbology introduced in the conditional rules section on page 28 of Chapter Two. To revisit those principles, consider the following example:

If J is selected, then R is selected.

Diagram:

$$J \longrightarrow R$$

In a Grouping game, this rule indicates then when J is chosen for a group, R must also be chosen for that group. Via the contrapositive, if R is not chosen for a group, then J cannot be chosen for that group.

A second example:

If R is selected, then H is not selected.

Diagram:

$$R \longrightarrow \cancel{H}$$

This rule indicates that when R is chosen for a group, H cannot also be chosen for that group. Via the contrapositive, if H is chosen for a group, then R cannot be chosen for that group.

The Double Not-Arrow

The double not-arrow is similar to a "not equal" sign; the two terms at the end of the sign cannot be selected at the same time.

This second example above bears further analysis. As stated after the rule, when R is selected, H is not selected, and, via the contrapositive, when H is selected, R is not selected. Thus, if R or H is selected, then the other cannot be selected, and we can infer that R and H can never be selected together. To represent this relationship accurately, we use the following super-symbol, known as the *double not-arrow*:

$$R \longleftarrow\!\!\!|\!\!\!\longrightarrow H$$

In the symbolization above, the two terms at the ends of the sign cannot be selected together. In this sense the double not-arrow is a "super-symbol," one that captures all meanings of the negative relationship. This symbol increases efficiency and speed when used in Grouping games.

If you diagram statements with the single arrow and slash as in the first diagram, you will not be making a mistake, but you will be using a less effective representation.

To review, the double not-arrow only prohibits one scenario—that where the two terms occur together. Using our R/H example, several possible scenarios can occur:

1. R is selected, H is not selected.   (R and H̶)
2. H is selected, R is not selected.   (R̶ and H)
3. Neither R nor H is selected.   (R̶ and H̶)

The only outcome that cannot occur is that both R and H are selected.

Returning to the prior page, if we link the very first arrow relationship with the double-not arrow relationship, the following diagram results:

$$J \longrightarrow R \longleftarrow\!\!\!|\!\!\!\longrightarrow H$$

Since J must be selected with R, and R cannot be selected with H, it can be inferred that J and H can never be selected together:

$$J \longleftarrow\!\!\!|\!\!\!\longrightarrow H$$

This particular rule combination and resulting inference appears frequently in Grouping games and you should familiarize yourself with it.

The Double Arrow

Many of the conditional statements in the Logic Games section feature arrows that point in only one direction. But, as you saw in the discussion of the double not-arrow, there are some statements that produce arrows that point in both directions. These arrows, also known as biconditionals, indicate that each term is both sufficient and necessary for the other. As such, they create a very limited set of possibilities. Consider the following example:

Arun will be selected if and only if Bai is selected.

As you can see, this sentence contains the conditional indicators "if" and "only if" connected by the term "and." This effectively creates two separate conditional statements:

1.   "A   if   B"

and

2.   "A   only if   B"

The "A if B" portion creates the following diagram:

$$B \longrightarrow A$$

The "A only if B" portion creates the following diagram:

$$A \longrightarrow B$$

Combined, the two statements create the double arrow:

$$A \longleftrightarrow B$$

Only two scenarios are possible under this double arrow:

1. A and B both selected   (A and B)
2. Neither A nor B are selected   (A̶ and B̶)

Any scenario where one of the two is selected but the other is not selected is impossible.

The double arrow is typically introduced in any of the following three ways:

1. Use of the phrase "if and only if" (as in the example above).
2. Use of the phrase "vice versa" (as in "If A is selected then B is selected, and vice versa.").
3. By repeating and reversing the terms (as in "If A is selected then B is selected, and if B is selected then A is selected.").

If you encounter a double-arrow statement in the rules, simply treat it as you would a grouping block.

Terms in a double arrow relationship always occur together

The Contrapositive in Grouping Games

Because arrows will still be used to display a number of the rules in Grouping games, you must be familiar with the inferences that result from conditional rules. As discussed previously, the contrapositive is an important tool for gaining insight into a game. For any complex or tricky conditional rule, always take the contrapositive:

S is not selected if R is not selected.

Diagram:

$$\cancel{R} \longrightarrow \cancel{S}$$

The rule can be interpreted as, "If R is not selected then S is not selected." Please note that the diagram above is correct since the "if" in the middle of the rule introduces the sufficient condition. But in this form the diagram is somewhat difficult to negotiate. Let us take the contrapositive of the diagram and observe how much easier it is to interpret (remember, reverse the terms and negate both):

$$S \longrightarrow R$$

The rule now reads, "If S is selected then R must be selected," and the elimination of the negatives makes the rule easier to grasp.

Consider another example:

If J is selected then exactly four variables total are selected.

Diagram:

$$J \longrightarrow 4$$

Contrapositive:

$$\cancel{4} \longrightarrow \cancel{J}$$

The contrapositive can be interpreted as, "If exactly 4 variables are not selected then J is not selected." In other words, a group of any size besides 4 cannot contain J.

Remember, there is a contrapositive for any conditional statement, and if the initial statement is true, then the contrapositive is also true. The contrapositive is simply a different way of expressing the initial statement. To analogize, it is like examining a penny: both sides look different but intrinsically the value is the same.

Now, let us take a moment to examine conditional statements that are a bit more complex, and to also observe how the contrapositive operates in such statements.

Always take the contrapositive of any unusual conditional rule.

Multiple Sufficient and Necessary Conditions

So far, all of the conditional statements we have examined have contained only one sufficient condition and one necessary condition. However, there are many statements on the LSAT that contain either multiple sufficient conditions or multiple necessary conditions. Consider the following statement:

> If R is selected, then both S and T must be selected.

In this statement there are two necessary conditions that must be satisfied in order for R to be selected: 1. S must be selected and 2. T must be selected. Thus, the proper diagram for this statement is:

A "+" sign can be substituted for the "and" in the diagram to the right.

The difficulty in handling multiple sufficient or necessary conditions is with the contrapositive. But, as we know from the prior page, the contrapositive is a critical tool in Logic Games, and so we must understand how to handle the contrapositive with these statements.

In the example above, if *either one* of the two necessary conditions is not met, then R cannot be selected. It is *not* required that both necessary conditions *fail* to be met in order to prevent the sufficient condition from occurring. Thus, the proper diagram of the contrapositive of the statement is:

Whenever you take a contrapositive of a statement with multiple terms in the sufficient or necessary condition, "and" turns into "or," and "or" turns into "and."

Note that in taking the contrapositive, the "and" in the necessary condition is changed to "or." The reverse would be true if the necessary conditions had originally been linked by the term "or." Consider the following statement:

> If R is selected, then S or T must be selected.

The proper diagram for this statement is:

In this case, for R to be selected, only one of the two necessary conditions need to be satisfied. This does not preclude the possibility of satisfying both conditions, but it is not necessary to do so. Now let's take the contrapositive of this statement:

This diagram indicates that if neither S nor T is selected (that is, both are not selected), then R cannot be selected. Again, note that as the contrapositive occurred, the "or" joining the original necessary conditions changed to "and."

Now, let us examine a statement with two sufficient conditions. Consider the following statement:

If C and D are selected, then E must be selected.

The proper diagram for this statement is:

Note that *both* C and D must be selected in order to meet the sufficient condition, and when both C and D are selected then E must be selected as well. Now, let us take the contrapositive:

The contrapositive indicates that if E is not selected, then either C or D is not selected. Thus, if E is not selected, then C is not selected, or D is not selected, or both are not selected. Note that once again the "and" has become "or."

Of course, just as with the statement with two necessary conditions, if a statement with two sufficient conditions were to appear and those conditions were linked by "or," then the contrapositive of that statement would change the "or" to "and."

Linear versus Grouping Symbolizations

Symbolizations in the two major game types generally indicate different concepts. Although they can be substituted at times, it is important to understand the underlying intent of each symbolization. Consider the aforementioned inference:

J and H cannot be selected together.

In Grouping games both arrows and blocks are used, depending on the specific components of the game.

Linear Game Diagram: Grouping Game Diagram:

                         J ←——→ H

The block diagram used in Linear games typically indicates adjacency. The arrow diagram used in Grouping games typically indicates association.

In Grouping games we use blocks in three specific situations:

1. When working with diagrams that have vertical components. Blocks represent the relationship between the variables in a visually powerful way, and are therefore the best diagramming choice. For example, "In a game involving two groups—group 1 and group 2—of four children each, A must be in the same group as B," the diagram is as follows:

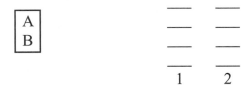

2. When diagramming rules that contain three or more variables in a positive or negative grouping relationship, such as "D, F, and G cannot all be selected together." This is diagrammed as:

3. To represent groups that must occupy a specified number of spaces, such as "In a game where four horses are selected, exactly two horses from the group H, J, K must be selected." The diagram is:

2 of H, J, K

Grouping Games Rule Diagramming Drill

In the space provided, supply the best symbolic representation (if any) of each of the following rules. If applicable, show any corresponding implications on the diagram provided. *Answers on the next page*

1. Of the four applicants R, S, T, and V, exactly three are hired.

— — — — —

Group of 5 Hirees

2. W, X, and Y cannot all be selected together.

— — — — —

Group of 5 Selections

3. D and E cannot be selected for the same team, and every player is assigned to exactly one of the teams.

— —
— —
— —
— —
1   2

4. If M and N are not assigned, then O must be assigned.

5. R and X cannot be selected together.

— — — — —

Group of 5 Selections

6. Either F or G, but not both, must be selected.

— — — — —

Group of 5 Selections

Grouping Games Rule Diagramming Drill Answer Key

1. 3 of R, S, T, and V

| R | S | T | V | ___ | ___ |
Group of 5 Hirees

2. [W X̷ Y]   No representation can be made on the diagram.

___ ___ ___ ___ ___
Group of 5 Selections

3. [D̷/E]   Remember to show the D/E dual-option on the diagram. D and E are represented in a block to the side since there is a vertical element in the setup.

   ___   ___
   ___   ___
   ___   ___
   D/E   E/D
    1   2

4. Diagram: M̷
                 and ——→ O
                 N̷

    Contrapositive: M
                 Ø̷ ——→ or
                        N

5. R ←—|—→ X   The rule is shown with the double not-arrow since there is no vertical element in the setup.

___ ___ ___ ___ ___
Group of 5 Selections

6. F ←—|—→ G   Reserve one space for the choice of F or G since exactly one must be selected.

F/G   ___   ___   ___   ___
Group of 5 Selections

Making Inferences

Making inferences is one of the keys to attacking the Logic Games section. In Grouping games, there are always several steps to take.

Linkage

As discussed in Chapter Two, the first step in making inferences is to find a variable that appears in at least two rules, combine the two rules, and then evaluate the implications.

When looking for inferences always start by linking the rules together.

In addition, combine any sub-groups that appear in the game, as in the following example:

> Nine people—five adults and four children—take a trip in two cars, car 1 and car 2. The adults are A, B, C, D, and E; the children are V, W, X, and Y. The following conditions apply:
> > Three adults ride in Car 1.
> > If A rides in car 2 then B also rides in car 2, and if B rides in car 2 then A must also ride in car 2.

The cars are two "main" groups, and the adults and children are each a "sub-group." At first the two rules above may not appear to be connected, but since A and B are both members of the adult sub-group, the two rules can be combined in the following way:

> Because the first rule states that three adults must ride in car 1, it follows that the remaining two adults must ride in car 2. According to the second rule, A and B must always ride together: they are either together in car 2 or they are together in car 1. Thus, if A or B rides in car 2, they both ride in car 2, and the other three adults—C, D, and E—would have to ride in car 1. Conversely, if A and B ride in car 1, then one of C, D, and E must ride in car 1, and the remaining two would have to ride in car 2.

Thus, by combining the sub-groups in the two rules, we have discovered a controlling inference in the game, and one that we could display within our diagram.

Always begin your inference search by linking the rules together.

Negative Grouping Rules

Negative grouping rules state that two or more variables *cannot* be selected together. As previously discussed, negative grouping rules can be displayed either with not-blocks or with the double-not arrow. In Grouping games, negative rules are as equally important as positive rules (rules that state two or more variables must be selected together). This is in contrast

In Grouping games, negative rules appear as frequently as positive rules.

to Linear games, where blocks are typically far more useful than not-blocks.

In grouping, negative and positive rules are of equal importance since both equally affect the selection of variables, albeit in opposite ways. Just as a set of positive grouping rules can yield powerful inferences, a collection of negative grouping rules can do the same. Thus, you should always carefully consider any collection of negative grouping rules to see if some powerful relationship is revealed.

Restrictions

Examining restrictions can sometimes lead to dramatic, game-changing inferences.

Restrictions are areas in a game where the number of options are limited. Restrictions can occur with almost any game element, but most notably with variables and available spaces. Because points of restriction almost always yield useful inferences, they are one of the first areas to search for when seeking to make inferences. Here are several areas of restriction to check within games:

Limited variable placement options

When a variable can only be placed into a limited number of places—such as with a split-option—the situation is inherently restricted and inferences often result. For example, rules such as the following must be considered constantly:

> "Janara must be assigned to either Group 1 or Group 2."

> "C is performed either second or fifth."

Restrictions can be so powerful that they sometimes lead to Identifying the Possibilities, a technique that will be discussed in a later chapter.

These rules will often come into play as other variables are placed, and spaces are thereby occupied.

Restrictions on a space or spaces

When a single space or set of spaces has a limited number of variables available for placement, the situation is restricted. Here are several rules featuring this concept:

> "Either the Q or R must be third."

> "There must be exactly one student on the committee."

> "Exactly two teachers from the group of F, G, and H must teach."

Space restrictions can also result from a combination of rules. For example, a large number of Not Laws for a single space can leave only one or two variables available to fill that space.

Structural Limitations

In certain games there are structural limitations that automatically spawn inferences. Here are two situations in which this occurs:

1. Small Group Size

In a game with multiple groups, when one of the groups is relatively small there is the potential for inferences. For example, a game with a group of two members and a group of five members would likely have limitations created by the fact that the group with two spaces would tend to fill up very quickly.

Also, keep in mind that group size can be affected by the rules. For example, a game with three groups of three members each would at first seem like infertile ground for a structural analysis based on group size. However, if one of the rules permanently placed a variable in one of the groups, then that group would only have two remaining spaces, and you would be well advised to always analyze those two spaces as you attacked the questions.

2. Two-Value Systems

A two-value system occurs in Defined, Balanced games that feature two groups (that is, there are two groups and all of the variables are assigned to one of the two groups). When a two-value system is present, there are often rules that create powerful inferences. Consider the following example:

> Exactly eight products—H, K, L, M, P, Q, R, and S—will be divided into exactly two 4-product testing groups—group 1 and group 2. Each product is assigned to exactly one of the two groups according to the following condition:
>> If H is in group 1, then L must be in group 1.

This Defined-Fixed, Balanced game would be diagrammed as follows:

H K L M P Q R S ^{8}

$H_1 \longrightarrow L_1$

$$
\begin{array}{cc}
\underline{} & \underline{} \\
\underline{} & \underline{} \\
\underline{} & \underline{} \\
\underline{} & \underline{} \\
1 & 2
\end{array}
$$

Because all eight variables must be assigned to exactly one of the two groups, the game uses a "two-value system," which means that if a variable is not assigned to one group, it must automatically be assigned to the other group. Because of this feature, an unusual contrapositive arises from the rule:

Rule: $$H_1 \longrightarrow L_1$$

Contrapositive: $$\cancel{L_1} \longrightarrow \cancel{H_1}$$

Applying the two-value system, we can infer that if L is not assigned to group 1 then L must be assigned to group 2, and if H is not assigned to group 1 then H must be assigned to group 2. Consequently, the contrapositive is properly diagrammed as:

$$L_2 \longrightarrow H_2$$

The proper representation of the rule allows for much greater insight into the game and is thus significantly more valuable. Always take the contrapositive in a two-value system game!

In short, although structural limitations do not occur in every game, you should always check to see if they exist, and if so, consider the implications as they may have a dramatic effect on your ability to complete the game quickly.

Hurdle the Uncertainty™

This powerful technique can be used in many different games, and it attacks a concept frequently used by the test makers. In games, during the placement of variables, situations occur where even though you cannot determine the exact variables being selected, you can "leap" that uncertainty to determine that other variables must be selected. Here is the simplest example:

> Three variables—A, B, and C—are available to fill two spaces.
> Rule: A and B cannot be selected together.

Because A and B cannot be selected together, it follows that they can only "fill" one of the two spaces. And, although we cannot be certain whether A or B is selected, we can "hurdle" that uncertainty and determine that C must fill the remaining space. Note how the choice of A or B is shown as a dual-option, as in Linear games:

$$\underline{A/B} \quad \underline{C}$$

Hurdle the Uncertainty appears at some point in virtually every Grouping game.

This situation can also occur with more than three variables:

Four variables—A, B, C, and D—are available to fill three spaces.
Rule: A, B, and C cannot be selected together.

In this scenario, A, B, and C can "fill" only two of the spaces, and thus we can determine that D must fill the remaining space. So, even though we are uncertain about which variable—A, B, or C—is selected, we can still use the knowledge that they can occupy only two of the three spaces in order to conclude that D must be selected, resulting in the following diagram:

Here is a more complex situation that uses the same idea:

Five variables—A, B, C, D, and E—are divided into two groups: a group of three and a group of two.
Rules: A and B cannot be in the same group.
          C and D must be in the same group.

Because A and B cannot be in the same group, we know that one of A or B must be in the group of three and the remainder must be in the group of two. But, we cannot be certain exactly which group contains A or B. The best way to handle this uncertainty is to reserve a space in each group for the choice of A or B. This should be shown as an A/B dual-option:

$$\frac{\overline{\quad}}{\underset{3}{A/B}} \quad \frac{\overline{\quad}}{\underset{2}{B/A}}$$

This leaves only one remaining space in the group of two, and it follows that the CD block must then be placed into the group of three. Since this fills all the available spaces in the group of three, E must then fill the remaining space in the group of two:

$$\frac{\dfrac{D}{C}}{\underset{3}{A/B}} \quad \frac{E}{\underset{2}{B/A}}$$

Again, although it cannot be determined exactly in which group A or B is placed, the fact that a space must be reserved in each group affects the other variables; and in spite of the A/B uncertainty we can conclude that C and D must be in the group of three and E must be in the group of two.

Hurdling the Uncertainty often occurs in "end-of-question" scenarios where some of the variables have been placed and only a few remain unplaced.

The example to the left is based on an LSAT game from 1990s. That game featured five students in two groups visiting three cities—Montreal, Toronto, and Vancouver. The test makers knew the two groups were the key to the game, and they attempted to hide the grouping element in a convoluted rule.

Here is another variation on the same theme:

Five variables—A, B, C, D, and E—are available to fill three spaces.

Rules: A and B cannot be selected together.
C and D cannot be selected together.

Since A and B can only fill one space, and C and D can only fill one space, it follows that E must fill the remaining space:

<u>A/B</u>   <u>C/D</u>   <u>E</u>

At this point you may have noticed that every example is built around a fairly tight numerical scenario: in each case there are exactly the right amount of variables to fill the spaces, or there are only one or two extra variables available. From this perspective, Hurdle the Uncertainty situations often arise when there are a limited number of variables available to fill the given positions.

Recycling Inferences

Once you have made an inference in a game, do not forget to consider the implications of that inference on rules that you have already processed. New inferences sometimes appear as a result of combining a previously discovered inference with the original rules. For example, consider the following three rules:

Rules: If F is selected, then G is selected.
G and H cannot be selected together.
If F is not selected, then I is not selected.

Most students successfully combine the first two rules in the following fashion:

F $\longrightarrow$ G $\longleftrightarrow$ H

Based on this relationship, they correctly infer that F and H cannot be selected together:

F $\longleftrightarrow$ H

The reasoning behind this inference is that if F requires G, and G and H cannot be selected together, then F cannot be selected with H.

Fewer students recycle the F $\longleftrightarrow$ H inference and combine it with the third rule. This oversight occurs because the third rule is presented with negatives, and some students make the mistake of believing that the first and third rules are unrelated, and that consequently there is no further reason to assess the relationship between the first and third rules, or the relationship between the third rule and any inference related to the first rule.

In order to better understand this phenomenon, let us examine the third rule more closely. The third rule is diagrammed as:

The contrapositive of this rule eliminates the negatives:

$$I \longrightarrow F$$

With the negatives removed, the relationship between the first rule and the previously-made inference should be clearer.

$$I \longrightarrow F \longleftarrow\!\!|\!\!\longrightarrow H$$

The relationship yields a powerful new inference:

$$I \longleftarrow\!\!|\!\!\longrightarrow H$$

Of course, we could have used a different recycling path to arrive at the same inference. By linking the first and third rules, we can deduce that:

$$I \longrightarrow F \longrightarrow G$$

This relationship yields the new inference that:

$$I \longrightarrow G$$

Recycling this inference with the second rule yields:

$$I \longrightarrow G \longleftarrow\!\!|\!\!\longrightarrow H$$

This relationship allow us to arrive at the same inference we previously deduced:

$$I \longleftarrow\!\!|\!\!\longrightarrow H$$

Even after you have made an inference, do not forget that the inference might be reusable, and actively search *all* of the rules to see if you can make a further connection.

Correctly interpreting the rules is crucial to success in the Games section. As you know, some rules and situations more frequently lead to misinterpretation. Here are several mistakes that students often make:

Conditional Rule Reversal

Because conditional rules play such a large role in Grouping games, you must guard against making a Mistaken Reversal.

Mistaken Reversals are one of the most frequent errors made by students.

As previously discussed, a conditional rule is triggered when the sufficient condition occurs. For example, consider the following rule:

When P is selected, then Q is selected.

This rule would be diagrammed as:

$$P \longrightarrow Q$$

When P is selected, then Q *must* also be selected. However, many test takers make the mistake of reversing the relationship, and when faced with Q being selected, they assume that P must also be selected. This error is known as a Mistaken Reversal.

Negative Grouping Rule Misinterpretation

Negative grouping rules can be tricky to work with in practice, and students often make one of the following two errors when working with the double not-arrows that these statements produce.

1. Mistaking the Possibilities

    Consider the following relationship:

    Some students make the error of believing that the statement implies that one and only one of A and B must be selected. While it is the case that A and B cannot be selected together, some students also mistakenly believe that it is impossible for A and B to both be absent. This is incorrect because the statement merely indicates that when one of A or B is present, then the other cannot be present. Thus, it is possible for both to be absent. Remember, under the double not-arrow, the following three results can occur:

- A is selected, and B is not selected.
- B is selected, and A is not selected.
- Neither A nor B is selected.

The only result that cannot occur is both A and B being selected.

2. Mistaking the Connections

Linking related statements is a powerful method for producing inferences. With the double not-arrow, we have already reviewed the following inference-producing relationship:

$$F \longrightarrow G \longleftarrow\!\!\!\!|\!\!\!\!\longrightarrow H$$

Based on this relationship, the correct inference is that F and H cannot be selected together:

$$F \longleftarrow\!\!\!\!|\!\!\!\!\longrightarrow H$$

The nature of the relationships given above is critical, and changing just a small portion can lead to a different result. Consider the following two rules:

M and N cannot be selected together.
When N is selected, then O is selected.

These two rules can be combined to produce the following diagram:

$$M \longleftarrow\!\!\!\!|\!\!\!\!\longrightarrow N \longrightarrow O$$

Compare this relationship with the one above. Both contain a double not-arrow and a single arrow, but the relationships are different in that the single arrow in the bottom diagram "leads away" from the double not-arrow relationship. This seemingly insignificant difference has a large effect. While an inference was possible in the first relationship, no inference can be drawn in the second relationship. Here is the reasoning behind this fact:

Although M and N cannot be selected together, it is possible for M and O to be selected together. If O is selected, N does not have to be selected, and thus, if M and O are selected together, there is no violation.

You must be very alert for the relationship discussed in this item because when the test takers present it in a game, they expect that a large number of students will misinterpret the relationship and draw a mistaken deduction.

The relationship to the left yields the inference, "Some O's are not M's," but that inference is largely useless in Logic Games. That inference is tested in Logical Reasoning, however, and so we cover that concept in more detail in the Logical Reasoning Bible.

Negative Sufficient Condition Confusion

Conditional statements with a negative sufficient condition often cause a large number of mistakes. Consider the following rule:

When A is not selected, then B is selected.

This rule would be diagrammed as:

Although this rule appears the same as any other single arrow relationship, the negative on the sufficient condition has a dramatic effect. In essence, the sufficient condition in this statement is one where something does not occur; in this case, A is not selected. The fact that an act of omission then indicates that something must occur is confusing for most people. Let us examine the contrapositive:

$$\cancel{B} \longrightarrow A$$

The two diagrams, when combined, indicate that when one of the variables is *not* selected, then the other must be selected. Thus, one of the two must always be in the selection group. Many students understand this point, but then they make the mistake of assuming that this rule relationship precludes the possibility of both A and B being selected together. The rule, as stated, above does not prohibit both A and B from appearing in the selection group. Here is why:

> All that is indicated from the rule and its contrapositive is that A and B will never both be unselected, because as soon as one is not selected then the other must be selected. They could, however, both be selected at the same time because the rules never address what happens when either A or B is selected, only what happens when A or B is not selected. Thus, when A is selected, B could be selected or B might not be selected. When B is selected, A could be selected or A might not be selected.

Thus, there are three possible outcomes under the rule given above:

- A is not selected and B is selected.
- B is not selected and A is selected.
- Both A and B are selected.

When you encounter a rule such as the one under discussion, remember that it is possible for the two variables to occur together.

There have been a number of games in recent years that featured rules like the one to the right.

Ultimately, this rule means that A and B cannot both be absent.

One final note on diagramming this relationship. Because the one outcome that is prohibited by this rule involves both variables being unselected, we could represent this relationship with a double not-arrow, as follows:

$$\cancel{A} \longleftrightarrow\!\!\!| \longrightarrow \cancel{B}$$

However, in the diagrams in this book we usually will not represent this relationship with the double-not arrow since so many people find it too difficult to work with. Regardless, the diagram simply indicates that A and B cannot be left unselected.

Overall, the rule discussed in this section is a tricky one because the negative is on the sufficient condition, and that has a powerful effect on how the rule operates. Fortunately, this type of statement appears less frequently on the test than statements where the negative is on the necessary condition.

Multi-Condition Contrapositive Errors

As discussed previously, when you encounter statements with multiple sufficient or multiple necessary conditions, you must be careful when taking the contrapositive.

Whenever you take a contrapositive of a statement with multiple terms in the sufficient or necessary condition, remember that "and" turns into "or," and "or" turns into "and." This is true regardless of whether the term is in the sufficient or necessary condition.

Two-value System Errors

Two-value systems can allow for powerful inferences, but there is one false inference that you must avoid. Let us take a moment to revisit the game scenario we used when we first discussed this concept:

> Exactly eight products—H, K, L, M, P, Q, R, and S—will be divided into exactly two 4-product testing groups—group 1 and group 2. Each product is assigned to exactly one of the two groups according to the following condition:

Now, let us discard the rule used previously and instead add a new rule:

> If K is in group 1, then M must be in group 2.

Rules with multiple sufficient or necessary conditions most frequently appear in Undefined games.

This Defined-Fixed, Balanced game would be diagrammed as follows:

H K L M P Q R S [8]

$$K_1 \longrightarrow M_2$$

$$\underline{\quad} \quad \underline{\quad}$$
$$\underline{\quad} \quad \underline{\quad}$$
$$\underline{\quad} \quad \underline{\quad}$$
$$\underline{\quad} \quad \underline{\quad}$$
$$\quad 1 \qquad 2$$

Most students, upon encountering this rule, take the contrapositive:

$$\cancel{M_2} \longrightarrow \cancel{K_1}$$

Of course, because this is a two-value system, when M is not in group 2 then M must be in group 1, and when K is not in group 1 then K must be in group 2. This insight allows the rule to be represented in more efficient fashion:

$$M_1 \longrightarrow K_2$$

So far, every step we have taken is correct. However, at this point some students, after observing that K and M *seem* to be in different groups, assume that K and M can never be in the same group together. This is not the case. The rule and its contrapositive both reference what occurs when one of the variables is assigned to group 1. When one of the variables is assigned to group 1, then the other must be assigned to group 2. However, both variables can be assigned to group 2 because the rule does not address what occurs when either K or M is assigned to group 2. If K is assigned to group 2, then M could be assigned to group 1 or group 2. If M is assigned to group 2, then K could be assigned to group 1 or group 2.

Here is a similar error that also occurs in two-value systems. Using the same setup as before, let us discard the previous rule and consider an entirely new, unrelated rule:

If P is in group 2, then Q must be in group 2.

This rule is properly diagrammed as:

$$P_2 \longrightarrow Q_2$$

The contrapositive, after accounting for the effect of the two-value system, is diagrammed as:

$$Q_1 \longrightarrow P_1$$

Remember, just because a term or variable appears in the necessary condition does not by itself indicate that anything will occur. To believe that it does is to make a Mistaken Reversal.

Again, each step taken thus far is correct. However, some students, after observing that P and Q *seem* to be in the same group, assume that P and Q are a block that must be assigned to the same group together. This is not the case.

The rule references what occurs when P is assigned to group 2, and the contrapositive references what occurs when Q is assigned to group 1. The statements do not address what occurs when Q is assigned to group 2 or when P is assigned to group 1. When P is assigned to group 1, Q could be assigned to group 1 or group 2 (no sufficient condition addresses P in group 1, so anything could occur). When Q is assigned to group 2, P could be assigned to group 1 or group 2 (again, no sufficient condition addresses Q in group 2, so anything could occur). Thus, P and Q are not a block, and it can occur that P is assigned to group 1 while G is assigned to group 2 (note that P being assigned to group 2 while Q is assigned to group 1 cannot occur because that would violate the rule).

Remember, when you encounter two-value systems and conditional rules, focus on the sufficient condition in each rule, the meaning of the conditional relationship created by the rule, and the contrapositive of the rule. Avoid making assumptions based on surface appearances or a cursory glance at the rule.

Final Section Note

Grouping is a challenging concept, and many students find these games to be among the most difficult on the LSAT. If you have the opportunity, go back and review the discussions of rule representation, inference making, and avoiding false inferences. Then, try your hand at the drill on the next page, and eventually on the six games that follow the drill.

As always, please read the explanations to each drill and game carefully, as they will give you a true sense of how to best attack Grouping games.

When you get to the six games, if you would like to test yourself under timed conditions, you should give yourself 8 minutes and 45 seconds for each game.

Grouping Setup Practice Drill

Each of the following items presents a scenario and corresponding rules similar to those found in actual Logic Games. Using the space provided, diagram the setup and include a representation of all rules and inferences. Each problem contains a corresponding question or questions. Use your knowledge of the rules and the setup to answer the question. After you complete *each* item, check your work against the diagram in the answer key, and carefully read the comments concerning each diagram. *Answers begin on Page 210*

1. A hiring committee must select three people from a group of five applicants—A, B, C, D, and E—in accordance with the following conditions:
   If C is not selected, then B is not selected.
   D and E cannot both be selected.
   In order for A to be selected, B must be selected.

Question 1.1. Which one of the following must be true?

(A) A is selected for the committee.
(B) B is selected for the committee.
(C) C is not selected for the committee.
(D) D is not selected for the committee.
(E) E is not selected for the committee.

Grouping Setup Practice Drill

2. A business school offers at least one of the following seven courses during the winter term: accounting, economics, finance, law, marketing, operations, and sales. The following restrictions apply:

    If accounting is offered, then finance is also offered but economics is not.

    If law is offered, then economics is also offered but marketing is not.

    If operations or sales is offered, then accounting is also offered.

Question 2.1. If law is offered, then each of the following must be false EXCEPT:

(A) Accounting is offered.
(B) Finance is offered.
(C) Marketing is offered.
(D) Operations is offered.
(E) Sales is offered.

3. Seven senators—P, Q, R, S, T, V, and X—serve on two subcommittees. Each subcommittee has
    at least three members. The following is known about the two subcommittees:
    >   Every senator serves on at least one subcommittee, and no senator serves on both
    >   subcommittees.
    >   If P serves on a subcommittee, then Q does not serve on that subcommittee.
    >   R and S do not serve on the same subcommittee.
    >   T serves on a subcommittee only if V serves on the same subcommittee.

Question 3.1. Which one of the following must be true?

(A) P must serve on the subcommittee that has three members.
(B) Q must serve on the subcommittee that has three members.
(C) R must serve on the subcommittee that has four members.
(D) S must serve on the subcommittee that has four members.
(E) T must serve on the subcommittee that has four members.

Question 3.2. Which one of the following CANNOT be true?

(A) P and R serve on the same subcommittee.
(B) Q and S serve on the same subcommittee.
(C) T and R serve on the same subcommittee.
(D) V and X serve on the same subcommittee.
(E) X and Q serve on the same subcommittee.

4. A set of five products—D, E, F, G, and H—is assigned to two product testers—tester 1 and tester 2. Each product must be tested at least once, and each tester conducts three tests. Once a tester has tested a product she cannot test that product again. The testing meets the following conditions:

    If D is assigned to tester 1, then E is assigned to tester 2.

    F and G cannot be assigned to the same tester.

    D is tested twice.

Question 4.1. Each of the following could be true EXCEPT:

(A) D and E are each tested by the same tester.
(B) D and F are each tested by the same tester.
(C) E and G are each tested by the same tester.
(D) E and H are each tested by the same tester.
(E) G and H are each tested by the same tester.

5. The members of a six-person panel will be selected from among four parents—J, K, L, and M—and four students—W, X, Y, and Z. The selection of panel members will meet the following conditions:

    The panel will include exactly three parents and exactly three students.
    W and X cannot both be selected.
    J cannot be selected unless W is selected.
    K cannot be selected unless X is selected.

Question 5.1. If X is not selected, then which one of the following cannot be selected?

(A) J
(B) K
(C) L
(D) W
(E) Y

6. Chris is choosing flowers for his garden from among the following choices: B, C, D, F, G, H, L, and M. Chris chooses the flowers in a manner consistent with the following conditions:

    If he chooses B, he does not choose D.

    If he chooses B, then he chooses G.

    If he chooses C, then he chooses D.

    If he chooses G, then he chooses B.

    If he does not choose H, then he chooses L.

    If he chooses M, he does not choose L.

Question 6.1. If Chris chooses G but not H, then it could be true that he also chooses

(A) B and C

(B) B and F

(C) B and M

(D) C and L

(E) C and M

Grouping Setup Practice Drill Answer Key

<u>Drill #1</u>. The scenario states that there are five applicants for three positions, and thus the grouping classification of this drill is Defined-Fixed, Unbalanced: Overloaded.

A B C D E ^{5}

____ ____ ____
3 Selections

The first rule states that if C is not selected, then B is not selected. This conditional rule should be diagrammed as follows:

$$\cancel{C} \longrightarrow \cancel{B}$$

When you see a conditional rule or inference where both the sufficient condition and the necessary condition are negative, always take the contrapositive, which, in this case is:

$$B \longrightarrow C$$

The second rule indicates that both D and E cannot be selected, and this rule can be represented as:

$$D \longleftarrow\!\!\!|\!\!\!\longrightarrow E$$

The third rule is diagrammed as:

$$A \longrightarrow B$$

Using linkage, the first and third rules can be connected to create a chain relationship:

$$A \longrightarrow B \longrightarrow C$$

Thus, we have the following situation:

A B C D E ^{5}

$A \longrightarrow B \longrightarrow C$ ____ ____ ____
$D \longleftarrow\!\!\!|\!\!\!\longrightarrow E$ 3 Selections

At this point, many students choose to move on to the question. This is a premature move. We have one powerful conditional chain and one powerful negative grouping rule. Just considering the second rule, our selection pool is down to the choice of A, B, C, or D/E:

| A | B | C | D/E |

Grouping Setup Practice Drill Answer Key

Of course, we still have our conditional chain to consider. The selection of A would automatically force the selection of B and C, and so if A is selected then there is only one solution. But, what would occur if one of the variables in the chain was not selected? Remember, when a necessary condition does not occur in a conditional chain, then all of the sufficient conditions also cannot occur. Thus, in Grouping games, *always* examine the necessary conditions of any chain relationship to see if the non-occurrence of those variables will have a significant effect. In this drill, we must always have three variables selected, but the second rule has already removed at least one of the five candidates from the pool (either D or E, or both, cannot be selected). This leaves only four variables for three spaces, and therefore problems would result if one of the necessary conditions were not selected.

For example, if C were not selected, the following contrapositive would occur:

The removal of C would thus eliminate three variables (A, B, and C), leaving only D or E to fill the selection group. Because this would violate the scenario, this cannot occur, and we can conclude that C must always be selected.

This is a powerful inference, but do not stop there. What about the other necessary condition within the chain, B? If B is removed, the following contrapositive occurs:

$$\cancel{B} \longrightarrow \cancel{A}$$

With both A and B removed from the candidate pool, only C and the choice of D/E would be available to fill the selection group. Because this would also violate the scenario, this cannot occur, and we can conclude that B must also always be selected.

Thus, both B and C must always be selected, and the only remaining choice is whether A, D, or E is the final applicant selected. Consequently, the game has only three solutions:

Solution 1: A, B, C
Solution 2: B, C, D
Solution 3: B, C, E

Question 1.1. The correct answer is (B). As discussed above, no viable solution can be created without the presence of B, and thus B must be selected to the committee.

Answer choice (A) is incorrect because A does not have to be selected to the committee.
Answer choice (C) is incorrect because C must be selected to the committee.
Answer choice (D) is incorrect because D could be selected to the committee.
Answer choice (E) is incorrect because E could be selected to the committee.

Grouping Setup Practice Drill Answer Key

Drill #2. Although the scenario states that there are seven courses in the selection pool, the exact number of courses offered by the school is never defined. Thus, the grouping classification of this drill is Undefined.

The first two rules each have two necessary conditions. The first rule is diagrammed as:

The second rule is diagrammed as:

At first, these two rules may not appear to be capable of being linked, but they can be, through the presence of E. Because the first rule requires E to not be offered and the second rule requires E to be offered, the necessary conditions are opposite, and we can infer that the two sufficient conditions—A and L—cannot both be offered together. In short, if A is offered then E is not offered, but when L is offered E must be offered. Thus, there is no way to offer both A and L because they have needs that are exactly opposite, and we can draw the following inference:

$$A \longleftarrow\!\!\!|\!\!\!\longrightarrow L$$

Consider an analogy to help make this point clear.

> Statement 1: To get into Harvard you must be rich.
> Statement 2: To get into Harvard you must be poor.

If the two statements above are true, is it possible for anyone to attend Harvard? No, because no one can be both rich and poor at the same time (and yes, for the purposes of discussion let's assume that rich and poor in this context refer to monetary wealth, and not spiritual wealth, etc.). Our situation here is slightly different, but the underlying principle is the same.

If the above discussion still does not make sense, take the contrapositive of one of the two rules and then link them together. The result will be the same.

The third rule has two sufficient conditions:

$$\begin{array}{c} O \\ \text{or} \longrightarrow A \\ S \end{array}$$

Grouping Setup Practice Drill Answer Key

Because the necessary condition of the third rule is identical to the sufficient condition in the first rule, the two can be combined to create a super-rule:

Note that this relationship leads to host of sub-inferences, including the following:

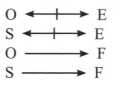

However, because the super-rule contains those inferences inherently as part of the chain, we will not draw them on the final diagram. This final diagram thus appears as:

A E F L M O S [7]

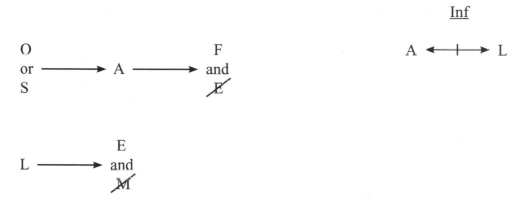

Remember, Undefined games do not allow you to specify the number of variables being selected.

Question 2.1. The correct answer is (B). When L is offered, according to the second rule E is offered and M is not offered. This information eliminates answer choice (C). We also know from the inference that when L is offered then A is not offered. This eliminates answer choice (A). When A is not offered, via the contrapositive of the third rule, both O and S are not offered. This inference eliminates answer choices (D) and (E).

Also, always remember to convert false into true in question stems. Applying that process, the "must be false" portion of this question asks for what "cannot be true," and then the "except" portion turns that around so that this question actually asks for which one of the following Could Be True.

Grouping Setup Practice Drill Answer Key

<u>Drill #3</u>. The scenario states that there are seven senators serving on two subcommittees of at least three members each. This makes the game appear Partially Defined, but then the first rule specifies that no senator serves on both subcommittees but that all senators must serve. This means that one of the subcommittees must have three members and the other subcommittee must have four members. This makes the game Defined, and although the game appears to be moving, no subcommittee names are ever specified, and so we simply have the "subcommittee of three" and the "subcommittee of four," leading this game to be Fixed. The final classification is Defined-Fixed, Balanced.

The initial numerical scenario appears as follows:

P Q R S T V X [7]
    *

$$
\begin{array}{cc}
& \overline{} \\
\overline{} & \overline{} \\
\overline{} & \overline{} \\
\overline{} & \overline{} \\
3 & 4
\end{array}
$$

The first two rules are fairly easy to diagram as they are both negative grouping rules.

First rule:

P̸/Q̸

Second rule:

R̸/S̸

The third rule can be a bit more challenging, but remember that "only if" introduces a necessary condition. The proper diagram is thus:

$$T \longrightarrow V$$

Applying the first two rules to the diagram, although we cannot ascertain where each variable serves, we do know that one of P or Q serves on each subcommittee, and one of R or S must serve on each subcommittee. These relationships can be shown as split dual-options:

$$
\begin{array}{cc}
& \overline{} \\
\overline{R/S} & \overline{S/R} \\
\overline{P/Q} & \overline{Q/P} \\
3 & 4
\end{array}
$$

Grouping Setup Practice Drill Answer Key

With so many spaces on the diagram occupied, the situation is restricted, and we can now examine the effects of that restriction on the third rule. Because when T serves on a subcommittee then V must also serve on that same subcommittee, we can infer that T cannot serve in the group of three (because then there would be no space for V). Thus, T must serve on the subcommittee with four members, and by applying the third rule we can conclude that V must serve on that subcommittee as well. The only remaining variable is X, the random, and the only remaining space is in the group of three, and so X must serve on the subcommittee with three members. The complete diagram is:

$$
\begin{array}{cc}
 & V \\
 & \overline{T} \\
X & T \\
\overline{R/S} & \overline{S/R} \\
\underline{P/Q} & \underline{Q/P} \\
3 & 4
\end{array}
$$

Question 3.1. The correct answer is (E). As explained above, the actions of the two pairs of variables involved in the negative grouping rules—P and Q, and R and S—force T to serve on the subcommittee of four. Each of the variables cited in the first four answers (not surprisingly, P, Q, R, and S) could serve on either subcommittee. In a Must Be True question such as this one, you should immediately avoid answers that contain moving variables such as P, Q, R, or S.

Question 3.2. The correct answer is (D). The answer choices present pairs of variables, and you are asked to identify the pair that cannot serve together. As discussed in the explanation to the first question, we know that P, Q, R, and S could serve on either subcommittee. Thus, answers that contain any of those four variables would be a poor choice (unless it was two variables known to be locked in a negative grouping rule, such as P and Q. But, the test makers would never make it that easy.). Answer choices (A), (B), (C), and (E) all contain one or more of those variables, and in each instance, the cited pairs can serve together.

Answer choice (D) is correct because we determined that V serves on the subcommittee of four and X must serve on the subcommittee of three. Consequently, V and X cannot serve on the same subcommittee.

Grouping Setup Practice Drill Answer Key

Drill #4. The scenario states that there are two testers who each test three products. Thus, the selection group is Defined-Fixed. There are five products assigned to the two tests, and thus the variable pool is Unbalanced: Underfunded. Fortunately, the final rule specifies that D is tested twice, and this balances out the scenario, and creates the following 2-1-1-1-1 numerical distribution:

Six tests =	2	-	1	-	1	-	1	-	1
"Six" products =	D		E		F		G		H

The quote marks appear on the "six" with products because there are really five products, but because one is tested twice, those products are used six times.

The initial scenario appears as follows:

D D E F G H [6]

$$\frac{\quad}{1} \quad \frac{\quad}{2}$$

The first rule can be diagrammed as follows:

$$D_1 \longrightarrow E_2$$

The second rule is a negative grouping rule:

$$\boxed{\frac{F}{G}}\!\!\!\!\diagup$$

We have already discussed the numerical impact of third rule in our discussion above, but functionally, if D is tested twice and no product is tested twice by the same tester, then D must be assigned to both testers:

$$\frac{\quad}{\underset{1}{D}} \qquad \frac{\quad}{\underset{2}{D}}$$

The second rule also has an impact on the diagram because F and G cannot be tested by the same tester:

$$\frac{F/G}{\underset{1}{D}} \qquad \frac{G/F}{\underset{2}{D}}$$

Grouping Setup Practice Drill Answer Key

The situation is now quite restricted because there is only one space left in each group. However, we have yet to consider the impact of the first rule on the two remaining products—E and H. When D is tested by tester 1, as is the case in this scenario, the E must be tested by tester 2:

$$
\begin{array}{cc}
 & E \\
\overline{F/G} & \overline{G/F} \\
\underline{D} & \underline{D} \\
1 & 2
\end{array}
$$

The remaining unused product—H—must then be assigned to the only remaining space, and we arrive at the final diagram:

$$
\begin{array}{cc}
\overline{H} & \overline{E} \\
\overline{F/G} & \overline{G/F} \\
\underline{D} & \underline{D} \\
1 & 2
\end{array}
$$

Note that reading all of the rules before diagramming makes this game easier to handle, because you can place both D's, and then the remaining variables fall into place. Students who start diagramming immediately will operate less efficiently and will possibly be forced to rework their diagram when they encounter the third rule.

Question 4.1. The correct answer is (D). As explained above, E must be assigned to tester 2 and H must be assigned to tester 1.

Answer choices (A) and (B) both contain D, and we know that because D is assigned to both testers, then every variable is, at some point, assigned to the same tester as D.

Answer choices (B), (C) and (E) each contain F or G, and we know that F and G rotate between the two testers. Thus, F and G could, depending on the scenario, be assigned to the same tester as every other product. These answer choices are thus incorrect. Note again how the uncertainty of placement of variables involved in a negative grouping rule plays a role in a question with a strong Could Be True element (in this Could Be True Except question, the correct answer choice Cannot Be True and the four incorrect answer choices Could Be True). In this sense, this question is similar to questions 3.1 and 3.2.

Grouping Setup Practice Drill Answer Key

<u>Drill #5</u>. The scenario states that a six-person panel will be selected, so the selection group is Defined-Fixed. There are eight candidates for the panel, so the selection Pool is Unbalanced, Overloaded. The candidates are also divided into two groups—parents and students—and so the pool is Subdivided.

Note that an 8 into 6 scenario such as this one is quite restricted because when any two variables are eliminated then the remaining six variables must be selected. The first rule further limits the game by establishing that exactly three members from each group must be selected:

Par: J K L M ^{4}
Stu: W X Y Z ^{4}

Panel of 6

The second rule reveals that W and X cannot be selected together, creating further restrictions on the student group. In fact, because the student group only has one "extra" member, the second rule leads to the inference that both Y and Z must be selected:

Panel of 6

The third and fourth rules are conditional, and can be diagrammed as follows:

$$J_P \longrightarrow W_S$$

$$K_P \longrightarrow X_S$$

The "P" and "S" subscripts designate the parent and student groups, respectively.

Interestingly, these rules can both be connected to the second rule. The second rule and third rule combine to form the following chain:

$$J_P \longrightarrow W_S \longleftarrow\!\!\!|\!\!\!\longrightarrow X_S$$

From this relationship we can infer that:

$$J_P \longleftarrow\!\!\!|\!\!\!\longrightarrow X_S$$

Of course, we can also recycle this inference with the fourth rule to create the following relationship:

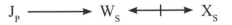

From this relationship we can infer that:

$$K_P \longleftrightarrow J_P$$

This is a powerful inference because it removes one of the parents from consideration. Note that we could have also drawn this inference by starting with the second and fourth rules:

$$K_P \longrightarrow X_S \longleftrightarrow W_S$$

This relationship yields the following inference:

$$K_P \longleftrightarrow W_S$$

When this inference is recycled and combined with the third rule, the following relationship results:

$$J_P \longrightarrow W_S \longleftrightarrow K_P$$

This relationship produces the same inference drawn at the top of this page:

$$J_P \longleftrightarrow K_P$$

Thus, on the parent side, there is also a limitation. Because J and K cannot both be selected, and the parent group originally had only one "extra" member, we can infer that both L and M must be selected, leading to our final setup:

Par: J K L M [4]
Stu: W X Y Z [4]

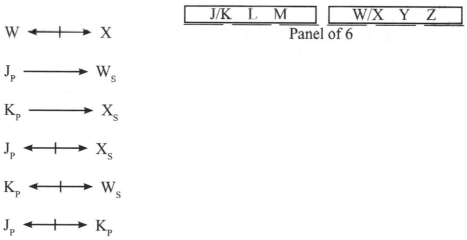

| J/K | L | M | | W/X | Y | Z |

Panel of 6

This final setup leaves us in a strong position to answer the question.

Grouping Setup Practice Drill Answer Key

Question 5.1. The correct answer is (B). When X is not selected, then W must be selected in order to create a workable group of students. When W is selected, we know from our inferences that K cannot be selected. Because K cannot be selected, J must be selected in order to create a workable group, leading to only one solution for this question:

From the analysis above, answer choice (B) is proven correct.

Grouping Setup Practice Drill Answer Key

Drill #6. This game is classified as Undefined because no specification is made as to how many flowers will be selected.

Because there are six rules, we will number them for easy reference. The six rules, as stated, can be diagrammed as follows:

1. B $\longleftrightarrow\!\!\!|\!\!\!\longrightarrow$ D

2. B $\longrightarrow$ G

3. C $\longrightarrow$ D

4. G $\longrightarrow$ B

5. $\cancel{H} \longrightarrow$ L

6. M $\longleftarrow\!\!\!|\!\!\!\longrightarrow$ L

The second and fourth rules should immediately be combined to create a single super-rule:

2 + 4. B $\longleftrightarrow$ G

This rule combination forces B and G to act as a block.

With these rules in place, we can begin to make inferences. The first four rules can be combined to create the following inferences:

Combination of 1 + 3.   C $\longleftrightarrow\!\!\!|\!\!\!\longrightarrow$ B

Combination of 1 + 4.   G $\longleftrightarrow\!\!\!|\!\!\!\longrightarrow$ D

The first inference can be combined with our super-rule to create the following inference:

C $\longleftrightarrow\!\!\!|\!\!\!\longrightarrow$ G

The fifth and sixth rules can also be combined:

$\cancel{H} \longrightarrow$ L $\longleftarrow\!\!\!|\!\!\!\longrightarrow$ M

This relationship yields the following inference:

$\cancel{H} \longrightarrow \cancel{M}$

The contrapositive of this inference is:

$$M \longrightarrow H$$

Thus, we can collect all of the rules and inferences into one main diagram:

B C D F G H L M [8]
   *

Rules		Inferences	
1.	B ←—|—→ D	C ←—|—→ B	
2 + 4.	B ←——→ G	G ←—|—→ D	
3.	C ——→ D	C ←—|—→ G	
5.	H̸ ——→ L	M ——→ H	
6.	M ←—|—→ L		

Question 6.1. The correct answer is (B).

When G is chosen, from the rules we know that B must also be chosen. From the inferences, we know that when G is chosen that C and D cannot be chosen. This information eliminates answer choices (A), (D), and (E), each of which contain C.

When H is not chosen, the L must be chosen, and when L is chosen then M cannot be chosen. This information eliminates answer choices (C) and (E), both of which contain M. Consequently, the only remaining answer choice is (B).

Note that once you ascertain that B is chosen, you could select answer choice (B) because F, the other flower in that answer choice, is a random that does not appear in any rule, and thus can always be chosen regardless of what other variables are chosen or not chosen.

Game #1: October 1996 Questions 6-12

A university library budget committee must reduce exactly five of eight areas of expenditure—G, L, M, N, P, R, S, and W—in accordance with the following conditions:

If both G and S are reduced, W is also reduced.
If N is reduced, neither R nor S is reduced.
If P is reduced, L is not reduced.
Of the three areas L, M, and R, exactly two are reduced.

6. Which one of the following could be a complete and accurate list of the areas of expenditure reduced by the committee?

(A) G, L, M, N, W
(B) G, L, M, P, W
(C) G, M, N, R, W
(D) G, M, P, R, S
(E) L, M, R, S, W

7. If W is reduced, which one of the following could be a complete and accurate list of the four other areas of expenditure to be reduced?

(A) G, M, P, S
(B) L, M, N, R
(C) L, M, P, S
(D) M, N, P, S
(E) M, P, R, S

8. If P is reduced, which one of the following is a pair of areas of expenditure both of which must be reduced?

(A) G, M
(B) M, R
(C) N, R
(D) R, S
(E) S, W

9. If both L and S are reduced, which one of the following could be a pair of areas of expenditure both of which are reduced?

(A) G, M
(B) G, P
(C) N, R
(D) N, W
(E) P, S

10. If R is not reduced, which one of the following must be true?

(A) G is reduced.
(B) N is not reduced.
(C) P is reduced.
(D) S is reduced.
(E) W is not reduced.

11. If both M and R are reduced, which one of the following is a pair of areas neither of which could be reduced?

(A) G, L
(B) G, N
(C) L, N
(D) L, P
(E) P, S

12. Which one of the following areas must be reduced?

(A) G
(B) L
(C) N
(D) P
(E) W

The game should be set up as follows:

GLMNPRSW[8]

Exactly 2 of L, M, R must be reduced.

The selection of exactly five variables means the game is Defined-Fixed. Since there are eight variables from which to select, the game is Unbalanced: Overloaded.

The second rule bears further analysis. When N is reduced, neither R nor S is reduced, and it can be inferred from the contrapositive that when R or S is reduced, N cannot be reduced. Thus, N and R cannot be reduced together, and N and S cannot be reduced together. Consequently, we have written the rule in two separate parts to fully capture this powerful information.

Because the last rule reserves two of the five spaces, it is the most important one. Any rule that controls the numbers in a game is always important, and this rule is no exception. If two of L, M, and R are reduced, then of the remaining five areas of expenditure—G, N, S, P, and W—exactly three must be reduced. And since N and S cannot be reduced together, the choice is further limited. On the diagram this has been represented with the two blocks. This separation of the variables into two groups is the key to making several powerful inferences:

1. Because two of the group of L, M, and R must be reduced:

> When L is not reduced, M and R must be reduced.
> When M is not reduced, L and R must be reduced.
> When R is not reduced, L and M must be reduced.

2. Because three of the group of G, P, W, N/S must be reduced:

> If G is not reduced, then P, W, and N/S must be reduced.
> If P is not reduced, then G, W, and N/S must be reduced.
> If W is not reduced, then G, P, and N/S must be reduced.
>> (Later it will be discovered that W must always be reduced so this final inference will not be applicable.)

3. If G and S are reduced, then W is reduced. Since these three variables fill the reduction allotment of G, N, S, P, and W, it follows that when G and S are reduced, N and P are not reduced:

4. When N is reduced, R and S are not reduced. When R is not reduced, L and M must be reduced. When L and M are reduced, P is not reduced. Thus, when N is reduced, R, S, and P are not reduced. Since there are only eight variables for five slots, when R, S, and P are not reduced, it follows that all five of the remaining variables must be reduced. Thus, when N is reduced, G, L, M, and W must also be reduced.

5. When L is not reduced, M and R must be reduced, and when R is reduced, N is not reduced. Thus, when L is not reduced, N is not reduced. By the same reasoning, when M is not reduced, N is not reduced.

6. When P is reduced, L is not reduced. When L is not reduced, M and R must be reduced. Thus, when P is reduced, M and R must also be reduced. This inference is tested directly on question #8.

Understanding how the two groups work—both separately and together—is clearly a powerful weapon against the questions. In this instance the groups are originated by the final rule, a rule concerning numbers. Always be on the lookout for rules that address the numbers in a game!

Question #6: Global, Could Be True, List. The correct answer choice is (A)

The application of proper List question technique (take a single rule and apply it to all five answer choices consecutively; take another rule and apply it to the remaining answer choices, etc.) eliminates every answer except for answer choice (A). Answer choice (B) is incorrect since both P and L are reduced. Answer choice (C) is incorrect since both N and R are reduced. Answer choice (D) is incorrect since G and S are reduced and W is not reduced. Answer choice (E) is incorrect because all three of L, M, and R are reduced. Consequently, answer choice (A) is correct. Of course, one of the most valuable results of answering a List question correctly is that we now know that the hypothetical G-L-M-N-W is a valid solution to the game.

Question #7: Local, Could Be True, List. The correct answer choice is (E)

Another List question, this time a Local question with the stipulation that W is selected. Do not make the mistake of thinking that because W is reduced that G and S are both reduced! This is a mistaken reversal of the rule. Answer choice (A) is incorrect since two of L, M, and R must be reduced and only M is reduced. Answer choice (B) is incorrect since both N and R are reduced, or alternately, because all three of L, M, and R are reduced. Answer choice (C) is incorrect because both P and L are reduced. Answer choice (D) is incorrect since both N and S are reduced. Consequently, answer choice (E) is correct, and we now know that the hypothetical W-M-P-R-S is a valid solution to the game.

Question #8: Local, Must Be True. The correct answer choice is (B)

As described earlier, when P is reduced, L cannot be reduced. When L is not reduced, M and R must be reduced, and hence answer choice (B) is correct.

Question #9: Local, Could Be True. The correct answer choice is (A)

When L is reduced, P cannot be reduced. Consequently, any answer choice that contains P can be eliminated, and answer choices (B) and (E) can be discarded. When S is reduced, N cannot be reduced and it follows that answer choices (C) and (D) are incorrect. Thus, answer choice (A) is correct.

Question #10: Local, Must Be True. The correct answer choice is (A)

This is one of the key questions of the game. The initial approach taken by most students is to consider the implications of R not being reduced. When R is not reduced, L and M must be reduced, and when L is reduced, P is not reduced. This provides sufficient information to eliminate answer choice (C). At this point the diagram next to the question looks like this:

$$\underline{\text{L}} \quad \underline{\text{M}} \quad \underline{} \quad \underline{} \quad \underline{}$$
$$\text{5 Reductions}$$
$$\cancel{R} \; \cancel{P}$$

But this leaves four answer choices in contention with no obvious path towards the correct solution. However, there are several approaches to finding the correct answer:

1. Based on our discussion of the reduction of three of the five expenditures G, N, S, P, and W, when P is not reduced then G, W, and N or S must be reduced:

$$\boxed{\underline{\text{L}} \quad \underline{\text{M}}} \; \boxed{\underline{\text{G}} \quad \underline{\text{W}} \quad \underline{\text{N/S}}}$$
$$\text{5 Reductions}$$

   Consequently, only answer choice (A) must be true.

2. Another approach is to make a few hypotheticals based on L and M being selected. The various hypotheticals can then be used to eliminate answer choices.

3. Since making new hypotheticals is useful, checking the hypotheticals created in questions #6 and #7 to see if they apply to question #10 might be even better. Although the W-M-P-R-S hypothetical in question #7 answer choice (E) is inapplicable since R is reduced, the hypothetical in question #6 answer choice (A) meets the criteria in question #10. By applying the G-L-M-N-W solution, we can eliminate answer choices (B), (C), (D), and (E), leaving only answer choice (A).

   Remember, always check back to earlier problems to see if you already have enough information to solve the current problem. Of course, only applicable work can be used. Do not forget that you should only use work that you are fully confident is correct. That is why answering List questions correctly is so important!

Question #11: Local, Cannot Be True. The correct answer choice is (C)

When R is reduced, N cannot be reduced. When both M and R are reduced, L cannot be reduced. Answer choice (C), which contains both L and N, is therefore correct.

Question #12: Global, Must Be True. The correct answer choice is (E)

This global question may come as somewhat of a surprise: apparently there is an area of expenditure that is always reduced. Yet this inference did not appear in our initial diagram! To have had this inference would have made the game easier, but it goes to show that there are times where you can miss an inference and still complete the game successfully.

The best way to attack this question is to use previous work. As in question #10, start with the hypotheticals created by questions #6 and #7. G-L-M-N-W, the hypothetical from question #6, shows that P does not have to be reduced, and therefore answer choice (D) can eliminated. W-M-P-R-S, the hypothetical from question #7, shows that G, L, and N do not have to be reduced, and therefore answer choices (A), (B), and (C) can be eliminated. Thus, with little or no work, it can be determined that answer choice (E) is correct. Consider how much faster and easier using this mode of attack is than the alternative of working out several independent solutions.

Abstractly, answer choice (E) is correct because ultimately no valid solution to the game can be created unless that solution contains W. If W is not reduced, then G, P and N must be reduced (see the GSW rule and the group of 3), but when G, P, and N are reduced you cannot reduce R or L (see the second and third rules), and thus the maximum number of reductions that could be made would be four: G, P, N, and M. Because there must be exactly five reductions and eliminating W does not allow for five reductions, it follows that W must be reduced.

One final point must be made about the restriction inherent in the L, M, and R rule. Since only three basic scenarios result under that rule—LM, LR, and MR—one entirely different approach to this game involves creating three templates based on each of those options. Although we feel this approach can be quite effective, its usefulness is dependent on making the inference regarding the three reductions from G, N, S, P, and W. As many students fail to make this inference, the value of the template approach is diminished here. In a later section the Identify the Templates approach will be revisited, and we will see that at times there is no better way to attack a game.

In order to separate the game from its answer key and explanations,
the second game is on the next page.

At a benefit dinner, a community theater's seven sponsors—K, L, M, P, Q, V, and Z—will be seated at three tables—1, 2, and 3. Of the sponsors, only K, L, and M will receive honors, and only M, P, and Q will give a speech. The sponsors' seating assignments must conform to the following conditions:

Each table has at least two sponsors seated at it, and each sponsor is seated at exactly one table.

Any sponsor receiving honors is seated at table 1 or table 2.

L is seated at the same table as V.

1. Which one of the following is an acceptable assignment of sponsors to tables?

    (A)   Table 1: K, P; Table 2: M, Q; Table 3: L, V, Z
    (B)   Table 1: K, Q, Z; Table 2: L, V; Table 3: M, P
    (C)   Table 1: L, P; Table 2: K, M; Table 3: Q, V, Z
    (D)   Table 1: L, Q, V; Table 2: K, M; Table 3: P, Z
    (E)   Table 1: L, V, Z; Table 2: K, M, P; Table 3: Q

2. Which one of the following is a list of all and only those sponsors any one of whom could be among the sponsors assigned to table 3 ?

    (A)   P, Q
    (B)   Q, Z
    (C)   P, Q, Z
    (D)   Q, V, Z
    (E)   P, Q, V, Z

3. If K is assigned to a different table than M, which one of the following must be true of the seating assignment?

    (A)   K is seated at the same table as L.
    (B)   L is seated at the same table as Q.
    (C)   M is seated at the same table as V.
    (D)   Exactly two sponsors are seated at table 1.
    (E)   Exactly two sponsors are seated at table 3.

4. If Q is assigned to table 1 along with two other sponsors, which one of the following could be true of the seating assignment?

    (A)   K is seated at the same table as L.
    (B)   K is seated at the same table as Q.
    (C)   M is seated at the same table as V.
    (D)   M is seated at the same table as Z.
    (E)   P is seated at the same table as Q.

5. If the sponsors assigned to table 3 include exactly one of the sponsors who will give a speech, then the sponsors assigned to table 1 could include any of the following EXCEPT:

    (A)   K
    (B)   M
    (C)   P
    (D)   Q
    (E)   Z

6. If three sponsors, exactly two of whom are receiving honors, are assigned to table 2, which one of the following could be the list of sponsors assigned to table 1 ?

    (A)   K, M
    (B)   K, Z
    (C)   P, V
    (D)   P, Z
    (E)   Q, Z

7. Which one of the following conditions, if added to the existing conditions, results in a set of conditions to which no seating assignment for the sponsors can conform?

    (A)   At most two sponsors are seated at table 1.
    (B)   Any sponsor giving a speech is seated at table 1 or else table 2.
    (C)   Any sponsor giving a speech is seated at table 2 or else table 3.
    (D)   Exactly three of the sponsors are seated at table 1.
    (E)   Any table at which both L and V are seated also has a third sponsor seated at it.

Analysis of Grouping Game #2: June 1997 Questions 1-7

It is immediately apparent that this game differs from the previous game in that the groups are not fixed. Although the number of variables—sponsors in this case—being placed is Defined at seven, the number of spaces per table is not precisely defined, and therefore the game is Moving. This type of uncertainty almost always increases the difficulty of a game because it introduces another element that must be tracked during the game. In addition, each of the seven sponsors will be seated at one of the three tables and thus the game is Balanced. Therefore, the game is Defined-Moving, Balanced.

The first rule establishes that each table must have at least two sponsors seated at it, and since there are a total of seven sponsors, it can be deduced that one of the three tables will have three sponsors seated at it and the other two tables will each seat two sponsors. This is a 3-2-2 numerical distribution. In this case, the 3-2-2 distribution is considered "unfixed," since the three sponsors could be seated at either table 1, table 2, or table 3. In some games "fixed" distributions occur, and these fixed distributions are generally a benefit since they limit the possibilities within a game.

The other rules of the game are relatively straightforward, and the initial setup should appear similar to the following:

K L M P Q V Z⁷

Honors: K L M
Speech: M P Q

3-2-2 distribution:

Since K, L, and M must sit at either table 1 or table 2, they cannot sit at table 3. Since V must sit at the same table as L, it follows that V cannot sit at table 3. Since K, L, M, and V cannot sit at table 3, only P, Q, and Z can possibly sit at table 3. Clearly then, table 3 is extremely restricted. As in any game, always examine the points of restriction since they often yield powerful inferences. In this case, since table 3 must have at least two sponsors, and only P, Q, and Z can possibly sit at table 3, at least two of the P, Q, Z group must always sit at table 3. Therefore, if a question states that one of the P, Q, Z group is seated at table 1 or table 2, then the remaining two sponsors must *automatically* be seated at table 3. Furthermore, any arrangement that attempts to seat two of the P, Q, or Z group at table 1 or table 2 will violate the rules and thus cannot occur. Ultimately, this simple analysis has uncovered the most important inference of the game. To reiterate, since table 3 has only three available sponsors to fill at least two seats, if any one of the sponsors is seated elsewhere, the remaining two sponsors must be seated at table 3. This is a variation of the type of inferences common when a dual-option is present, and you can expect at least one or two of the questions to directly test your knowledge of this inference.

Question #1: Global, Could Be True, List. The correct answer choice is (D)

As in many games, the first question in this game is a List question. The optimal attack for List questions is as always to apply one rule at a time to each of the five answer choices, eliminating answer choices from consideration until only one answer choice remains. In choosing the first rule to apply, try to choose a rule that can be easily applied from a visual standpoint. In this game, the LV block and the Not Laws on table 3 are the easiest to apply. The 3-2-2 distribution, although not difficult to apply, is more time consuming than the other two rules and thus should be applied last.

Applying the LV block rule eliminates answer choice (C). Applying the Not Laws on table 3 eliminates answer choices (A) and (B), as well as (C) again. Finally, applying the 3-2-2 numerical distribution rule eliminates answer choice (E). Answer choice (D) is thus proven correct by process of elimination.

Question #2: Global, Could Be True, List. The correct answer choice is (C)

From our earlier analysis of table 3 we know that answer choice (C) is correct.

Question #3: Local, Must Be True. The correct answer choice is (E)

If K and M are assigned to different tables, one must be assigned to table 1 and the other must be assigned to table 2. Since we cannot be certain which is assigned to table 1 or table 2, it is best to display this situation as a dual option and then Hurdle the Uncertainty:

$$\frac{\text{K/M}}{1} \quad \frac{\text{M/K}}{2} \quad \frac{\quad}{3}$$

Since the LV block must be seated at either table 1 or table 2, it follows that table 1 or table 2 must have three sponsors seated at it. Therefore, table 3 can only have two sponsors seated at it and answer choice (E) is proven correct. Answer choice (D) is incorrect since it is possible for three sponsors to sit at table 1. Answer choices (A) and (C) are both incorrect since the LV block can sit at either table 1 or table 2, as can K or M. Thus, although many combinations of K, M, and the LV block are possible, none must occur. Answer choice (B) is incorrect since L and Q can never sit together given the condition in the question stem.

Question #4: Local, Could Be True. The correct answer choice is (B)

If Q is assigned to table 1, P and Z must be assigned to table 3:

$$\frac{\quad}{\underset{1}{Q}} \quad \frac{\quad}{2} \quad \frac{\overset{Z}{\underset{}{P}}}{3}$$

Since the question stem also states that table 1 has three sponsors, the numerical distribution is now fixed at 3-2-2:

$$\frac{\quad}{\underset{1}{Q}} \quad \frac{\quad}{2} \quad \frac{\overset{Z}{\underset{}{P}}}{3}$$

Since the four remaining unseated sponsors are K, M, L, and V, two of that group must sit at table 1 and the other two must sit at table 2. Because L and V must sit together as a block, it follows that K and M must also sit together as a block. Thus, the KM block and the LV block cannot sit together:

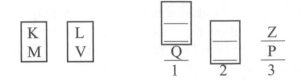

This information is sufficient to prove answer choice (B) correct.

Question #5: Local, Could Be True, Except. The correct answer choice is (E)

Remember, a Could Be True EXCEPT question asks for what Cannot Be True. This is the first question to address the "speech" subgroup established in the initial conditions of the game. Since M, P, and Q form the speech subgroup, and M cannot be seated at table 3, it follows that the one sponsor seated at table 3 who gives a speech must be either P or Q. Additionally, since at least two sponsors from the group P, Q, and Z must be seated at table 3, we can Hurdle the Uncertainty and infer that Z must be seated at table 3:

$$\underset{1}{\underline{}} \quad \underset{2}{\underline{}} \quad \underset{3}{\underline{\begin{array}{c} Z \\ P/Q \end{array}}}$$

Thus, answer choice (E) is correct.

Question #6: Local, Could Be True, List. The correct answer choice is (B)

This is the first question to address the "honors" subgroup established in the initial conditions of the game. The conditions in the question stem establish the following 2-3-2 fixed numerical distribution setup:

Fixed Numerical Distribution 2-3-2:

Honors block ⟶

Since table 1 can only have one sponsor from the honors subgroup, answer choice (A) can be eliminated. Conversely, answer choices (C), (D), and (E) can be eliminated since table 1 must have exactly one sponsor from the honors subgroup, and none of these answer choices meet that criterion. Alternately, answer choices (D) and (E) can be eliminated since they contain two sponsors from the P, Q, and Z group that must supply table 3 with two sponsors. By process of elimination, answer choice (B) is proven correct.

Question #7: Global, Cannot Be True, Justify. The correct answer choice is (B)

Justify questions, which appear infrequently in the Logic Games section, require you to select an answer choice that, when added to the initial rules of the game, forces the condition requested in the question stem to occur. In this case, the answer choice must force a situation in which no possible hypothetical can meet all of the conditions of the game. Since we know table 3 is the most restricted point in the game, it is a good bet that the answer choice will in some way affect the sponsors available to meet the table 3 requirements. This occurs in answer choice (B), which places P and Q at tables 1 or 2, leaving only Z to fulfill the requirement that two sponsors sit at table 3.

This question also provides an excellent example of the technique of using hypotheticals from other questions to eliminate incorrect answer choices. For example, answer choice (A) states that "At most two sponsors are seated at table 1." From question #6 we know that this scenario produces several workable hypotheticals. Since any workable hypothetical would conflict with the desired result of question #7, answer choice (A) must be wrong. Answer choice (D) can be eliminated by the same process. Answer choice (D) states, "Exactly three of the sponsors are seated at table 1." The information in the stem from question #4 and also answer choice (D) in question #1 shows that this occurrence also allows several workable hypotheticals. Thus, answer choice (D) is incorrect. Answer choice (E) can be eliminated by examining the hypotheticals from question #3 as well as answer choice (D) in question #1. Remember, when a working hypothetical from another question meets the required conditions of a particular question, that hypothetical can be used to eliminate wrong answers or confirm the correct answer.

This game, from the June 1997 LSAT, is representative of the type of Grouping games that frequently appear on the LSAT. There are two powerful lessons to learn from this game. First, always examine the restricted points in a game. In a Grouping game this often means examining the available variables for a particular group, or examining the variables that cannot be placed together. Second, always examine any rule that deals with numbers. Often these numerical rules introduce a controlling factor into a game, such as a numerical distribution. Numerical Distributions will be discussed in more detail in Chapter Eight.

In order to separate the game from its answer key and explanations,
the third game is on the next page.

An album contains photographs picturing seven friends: Raimundo, Selma, Ty, Umiko, Wendy, Yakira, Zack. The friends appear either alone or in groups with one another, in accordance with the following:

Wendy appears in every photograph that Selma appears in.

Selma appears in every photograph that Umiko appears in.

Raimundo appears in every photograph that Yakira does not appear in.

Neither Ty nor Raimundo appears in any photograph that Wendy appears in.

13. Which one of the following could be a complete and accurate list of the friends who appear together in a photograph?

(A) Raimundo, Selma, Ty, Wendy
(B) Raimundo, Ty, Yakira, Zack
(C) Raimundo, Wendy, Yakira, Zack
(D) Selma, Ty, Umiko, Yakira
(E) Selma, Ty, Umiko, Zack

14. If Ty and Zack appear together in a photograph, then which one of the following must be true?

(A) Selma also appears in the photograph.
(B) Yakira also appears in the photograph.
(C) Wendy also appears in the photograph.
(D) Raimundo does not appear in the photograph.
(E) Umiko does not appear in the photograph.

15. What is the maximum number of friends who could appear in a photograph that Yakira does not appear in?

(A) six
(B) five
(C) four
(D) three
(E) two

16. If Umiko and Zack appear together in a photograph, then exactly how many of the other friends must also appear in that photograph?

(A) four
(B) three
(C) two
(D) one
(E) zero

17. If exactly three friends appear together in a photograph, then each of the following could be true EXCEPT:

(A) Selma and Zack both appear in the photograph.
(B) Ty and Yakira both appear in the photograph.
(C) Wendy and Selma both appear in the photograph.
(D) Yakira and Zack both appear in the photograph.
(E) Zack and Raimundo both appear in the photograph.

Analysis of Grouping Game #3: December 2004 Questions 13-17

This is an Undefined Grouping game. The game is Undefined because we do not know how many photographs are displayed in the album, nor do we know exactly how many people are in a photograph. With these elements unspecified, we cannot create a diagram in the traditional sense; that is, we cannot create a group of say, five spaces and then place variables in those spaces. Instead, we must diagram the rules and make inferences, and then proceed to the questions without a defined group in place. Although this task sounds difficult, it is not, and games of this nature are not unusual on the LSAT. Some similar games are: October 2005 #2 (Light Switches), December 2005 #1 (Electrical Appliances), and June 2006 #3 (Summer Courses).

Instead of showing an initial diagram, we will begin by examining each rule and then at the end of the rule analysis and inference we will present the completed setup.

The Rules

Rule #1. One of the easiest mistakes to make in this game is to misinterpret the wording in each of the rules. This rule indicates that whenever S appears in a photograph, then W appears in that same photograph. The correct diagram for that relationship is:

$$S \longrightarrow W$$

Many students mistakenly reverse the above diagram. To avoid doing so, consider the rule for a moment: does the rule say that every time W appears in a photograph that S also appears? No. Although the difference is subtle, the wording in the rule is that W appears in every photograph *that S appears in*. Thus, S is the sufficient condition, and the appearance of S indicates that W will appear in that same photograph.

Rule #2. The wording in this rule is identical to the wording in rule #1, and so it is just as easy to make an error when diagramming this rule. The correct diagram is:

$$U \longrightarrow S$$

When we get to the "Inference" section we will discuss how the first and second rules can be linked. Also, note that since both of the first two rules are "positive" (no negative terms involved) we are not diagramming contrapositives since you should know those as an automatic result of seeing any conditional statement.

Rule #3. This is also a tricky rule, not only because of the wording, but also because the conditional relationship between R and Y is easy to misunderstand. First, let us diagram the rule:

$$\cancel{Y} \longrightarrow R$$

Since this rule contains a negative, let us also diagram the contrapositive:

$$\cancel{R} \longrightarrow Y$$

Many students will interpret these two diagrams as a reduced to a simple double-not arrow relationship:

Y ◄──┼──► R. This is *not* the meaning of the rule! Instead, consider the exact relationship between Y and R: when Y is not in the photograph, then R must be in the photograph; and, via the contrapositive, when R is not in the photograph, then Y must be in the photograph. Thus, when one of the two is *not* in the photograph, the other *must* be in the photograph, and that relationship can best be expressed by stating that both cannot be absent from the photograph. The correct double-not arrow diagram, then, is:

$$\cancel{R} \longleftarrow\!\!\!\!\mid\!\longrightarrow \cancel{Y}$$

The operating result of this rule is that *either Y or R, or both, must appear in each photograph* (note that R and Y *can* appear in a photograph together; the rule does not prohibit this occurrence).

Rule #4. This rule is actually two rules in one: one rule states that T and W do not appear in the same photograph, and the other states that R and W do not appear in the same photograph. Let's consider each part separately.

As stated directly, when W is in a photograph, T is not in that same photograph:

$$W \longrightarrow \cancel{T}$$

This rule can be turned into the a double-not arrow indicating that T and W are never in the same photograph:

$$W \longleftarrow\!\!\!\!\mid\!\longrightarrow T$$

The other part of the rule states that when W is in a photograph, R is not in that same photograph:

$$W \longrightarrow \cancel{R}$$

This rule can be turned into the a double-not arrow indicating that R and W are never in the same photograph:

$$W \longleftarrow\!\!\!\!\mid\!\longrightarrow R$$

One note about the rules: every variable is mentioned in the rules except Z. Thus, Z is a random in this game, and since there is not a specified number of spaces, Z is largely powerless in this game. If a question stem includes Z as part of a local condition, there *must* be other information included in the question stem, and you should focus on the other information first.

In review, the four rules contain five basic grouping relationships that create many different inferences. When you consider the four rules, you can see that the test makers placed a trap for the unwary student. A student who quickly reads through the rules and does not read for meaning can easily mis-diagram one or more of the rules, and of course mis-diagramming during the setup is almost always costly.

After correctly negotiating each of the rule diagrams, the next step is to make inferences by connecting the rules. In this game, there are many inferences, and so the challenge becomes managing the information.

<u>The Inferences</u>

Inference #1. By connecting the first and second rules, we can create the following chain:

$$U \longrightarrow S \longrightarrow W$$

This connection is important because it shows that if U appears in a photograph then two other friends must also appear in that same photograph. Via the contrapositive, the relationship also indicates that if W does not appear in a photograph, then neither S nor U can appear in that photograph.

Inferences #2 and #3. The first and fourth rules can be connected through W:

$$S \longrightarrow W \longleftarrow\!\!\mid\!\longrightarrow T$$

and

$$S \longrightarrow W \longleftarrow\!\!\mid\!\longrightarrow R$$

These two relationships yield the following inferences:

$$S \longleftarrow\!\!\mid\!\longrightarrow T$$

and

$$S \longleftarrow\!\!\mid\!\longrightarrow R$$

Inferences #4 and #5. The two previous inferences connected S to T and R through S's relationship with W. Since U also has a relationship with S from the second rule, we can connect the second rule to inferences we just made:

$$U \longrightarrow S \longleftarrow\!\!\mid\!\longrightarrow T$$

and

$$U \longrightarrow S \longleftarrow\!\!\mid\!\longrightarrow R$$

These two relationships yield the following inferences:

$$U \longleftarrow\!\!\mid\!\longrightarrow T$$

and

$$U \longleftarrow\!\!\mid\!\longrightarrow R$$

Inference #6. Because R appears in the third and fourth rules, we can make a connection using R:

This relationship results in the unique inference that:

$$\cancel{Y} \longrightarrow \cancel{W}$$

Because both conditions are negative, take the contrapositive:

$$W \longrightarrow Y$$

Thus, if W appears in a photograph, then Y must appear in that photograph as well.

Inferences #7 and #8. From the inference we just made we know that when W is in a photograph, then Y must also be in that photograph. We can add this to the chain that appeared in inference #1 (which was the combination of the first two rules):

$$U \longrightarrow S \longrightarrow W \longrightarrow Y$$

These relationships yield the following two inferences:

$$S \longrightarrow Y$$

and

$$U \longrightarrow Y$$

Thus, the appearance of either S or U will ultimately force Y to appear. This makes U a powerful variable. when U appears in a photograph, then S, W, and Y must also appear, and R and T cannot appear. Thus, the appearance of U allows for only two solutions, depending on whether Z is in the photograph.

There are other ways to arrive at some of these inferences (for example, when S has a relationship with a variable, U has the same relationship because of the second rule), but each inference above is a product of combining the rules or of combining the rules and inferences (do not forget to recycle your inferences!).

Compiling all of the information above, we arrive at the final setup for this game:

R or Y must appear in each picture: R/Y

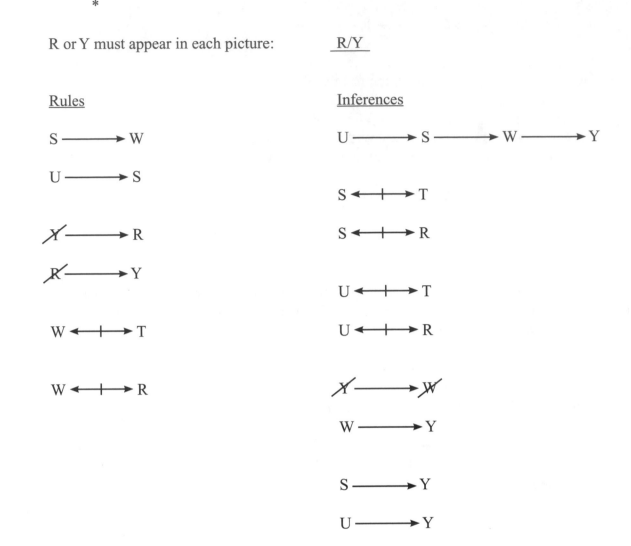

Rules

Inferences

As long as you focus on connecting the variables in the rules and inferences, you can attack the questions and complete each problem with relative ease. Remember, this game is not logically difficult; it is simply an information management game, so do not be intimidated!

Question #13: Global, Could Be True, List. The correct answer choice is (B)

Because there is no lack of rules or inferences to apply to this List question, this should be a relatively easy question.

Answer choice (A): This answer choice is incorrect because W cannot appear in a photograph with R or T. Alternately, this answer could be eliminated because when W is in a photograph then Y must be in that photograph.

Answer choice (B): This is the correct answer choice.

Answer choice (C): This answer choice is incorrect because W cannot appear in a photograph with R.

Answer choice (D): This answer choice can be eliminated because when S appears in a photograph, W must also appear in that photograph. Alternately, this answer can be eliminated because T cannot appear in a photograph with S or U.

Answer choice (E): This answer choice can be eliminated because when S appears in a photograph, W must also appear in that photograph. Alternately, this answer can be eliminated because either Y or R must appear in the photograph, or because T cannot appear in a photograph with S or U.

Question #14: Local, Must Be True. The correct answer choice is (E)

The question stem indicates that T and Z appear in a photograph. As discussed before, because Z is a random you should ignore Z in your consideration of who can and cannot appear together in a photograph. Consequently, let's revisit what we know about T:

From the fourth rule: W ◄───┼───► T

From the second inference: S ◄───┼───► T

From the fourth inference: U ◄───┼───► T

Thus, when T is in a photograph, then W, S, and U cannot appear in that photograph. Consequently, answer choice (E) must be correct.

Another way of thinking about this question would be to apply the fourth rule and conclude that when T is in a photograph then W is not in that photograph. Then, using the contrapositive of the first two rules, we can conclude that when W is not in a photograph, then S is not in that photograph, and U is not in that photograph.

Answer choice (A). This answer is incorrect because S cannot appear in any photograph that T appears in.

Answer choice (B): This answer choice is incorrect because although Y could appear in a photograph with T, Y does not have to appear in a photograph when T is in that photograph.

Answer choice (C): This answer is incorrect because S cannot appear in any photograph that T appears in.

Answer choice (D): This answer choice is incorrect because although R does not have to appear in a photograph with T, R could appear in a photograph when T is in that photograph.

Note how the first three answer choices specify variables that must appear with T, whereas the last two answers specify variables that *cannot* appear with T. Always make sure to read each answer choice closely!

Question #15: Local, Must Be True, Maximum. The correct answer choice is (D)

In this question you are asked to find the maximum number of friends that can appear in a photograph when Y does not appear in the photograph. This requires two steps: first you must establish what must be true and what cannot be true when Y does not appear, and second you must then arrange the other variables in a way that allows for the most number of friends to appear in the picture. Let's examine both steps:

Step 1: From the third rule, when Y does not appear in a photograph, then R must appear in that photograph:

From the fourth rule, when R appears in a photograph, then W cannot appear in that photograph:

R ⟶ W̸

Via the contrapositive of the first and second rules, when W does not appear in a photograph, then S and U cannot appear in that photograph:

Thus, when Y does not appear in a photograph, then R must appear in the photograph, and W, S, and U cannot appear in the photograph.

Step 2: The remaining two variables that have not yet been addressed are T and Z. Because Z is a random, Z can automatically be included in the photograph. So, the final question is whether T is compatible with R, and the answer is yes. Although R and T both figure in the fourth rule, that rule individually relates R and T to W, and it does not make a direct connection between R and T. Thus, R and T can appear in a photograph together, and the maximum number of friends that can appear is three—R, T, and Z. Answer choice (D) is correct.

Answer choices (A), (B), (C): Each of these answer choice is incorrect because more than three friends cannot appear in the photograph when Y does not appear.

Answer choice (D): This is the correct answer choice.

Answer choice (E): This answer choice is incorrect because the question asks for the *maximum* number friends who can appear in the photograph when Y does not appear, and this answer is not the maximum.

Question #16: Local, Must Be True. The correct answer choice is (B)

The question stem asks for the number of *other* friends who must appear when U and Z appear together in a photograph.

As we have already established, Z is irrelevant in this type of question because Z is a random. Thus, the question revolves around U. From the first two rules, we know that when U appears in a photograph then S and W must also appear in that photograph. The appearance of W in the photograph (and S and U), forces Y to appear in the photograph. None of the other friends must appear, and thus the correct answer is three: S, W, and Y.

Answer choices (A), (C), (D), and (E): These answer choices are incorrect because they do not contain a number that equals the number of other friends who *must* appear in the photograph.

Question #17: Local, Could Be True Except. The correct answer choice is (A)

This is the only question of the game to define the number of friends who can appear in a photograph; in this case, three. With only three spaces in the photograph, every variable becomes important, especially those that bring along other variables.

Because this is a Could Be True Except question, the correct answer choice Cannot Be True, and is one that provides a pair of friends that together result in four or more friends appearing in the photograph. Thus, you should immediately scan the answers for a variable such as U, who by itself brings S, W, and Y. Unfortunately, U does not appear in the answers (but it is worth taking the time to see if the question could be solved that easily).

Answer choice (A): This is the correct answer choice. When S appears in a photograph, then W and Y must also appear in that photograph. Since the answer choice also establishes that Z is in this photograph, that totals four friends (S, W, Y, and Z), and thus this answer cannot be true and is correct.

Answer choice (B): This answer choice is incorrect. T and Y could appear in a photograph of exactly three friends, as proven by the following hypothetical: T-Y-Z.

Answer choice (C): This answer choice is incorrect. W and S could appear in a photograph of exactly three friends, as proven by the following hypothetical: W-S-Y.

Answer choice (D): This answer choice is incorrect. Y and Z could appear in a photograph of exactly three friends, as proven by the following hypothetical: T-Y-Z.

Answer choice (E): This answer choice is incorrect. Z and R could appear in a photograph of exactly three friends, as proven by the following hypothetical: R-T-Z.

Remember, if you do not see a quick solution to a problem such as this one, you should immediately make hypotheticals from the answer choices to see what is possible. Never waste time on the LSAT simply staring at a problem!

In order to separate the game from its answer key and explanations,
the fourth game is on the next page.

To prepare for fieldwork, exactly four different researchers—a geologist, a historian, a linguist, and a paleontologist—will learn at least one and at most three of four languages—Rundi, Swahili, Tigrinya, and Yoruba. They must learn the languages according to the following specifications:

Exactly one researcher learns Rundi.
Exactly two researchers learn Swahili.
Exactly two researchers learn Tigrinya.
Exactly three researchers learn Yoruba.
Any language learned by the linguist or paleontologist is not learned by the geologist.
Any language learned by the geologist is learned by the historian.

6. Which one of the following could be true?

   (A) The linguist learns three languages—Rundi, Swahili, and Tigrinya.
   (B) The linguist learns three languages—Swahili, Tigrinya, and Yoruba.
   (C) The historian learns three languages—Rundi, Swahili, and Tigrinya.
   (D) The historian learns three languages—Swahili, Tigrinya, and Yoruba.
   (E) The paleontologist learns three languages—Rundi, Swahili, and Tigrinya.

7. If the linguist learns three of the languages, then which one of the following must be true?

   (A) The linguist learns Tigrinya.
   (B) The linguist learns Rundi.
   (C) The linguist learns Swahili.
   (D) The paleontologist learns Rundi.
   (E) The paleontologist learns Swahili.

8. Each of the following could be true of the researcher who learns Rundi EXCEPT:

   (A) The researcher also learns Tigrinya but not Swahili.
   (B) The researcher learns neither Tigrinya nor Swahili.
   (C) The researcher also learns Tigrinya but not Yoruba.
   (D) The researcher also learns both Tigrinya and Yoruba.
   (E) The researcher also learns Yoruba but not Tigrinya.

9. Each of the following could be a complete and accurate list of the researchers who learn both Swahili and Yoruba EXCEPT:

   (A) the historian
   (B) the paleontologist
   (C) the historian, the linguist
   (D) the historian, the paleontologist
   (E) the linguist, the paleontologist

10. If the geologist learns exactly two of the languages, then which one of the following could be true?

    (A) The paleontologist learns Rundi.
    (B) The paleontologist learns Swahili.
    (C) The historian learns Rundi.
    (D) The paleontologist learns exactly three of the languages.
    (E) The historian learns exactly two of the languages.

11. Which one of the following must be true?

    (A) Fewer of the languages are learned by the historian than are learned by the paleontologist.
    (B) Fewer of the languages are learned by the geologist than are learned by the historian.
    (C) Fewer of the languages are learned by the geologist than are learned by the linguist.
    (D) Fewer of the languages are learned by the paleontologist than are learned by the linguist.
    (E) Fewer of the languages are learned by the paleontologist than are learned by the historian.

12. If exactly two of the languages are learned by the historian, then which one of the following must be true?

    (A) The paleontologist does not learn Rundi.
    (B) The geologist does not learn Swahili.
    (C) The linguist does not learn Rundi.
    (D) The historian does not learn Rundi.
    (E) The paleontologist does not learn Swahili.

Analysis of Grouping Game #4: June 1999 Questions 6-12

Like game #2, and in contrast to games #1 and #3, the variables in this game are separated into different selection groups. Unlike the last game, the size of each group is fixed. Thus, the game is Defined-Fixed. And unlike either of the two previous games, there are fewer variables (four researchers) than spaces available (eight language slots) and so the game can be classified as Unbalanced: Underfunded. The complete classification is Defined-Fixed, Unbalanced: Underfunded.

When you create the setup, it is critical that the correct base be selected. There are two choices: the four researchers or the four languages. Since the researchers can learn one to three languages but it is uncertain exactly how many languages each researcher learns, the researchers seem a poor choice for the base. On the other hand, the number of researchers learning each language is clearly specified in the rules and as such the languages are the best choice for the base:

The distribution of researchers to languages is thus fixed at 1-2-2-3, and since there are only four researchers, it is clear that at least two researchers will have to learn more than one language (in fact, at least two researchers and at most three researchers will learn more than one language). Using the above base, we can set up the game as follows:

G H L P ⁴

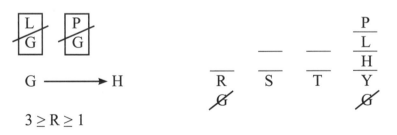

From the rules it is clear that G is a power variable, since G appears in both the non-numerical rules. The key inference involving G comes with Yoruba. Because Yoruba must be learned by exactly three researchers, and G cannot be selected with either L or P, it can be inferred that G cannot learn Yoruba, and the other three researchers must learn Yoruba. Additionally, since when G is selected H must also be selected, it is not possible for G to learn Rundi, as there is no room for H to be selected. Consequently, since G must learn at least one language, G (in the form of a GH block) must learn either Swahili or Tigrinya or both. From this inference it follows that neither L nor P can learn *both* Swahili and Tigrinya.

Question #6: Global, Could Be True. The correct answer choice is (D)

Since it has already been established that H, L, and P must each learn Yoruba, answer choices (A), (C), and (E) can be eliminated. Since we have established that G must at a minimum learn either Swahili or Tigrinya, and it is therefore known that neither L or P can learn *both* Swahili and

Tigrinya, answer choice (B) (as well as answer choices (A) and (E)) can be eliminated. Thus, answer choice (D) is proven correct by process of elimination.

Question #7: Local, Must Be True. The correct answer choice is (B)

Keeping in mind the inference that L cannot learn both Swahili and Tigrinya, when L learns three languages, we can Hurdle the Uncertainty to determine those languages must be Yoruba, Rundi, and either Swahili or Tigrinya. Consequently, answer choice (B) is correct.

Question #8: Global, Cannot Be True. The correct answer choice is (C)

Since G cannot learn Rundi, it can automatically be deduced that either H, L, or P must learn Rundi. Since H, L, and P each learn Yoruba, it must be the case that the researcher who learns Rundi also learns Yoruba. It follows that answer choice (C) cannot occur and is therefore correct.

Question #9: Global, Cannot Be True, List. The correct answer choice is (B)

In a question requiring a complete list of researchers who cannot learn both Swahili and Yoruba, the first researcher to check is G, because G cannot learn Yoruba. Unfortunately, G does not appear in any answer choice. The next step is to consider the implications of learning both Swahili and Yoruba. Since H, L, and P each learn Yoruba, it seems likely that any combination of two of those three researchers could learn Swahili. Since answer choice (C), (D), and (E) each list two of H, L, or P, it seems unlikely that any of those answer choices are correct. Thus, let us focus on answer choices (A) and (B). Answer choice (A) lists just H, but under the following hypothetical H can be the only researcher who learns both Swahili and Yoruba:

$$
\begin{array}{cccc}
 & \begin{array}{c}H\\\hline G\end{array} & \underline{} & \begin{array}{c}P\\L\\H\end{array} \\
\underline{} & \\
R & S & T & Y
\end{array}
$$

Let us check answer choice (B):

$$
\begin{array}{cccc}
 & \underline{} & \underline{} & \begin{array}{c}P\\L\\H\end{array} \\
\underline{} & P & \\
R & S & T & Y
\end{array}
$$

In this instance the second researcher who learns Swahili cannot be H or L since neither is listed in the answer choice. G also cannot learn Swahili since there is no room for H. Thus P cannot be the only person who learns both Swahili and Yoruba and answer choice (B) is correct.

With answer choice (B), when P is the sole researcher learning both Swahili and Yoruba, a problem arises because a second researcher is needed to learn Swahili, but according to the conditions of the question it must be one who does not also learn Yoruba. In this situation, who could you choose? You cannot choose L or H because they already learn Yoruba. That leaves only G, but if you select G for the second researcher slot in Swahili, you immediately violate the last rule because there is no room for H (and H could not be chosen anyway because that would be a violation as H learns Yoruba already). Hence, answer choice (B) cannot be a complete and accurate list of researchers who learn both Swahili and Yoruba.

When you are trying to figure out a situation such as the one above, always remember to try to work out the solution by creating hypotheticals. In this instance you can create viable hypotheticals for (A), (C), (D), and (E), but you cannot create on for (B).

Question #10: Local, Could Be True. The correct answer choice is (A)

If G learns exactly two languages, those languages must be Swahili and Tigrinya:

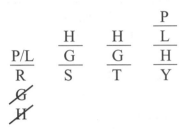

Since H will then learn Swahili, Tigrinya, and Yoruba, due to the rule that limits a researcher to learning at most three languages, it follows that H cannot learn Rundi, and only P or L can learn Rundi. Answer choice (A) is thus correct.

Question #11: Global, Must Be True. The correct answer choice is (B)

The correct answer choice, answer choice (B), partially tests your understanding of the conditional relationship between G and H. According to the rule, every time G learns a language then H must also learn that same language. Consequently, H must learn at least as many languages as G. And since H also learns Yoruba and G cannot learn Yoruba, it must be that G learns fewer languages than H. The hypothetical from question #10 can be used to disprove answer choices (A), (C), and (D).

Question #12: Local, Must Be True. The correct answer choice is (D)

Since it has already been established that H learns Yoruba, the second language that H learns must come in conjunction with G, since G must learn at least one language. Since G must learn either Swahili or Tigrinya, it follows that H cannot learn Rundi and thus answer choice (D) is correct.

Like game #1, one possible approach to this game is to create three basic templates based on the position of G: G learning Swahili only, G learning Tigrinya only, and G learning both Swahili and Tigrinya. As with the first game, we believe this approach is less efficient than using the diagram and inferences described earlier, in part because the templates still leave a large number of possibilities unrealized.

Bird-watchers explore a forest to see which of the following six kinds of birds—grosbeak, harrier, jay, martin, shrike, wren—it contains. The findings are consistent with the following conditions:

> If harriers are in the forest, then grosbeaks are not.
> If jays, martins, or both are in the forest, then so are harriers.
> If wrens are in the forest, then so are grosbeaks.
> If jays are not in the forest, then shrikes are.

6. Which one of the following could be a complete and accurate list of the birds NOT in the forest?

   (A)   jays, shrikes
   (B)   harriers, grosbeaks
   (C)   grosbeaks, jays, martins
   (D)   grosbeaks, martins, shrikes, wrens
   (E)   martins, shrikes

7. If both martins and harriers are in the forest, then which one of the following must be true?

   (A)   Shrikes are the only other birds in the forest.
   (B)   Jays are the only other birds in the forest.
   (C)   The forest contains neither jays nor shrikes.
   (D)   There are at least two other kinds of birds in the forest.
   (E)   There are at most two other kinds of birds in the forest.

8. If jays are not in the forest, then which one of the following must be false?

   (A)   Martins are in the forest.
   (B)   Harriers are in the forest.
   (C)   Neither martins nor harriers are in the forest.
   (D)   Neither martins nor shrikes are in the forest.
   (E)   Harriers and shrikes are the only birds in the forest.

9. Which one of the following is the maximum number of the six kinds of birds the forest could contain?

   (A)   two
   (B)   three
   (C)   four
   (D)   five
   (E)   six

10. Which one of the following pairs of birds CANNOT be among those birds contained in the forest?

   (A)   jays, wrens
   (B)   jays, shrikes
   (C)   shrikes, wrens
   (D)   jays, martins
   (E)   shrikes, martins

11. If grosbeaks are in the forest, then which one of the following must be true?

   (A)   Shrikes are in the forest.
   (B)   Wrens are in the forest.
   (C)   The forest contains both wrens and shrikes.
   (D)   At most two kinds of birds are in the forest.
   (E)   At least three kinds of birds are in the forest.

12. Suppose the condition is added that if shrikes are in the forest, then harriers are not. If all other conditions remain in effect, then which one of the following could be true?

   (A)   The forest contains both jays and shrikes.
   (B)   The forest contains both wrens and shrikes.
   (C)   The forest contains both martins and shrikes.
   (D)   Jays are not in the forest, whereas martins are.
   (E)   Only two of the six kinds of birds are not in the forest.

Similar to the third game, the number of variables being selected—birds in this case—is left open, and so the game is classified as Undefined. Although a maximum of six birds can be in the forest (remember, there are only six birds total), prior to consideration of the rules there could be anywhere from zero to six birds in the forest. This uncertainty increases the difficulty of the game and is an element that must be tracked throughout the game. Of course, since it cannot be determined how many birds are in the forest, there is no "selection group" as in a Defined game:

G H J M S W [6]

Inferences:

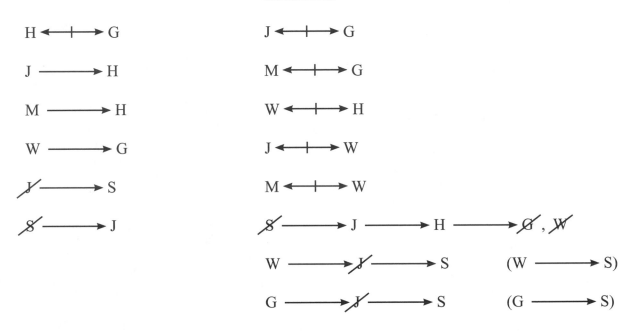

Like many Undefined Grouping games, this one contains a large number of conditional rules. By using basic linkage, we can draw a slew of inferences. Let us examine these in greater detail:

1. J ←—|—→ G. This inference results from linking the first two rules.

2. M ←—|—→ G. This inference results from linking the first two rules.

3. W ←—|—→ H. This inference results from linking the first and third rules.

4. J ←—|—→ W. This inference results from linking the first inference and the third rule. Note how the first inference has been recombined or "recycled" with the original rules.

5. M ←—|—→ W. This inference results from linking the second inference and the third rule. The third rule here refers to the rules as listed in the game.

6. S̶ ——→ J ——→ H ——→ G̶, W̶. The final rule is tricky and bears further analysis. When J is not in the forest, then S must be in the forest. Via the contrapositive, when S is not in the forest, then J must be in the forest. In each case, the absence of one of the birds forces the other bird to appear in the forest. This type of "omission" rule appears infrequently on LSAT games, but when

it does, it tends to cause problems. It is easy to forget that the absence of a variable forces other variables to be present. In this case, when S is not in the forest, then J must be in the forest, and from the second rule, when J is in the forest, it follows that H must be in the forest. Of course, from the first rule and third inference, when H is in the forest, then G cannot be in the forest and W cannot be in the forest.

7. W ———→ ̷J ———→ S. From the fourth inference it is known that W and J cannot be in the forest together. Thus, when W is in the forest, then J cannot be in the forest, and from the last rule it follows that S must be in the forest (W ———→ S). This is another classic example of recycling an inference.

8. G ———→ ̷J ———→ S. Similar to the previous inference, when G is in the forest, then J cannot be in the forest, and from the last rule it follows that S must be in the forest (G ———→ S).

In light of all these inferences, the bigger question becomes, "When do you know you have made all of the inferences?" In this case the application of basic Linkage creates a large number of inferences, and then the recycling of those inferences leads to even more inferences. At some point the time pressure of this section demands that you move on to the questions. Although in our diagram we could continue to make inferences (for example, if H is not in the forest, then J is not in the forest and S must be in the forest), there comes a point when you must ask yourself, "Do I have enough information to effectively attack the questions?" The answer here is undeniably "yes." It may be that you do not discover every inference in the game (as with the first game in this section), but when you feel you have exhausted all the obvious routes of inference-making, it is time to move on to the questions. The challenge in the questions then becomes keeping track of all the information at your disposal.

Question #6: Global, Cannot Be True, List. The correct answer choice is (D).

In attacking this question, keep in mind that since each answer choice is supposed to be a complete and accurate list of the birds not in the forest, all of the birds not named on each list will be in the forest. Given the number of negative grouping rules in play, that is an important consideration. For example, in answer choice (B), when only H and G are not in the forest, J, M, S, and W are in the forest. But, according to the fourth inference, J and W cannot both be in the forest and therefore answer choice (B) is incorrect. Answer choice (E) can be eliminated by identical reasoning. Answer choice (C) can be eliminated because, via the third inference, H and W cannot both be in the forest. Answer choice (A) can be eliminated by applying the last rule. Answer choice (D) is therefore proven correct by process of elimination.

Question #7: Local, Must Be True. The correct answer choice is (E)

If H is in the forest, then G cannot be in the forest. If G cannot be in the forest, then W cannot be in the forest. At this point it has been established that H and M are in the forest and G and W are not in the forest. The only unaddressed birds are S and J, and at least one of them, possibly both, must be in the forest. Answer choices (A) and (B) are therefore incorrect because it is possible that both S and J can be in the forest. Answer choice (C) is incorrect because, due to the final rule, the forest always contains at least S or J. Answer choice (D) is incorrect because it is possible there is only one other kind of bird in the forest (S or J). Answer choice (E) is thus correct since at most S and J can be in the forest in addition to M and H.

Question #8: Local, Cannot Be True. The correct answer choice is (D)

This question has been phrased in terms of falsity. Remember, always convert "false" questions into terms of "true." As discussed earlier, "Must Be False" is identical to "Cannot Be True," and so this question simply asks which one of the following Cannot Be True. If J is not in the forest, then according to the last rule, S must be in the forest, and answer choice (D) cannot be true and is therefore correct.

Question #9: Global, Must Be True, Maximum. The correct answer choice is (C)

In this question you must select the variables in such a way as to maximize the number of birds in the forest. This means that birds that tend to knock out several other birds must be removed. An examination of the list of inferences indicates that W must be removed since, when W is in the forest, then H, J, and M cannot be in the forest. The other bird that must be removed is G since, when G is in the forest, then H cannot be in the forest, and when H is not in the forest, then neither J nor M can be in the forest. If G and W are removed from consideration, then the remaining four birds are J, H, M, and S. Ultimately, four is the maximum number of birds in the forest, and answer choice (C) is correct.

Another approach to this question involves referring to work done on other questions. When this approach is used, hypotheticals are examined to eliminate certain answer choices. For example, in question #7 we were able to determine that four birds could be in the forest: M, H, S, and J. This hypothetical eliminates answer choices (A) and (B). To effectively use this approach, however, it would be best to skip this question and return after completing all other questions in order to have as many hypotheticals as possible.

A third approach involves considering the negative grouping rules in the setup. For example, since the first rule establishes that H and G cannot both be in the forest, answer choice (E) can be rejected. And since at least one of H and G cannot be in the forest and at least one of W and H (or W and J for that matter) cannot be in the forest, a case can also be made against answer choice (D). When you examine these rules, it is important to consider negative grouping rules that contain entirely different sets of variables. You cannot simply count all the negative rules and arrive at an answer because some of the rules will revolve around the same variable, and when that variable is removed the other variables can be selected.

Finally, let's take a moment to examine a mistake that is made by a number of test takers. Some students, upon encountering the final rule, make the classic error of assuming that the jays and the shrikes cannot be in the forest together. As discussed in the Avoiding False Inferences section on page 200, this is a false inference, and thus it is possible for J and S to be in the forest together. Let us take a moment to review:

> Most LSAT Logic Game conditional rules place the "not" on the necessary condition, but in this rule, the "not" is on the sufficient condition. While that difference may seem minor, in effect it completely changes the meaning of the rule.

> According to the rule, if J is not in the forest, then S must be in the forest, and via the contrapositive if S is not in the forest, then J must be in the forest. Essentially, this means that

if either bird (S or J) is absent (not in the forest), then the other bird cannot also be absent (they cannot both be out of the forest at the same time; at least one must always be in the forest). In other words, all we know from the fourth rule is that they will never both be *out* of the forest, because as soon as one is out the other must be in. They could, however, both be in the forest at the same time. The rules never tell us anything about what happens when either J or S is *in* the forest, only what happens when J or S is not in the forest.

Since it is possible for both J and S to be in the forest at the same time, that possibility impacts the choices you have in questions #9 and #10. In #9, most people assume that one of J or S is always out of the forest. Obviously, that is not the case, and when arriving at the maximum number of birds in the forest you should include both J and S. In question #10, many people select answer choice (B) because they misinterpret the fourth rule. As explained above, J and S—the pair in answer choice (B) of question #10—can both be in the forest at the same time.

Question #10: Global, Cannot Be True. The correct answer choice is (A)

With Global Must Be True or Global Cannot Be True questions always make sure to check your inferences as the first step in attacking the question. Per inference #4 answer choice (A) is correct.

Note that this possibility is also discussed in the solution to question #9.

Question #11: Local, Must Be True. The correct answer choice is (A)

Per the final inference, when G is in the forest, then S must be in the forest, and answer choice (A) is proven correct. A review of the entire inference chain shows that, when G is in the forest, then H is not in the forest (from rule #1), and when H is not in the forest, then neither J or M is in the forest (from rule #2). When J is not in the forest, then S must be in the forest (from rule #4).

In this question, be sure to avoid making a Mistaken Reversal: although from the third rule we know that when W is in the forest then G must be in the forest, this does not mean that when G in the forest that W must also be in the forest.

Question #12: Local, Could Be True. The correct answer choice is (B)

This is not a Suspension question because the rule is simply added on to the given information. In this way it acts like a normal Local question. The extra condition stipulates that S and H cannot both be in the forest. This affects both J and M because, when either J or M is in the forest, then H is in the forest. Thus, neither J and S nor M and S can be in the forest at the same time. This information is sufficient to reject answer choices (A) and (C). Answer choice (D) can also be rejected since, when J is not in the forest, then S must be in the forest, and when S is in the forest, then H is not in the forest, and when H is not in the forest, then neither J nor M is in the forest. Finally, answer choice (E) can be disproven since if H, for example, is in the forest, then G, S, and W are not in the forest. It follows that answer choice (B) is correct.

Despite the large number of inferences in this particular game, the typical student eventually comes to find this type of game completely reasonable, and certainly doable in the allotted time. As you develop the ability to make inferences more quickly, you will begin to see a game like this one as an opportunity to make up time, especially if you know how to handle the last rule.

The Export Alliance consists of exactly three nations: Nation X, Nation Y, and Nation Z. Each nation in the Alliance exports exactly two of the following five crops: oranges, rice, soybeans, tea, and wheat. Each of these crops is exported by at least one of the nations in the Alliance. The following conditions hold:

> None of the nations exports both wheat and oranges.
> Nation X exports soybeans if, but only if, Nation Y does also.
> If Nation Y exports rice, then Nations X and Z both export tea.
> Nation Y does not export any crop that Nation Z exports.

18. Which one of the following could be an accurate list, for each of the nations, of the crops it exports?

   (A)   Nation X: oranges, rice; Nation Y: oranges, tea; Nation Z: soybeans, wheat
   (B)   Nation X: oranges, tea; Nation Y: oranges, rice; Nation Z: soybeans, wheat
   (C)   Nation X: oranges, wheat; Nation Y: oranges, tea; Nation Z: rice, soybeans
   (D)   Nation X: rice, wheat; Nation Y: oranges, tea; Nation Z: oranges, soybeans
   (E)   Nation X: soybeans, rice; Nation Y: oranges, tea; Nation Z: soybeans, wheat

19. If Nation X exports soybeans and tea, then which one of the following could be true?

   (A)   Nation Y exports oranges.
   (B)   Nation Y exports rice.
   (C)   Nation Y exports tea.
   (D)   Nation Z exports soybeans.
   (E)   Nation Z exports tea.

20. If Nation Z exports tea and wheat, then which one of the following must be true?

   (A)   Nation X exports oranges.
   (B)   Nation X exports tea.
   (C)   Nation X exports wheat.
   (D)   Nation Y exports rice.
   (E)   Nation Y exports soybeans.

21. It CANNOT be the case that both Nation X and Nation Z export which one of the following crops?

   (A)   oranges
   (B)   rice
   (C)   soybeans
   (D)   tea
   (E)   wheat

22. Which one of the following pairs CANNOT be the two crops that Nation Y exports?

   (A)   oranges and rice
   (B)   oranges and soybeans
   (C)   rice and tea
   (D)   rice and wheat
   (E)   soybeans and wheat

At first, this appears to be a standard Grouping game, but the test makers use the Numerical Distribution to raise the level of difficulty.

The game scenario establishes that three nations—X, Y, and Z—each export exactly two crops from a group of five:

O R S T W [5]

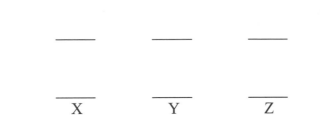

Since there are only five crops (and each crop must be exported by at least one nation), but there are six exporting slots to be filled, exactly one of the crops must exported twice, and there is a 2-1-1-1 Numerical Distribution present. This distribution is critical, because any time one of the crops is known to be exported twice, then no other crop can be exported twice. Since some of the rules result in a crop being exported twice, this distribution comes up in many of the questions. As we analyze the rules, we will discuss how each rule affects the distribution, where applicable.

Note that we have chosen the nations as the base because they establish a fixed 2-2-2 spread; if we chose the crops as the base, then we would have to deal with the uncertainty of which crop is doubled in our diagram.

Rule #1. This is the least complex of the four rules, and the correct diagram is:

This rule does not allow us to make any powerful inferences, but can infer that if O is the crop exported twice, then W would have to be exported by the country that does not export O; if W is the crop exported twice, then O would have to be exported by the country that does not export W.

Rule #2. This can be a tricky rule to diagram if you are not familiar with the phrasing used by the test makers. The phrase "if but only if" is identical to the phrase "if and only if," which produces a double-arrow diagram. The proper diagram for "if but only if" is also a double arrow:

$$X_S \longleftrightarrow Y_S$$

Functionally, this rule means that if X exports S, then Y exports S; and if Y exports S, then X exports S.

A horizontal block could be used to show this relationship, but a block would not show the conditional aspect of this rule, which is that if one of the two countries exports S, then the other must do so as well (a block might imply to someone that both countries must always export S, which is not true).

From a numerical standpoint, this is a powerful rule because if either X or Y exports S, then the other country must do so as well, and that means that S would be the one and only crop that is exported twice. The other four crops would then be exported a single time.

We can also infer that if either X or Y exports S, then Z cannot export S:

$$X_S \longleftrightarrow\hspace{-0.7em}\vert\hspace{0.7em} Z_S$$

and

$$Y_S \longleftrightarrow\hspace{-0.7em}\vert\hspace{0.7em} Z_S$$

This occurs because if once X or Y exports S, then the other must also export S, and if Z also attempts to export S, then each nation would export S. With all three nations exporting S, the Numerical Distribution is violated (S would occupy three of the six available exportation slots, leaving an insufficient number of spaces to export each of O, R, T, and W).

Rule #3. This is a conditional rule with two necessary conditions:

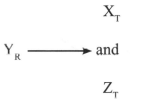

$$X_T$$
$$Y_R \longrightarrow \text{and}$$
$$Z_T$$

Like the previous rule, this rule also results in one of the crops being exported twice, in this case T. So, the immediate inference we can draw is that the second and third rules pose a conflict because both result in different crops being exported twice, and if one rule is enacted, then the other one cannot be enacted:

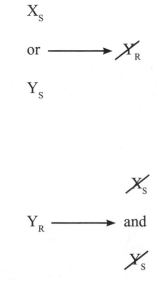

$$X_S$$
$$\text{or} \longrightarrow \cancel{X_R}$$
$$Y_S$$

and

$$\cancel{X_S}$$
$$Y_R \longrightarrow \text{and}$$
$$\cancel{Y_S}$$

The two diagrams one the previous page, although perfectly accurate, are a bit unwieldy. A simplified representation would be these two double-not arrow diagrams:

$$Y_R \longleftrightarrow X_S$$

and

$$Y_R \longleftrightarrow Y_S$$

The inferences above are easily missed, so let us cover the reasoning behind them again:

> The game scenario establishes that the five exported crops must fill a total of six exportation slots (two per nation). Thus, exactly one of the crops must be exported twice (this balances the crops to export slots at six to six, eliminating the underfunded aspect of the game). Because only one crop can be exported twice, any rule that results in a crop being exported twice automatically prohibits any other rule from being enacted that results in a crop being exported twice. Since both the second and third rules result in different crops being exported twice, those two rules cannot both occur in a viable solution to the game. Therefore, if one of those two rules occurs, the other will not occur. This can be directly stated as if X or Y exports S (the second rule), then Y cannot export R (the sufficient condition of the third rule), and if Y exports R (the sufficient condition of the third rule), then neither X nor Y cannot export S.

Rule #4. This rule can be diagrammed as:

$$Z \longrightarrow \cancel{X}$$

The contrapositive is:

$$Y \longrightarrow \cancel{Z}$$

The combination of those two diagrams creates a double-not arrow relationship, where Y and Z cannot have any exports in common:

$$Y \longleftrightarrow Z$$

However, if you diagram this relationship off to the side, you might forget the rule, so a better approach is to diagram the rule internally by placing it right into the main diagram:

O R S T W [5]

$$X \qquad Y \longleftrightarrow Z$$

The other rules and inferences can be diagrammed on the side, creating the following master setup:

O R S T W [5]

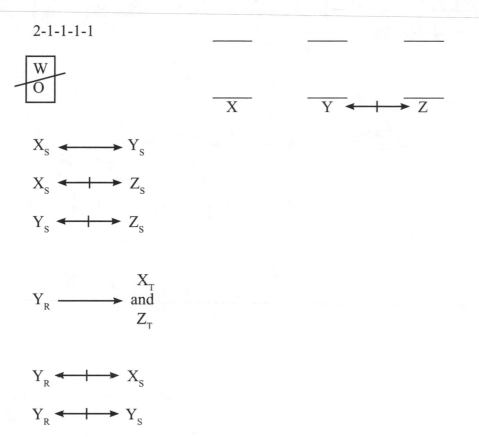

2-1-1-1-1

Using the setup above and keeping the Numerical Distribution firmly in mind, we are ready to attack the questions.

Question #18: Global, Could Be True, List. The correct answer choice is (A)

To attack this List question apply the rules in the following order: Rule #1, Rule #4, Rule #2, Rule #3.

Answer choice (A): This is the correct answer choice.

Answer choice (B): This answer choice violates the third rule because Y exports R, but Z does not export T.

Answer choice (C): This answer choice violates the first rule because X exports both O and W.

Answer choice (D): This answer choice violates the fourth rule because Y and Z both export O.

Answer choice (E): This answer choice violates the second rule because X exports S, but Y does not export S.

Question #19: Local, Could Be True. The correct answer choice is (A)

The question stem indicates that X exports S and T, so from the second rule since X exports S then Y must also export S as well (and Z cannot export S):

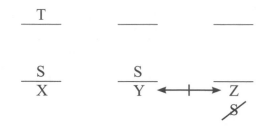

Because S is now exported by two countries, we know that every other crop is exported just once. This means that Y cannot export R, as discussed in the analysis of rule #3:

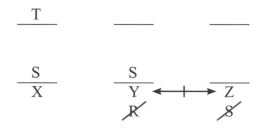

Answer choice (A): This is the correct answer choice. It is proven by the following hypothetical:

Answer choice (B): This answer choice cannot be true, and is therefore incorrect. If Y exports R, then X and Z would have to export T. This results in a scenario where S is exported twice, T is exported twice, R is exported once, and then there is not sufficient space to export both O and W.

Answer choice (C): If Y exports T, then in this question both X and Y export S and T. In somewhat of a similar manner as answer choice (B), this results in a scenario where S is exported twice and T is exported twice, and then there is not sufficient space to export all three of O, R and W. Thus, this answer is incorrect.

Answer choice (D): This answer choice is incorrect for two reasons. First, if Z exports S, then both Y and Z would export S, a violation of the last rule. Second, if Z exports S, then X, Y, and Z each export S, a violation of the numerical possibilities within the game.

Answer choice (E): If Z exports T, then in this question X and Y both export S, and X and Z both export T. Similar to answer choices (C), this results in a scenario where S is exported twice and T is exported twice, and then there is not sufficient space to export all three of O, R and W. Thus, this answer is incorrect.

Note that every single wrong answer choice plays upon the limitations created by the Numerical Distribution.

Question #20: Local, Must Be True. The correct answer choice is (E)

This is the most difficult question of the game. The question stem indicates that Z exports T and W, and as a consequence of the fourth rule, we can immediately infer that Y does not export T and W:

With nation Z's exports fully assigned, crops O, R, and S must be exported by X and Y. Of course, from the second rule we know that when X or Y exports S, then the other must also export S, and we can then infer that S is exported by both:

O and R are the two remaining crops to be assigned. Because of the third rule, however, we can infer that R cannot be exported by Y because if R was exported by Y, we could not meet the condition of nations X and Z both exporting T. Thus, X must export R, and Y must export O:

This is the only solution to this question, and thus answer choice (E) is the correct answer.

The inference above that X and Y must export S is not easy to see, especially under the time pressure of the test. If you did not see the inferences above, you can still solve this problem effectively by using hypotheticals. The best approach for creating hypotheticals in this question would be to attack Y because we already have two Not Laws on Y. Because Y cannot export T or W, there are only three crops—O, R, and S—available for Y to export. Making hypotheticals that use two of these three crops for Y will quickly and effectively help you see why crop S must be exported by Y.

Answer choices (A), (B), (C), and (D): As shown in the diagram above, none of the statements in these answer choices can be true.

Question #21: Global, Cannot Be True. The correct answer choice is (C)

As mentioned in the discussion of Rule #2, when X or Y exports S, then Z cannot export S. Let us revisit the reasoning behind this inference, as it applies to this question stem:

> If both X and Z export S, then from the second rule we know Y will also export S. Thus, each nation would export S. This assignment would occupy three of the six available exportation slots, leaving an insufficient number of spaces available to export each of O, R, T, and W.

Answer choices (A), (B), (D), and (E): These answer choices are incorrect because X and Z can both export each listed crop.

Answer choice (C): This is the correct answer choice.

Question #22: Global, Cannot Be True. The correct answer choice is (C)

Given that three of the rules directly reference Y, it is not surprising that there is a pair of crops that Y cannot export. And, as you might expect, the reasoning behind the inference centers on the way these rules interact with the Numerical Distribution.

To initially attack this question, most students link the second and third rules together and immediately look for R and S as the answer. This is exactly the right approach, because if Y exports R and S, then the Numerical Distribution would be violated since S would be exported twice (from the second rule) and T would be exported twice (from the third rule). However, the test makers choose not to use R and S as the answer to this problem.

Focusing on R and S is not a mistake, and the role played by R ultimately leads to the correct answer. When Y exports R we know from the third rule that both X and Z must export T. Thus, if Y tried to export T in addition to R, the result would be a violation of the Numerical Distribution because all three nations would export T. Thus, Y cannot export both R and T, and answer choice (C) is correct. Note that the reasoning behind this question is very similar to that in question #21, another Global, Cannot Be True question.

If you did not see the reasoning path behind the correct answer, remember that you can always rely on hypotheticals to attack and eliminate answers. This approach works perfectly on a question such as this one, where you will immediately see why a certain pair of answers would or would not work.

If you have very little time to solve this problem, one way to make an informed guess would be to consider each of the five answers by their similarities to other answer choices. For example, O and W are functionally interchangeable variables in this game. Answer choices (A) and (D), which pair R with O and W, respectively, are therefore very similar in the results they produce and are less likely to be correct. The same reasoning holds for answer choices (B) and (E), which pair S with O and W, respectively. Remember, the correct answer to any LSAT problem must be wholly unique, and if two answer choices are functionally identical, then both answers are incorrect. Using this reasoning, we can eliminate the four incorrect answer choices in this problem, leaving only answer choice (C).

Answer choices (A) and (D): These two answers can be eliminated by the following hypothetical, which uses a dual-option to show how R and either O or W can be exported by Y without causing a problem. To eliminate (A), simply consider the scenario as if Y exported O and R; to eliminate (D), consider the scenario in reverse, as if Y exported W and R.

Answer choices (B) and (E): These two answers can be eliminated by the following hypothetical, which uses a dual-option to show how S and either O or W can be exported by Y without causing a problem. To eliminate (B), simply consider the scenario as if Y exported S and O; to eliminate (E), consider the scenario in reverse, as if Y exported S and W.

$$\underline{\text{W/O}} \qquad \underline{\text{O/W}} \qquad \underline{\text{T}}$$

$$\frac{S}{X} \qquad \frac{S}{Y} \longleftarrow \mid \longrightarrow \frac{R}{Z}$$

Answer choice (C): This is the correct answer choice. If Y exports both R and T, then all three nations would export T, violating the Numerical Distribution and not leaving sufficient room to export the other three crops.

Chapter Five: Grouping/ Linear Combination Games

Working with the Combination of Major Principles

Grouping and linearity are the two fundamental principles test makers use to form the Logic Games section, and typically at least 75% of the games in each section feature at least one of these ideas. It is not surprising, therefore, to see a number of games that combine these ideas.

Because Chapters Two, Three, and Four covered the basic principles of linearity and grouping, an extensive review of those ideas is unnecessary. However, when attacking games that combine these principles, keep in mind this basic Hierarchy of Game Power™:

Grouping

↓

Linearity

The Hierarchy of Game Power will be revisited in Chapter Eight in the Numerical Distribution section. At that time the Hierarchy will be expanded to include numerical ideas.

The diagram above indicates that the higher term dominates the lower term. When you set up a game, always consider the dominant term first. Because a group must be established before the members of that group can be lined up, always examine the grouping elements first and then examine the linear elements. Although this may seem like a logical recommendation, students often tend to gravitate towards examining linearity first because they often feel most comfortable with that concept. Naturally, this hierarchy can also be seen in real life:

> Suppose that you are offered six free Super Bowl tickets. Your first reaction wouldn't be to start putting people in the first seat, or sixth seat, etc. Instead, you would first select the group of six people to attend the game and then, once at the game, consider how to line up the individuals in the seats.

This example will also be expanded in Chapter Eight.

Typically, in Grouping/Linear combination games an Unbalanced: Overloaded set of variables must be narrowed down and then the remaining variables must be placed into a diagram that has a linear element. For example, consider the following:

> A theater director must select exactly seven of nine plays to be presented over seven consecutive months, January through July.

The first point of emphasis will be to watch the grouping rules, especially since the nine-into-seven relationship leaves only two "extra" plays to be presented. If any two plays are knocked out by the rules then each of the remaining seven plays must be presented. When a play is known to be presented—whether from the rules or from a question—first examine how that affects the plays still under consideration.

The second point of emphasis will be to consider how the linear rules affect the plays being presented. Although in each case it may be impossible to determine every play presented, the rules will undoubtedly allow for linear inferences irrespective of the grouping element.

Thus, we can distill the correct approach to these games into two steps:

1. Focus on the Grouping aspect of the game and determine if any variables must be selected and which variables are the most powerful. In any question, first attempt to determine the group of variables that must be selected.

2. In each question, once you have isolated as many of the variables in use as possible, next focus on the ordering rules and use your knowledge of Linear games to manipulate the rules, make inferences, and solve the questions.

Final Pregame Note

More games featuring grouping will appear in Chapter Eight.

Because these games are a combination of the Grouping and Linear games discussed in the previous chapters, there are only two examples provided.

Please make sure to read the explanations carefully as they will give you a true sense of how to best attack each game, and the explanations always include points that expand the discussion given above.

If you would like to test yourself under timed conditions, you should give yourself 8 minutes and 45 seconds for each game. Good luck on the games!

A soloist will play six different guitar concertos, exactly one each Sunday for six consecutive weeks. Two concertos will be selected from among three concertos by Giuliani—H, J, and K; two from among four concertos by Rodrigo—M, N, O, and P; and two from among three concertos by Vivaldi—X, Y, and Z. The following conditions apply without exception:

If N is selected, then J is also selected.

If M is selected, then neither J nor O can be selected.

If X is selected, then neither Z nor P can be selected.

If both J and O are selected, then J is played at some time before O.

X cannot be played on the fifth Sunday unless one of Rodrigo's concertos is played on the first Sunday.

19. Which one of the following is an acceptable selection of concertos that the soloist could play on the first through the sixth Sunday?

	1	2	3	4	5	6
(A)	H	Z	M	N	Y	K
(B)	K	J	Y	O	Z	N
(C)	K	Y	P	J	Z	M
(D)	P	Y	J	11	X	O
(E)	X	N	K	O	J	Z

20. If the six concertos to be played are J, K, N, O, Y, and Z and if N is to be played on the first Sunday, then which one of the following concertos CANNOT be played on the second Sunday?

(A) J
(B) K
(C) O
(D) Y
(E) Z

21. If J, O, and Y are the first three concertos to be played, not necessarily in the order given, which one of the following is a concerto that CANNOT be played on the fifth Sunday?

(A) H
(B) K
(C) N
(D) P
(E) X

22. If O is selected for the first Sunday, which one of the following is a concerto that must also be selected?

(A) J
(B) K
(C) M
(D) N
(E) X

23. Which one of the following is a concerto that must be selected?

(A) J
(B) K
(C) O
(D) Y
(E) Z

24. Which one of the following is a concerto that CANNOT be selected together with N?

(A) M
(B) O
(C) P
(D) X
(E) Z

Since the concertos from each composer produce the variables that are used in the linear setup, they are the logical starting point for our analysis. Each composer supplies two concertos, and the groups are as follows:

Giuliani: H, J, K   _____ _____
Rodrigo: M, N, O, P   _____ _____
Vivaldi: X, Y, Z   _____ _____

Of the three groups, Giuliani and Vivaldi are the most restricted, since they only have three concertos to fill the required two selections per composer. Thus, if any one concerto is unavailable from either the Giuliani or Vivaldi group, then the other two concertos must be selected. In a situation such as this, it is always best to immediately check the rules for any negative grouping rules among the members of the restricted groups. The third rule contains such a relationship:

$$X \longleftrightarrow\!\!\!| \longrightarrow Z$$

Since X and Z can never be selected together, we can Hurdle the Uncertainty and infer that Y must be selected from Vivaldi's group:

Y   X\Z

The scenario above, three variables for two spaces, is perhaps the most common inference scenario that appears in Grouping games. Any negative grouping rule or any question stem that knocks out one of the three variables leads to the inference that some other variable must be selected. In the above scenario, the rule involving X and Z effectively knocks one of those two variables out of the selection pool, forcing Y to be selected. One of the best examples of this type of inference occurred in a game from the 1980s. In that game, seven basketball players were selected for five starting spots. Clearly, this leaves only two extra variables in the selection pool. However, as the rules unfold it turns out that two separate pairs of variables could not be selected together, in each case effectively reducing the candidate pool by one player. Since this occurred twice, it had to be that the three players not involved in the negative grouping rules were selected, a classic Hurdle the Uncertainties situation:

R S T U V W X [7]

U $\longleftrightarrow\!\!\!| \longrightarrow$ S   R   T   X   U/S   W/V
                                         5 Players

W $\longleftrightarrow\!\!\!| \longrightarrow$ V

Of course, a similar scenario can be produced with a wide variety of numerical combinations, four candidates for three spaces, eight candidates for six spaces, etc. It is also important to note that many questions introduce "if" statements that ultimately result in limited scenarios, such as three candidates for two spaces or four candidates for three spaces. The point is that any selection group that is limited in size relative to the number of members that must be selected will probably yield an important inference, and you must always watch for situations such as these in games. In the guitar concerto game under consideration, in Question #23 we benefit directly from our inference that Y must always be selected. Continuing with the setup of the game, we arrive at the following representation of the rules:

A combination of the first and second rules produces the following additional deduction:

$$N \longleftrightarrow M$$

This deduction provides the answer to Question #24. There are also several other, less important inferences that can be made. For example, according to the second rule, when M is selected, J and O cannot be selected. Via the contrapositive, when J is not selected then N cannot be selected. From Rodrigo's group then, when M is selected, P is also selected:

$$M \longrightarrow P$$

And since J is not selected, H and K must be selected from Giuliani's group:

$$M \longrightarrow P, H, K$$

However, when P is selected, then X is not selected, and thus from Vivaldi's group Y and Z must be selected:

$$M \longrightarrow P, H, K, Y, Z$$

So, if M is selected, the other five positions are automatically filled. A similar situation arises with X. When X is selected, Z and P are not selected. Since P is not selected, M cannot be selected (see the inference above). Since both M and P are not selected, N and O must be selected from Rodrigo's group. Of course, Y is always selected:

$$X \longrightarrow Y, N, O$$

According to the first rule, if N is selected, then J must be selected:

$$X \longrightarrow Y, N, O, J$$

These last two major inferences involving M and X are helpful, but they are not essential to answering the questions in the game. We discuss them here simply to indicate the type of inferences that can follow from restricted situations. The only other rule of note is the last rule, which states that if X is played on the fifth Sunday then one of Rodrigo's concertos must be played on the first Sunday. This rule is noteworthy because it is so specific. It should be easy to track while answering the questions, because it relies so heavily on two designated spaces.

Question #19: Global, Could Be True, List. The correct answer choice is (B)

This List question is easily answered by a systematic application of the rules. Answer choice (B) is correct. Answer choice (A) is incorrect because N is selected but J is not selected. Answer choice (C) is incorrect because both M and J are selected. Answer choice (D) is incorrect because both X and P are selected. Answer choice (E) is incorrect because J and O are both selected yet O is played before J.

Question #20: Local, Cannot Be True. The correct answer choice is (C)

This question provides a nice test of your linkage ability. Since the six variables are selected by the question stem, only the last two rules are applicable (both deal with the ordering of the variables). Since N (a concerto by Rodrigo) is to be played on the first Sunday, the conditions for the last rule (X on the fifth Sunday) are satisfied and this rule is not likely to play a role in answering the questions. However, since both J and O have been selected, the rule that states that J must be played before O is still in force. Since N will be played on the first Sunday, the sequencing relationship between J and O yields the Not Laws that J cannot be played on the sixth Sunday and O cannot be played on the second Sunday. Accordingly, answer choice (C) is correct.

Question #21: Local, Cannot Be True. The correct answer choice is (E)

The linkage chain in this question should be obvious. The question stem specifically refers to the fifth Sunday, a reference that also appears in the last rule. For X to play on the fifth Sunday, one of Rodrigo's concertos must be played on the first Sunday. According to the question stem, the only Rodrigo concerto that could be played on the first Sunday is O, but since J and O have both been selected, their sequencing relationship precludes O from being played on the first Sunday. It follows that X cannot be played on the fifth Sunday and thus answer choice (E) is correct.

Question #22: Local, Must Be True. The correct answer choice is (B)

If O is selected for the first Sunday, according to the sequencing rule involving J, J cannot be selected, and answer choice (A) is incorrect. Since J cannot be selected, the grouping restrictions come into play and H and K must be selected to represent Giuliani. Answer choice (B) is thus correct.

Question #23: Global, Must Be True. The correct answer choice is (D)

As previously discussed, answer choice (D) is correct.

Question #24: Global, Cannot Be True. The correct answer choice is (A)

As previously discussed, by combining the first two rules, we can infer that answer choice (A) is correct.

Perhaps the most important lesson of this game is to be mindful of the candidate restrictions in Grouping games. When some variables must be selected from a limited pool of candidates, invariably some powerful inferences will arise during the game, whether at the outset or during the questions.

In order to separate the game from its answer key and explanations,
the second game is on the next page.

An art teacher will schedule exactly six of eight lectures—fresco, history, lithography, naturalism, oils, pastels, sculpture, and watercolors—for three days—1, 2, and 3. There will be exactly two lectures each day—morning and afternoon. Scheduling is governed by the following conditions:

Day 2 is the only day for which oils can be scheduled.

Neither sculpture nor watercolors can be scheduled for the afternoon.

Neither oils nor pastels can be scheduled for the same day as lithography.

If pastels is scheduled for day 1 or day 2, then the lectures scheduled for the day immediately following pastels must be fresco and history, not necessarily in that order.

12. Which one of the following is an acceptable schedule of lectures for days 1, 2, and 3, respectively?

(A) Morning: lithography, history, sculpture
     Afternoon: pastels, fresco, naturalism
(B) Morning: naturalism, oils, fresco
     Afternoon: lithography, pastels, history
(C) Morning: oils, history, naturalism
     Afternoon: pastels, fresco, lithography
(D) Morning: sculpture, lithography, naturalism
     Afternoon: watercolors, fresco, pastels
(E) Morning: sculpture, pastels, fresco
     Afternoon: lithography, history, naturalism

13. If lithography and fresco are scheduled for the afternoons of day 2 and day 3, respectively, which one of the following is a lecture that could be scheduled for the afternoon of day 1?

(A) history
(B) oils
(C) pastels
(D) sculpture
(E) watercolors

14. If lithography and history are scheduled for the mornings of day 2 and day 3, respectively, which one of the following lectures could be scheduled for the morning of day 1?

(A) fresco
(B) naturalism
(C) oils
(D) pastels
(E) sculpture

15. If oils and lithography are scheduled for the mornings of day 2 and day 3, respectively, which one of the following CANNOT be scheduled for any day?

(A) fresco
(B) history
(C) naturalism
(D) pastels
(E) sculpture

16. If neither fresco nor naturalism is scheduled for any day, which one of the following must be scheduled for day 1?

(A) history
(B) lithography
(C) oils
(D) pastels
(E) sculpture

17. If the lectures scheduled for the mornings are fresco, history, and lithography, not necessarily in that order, which one of the following could be true?

(A) Lithography is scheduled for day 3
(B) Naturalism is scheduled for day 2.
(C) Fresco is scheduled for the same day as naturalism.
(D) History is scheduled for the same day as naturalism.
(E) History is scheduled for the same day as oils.

This Grouping/Linear combination game features eight lectures filling six spaces, and thus whenever two lectures are eliminated from the scheduling, the remaining six lectures must be scheduled. Questions #16 and #17 are excellent examples of this principle in action. The morning and afternoon variable sets also add an advanced linear element to the game, and consequently the game is more difficult than game #1 in this section. The setup to the game is as follows:

Since the three days contain an inherent sense of order, they are chosen as the base and the morning and afternoon variable sets are stacked on top. "Morning" and "afternoon" have been abbreviated as AM and PM because they are too time-consuming to write out. It makes no difference whether your diagram has the AM set as the top row or as the bottom row.

Because of the vertical component, the OL and PL rules are written in block form. For convenience L has been placed on the bottom in both rules, but it is essential to understand that O and L (and P and L) can never be scheduled for the same day, regardless of which one is in the AM or PM. If this confuses you, each rule can be written out both ways for clarity:

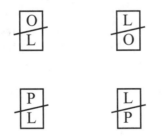

Note also that the first rule has not been written out. Instead of showing that O could go on day 2 (O should not be placed on day 2 on the diagram because we cannot be sure O is one of the six scheduled lectures), it is preferable to show that O cannot go on day 1 and day 3. Superior representations always reflect the absolutes—what must occur and what cannot occur. In examining the diagram it is also important to note that the O Not Laws on day 1 and day 3 apply to both the AM and PM. They can be placed on each row for each day if you feel that is necessary.

The last rule is difficult to diagram concisely. There are two scenarios under the rule: when P is scheduled for day 1, then F and H are scheduled for day 2, and when P is scheduled for day 2 then F and H are scheduled for day 3. In the form we have chosen, we have combined the two possibilities and represented them through the "1, 2" and "2, 3" subscripts. If you find this confusing, write out each scenario separately. This rule is especially important because it needs a lot of space. Also, do not forget to take the contrapositive of the rule: if any variable other than F or H is scheduled for day 2, then P cannot be scheduled for day 1, and if any variable other than F or H is scheduled for day 3, then P cannot be scheduled for day 2. This important inference is tested.

Because each appears in two rules, O and P are the key variables in the game and you must always be aware of them. In contrast to O and P, N is a random and relatively weak variable. Remember that in games with a large number of variables—say 9 or 10—randoms are relatively weak, and that in games with few variables—5 or 6—randoms are stronger and need to be given more consideration.

Finally, it is notable that this game does not contain any extremely deep inferences. There are some obvious inferences—for example, if L is scheduled for day 2, then O cannot be scheduled at all—but nothing truly challenging. This may in part explain why five of the six questions are local: to create challenging situations the test makers had to supply local conditions to create limitation. Some games with deep inferences or limited possibilities have a large number of global questions to test your knowledge of the inferences. The first game from the June 1999 LSAT is a good example (only several possibilities exist and consequently all five questions are global).

Question #12: Global, Could Be True, List. The correct answer choice is (B)

Remember to apply the simplest and most visually powerful rules first. In this case that happens to be the order in which the rules are presented. The first rule eliminates answer choice (C). The second rule eliminates answer choice (D). The third rule eliminates answer choice (A). And the fourth rule eliminates answer choice (E). Answer choice (B) is thus correct.

Question #13: Local, Could Be True. The correct answer choice is (A)

Irrespective of the Local conditions, answer choices (B), (D), and (E) can be eliminated by the PM and day 1 Not Laws. With the answers narrowed to (A) and (C), we can consider the Local condition in the question stem. The stem produces the following mini-diagram next to the question:

$$
\begin{array}{cccc}
\text{PM} & \underline{} & \underline{\text{L}} & \underline{\text{F}} \\
\text{AM} & \underline{} & \underline{} & \underline{} \\
 & 1 & 2 & 3
\end{array}
$$

Note that in doing the question on the test, we would not take the time to write out AM, PM, 1, 2, and 3.

This setup automatically rules out P's being scheduled on day 1, since if P is scheduled for day 1, then both F and H have to be scheduled for day 2. Since F is already scheduled for day 3, answer choice (C) can be eliminated. Answer choice (A) is therefore correct.

Question #14: Local, Could Be True. The correct answer choice is (E)

Irrespective of the Local conditions, answer choice (C) can be eliminated by applying the Not Laws. The conditions produce the following diagram:

$$\frac{\quad}{\not{\emptyset}} \quad \frac{L}{\not{\emptyset}} \quad \frac{H}{\not{\emptyset}}$$

Once L is scheduled for day 2, O cannot be scheduled for day 2, and, consequently O cannot be scheduled for any of the days. The other lecture affected by the local conditions is P. As in question #2, P cannot be scheduled on day 1, since if P is scheduled for day 1 then both F and H have to be scheduled for day 2. Since H is already scheduled for day 3, answer choice (D) can be eliminated.

There are now three answer choices remaining: F, N, and S. Forced to guess with just the information at hand, you might suspect that S could be scheduled for the morning of day 1 because S is a variable already confined to the morning spaces. Although answer choice (E) is correct, it is important to understand why both answer choices (A) and (B) are incorrect. Consider that for the three afternoon spaces there are initially eight lectures: F, H, L, N, O, P, S, and W. From the second rule both S and W cannot lecture in the afternoon, so the pool is now down to six: F, H, L, N, O, and P. The conditions in the question place L and H in the morning and eliminate O from scheduling, and so the candidate pool is now three: F, N, and P. Thus, F, N, and P must be the three afternoon lectures in this question. If any of the three is placed in a morning space then there would not be enough lectures for the afternoon. **This illustrates a critical grouping concept: it is as important to evaluate the variables left for consideration as it is to evaluate the variables already placed.**

Question #15: Local, Cannot Be True. The correct answer choice is (D)

Since L is scheduled for day 3, P cannot be scheduled for day 2 (because of the contrapositive of the last rule) or day 3 (because of the third rule). Since O is scheduled for day 2, again because of the second rule, P cannot be scheduled for day 1. It follows that answer choice (D) is correct.

Question #16: Local, Must Be True. The correct answer choice is (B)

Irrespective of the Local conditions, answer choice (C) can be eliminated by applying the Not Laws.

Since neither F nor N is scheduled, it follows that H, L, O, P, S, and W must be scheduled. And since F is not scheduled, P cannot be scheduled for day 1 or day 2 (the contrapositive of the final rule). Consequently P must be scheduled for day 3 and thus answer choice (D) is incorrect. Since O is scheduled for day 2 and P is scheduled for day 3, the third rule can be applied, and it follows that since L cannot be scheduled with O or P, then L must be scheduled for day 1. Thus, answer choice (B) is correct.

Question #17: Local, Could Be True. The correct answer choice is (E)

Since F, H, and L are scheduled for the three morning slots, the pool of afternoon lectures is S, W, N, O, and P. However, because S and W cannot be scheduled in the afternoon, only N, O, and P can be scheduled for the afternoon slots. Accordingly, O must be scheduled for day 2, P must be scheduled for day 3 (apply the last rule!), and thus N is scheduled for day 1. Since O and P are scheduled for days 2 and 3 respectively, L must be scheduled for day 1. F and H represent a dual-option on the mornings of days 2 and 3:

$$
\begin{array}{cccc}
\text{PM} & \underline{\text{N}} & \underline{\text{O}} & \underline{\text{P}} \\
\text{AM} & \underline{\text{L}} & \underline{\text{H/F}} & \underline{\text{F/H}} \\
 & 1 & 2 & 3
\end{array}
$$

Answer choice (E) is therefore correct.

CHAPTER SIX: PURE SEQUENCING GAMES

Pure Sequencing Games

Pure Sequencing games use the sequencing principles introduced in Chapter Two. Although the sequences usually overlay a linear scenario, the game is called *Pure Sequencing* because all of the rules are sequential in nature, and thus your primary task is tracking the relative positions of the variables.

Linear games with sequencing rules appear very frequently, so you must have the ability to handle these types of rules. Games based solely on sequencing rules, such as the ones in this chapter, have appeared less frequently, but at times the test makers have presented these games with high frequency. Consider the history of Pure Sequencing games thus far on the modern LSAT (June 1991 to the present):

1. Between June 1991 and February 1994, five different LSATs contained a Pure Sequencing game.

2. Between June 1994 and December 1998, no released LSAT contained a Sequencing game (This time lapse between the appearances of Pure Sequencing games is not unprecedented: there was a three-year gap in the appearance of Pure Sequencing between the October 1983 LSAT and the June 1986 LSAT.).

3. From February 1999 to the present, Pure Sequencing games have appeared over ten times. The September 2007 LSAT actually contained two Pure Sequencing games, meaning that games of this type comprised 50% of the Logic Games section of that exam.

Thus, although Sequencing games go in and out of favor with the test makers, you should fully master the principles presented on the following pages because there is an extremely high probability that a future LSAT will contain a Pure Sequencing game, and it is certain that future Linear games will contain sequencing elements.

Pure Sequencing Diagramming Guidelines

Linear games contain rules that fix the position of variables, such as "P must be third."

Sequencing games contain rules that place variables in relative positions.

Pure Sequencing games involve the ranking or ordering of variables. The key to recognizing a Pure Sequencing game is that the relationships among the variables are relative and not precisely fixed. For example, a rule might state, "Lopez's salary is greater than Nassar's salary." From this rule, it is known only that Lopez makes more than Nassar, but not how much more. Lopez could make just a dollar more than Nassar, or thousands of dollars more than Nassar. There is also no indication of where they stand on the salary scale: Lopez could be making a $100,000 a year or a $100 a year. This uncertainty about the specifics of each relationship is inherent in Sequencing games and is the focus of the questions. In each game you must attempt to determine what must be true, and at the same time avoid making any unwarranted assumptions. Use the following guidelines to create ideal Pure Sequencing setups:

1. Use either "greater than" signs (>) or "less than" signs (<) to represent relative relationships, and always make sure that the signs are of the same type and direction.

    Example: Petra is faster than Tai and slower than Sara.

    $$S > P > T$$

    In the context of sequencing, the "greater than" sign simply means "to the left of." Thus, "S > P" indicates that S is to the left of P on the diagram. There is no implied numerical value or mathematical value.

2. Keep in mind that unless otherwise ruled out by the game scenario, variables can be equal. If equality is part of a relationship in a sequencing game, expect to be tested on that relationship at least once during the course of the game.

    Example: Jahru is not faster than Miles.

    $$M \geq J$$

3. Search for variables that appear in more than one rule and link them together in order to build the most complete chain sequence.

    Example: Jahru is not faster than Miles.
    Miles is slower than Noguchi.

    $$N > M \geq J$$

4. Always test the limits of the game by checking the first and last positions.

   Example: Who could be fastest and who could be slowest?

   This process is critical because it helps you establish the range of possibilities at the endpoints, and thus within the game as a whole.

5. Use Multi-Branched Verticals to represent variables whose relationship is uncertain.

   Double Branched Vertical Example: Tai is faster than both Vernon and Wendy.

```
                V
        T > - - - - - -
                W
```

Branched Verticals were introduced in Chapter Two during the Linear games discussion.

The dotted line visually separates V and W into two separate "branches." Beyond the fact that V and W are both slower than T, the variables in each branch are completely unrelated to each other. Thus, V or W could be slowest, or both could be equally slow. If the rules stipulate that there can be no ties, then the possibility of V and W being equally slow would be eliminated.

Double Branched Vertical Example: Vernon and Wendy are both faster than Tai.

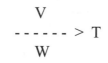

```
        V
  - - - - - - > T
        W
```

V and W are both faster than T, but no relationship can be inferred between V and W. V could be fastest, W could be fastest, or they could be equally fast.

Triple Branched Vertical Example: Vernon, Wendy, and Zazi are all faster than Tai.

V, W, and Z are each faster than T, but again the variables in each branch are completely unrelated to each other. Thus, V could be fastest, W could be fastest, or Z could be fastest. Or, all three could be equally fast.

6. If your diagram becomes too complex to use "greater than" or "less than" signs, use arrows to clarify the relationship between variables. The arrows have the same meaning as the "greater than" or "less than" signs, but they can represent the same idea more cleanly. Note that the arrow in this context is not conditional.

    Example: Paula is faster than Tai and slower than Sara.
    Noguchi is slower than Tai.
    Jahru is not faster than Miles.
    Miles is slower than Noguchi.

$$S > P > T > N > M \geq J$$

    If Fuad > Tai, you can diagram the new rule as:

$$S > P > T > N > M \geq J$$

F is now in a second branch and no assumption can be made about the relationship between F and S or F and P.

Arrows are also particularly good at handling this thorny rule configuration:

    Example: A is heavier than B and lighter than C.
    B is heavier than D, and D is heavier than E.
    F is heavier than B.
    G is lighter than F

The dotted line separator can be used with the arrow. The meaning is the same as with the "greater than" signs.

Most students handle the first two rules fairly easily, and create a diagram that appears as follows:

$$C > A > B > D > E$$

However, the third and fourth rules present a problem because they connect to B, which is in the middle of the chain sequence. Handling one of the rules with an arrow is easy, but so is handling both rules:

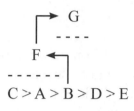

$$C > A > B > D > E$$

The diagram above indicates that F "floats" relative to B, and that G "floats" relative to F. Yes, this is a tougher diagram form to handle, but the test makers typically construct games with the intention of making the setup challenging. How you handle the rules will have a direct effect on your success on the game.

7. Watch for rules that create two separate, mutually exclusive possibilities. If you encounter such a rule, you must diagram both chain possibilities.

    Example: C is faster than D, or else D is faster than C, but not both.

    This rule allows for only two outcomes, each of which excludes the other:

    $$C > D$$
    or
    $$D > C$$

    Unless one of the other rules in the game eliminates one of the two possibilities, you must proceed as if the game itself has two branches, and create a diagram for each branch—one built around C > D, and one built around D > C.

8. Track the appearance of outside restrictions or occurrences by circling the affected variable.

Example: Vernon, Wendy, and Zazi are all faster than Tai.
            Wendy cannot be fastest, and there are no ties.

$$V$$
$$------$$
$$(W) \quad > T$$
$$------$$
$$Z$$

If the variables above are the only four in the game, then the only possibilities for Wendy are to be second or third. However, showing this within the diagram is difficult (in part because although at least one of V or Z is faster than W, both do not have to be faster). In order to help remember that W has a special restriction, circle W as indicated on the diagram above.

9. The key to superior performance on sequencing games is to avoid making unwarranted assumptions. Physical proximity within the diagram does not necessarily indicate an actual relationship; for example, R may be ahead of W on the diagram, but do not assume that R must be ahead of W in terms of the game. Consider the following example:

$$R > V$$
$$--------- > T$$
$$W$$

In this diagram, R appears to be physically ahead of W, but in fact W could be ahead of R. Since R and W are part of two separate branches, their relationship is unknown; R could be faster than W, R and W could be equally fast, or W could be faster then R. The same possibilities hold true for V and W.

In determining relationships between variables, do not let physical proximity influence your evaluation. Use only the rules of the game and your own diagram to establish the truth of each relationship.

Use the Pure Sequencing Diagramming Guidelines to set up sequencing chains for each of the following items. The rules may yield more than one chain per item. *Answers on Page 288*

1. Rules: E is taller than F.
              E is shorter than D.
              D is shorter than B and C.
              A is taller than B.

   A. Which of the variables in the chain could be tallest?

   B. Which of the variables in the chain could be shortest?

2. Rules: R and S are heavier than T.
              V is heavier than W and X.
              U is lighter than X.

   A. Which of the variables could be heaviest?

   B. Which of the variables could be lightest?

3. Rules: F is larger than G and H.
                  G is larger than I.
                  I is larger than J and K.
                  K is not the smallest.

A. Which of the variables in the chain could be largest?

B. Which of the variables in the chain could be smallest?

4. Rules: E is heavier than A.
                  A and B are heavier than C.
                  D and H are lighter than C.
                  F and G are lighter than D and H.

A. Which of the variables in the chain could be heaviest?

B. Which of the variables in the chain could be lightest?

5. Rules: Q and R are both larger than S.
              R and T are both larger than V.

   A. Which of the variables in the chain could be largest?

   B. Which of the variables in the chain could be smallest?

6. Rules: A is taller than B and C.
              D is not taller than C.
              G and H are taller than A.
              H is shorter than I and J.

   A. Which of the variables in the chain could be tallest?

   B. Which of the variables in the chain could be shortest?

Pure Sequencing Diagramming Drill Answer Key

1. Tallest: A, C

   Shortest: F

   ```
           A > B
           - - - - - > D > E > F
             C
   ```

2. Heaviest: R, S, V

   Lightest: T, U, W

   ```
          R
          - - - - > T
          S
   ```

   ```
            W
      V > - - - - - -
            X > U
   ```

3. Largest: F

   Smallest: H, J

   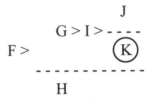

   ```
                       J
              G > I > - - - -
      F >              Ⓚ
            - - - - - - - - - - - -
              H
   ```

4. Heaviest: B, E

   Lightest: F, G

   ```
      E > A          D        F
      - - - - - - > C > - - - - > - - - -
          B              H        G
   ```

5. Largest: Q, R, T

   Smallest: S, V

   ```
          Q
          - - - - - > S
          Ⓡ      - - - -
          - - - - - > V
          T
   ```

   R is circled because R is uniquely connected by the rules to both S and V.

6. Tallest: G, I, J

   Shortest: B, C*, D
   *C could only tie
   for shortest.

   ```
                    G
          - - - - - - - -          B
          I            > A > - - - - - - -
          - - - - > H          C ≥ D
          J
   ```

Each of seven television programs—H, J, L, P, Q, S, V—is assigned a different rank: from first through seventh (from most popular to least popular). The ranking is consistent with the following conditions:

    J and L are each less popular than H.
    J is more popular than Q.
    S and V are each less popular than L.
    P and S are each less popular than Q.
    S is not seventh.

1. Which one of the following could be the order of the programs, from most popular to least popular?

    (A)   J, H, L, Q, V, S, P
    (B)   H, L, Q, J, S, P, V
    (C)   H, J, Q, L, S, V, P
    (D)   H, J, V, L, Q, S, P
    (E)   H, L, V, J, Q, P, S

2. If J is more popular than L, and S is more popular than P, then which one of the following must be true of the ranking?

    (A)   J is second.
    (B)   J is third.
    (C)   L is third.
    (D)   Q is third.
    (E)   P is seventh.

3. Which one of the following programs CANNOT be ranked third?

    (A)   L
    (B)   J
    (C)   Q
    (D)   V
    (E)   P

4. If V is more popular than Q and J is less popular than L, then which one of the following could be true of the ranking?

    (A)   P is more popular than S.
    (B)   S is more popular than V.
    (C)   P is more popular than L.
    (D)   J is more popular than V.
    (E)   Q is more popular than V.

5. If Q is more popular than L, then each of the following must be true of the ranking EXCEPT:

    (A)   H is first.
    (B)   L is fourth.
    (C)   V is not fourth.
    (D)   J is not third.
    (E)   Q is third.

Analysis of Pure Sequencing Game #1: December 2000 Questions 1-5

Because Pure Sequencing is generally favorable for most test takers, this was an excellent way to begin the December 2000 LSAT.

Use the Pure Sequencing Diagramming Guidelines to create the following diagram:

H J L P Q S V [7]

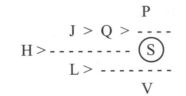

$$\frac{H}{1} \quad \frac{J/L}{2} \quad \frac{}{3} \quad \frac{}{4} \quad \frac{}{5} \quad \frac{}{6} \quad \frac{P/V}{7} \quad \frac{}{\cancel{8}}$$

In creating the sequence diagram, the most problematic television program is S. S is less popular than both Q and L, but Q and L are in separate branches. We have solved this problem by placing S at the terminus of the dotted line separator, and then circling S.

As with most Pure Sequencing games, this one is built on top of a linear relationship. H must be the most popular television program and only J or L could be second. Since S cannot be seventh, P or V must be the least popular. With this information we can attack the questions, watching the following two areas:

1. In Pure Sequencing games the test makers always check to see whether you will make unwarranted assumptions about the relationships between the variables.

2. The test makers typically introduce new relationships into the sequence to test your understanding of how the original relationships are affected.

Question #1: Global, Could Be True, List. The correct answer choice is (C)

Apply the rules and inferences in this order: inference that H must be first, fifth rule, second rule, and finally the first, third, and fourth rules can be applied in any order since they are roughly equivalent in form.

Answer choice (A) is incorrect because H must be more popular than J. Answer choice (B) is incorrect because J must be more popular than Q. Answer choice (D) is incorrect because L must be more popular than V. Answer choice (E) is incorrect because S cannot be seventh. Answer choice (C) is correct.

Question #2: Local, Must Be True. The correct answer choice is (A)

When examining the linear portion of the setup, take special note of the dual-options. A favorite trick of the test makers is to "take away" one of the variables in a dual-option to see if you recognize that the other variable is then forced into a position. Since either J or L must be second, and according to the question stem J is more popular than L, L cannot be second and J must be second. Answer choice (A) reflects that fact and is correct.

Question #3: Global, Cannot Be True. The correct answer choice is (E)

A program that cannot be ranked third is one that has either three or more variables ranked before it, or five or more variables ranked behind it (such as H). Applying the former criterion produces the following analysis:

H	minimum of 0 variables ranked ahead, cannot be ranked third since must be ranked first
J	minimum of 1 variable ranked ahead (H), can be ranked third
L	minimum of 1 variable ranked ahead (H), can be ranked third
P	minimum of 3 variables ranked ahead (H, J, Q), cannot be ranked third
Q	minimum of 2 variables ranked ahead (H, J), can be ranked third
S	minimum of 4 variables ranked ahead (H, J, Q, L), cannot be ranked third
V	minimum of 2 variables ranked ahead (H, L), can be ranked third

Accordingly, H, P, and S cannot be ranked third. Since only P appears among the answer choices, answer choice (E) is correct.

Note that this question does not require any writing. The listing above has been provided for the purposes of clarity. Since speed is a factor during the test, the number of variables ranked ahead should be visually scanned and counted.

Question #4: Local, Could Be True. The correct answer choice is (D)

The condition in the question stem produces the following mini-diagram:

$$\begin{array}{c} J \\ H > L > \text{-----}> Q > S > P \\ V \end{array}$$

S must be ranked ahead of P because otherwise S would be ranked seventh, a violation of the rules.

In a Could Be True question the correct answer choice could actually have the characteristic of Must Be True, but that usually does not occur on the LSAT. Consequently, since the correct answer will contain a scenario that is possible but not certain to occur, the best strategy is to look immediately for the uncertainty in the diagram and attack that area. Since the only uncertainty in this question involves J and V (J could be ranked ahead of V or V could be ranked ahead of J), immediately scan the answer choices for one that contains both J and V. In this case only answer choice (D) contains J and V. After a brief examination, it is apparent that answer choice (D) could be true and is therefore correct.

If the diagram to this question had more areas of uncertainty, the strategy above would still have been successful but would have taken more time to apply.

Question #5: Local, Must Be True, Except. The correct answer choice is (B)

Remember, *Must Be True EXCEPT* is the same as *Not Necessarily True*. The condition in the question stem produces the following diagram:

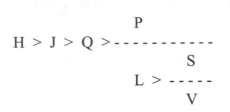

H, J, and Q must be ranked first, second, and third, respectively. Answer choices (A), (D), and (E) can thereby be eliminated. The highest V can be ranked is fifth and that eliminates answer choice (C). Since P could be fourth, it follows that L does not have to be fourth and answer choice (B) is correct.

For most test takers the appearance of a Pure Sequencing game is cause for celebration. Remember, Pure Sequencing games can be easily identified since the majority of rules are relative in nature. As you work through this book, keep in mind that part of your task is to learn how to quickly identify each game type.

A rowing team uses a boat with exactly six seats arranged in single file and numbered sequentially 1 through 6, from the front of the boat to the back. Six athletes—Lee, Miller, Ovitz, Singh, Valerio, and Zita—each row at exactly one of the seats, The following restrictions must apply:

Miller rows closer to the front than Singh.

Singh rows closer to the front than both Lee and Valerio.

Valerio and Zita each row closer to the front than Ovitz.

6. Which one of the following could be an accurate matching of athletes to seats?

    (A)   Miller: seat 1; Valerio: seat 5; Lee: seat 6
    (B)   Singh: seat 3; Valerio: seat 4; Zita: seat 5
    (C)   Miller: seat 1; Valerio: seat 3; Lee: seat 6
    (D)   Lee: seat 3; Valerio: seat 4; Ovitz: seat 5
    (E)   Zita: seat 2; Valerio: seat 3; Ovitz: seat 6

7. If Valerio rows at seat 5, then which one of the following must be true?

    (A)   Miller rows at seat 1.
    (B)   Singh rows at seat 2.
    (C)   Zita rows at seat 3.
    (D)   Lee rows at seat 4.
    (E)   Ovitz rows at seat 6.

8. If Lee rows at seat 3, then each of the following could be true EXCEPT:

    (A)   Zita rows immediately behind Valerio.
    (B)   Ovitz rows immediately behind Valerio.
    (C)   Ovitz rows immediately behind Zita.
    (D)   Valerio rows immediately behind Lee.
    (E)   Singh rows immediately behind Zita.

9. Which one of the following CANNOT be true?

    (A)   Ovitz rows closer to the front than Singh.
    (B)   Zita rows closer to the front than Miller.
    (C)   Lee rows closer to the front than Valerio.
    (D)   Singh rows closer to the front than Zita.
    (E)   Valerio rows closer to the front than Lee.

10. Exactly how many different seats could be the seat occupied by Zita?

    (A)   two
    (B)   three
    (C)   four
    (D)   five
    (E)   six

11. If Valerio rows closer to the front than Zita, then which one of the following must be true?

    (A)   Miller rows immediately in front of Singh.
    (B)   Lee rows immediately in front of Valerio.
    (C)   Zita rows immediately in front of Ovitz.
    (D)   Singh rows immediately in front of Lee.
    (E)   Singh rows immediately in front of Valerio.

12. Suppose the restriction that Miller rows closer to the front than Singh is replaced by the restriction that Singh rows closer to the front than Miller. If the other two restrictions remain in effect, then each of the following could be an accurate matching of athletes to seats EXCEPT:

    (A)   Singh: seat 1; Zita: seat 2; Miller: seat 6
    (B)   Singh: seat 1; Valerio: seat 3; Ovitz: seat 5
    (C)   Singh: seat 3; Lee: seat 4; Valerio: seat 5
    (D)   Valerio: seat 3; Miller: seat 4; Lee: seat 5
    (E)   Valerio: seat 4; Miller: seat 5; Ovitz: seat 6

This is a linear game controlled by pure sequencing rules, and because the sequential rules are so dominant, we classify this as a Pure Sequencing game. The key to this game is to make a usable sequence from the three rules, and then to understand the possibilities within that sequence.

From the game scenario, we know the following:

L M O S V Z [6]

Each of the rules can be diagrammed individually, but as you diagram, you should combine the rules in a super-sequence. First we will show the diagram for each rule:

Rule #1:

$$M > S$$

Rule #2:

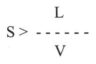

```
            L
   S > ------
            V
```

Rule #3:

```
   V
   ------ > O
   Z
```

Now, combine the rules.

Rule #1 and #2 combined:

```
                L
   M > S > ------
                V
```

The addition of the third rule is more problematic, and requires careful consideration. First, from the third rule we know that V > O:

```
                L
   M > S > ---------
              V > O
```

This leaves Z to be added to the diagram, a potential stumbling block because Z > O, but, unlike V, Z is not necessarily farther from the front than S. Use an arrow to show the relationship of O and Z:

Rule #1, #2, and #3 combined:

$$
\begin{array}{c}
\text{L} \\
\text{M} > \text{S} > ---------\\
\text{V} > \text{O} \\
\text{Z}
\end{array}
$$

Z is a very unrestricted variable in this game: Z could be as far forward as seat 1, or as far back as seat 5.

At this juncture we could choose to diagram all the Not Laws, but this would not be a wise choice since we already have the very powerful super-sequence to use to attack the questions. The one thing worth noting is which variables can be first or last. In this case, either M or Z must be first, and either L or O must be last:

$$
\underset{1}{\underline{\text{M/Z}}} \quad \underset{2}{\underline{\quad}} \quad \underset{3}{\underline{\quad}} \quad \underset{4}{\underline{\quad}} \quad \underset{5}{\underline{\quad}} \quad \underset{6}{\underline{\text{L/O}}}
$$

Question #6: Global, Could Be True, List. The correct answer choice is (C)

This is a harder-than-average List question. Our analysis of who is first and last only eliminates answer choice (D)—either L or O must be last, yet (D) features L in seat 3 and O in seat 5.

Answer choice (A): If V is in seat 5, then O must be in seat 6 since V > O. However, this answer features V in seat 5 and L in seat 6, and so it is incorrect.

Answer choice (B): There are two different ways this answer can be eliminated:

1. If S rows in seat 3, then M and Z must occupy seats 1 and 2 in some order. However, this answer features Z in seat 5, and that assignment does not leave enough athletes for seats 1 and 2.

2. According to the rules L must row behind S, and O must row behind V and Z. With S, V, and Z rowing at seats 3, 4, and 5, only seat 6 is available for both L and O, a violation of the rules.

Answer choice (C): This is the correct answer choice.

Answer choice (D): This answer choice is incorrect because either L or O must be in seat 6, and neither can be under this scenario.

Answer choice (E): According to the rules, M and S must row ahead of V. When Z and V row at seats 2 and 3, only seat 1 is available for both M and S, a violation of the rules.

Question #7: Local, Must Be True. The correct answer choice is (E)

If V rows at seat 5, then according to the third rule O must row in seat 6. Consequently, answer (E) must be correct.

Answer choices (A), (B), (C), and (D): Each of these answer choices could be true, but none of them have to be true and therefore each is incorrect.

Question #8: Local, Could Be True, Except. The correct answer choice is (E)

If L rows at seat 3, then according to our sequence, M must row at seat 1 and S must row at seat 2:

$$\frac{M}{1} \quad \frac{S}{2} \quad \frac{L}{3} \quad \frac{}{4} \quad \frac{}{5} \quad \frac{}{6}$$

Because either L or O must row last, and L is already assigned to seat 3, we can also deduce that O must row at seat 6:

$$\frac{M}{1} \quad \frac{S}{2} \quad \frac{L}{3} \quad \frac{}{4} \quad \frac{}{5} \quad \frac{O}{6}$$

The only remaining choice is the positioning of V and Z, and since the two do not have a direct relationship, either can row at seat 4 or 5:

$$\frac{M}{1} \quad \frac{S}{2} \quad \frac{L}{3} \quad \frac{V/Z}{4} \quad \frac{Z/V}{5} \quad \frac{O}{6}$$

Answer choices (A), (B), (C), and (D): Each of these answer choices could be true and therefore each is incorrect.

Answer choice (E): This is the correct answer choice. As proven by the diagram above, since S rows at seat 2, S can never row immediately behind Z, which must row at seat 4 or 5.

Question #9: Global, Cannot Be True. The correct answer choice is (A)

A Global question requires you to examine your diagram for the information needed to evaluate each answer choice. In this instance, our diagram primarily consists of the super-sequence, so use that to attack each answer choice.

Answer choice (A): This is the correct answer choice. As shown in the diagram, O must always row somewhere behind V, which rows somewhere behind S. Thus, O can never row ahead of S.

Answer choice (B): Because the only rule involving Z states that Z must row closer to the front than O, it is possible for Z to row closer to the front than M. Therefore, this answer choice could be true and it is incorrect.

Answer choice (C): The second rule states that L and V row somewhere behind S. However, this rule does not indicate that L rows ahead of V, or that V rows ahead of L. Consequently, it is possible for L to row closer to the front than V, and this answer choice is incorrect. The hypothetical produced in question #8 also helps show that this scenario could occur.

Answer choice (D): Although Z could be as far forward as seat 1, Z could also be as far back as seat 5. Hence, it is possible for S to row closer to the front than Z, and this answer choice is incorrect. As with answer choice (C), the hypothetical produced in question #8 helps show that this scenario is possible.

Answer choice (E): This answer choice can be eliminated by the similar reasoning used to eliminate answer choice (C). Just as we were able to show that L could row closer to the front than V, it is possible that V can row closer to the front than L.

Question #10: Global, Must Be True, Maximum. The correct answer choice is (D)

In our discussion of diagramming the sequence, we discussed the possibilities for Z: Z could row as far forward as seat 1, or as far back as seat 5. Consequently, Z could occupy any of five different seats, and answer choice (D) is correct.

Answer choices (A), (B), and (C): Because the question stem asks for how many different seats Z can occupy, these answer choices are insufficient since they each supply a number that is less than the maximum number of seats that Z can occupy.

Answer choice (E): From the third rule we know that Z must always row closer to the front than O. Consequently, Z can never row at seat 6, and therefore Z cannot row in all six different seats. This answer is therefore incorrect.

Question #11: Local, Must Be True. The correct answer choice is (A)

The question stem adds a condition that modifies the original sequence established by the rules. In this instance, the question stem stipulates that V > Z, and thus the original diagram can be re-diagrammed as follows:

$$
\begin{array}{c}
\quad\quad\quad\quad L \\
M > S > \text{- - - - - - - - - - -} \\
\quad\quad\quad V > Z > O
\end{array}
$$

Accordingly, we know that M must row at seat 1, and S must row at seat 2. V, Z, and O are in a sequence, but L can float freely among seats 3, 4, 5, and 6.

Answer choice (A): This is the correct answer choice. Answer choice (A) is shown to be true by the discussion of the placement of M and S.

Answer choices (B), (C), (D), and (E): Each of these answer choices could be true, but none of them has to be true and therefore each is incorrect.

Question #12: Local, Cannot Be True, Suspension. The correct answer choice is (C)

This is a suspension question, that is, a question that suspends one of the original rules of the game. This type of question requires the original sequence to be re-diagrammed before you attack the questions. And, in this case, because an additional condition is added to the mix, that must also be accounted for in the new diagram. Suspension questions are generally very time-consuming, and you should avoid them if you have difficulty completing the games section.

Because the first rule has been removed, only the combination of the second and third rules remains:

$$
\begin{array}{c}
\text{L} \\
\text{S} > \text{-------} \\
\text{V} > \text{O} \\
\text{Z} \hookleftarrow
\end{array}
$$

The question stem reverses the first rule, which by itself would be diagrammed as:

$$\text{S} > \text{M}$$

Adding this new condition to the diagram of the second and third rules, we arrive at the following diagram for question #12:

Although S may appear to row at seat 1, Z is still a virtual wild card in this question, and Z could also row at seat 1. However, the latest that S can row is at seat 2.

Answer choices (A), (B), (D), and (E): Each of these answer choices could be true, but because the question asks for an answer choice that cannot be true, each of these answers is incorrect.

Answer choice (C): This is the correct answer choice. As discussed above, the latest that S can row is at seat 2, and because this answer attempts to place S in seat 3, it cannot be true and is therefore correct.

CHAPTER SEVEN: THE FORGOTTEN FEW

Three Rare Game Types

In this chapter we will examine three game types that appear infrequently on today's LSAT: Pattern, Circular Linearity, and Mapping games. Although each of these types rarely appear, all three will likely appear in the future and thus a working knowledge of their basic principles is helpful. Remember, at least 75% of any Logic Games section will probably be made up of Grouping or Linear games, so it is unlikely that you would see more than one of these game types on a current LSAT.

Take a moment to consider why the test makers use different game types. As with the Logical Reasoning section, presenting different types of games helps the test makers keep you off balance. Imagine how easy a Logical Reasoning section would be if it was composed of 25 Weaken questions. You could establish a rhythm and pound out the questions quickly and efficiently. Of course, the test makers do not want that to occur, so they mix different types of questions. The same is true of the Games section. By using different game types—especially those rarely-seen game types—the test makers have a better chance of throwing you off. You can thwart this tactic by knowing the basics of every type of game that can occur on the LSAT.

Although the majority of your Logic Games section will be composed of Linear and Grouping games, it is worthwhile to prepare for any game type the test makers might use.

Pattern Games

The Linear Component

Pattern games are a variation of the Linear games discussed in Chapters Two and Three. In a Pattern game, the rules govern the general action of all variables, as opposed to the specific variable governance found in standard Linear games. Thus, instead of rules defining the specific placement of a variable, such as "P must speak third," Pattern game rules generally affect the action of all variables, as in "Each candidate must speak either first or second at at least one of the meetings." Consider the following game scenario:

Pattern games are a specific type of Linear game.

> A traveling salesman makes five sales trips around a circle of five cities—F, G, H, J, and K—stopping at exactly three of the cities on each trip. The salesman must conform to the following conditions:
>> The salesman stops at any given city on exactly of the three trips, but not on three consecutive sales trips.
>> The salesman stops at any given city at least once in any two consecutive sales trips.

Both of the rules in this game are equally directed at the five variables—F, G, H, J, and K—but neither rule mentions the variables by name. When the rules fail to mention the variables, the setup will often be devoid of solid information:

F G H J K [5]

The interaction of these broad rules often produces deep-seated patterns within the game but very little setup information. Unlike a typical linear game, none of the variables can be placed into the diagram, there are no Not Laws, etc. For this reason, most Pattern games have few global questions, and instead have a majority of local questions that provide the specific information lacking in the rules. If you have difficulty understanding a Pattern game, try a few hypotheticals after reading the rules to help clarify the patterns that result from the interaction of the rules. Alternately, look for the local question containing the greatest amount of information.

The name *Pattern game* is a reference to the fact that patterns exist within the placement of variables. If you can identify the patterns present in a game, then you usually have an advantage in attacking the questions. However, it is not essential for you to identify the patterns, and in some cases it is quite difficult. For example, in the game on the previous page, the two rules produce a set of five patterns that appear in every solution to the game:

Pattern #1:	1 - 3 - 5
Pattern #2:	1 - 3 - 4
Pattern #3:	1 - 2 - 4
Pattern #4:	2 - 3 - 5
Pattern #5:	2 - 4 - 5

(We have numbered the patterns for convenience; the patterns could be listed in any order. The numbers within each pattern—such as 1-3-5—refer to the stops for a city. For example, the first pattern indicates that the salesman will stop at one of the cities on the first trip, the third trip, and the fifth trip. Every solution to the game contains one city—it could be any one of the five—that fits this 1-3-5 pattern.)

Detecting the patterns while setting up the game would make the questions significantly easier; nevertheless, the game can still be attacked successfully without ever understanding the patterns if you identify

The complex pattern to the right reveals important information about the three cities where the salesman stops on each trip. For example, on the first trip, the three cities fit these three patterns: 1-3-5, 1-3-4, 1-2-4. Consequently it can be inferred that of the three cities on the first trip, one of those cities will be a stop on the second trip, two of those cities will be a stop on the third trip, two of those cities will be a stop on the fourth trip, and one city will be a stop on the fifth trip.

strongly with each individual rule. This is the key to Pattern games: since the rules are the only real weapons available to attack the questions, you must use the rules as a hammer against the questions. Although this is true of all games, it is even more important in Pattern games where there is not a conventional setup.

How to Identify Pattern Games

Pattern games can be difficult to identify. Here a few indicators:

1. The game is linear based, often with multiple stacks.

2. Typically, the rules do not name individual variables and instead the rules govern the action of all variables.

3. The setup is entirely free of placed or fixed variables. For this reason, creating a Pattern game setup usually takes a minimal amount of time.

4. There are very few Global questions but many Local questions.

Remember, the very nature of a Pattern game is somewhat abstract, and thus there are usually no obvious identifying features.

How to Attack Pattern Games

Once you recognize the presence of a Pattern game, there are several steps you can take to attack this unique game type:

1. Do not agonize over the fact that your setup seems "empty." The generalized nature of Pattern games usually leads to setups without a lot of information, so simply accept that fact and then move on.

2. Because the setup will be minimal, focus on fully understanding the rules. The rules are all that you will have to rely upon, so you must make certain that you completely understand each rule.

3. Do any List question first.

4. If the nature of the game is still causing you difficulty, create one or two hypotheticals to help you work with the rules and gain insight into how they interact with the variables.

5. If you continue to have difficulty, seek out the Local questions with the greatest amount of information and use those questions to create more hypotheticals. Remember to use those hypotheticals to attack other questions when applicable.

Final Pregame Note

Please be sure to read the explanations carefully as they will give you a true sense of how to best attack each game. In addition, the explanations include points that expand the discussion given above.

If you would like to test yourself under timed conditions, you should give yourself 8 minutes and 45 seconds for each game.

After these two games, this chapter will continue on to the next game type, Circular Linearity games, and thereafter, Mapping games.

Five candidates for mayor—Q, R, S, T, and U—will each speak exactly once at each of three town meetings—meetings 1, 2, and 3. At each meeting, each candidate will speak in one of five consecutive time slots. No two candidates will speak in the same time slot as each other at any meeting. The order in which the candidates will speak will meet the following conditions:

> Each candidate must speak either first or second at at least one of the meetings.
> Any candidate who speaks fifth at any of the meetings must speak first at at least one of the other meetings.
> No candidate can speak fourth at more than one of the meetings.

19. Which one of the following could be the order, from first to fifth, in which the candidates speak at the meetings?

    (A)   meeting 1: Q, U, R, T, S
          meeting 2: S, T, R, U, Q
          meeting 3: T, U, Q, R, S
    (B)   meeting 1: R, S, Q, T, U
          meeting 2: U, T, S, R, Q
          meeting 3: Q, R, T, U, S
    (C)   meeting 1: S, Q, U, T, R
          meeting 2: U, T, Q, R, S
          meeting 3: R, Q, S, T, U
    (D)   meeting 1: T, R, S, U, Q
          meeting 2: Q, R, S, T, U
          meeting 3: U, S, R, Q, T
    (E)   meeting 1: U, T, R, S, Q
          meeting 2: Q, R, S, T, U
          meeting 3: S, T, U, Q, R

20. If R speaks second at meeting 2 and first at meeting 3, which one of the following is a complete and accurate list of those time slots any one of which could be the time slot in which R speaks at meeting 1?

    (A)   fourth, fifth
    (B)   first, second, fifth
    (C)   second, third, fifth
    (D)   third, fourth, fifth
    (E)   second, third, fourth, fifth

21. If the order in which the candidates speak at meeting 1 is R, U, S, T, Q, and the order in which they speak at meeting 2 is Q, R, U, S, T, which one of the following could be true of meeting 3 ?

    (A)   Q speaks first.
    (B)   R speaks third.
    (C)   S speaks first.
    (D)   T speaks second.
    (E)   U speaks fifth.

22. If R speaks first at meetings 1 and 2, and S speaks first at meeting 3, which one of the following must be true?

    (A)   R speaks second at meeting 3.
    (B)   R speaks fourth at meeting 3.
    (C)   S speaks second at at least one of the meetings.
    (D)   S speaks fifth at exactly one of the meetings.
    (E)   S speaks fifth at exactly two of the meetings.

23. It could be true that at all three meetings T speaks

    (A)   first
    (B)   second
    (C)   in some time slot after the time slot in which R speaks
    (D)   in some time slot after the time slots in which S and U speak
    (E)   in some time slot before the time slots in which R and U speak

24. If S, T, and U speak second at meetings 1, 2, and 3, respectively, which one of the following must be true?

    (A)   The fifth speaker at at least one of the meetings is either Q or R.
    (B)   Either Q speaks first at exactly two of the meetings or else R does so.
    (C)   Neither S nor T speaks fifth at any of the meetings.
    (D)   Q speaks third at one of the meetings, and R speaks third at another of the meetings.
    (E)   Q speaks fourth at one of the meetings, and R speaks fourth at another of the meetings.

Analysis of Pattern Game #1: October 1997 Questions 19-24

As with virtually all Pattern games, the setup contains little in the way of concrete information:

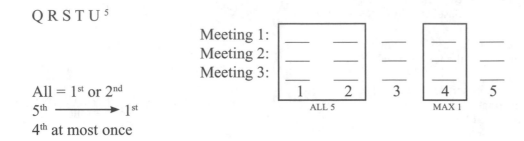

QRSTU⁵

All = 1ˢᵗ or 2ⁿᵈ
5ᵗʰ ⟶ 1ˢᵗ
4ᵗʰ at most once

Because the setup contains no "starting point" for analysis, the best approach is to review the rules in order to ensure a complete understanding of the game. As is often the case in Pattern games, the rules are difficult to diagram. However, it is important to symbolize the rules in some way since the focus of the game will be on their application. Fortunately, in this game the rules are relatively simple and thus easy to remember.

The first rule states that "Each candidate must speak either first or second at at least one of the meetings." This rule is represented off to the side of the diagram, and also as a block around the first two positions. Because there are three meetings, it follows that there are six available spaces for the candidates to meet this requirement. Since there are five candidates, each of whom must appear once in these six spaces, it can be inferred that exactly one candidate must appear twice within the first two speaking spaces of all three meetings, and the rest of the candidates appear only once. This is an unfixed numerical distribution of 2-1-1-1-1 for the six spaces that represent the first and second speaking slots of the three meetings. Essentially, this rule means that if one speaker speaks within the first two slots at two of the meetings, then the remaining slots must be filled with the rest of the speakers. For example, if Q speaks first at meeting 1 and second at meeting 2, then R, S, T, and U each speak once in the remaining first or second positions of the meetings. This inference comes into play on all of the questions, particularly questions #20 and #21.

The second rule states that "Any candidate who speaks fifth at any of the meetings must speak first at at least one of the other meetings." This is a powerful rule because it establishes a constant connection between the first and fifth spaces. Because the fifth space cannot be filled by the same candidate at all three meetings (that candidate would have to speak first at at least one of the meetings), it follows that there are always two or three different speakers in the fifth slot at all three meetings. If there are three different candidates speaking in the fifth slot, then those same three candidates will also speak in the first slot at a meeting in a different order. If there are two different candidates speaking in the fifth slot, then those same two candidates will speak in the first slot, with either another candidate in the remaining first slot or with one of the two candidates doubling up. Therefore, please note that if two different candidates fill all three of the fifth speaking slots, it is possible for a candidate to speak first at a meeting and not speak fifth (to think that if a candidate speaks first at a meeting that he or she must then speak fifth at another meeting would be to make a Mistaken Reversal). For example, if the fifth speaker at each of the three meetings, is R, R, and T respectively, then the first speaker at each of the three meetings could be T, Q, and R respectively.

Although the above explanation is complex, the application of the rule is much easier. Essentially, any candidate placed into the first or fifth slot immediately becomes subject to this rule. Combined with the first rule, slots one, two, and five appear to be the most controlling slots, thereby the most important ones.

Question #19: Global, Could Be True, List. The correct answer choice is (D)

In Pattern games always be sure to do List questions first, in order to establish a workable hypothetical. The easiest rule to apply from a visual standpoint is the last rule, "No candidate can speak fourth at more than one of the meetings." Answer choice (C) violates this rule and is thus incorrect. The next easiest rule to apply is probably the first rule. Answer choice (A) violates this rule (R does not appear) and is therefore incorrect. Finally, applying the second rule eliminates answer choices (B) and (E). Answer choice (D) is proven correct by process of elimination.

Question #20: Local, Could Be True, List. The correct answer choice is (D)

This is the first local question of the game. If R speaks second at meeting 2 and first at meeting 3, then according to our analysis of the first rule R cannot speak first or second at meeting 1. Accordingly, answer choices (B), (C), and (E) can be eliminated. The difference between the remaining two answer choices is whether R can speak third at meeting 1. Since there is no constraint on speaking third, and no violation caused by R speaking third, it follows that answer choice (D) is correct. Note that this answer choice reflects the fact that just because a candidate speaks first does not mean that candidate has to speak fifth. The second rule as stated and diagrammed can be paraphrased as "if a candidate speaks fifth at a meeting, then at some other meeting they must speak first."

Question #21: Local, Could Be True. The correct answer choice is (B)

The information in the question stem produces the following setup:

	1	2	3	4	5
Meeting 1:	R	U	S	T	Q
Meeting 2:	Q	R	U	S	T
Meeting 3:	T	S			

Since R, Q, and U speak first or second at meetings 1 and 2, T and S must speak in the first two slots of meeting 3. Since T speaks fifth at meeting 2, and fourth at meeting 1, T must speak first at meeting 3, and it follows that S must speak second at meeting 3. Accordingly, answer choices (A), (C), and (D) can be eliminated. Answer choice (E) can also be eliminated since if U spoke fifth, U would have to speak first at another meeting and that is not possible in this situation. Thus, answer choice (B) is correct.

In this question, the second rule often gives rise to a Mistaken Reversal. Remember, the second rule means that if a speaker speaks fifth at one of the meetings, then that speaker must speak first at one of the other meetings ($5^{th} \longrightarrow 1^{st}$). Many students wrongly interpret this rule to mean that if a speaker speaks first at one of the meetings that speaker must speak fifth at another meeting ($1^{st} \longrightarrow 5^{th}$). While that interpretation may sound logical, that is not actually what the second rule says, and it does not have to be true. For example, the following hypothetical for meeting 3 in this question satisfies all the rules: T-S-R-U-Q. Note that, with this hypothetical in question #21, anyone who speaks fifth (Q and T) also speaks first (in meetings 2 and 3). R, who speaks first at meeting 1, does not speak fifth at any meeting, and this is acceptable under the wording of the second rule.

Question #22: Local, Must Be True. The correct answer choice is (E)

If R speaks first at meetings 1 and 2, and S speaks first at meeting 3, then, according to our analysis of the second rule, R must speak fifth at meeting 3 and S must speak fifth at meetings 1 and 2. It follows that answer choice (E) is correct.

Specifically, in question #22, we know that:

Meeting 1:	R	__	__	__	__
Meeting 2:	R	__	__	__	__
Meeting 3:	S	__	__	__	__
	1	2	3	4	5

So, from the question stem we already know which speakers are first at each meeting. That brings up an interesting situation for the other speakers. For example, could T speak fifth at one of the meetings, say the meeting 1? No, because then there would be no meeting where T could speak first (those positions are already taken by R or S), and that would violate the second rule. The same situation would apply to Q and U, and so T, Q, and U can never speak fifth in the scenario presented in question #22. Hence, R and S must fill all of the fifth speaking spaces, and that means we can infer that S speaks fifth at meetings 1 and 2, R speaks fifth at meeting 3:

Meeting 1:	R	__	__	__	S
Meeting 2:	R	__	__	__	S
Meeting 3:	S	__	__	__	R
	1	2	3	4	5

This scenario proves answer choice (E) is correct.

Question #23: Global, Could Be True. The correct answer choice is (C)

From our discussion of the first rule, answer choices (A) and (B) can be eliminated. Answer choice (D) can be eliminated because if T always speaks after both S and U, T could never speak first or second, a violation of the first rule. Answer choice (E) can be eliminated since if T always speaks before R and U, then T would speak first at least twice, but could never speak fifth, which would ultimately cause a violation of the first rule. Thus, answer choice (C) is proven correct by process of elimination. Here is a hypothetical that satisfies all of the rules of the game and the condition in answer choice (C):

Meeting 1:	R	T	U	S	Q
Meeting 2:	S	R	T	U	Q
Meeting 3:	Q	U	R	T	S
	1	2	3	4	5

Note that Q and S are the only candidates who speak 5th. Since they both speak 1st at some point, the second rule is satisfied.

Question #24: Local, Must Be True. The correct answer choice is (A)

If S, T, and U speak second, then Q and R must each appear in the first speaking slot at least once. Because of this, either Q or R must speak in the fifth slot at one of the meetings, and it follows that answer choice (A) is correct. From a structural standpoint, answer choices (D) and (E) are very unlikely to be correct since they deal with the third and fourth slots.

Remember, in Pattern games the setup is generally easy to create, and therefore you have a greater amount of time to analyze the rules and ascertain their relationship to the pattern of the game (there are exceptions though!). And with the knowledge that Pattern games produce few inferences, you should not be unduly concerned when your setup seems relatively empty. Also, when in doubt, do the List questions or try a hypothetical to help gain an understanding of the nature of the game.

In order to separate the game from its answer key and explanations,
the second game is on the next page.

Three boys—Karl, Luis, and Miguel—and three girls—Rita, Sarah, and Tura—are giving a dance recital. Three dances—1, 2, and 3—are to be performed. Each dance involves three pairs of children, a boy and a girl partnering each other in each pair, according to the following conditions:

    Karl partners Sarah in either dance 1 or dance 2.
    Whoever partners Rita in dance 2 must partner Sarah in dance 3.
    No two children can partner each other in more than one dance.

14. If Sarah partners Luis in dance 3, which one of the following is a complete and accurate list of the girls any one of whom could partner Miguel in dance 1 ?

    (A)   Rita
    (B)   Sarah
    (C)   Tura
    (D)   Rita, Sarah
    (E)   Rita, Tura

15. If Miguel partners Rita in dance 2, which one of the following could be true?

    (A)   Karl partners Tura in dance 1.
    (B)   Luis partners Sarah in dance 2.
    (C)   Luis partners Sarah in dance 3.
    (D)   Miguel partners Sarah in dance 1.
    (E)   Miguel partners Tura in dance 3.

16. If Miguel partners Sarah in dance 1, which one of the following is a pair of children who must partner each other in dance 3 ?

    (A)   Karl and Rita
    (B)   Karl and Tura
    (C)   Luis and Rita
    (D)   Luis and Tura
    (E)   Miguel and Tura

17. If Luis partners Sarah in dance 2, which one of the following is a pair of children who must partner each other in dance 1 ?

    (A)   Karl and Rita
    (B)   Karl and Tura
    (C)   Luis and Rita
    (D)   Luis and Tura
    (E)   Miguel and Rita

18. If Miguel partners Rita in dance 1, which one of the following must be true?

    (A)   Karl partners Rita in dance 2.
    (B)   Karl partners Sarah in dance 3.
    (C)   Karl partners Tura in dance 1.
    (D)   Luis partners Rita in dance 2.
    (E)   Luis partners Tura in dance 3.

Some games are difficult because they contain a large number of rules or variables; other games are difficult because they are built around complex concepts that lead to several deep inferences. This Pattern game is one of the latter.

For a Pattern game it is somewhat unusual that the rules address specific variables, but this is not unprecedented. For example, the third game on the October 1996 LSAT contains similar rules. In this case the interaction of the partners helps establish the three patterns that exist in every game solution. Creating a setup that effectively captures this information is critical. The first important decision in this game is how to display the dancing couples for each dance. Many students attempt to use a basic setup similar to the following:

Unfortunately, this setup represents the information inefficiently. For each of the three dances, decisions must still be made for each of the six variables, eighteen total for all three dances. If at all possible, it would be preferable to fix some of the variables in the setup and thus reduce the number of variables to consider for each dance. By realizing that the individuals who dance with each girl are a single variable set, we can stack rows for R, S, and T above each of the three numbered dances:

The stacking of R, S, and T in the diagram leaves only the placement of the three boys in each of the three dances. This effectively reduces the total number of variables to be placed to nine, down from eighteen in the previous setup. Choosing to display R, S, and T is superior to choosing K, L, and M because it allows the second rule to be displayed within the diagram:

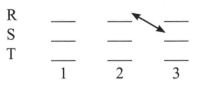

Note that the second rule is represented with a double arrow (if one occurs, then the other must occur). If we know who partners Rita in dance 2, that person must partner Sarah in dance 3, and if we know who partners Sarah in dance 3, that same person must partner Rita in dance 2.

According to the last rule, "No two children can partner each other in more than one dance." By combining this rule with the second rule, we can infer that the boy who partners Rita in dance 2 and Sarah in dance 3 must partner Tura in dance 1. This pattern holds true for every possible game configuration. This inference can also be added to the setup:

Since the game now has one established pattern, it is quite possible that other patterns exist. For example, examine the boy who dances with Rita in dance 1. In dance 2 this same boy can partner Sarah or Tura, and in dance 3 he can partner only Tura (remember, Sarah is already taken and he can't partner with Rita again). But wait—if he must partner Tura in dance 3, then he cannot partner her in dance 2, and thus he must partner Sarah in dance 2. It therefore follows that whomever partners Rita in dance 1 must partner Sarah in dance 2 and Tura in dance 3. Now that this second pattern exists, there can be only one possible pattern for the boy who partners Sarah in dance 1: Tura in dance 2 and Rita in dance 3 (remember each of the other two girls in dances 2 and 3 are involved in other patterns). Thus, by analyzing the interaction of the second and third rules, we have established that three patterns must exist in every game:

One boy must partner T in dance 1, R in dance 2, and S in dance 3. (T - R - S)
One boy must partner R in dance 1, S in dance 2, and T in dance 3. (R - S - T)
One boy must partner S in dance 1, T in dance 2, and R in dance 3. (S - T - R)

Obviously, uncovering this pattern within the rules makes the game easy to conquer. But, before beginning the questions, keep in mind that Karl must partner with Sarah in dance 1 or 2 (which means that he will be in either the STR pattern or the RST pattern).

Question #14: Local, Could Be True, List. The correct answer choice is (D)

If Luis partners Sarah in dance 3, he must partner Rita in dance 2 and Tura in dance 1. This leaves either Rita or Sarah for Miguel to partner in dance 1, and thus answer choice (D) is correct.

Question #15: Local, Could Be True. The correct answer choice is (B)

If Miguel partners Rita in dance 2, he must partner Sarah in dance 3 and Tura in dance 1. This information is sufficient to eliminate answer choices (A), (C), (D), and (E). It follows that answer choice (B) is correct.

Question #16: Local, Must Be True. The correct answer choice is (B)

If Miguel partners Sarah in dance 1, Karl must partner Sarah in dance 2. This being the case, Luis must partner Sarah in dance 3. Of course, if Luis partners Sarah in dance 3, he must partner Rita in dance 2 and Tura in dance 1. Adding this information to the patterns already established fills in the entire diagram:

	1	2	3
R	K	L	M
S	M	K	L
T	L	M	K

It follows that answer choice (B) is correct.

Question #17: Local, Must Be True. The correct answer choice is (C)

Like the previous question, the information in the question stem fills in the entire diagram:

$$
\begin{array}{cccc}
\text{R} & \underline{\text{L}} & \underline{\text{M}} & \underline{\text{K}} \\
\text{S} & \underline{\text{K}} & \underline{\text{L}} & \underline{\text{M}} \\
\text{T} & \underline{\text{M}} & \underline{\text{K}} & \underline{\text{L}} \\
 & 1 & 2 & 3
\end{array}
$$

Thus answer choice (C) is correct.

Question #18: Local, Must Be True. The correct answer choice is (D)

While the four previous questions can be answered without an understanding of the three patterns that control this game, this generally difficult question is made easy by applying the patterns:

$$
\begin{array}{cccc}
\text{R} & \underline{\text{M}} & \underline{\text{L}} & \underline{\text{K}} \\
\text{S} & \underline{\text{K}} & \underline{\text{M}} & \underline{\text{L}} \\
\text{T} & \underline{\text{L}} & \underline{\text{K}} & \underline{\text{M}} \\
 & 1 & 2 & 3
\end{array}
$$

The setup indicates that answer choice (D) is correct.

In retrospect, this game has a few unusual features for a Pattern game (deep inferences, variables mentioned in the rules), but it also displays features that are very patternistic, such as all five questions being Local. This game was universally considered by students to be the hardest game on the October 1993 LSAT, if not one of the hardest games of the modern era. However, an application of the basic rules allows any test taker to answer at least the first four questions, and those students who discovered the three patterns found the game quite easy. Remember, just because a game contains a few simple rules does not necessarily mean that the setup is also simple or uninformative. Always examine the interaction of the rules, even if there are only two or three.

Circular Linearity Games

Circular Linearity games consist of a fixed number of variables assigned to spaces distributed around a circle. Usually the scenario involves people sitting around a table. Essentially these games are Linear games wrapped around a circular diagram, hence the name. As linearity is still the controlling principle, the Linear games approach discussed in earlier chapters still applies. There are several effects of the circularity:

1. In a normal Linear game, the base is written out horizontally or vertically in consecutive slots. Since Circular Linearity games feature a table, the diagramming is a bit different. Consider the following example:

    > Eight individuals sit around a circular conference table with eight chairs. At most one individual sits in each chair.

    Most students attempt to diagram the game by drawing a circle with seats placed equidistantly around the circle:

    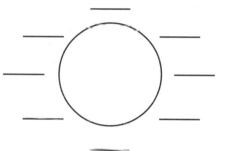

    Although visually appealing, this diagram is too time-consuming to draw, too space inefficient, and can be confusing to use. The following diagram captures the seating and can be drawn more quickly:

    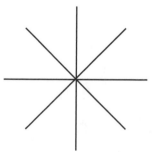

    Each seat is represented by the end of a "spoke." Since there are eight seats, four spokes are needed.

2. In Circular Linearity games the number of variables affects how you attack the game. In games with an even number of variables, rules involving opposite variables (such as "A must sit opposite of B")

Do not waste your time by drawing out a table!

When an even-number of individuals are seated around a table, divide by two and the quotient is the number of spokes that should be drawn.

are the most important rules. The "spoke" diagram above has the additional benefit of perfectly portraying opposites. In games without opposite rules, block rules are the most important.

In games with an odd number of variables, there can be no opposites (when seven people sit equidistantly around a table no person is directly opposite another). In these games, blocks are the most important rules and should be considered first.

3. Although most games do not have assigned seat numbers, when they do, remember that, since the linear diagram is wrapped around a circle, the person in the "first" seat and the person in the "last" seat are in fact seated next to each other. Knowledge of this fact is usually tested in List questions.

4. The phrases "to the left of" and "to the right of" refer to the left and right of the variable in question, not your left and right.

5. During the setup, some of the variables can usually be placed on the diagram in spite of the fact that you have to place them in an arbitrary fashion (you pick the spoke). If there are rules involving variables that are opposites, place those variables first. Opposites are powerful because they divide the table into two parts. If there are no opposites, then place any variables in a block. The following game will address this point.

In spite of the fact that only a few Circular Linearity games have appeared on a released section since 1991, we do expect that a future LSAT will contain a similar game.

Circular Linearity games have appeared very infrequently in the released sections of the modern LSAT, most notably in the June 1991 and October 2003 tests. The June 1991 game is presented on the next page.

Exactly six trade representatives negotiate a treaty: Klosnik, Londi, Manley, Neri, Osata, Poirier. There are exactly six chairs evenly spaced around a circular table. The chairs are numbered 1 through 6, with successively numbered chairs next to each other and chair number 1 next to chair number 6. Each chair is occupied by exactly one of the representatives. The following conditions apply:

> Poirier sits immediately next to Neri.
> Londi sits immediately next to Manley, Neri, or both.
> Klosnik does not sit immediately next to Manley.
> If Osata sits immediately next to Poirier, Osata does not sit immediately next to Manley.

1. Which one of the following seating arrangements of the six representatives in chairs 1 through 6 would NOT violate the stated conditions?

   (A) Klosnik, Poirier, Neri, Manley, Osata, Londi
   (B) Klosnik, Londi, Manley, Poirier, Neri, Osata
   (C) Klosnik, Londi, Manley, Osata, Poirier, Neri
   (D) Klosnik, Osata, Poirier, Neri, Londi, Manley
   (E) Klosnik, Neri, Londi, Osata, Manley, Poirier

2. If Londi sits immediately next to Poirier, which one of the following is a pair of representatives who must sit immediately next to each other?

   (A) Klosnik and Osata
   (B) Londi and Neri
   (C) Londi and Osata
   (D) Manley and Neri
   (E) Manley and Poirier

3. If Klosnik sits directly between Londi and Poirier, then Manley must sit directly between

   (A) Londi and Neri
   (B) Londi and Osata
   (C) Neri and Osata
   (D) Neri and Poirier
   (E) Osata and Poirier

4. If Neri sits immediately next to Manley, then Klosnik can sit directly between

   (A) Londi and Manley
   (B) Londi and Poirier
   (C) Neri and Osata
   (D) Neri and Poirier
   (E) Poirier and Osata

5. If Londi sits immediately next to Manley, then which one of the following is a complete and accurate list of representatives any one of whom could also sit immediately next to Londi?

   (A) Klosnik
   (B) Klosnik, Neri
   (C) Neri, Poirier
   (D) Klosnik, Osata, Poirier
   (E) Klosnik, Neri, Osata, Poirier

6. If Londi sits immediately next to Neri, which one of the following statements must be false?

   (A) Klosnik sits immediately next to Osata.
   (B) Londi sits immediately next to Manley.
   (C) Osata sits immediately next to Poirier.
   (D) Neri sits directly between Londi and Poirier.
   (E) Osata sits directly between Klosnik and Manley.

7. If Klosnik sits immediately next to Osata, then Londi CANNOT sit directly between

   (A) Klosnik and Manley
   (B) Klosnik and Neri
   (C) Manley and Neri
   (D) Manley and Poirier
   (E) Neri and Osata

Analysis of Circular Linearity Game #1: June 1991 Questions 1-7

This is the very first game of the first LSAT of the modern era (marked by the introduction of the 120-180 scoring scale). It is also the last time a Circular Linearity game appeared in a released LSAT section before another Circular game appeared in October 2003. The setup is as follows:

K L M N O P⁶

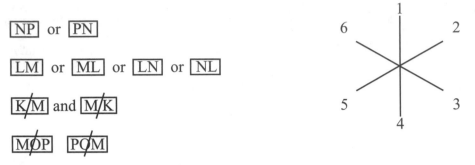

Since there are six chairs and six trade representatives, this is a Balanced game. The chair numbers prove to be relevant only on Question #1. Since the game contains no rules of opposition, the best defined block, PN, should be placed on the diagram:

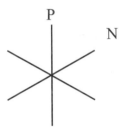

The placement of the PN block is arbitrary. They could be placed at the end of any pair of spokes, and could be in the order PN or NP. Do not assume that P and N are in chairs 1 and 2. Nevertheless, it is important to place the block on the diagram, as it will provide a starting point for adding other variables.

The final rule also bears further analysis. The rule states, "If O sits immediately next to P, O does not sit immediately next to M." Accordingly, every time O and P sit next to each other, then M cannot sit next to O and the configurations MOP and POM are impossible. Even though the rule can be written as a conditional, the representation we have provided is superior since it is easier to apply from a visual standpoint.

Question #1: Global, Cannot Be True, List. The correct answer choice is (B)

Employ the rules in order of ease of application: answer choice (E) can be eliminated since P and N are separated; an application of the KM rule eliminates answer choice (D) (Remember, chairs 1 and 6 are next to each on the circular table!); an application of the LM or LN rule eliminates answer choice (A); and finally, an application of the MOP rule eliminates answer choice (C). Answer choice (B) is correct.

Because none of the rest of the questions include the chair numbers, the rest of the game can be treated as a basic linear exercise.

Question #2: Local, Must Be True. The correct answer choice is (A)

The Local condition in the question stem produces the following mini-diagram:

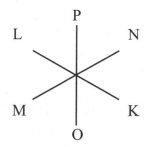

Since P and N are a block, when L sits next to P, either an LPN or NPL block is formed (the diagram above has LPN). Since L must sit next to N or M, and N is already occupied, it follows that M must sit next to L. There are now only two open spaces. Since K cannot sit next to M, K must sit next to N. O sits in the final chair, next to K and M. Answer choice (A) is correct.

Question #3: Local, Must Be True. The correct answer choice is (B)

The Local condition in the question stem produces the following mini-diagram:

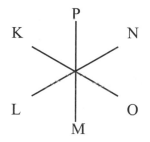

Adding the Local condition to the PN block produces a L-K-P-N sequence. Since L must sit next to M or N, M must sit next to L, and, again, O sits in the final chair. Answer choice (B) is correct.

Question #4: Local, Could Be True. The correct answer choice is (E)

Adding the Local condition to the PN block produces a P-N-M sequence. Since L must sit next to M or N, L must sit next to M. Since there are no restrictions on K or O, they form a dual-option:

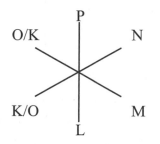

Consequently answer choice (E) is correct.

Question #5: Local, Could Be True, List. The correct answer choice is (E)

The question stem solidifies the second rule to establish that L is sitting next to M. Since this information does not allow a complete diagram to be created, the best approach is to quickly refer to previous questions to see if any meet the criteria that L and M sit next to each other. If so, the work in those questions can be used to attack question #5.

In question #1 L and M are seated next to each other, so the hypothetical created by the correct answer in #1, K-L-M-P-N-O, can be used to prove that L can sit next to K. Accordingly, any answer choice in question #5 that does not contain K must be eliminated. Answer choice (C) can be discarded. Next, consider the work done in question #2. The solution meets the criteria that L and M sit next to each other, and reveals that L can sit next to P. Again, any answer choice that does not contain P must be rejected. Answer choices (A) and (B) can now be discarded. Only answer choices (D) and (E) remain. Question #3 also applies but only reveals that L can sit next to K, a fact established by the analysis of question #1. In question #4 it is shown that O can sit next to L, but since both answer choices (D) and (E) contain O, no progress is made. Since answer choices (D) and (E) are differentiated only by the presence of N, make a quick hypothetical to test N. The following hypothetical proves that N can sit next to L when L and M are seated next to each other:

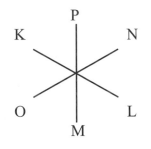

Answer choice (E) is therefore correct.

Question #6: Local, Cannot Be True. The correct answer choice is (C)

If L sits next to N, a P-N-L sequence is created:

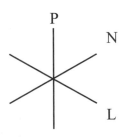

The three remaining variables are K, M, and O. Since K and M cannot sit next to each other, by Hurdling the Uncertainty we can infer that O must separate K and M:

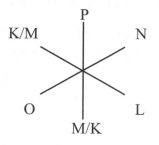

Since O is between K and M, answer choice (C) is correct.

Question #7: Local, Cannot Be True. The correct answer choice is (E)

The question stem creates a KO block. Since no obvious diagramming inferences can be made, reuse information, as was done in question #5.

The hypothetical from Question #1 applies since K and O are next to each other (remember, the first and last variables are next to each other); and this hypothetical proves that L can sit directly between K and M. That is sufficient to eliminate answer choice (A). The work from question #2 also applies and is sufficient to eliminate answer choice (D). Question #3 does not apply. Question #4 does apply and proves that L can sit between M and O (not in the answers) or M and K (already known from question #1). The hypothetical from question #6 must be examined closely. In spite of the fact that M and K rotate in the dual-option, K will always sit next to O, and thus the hypothetical reveals that L can sit between K and N as well as M and N. This information eliminates answer choices (B) and (C). Answer choice (E) is therefore correct via process of elimination.

This question again reveals the power of reusing previous work. With minimal effort all four incorrect answer choices are eliminated. And since the hypotheticals can be visually scanned at a high rate, the question takes less time than a question requiring a new diagram.

Circular Linearity games appear once in a blue moon, and it is not likely that one will appear on your test. Nevertheless, it is worthwhile to be acquainted with the basic principles in case such a game happens to appear.

Mapping Games

In many games
the numerical
aspect is as
simple as the
one-to-one
relationships
described earlier.

Pure Mapping
games contain
no numerical
element.

All Logic Games can be classified as numerical or non-numerical. The vast majority of games are numerical in nature, where numbers play an important role in the game solution (Linear, Grouping, Pattern, etc.). The only non-numerical game type is Mapping, and even within Mapping games, some contain enough grouping as to be numerical.

Mapping games appeared several times in the early 1990s on the LSAT, but recently they have been rare. Nevertheless, they can be quite troublesome to the unprepared student. There are three types of Mapping games:

1. Spatial Relations. The rules in these games do not fix the physical relationships among the variables. For example, a game involving shelter sites in a park simply states that certain shelters are one day's hike from each other. Using this information allows the test taker to ascertain the relationship among the variables, but not their exact positions. Whether a variable is north or south of another variable is generally meaningless in games of this type. The best approach for these games is to diagram the relationships with arrows or lines.

2. Directional. These games involve a fixed point, and all other variables are placed North, East, South, and West of that point. For example, one game fixes City Hall as the center of a town and then proceeds to place all variables directionally by referencing City Hall. The best approach to this type of game is to use the fixed center point and draw each of the four quadrants (NE, SE, SW, and NW) around the center point.

    Although Directional games appeared several times in the 1980s, there has not been a pure Directional game in the 1990s. At most some games have featured directional elements, such as the Park Bench game from the October 1992 LSAT.

3. Supplied Diagram. In these games the makers of the test supply a diagram intended to represent the relationship of the variables. Always use the diagram! A good example is the last game from the February 1992 LSAT about ski chalets.

For a reference
of all games that
have appeared on
LSATs released
since 1991, see
Appendix One.

THE POWERSCORE LSAT LOGIC GAMES BIBLE

Attacking Mapping Games

When drawing the diagram in a Mapping game, always consider the following three questions in the order given:

 A. What is the direction of the connection between the variables?

 B. Do the lines have to be straight?

 C. Can the lines intersect?

Although the questions may appear simple, perhaps even obvious, many students make assumptions that can be deadly. Consider this game scenario:

> Five boroughs of a city—B, M, Q, S, and X— are connected by highways. The highway connections accord with the following rules:
> The highways do not intersect.
> Each highways directly connects exactly two and only two boroughs with each other.
> No two boroughs are directly connected by more than one highway.

The game appears to be a drawing exercise connecting the five boroughs with highways. Since the highways cannot intersect, the key will be to line up the boroughs in such a way as to make sure there are no intersections, right? No. The rules never state that the highways are straight. And, of course, if the highways are not straight, they can loop around the other highways and the drawing aspect becomes meaningless. The game is actually a grouping exercise in matching boroughs to each other.

The first of the three questions above, "What is the direction of the connection between the variables," is useful since it indicates whether the connections are one-way or bi-directional. If connections are one-way, draw them with arrows. If connections are bi-directional, just use straight lines (otherwise the proper approach would be to draw double-arrows ($\longleftrightarrow$) and drawing the extra arrowheads is a waste of time).

The second question, "Do the lines have to be straight?" is especially important when there are rules prohibiting intersection. The Highways game demonstrates just how critical this question is.

The third question is especially important if the lines must be straight. If the lines are straight and there is no intersection, the game will have a limited number of solutions. The last game from the February 1992 LSAT (The Ski Chalets) contains straight lines with no intersection and there are only six solutions.

To summarize, if the lines are straight but intersection is allowed, the

The last game from February 1992 is a Pure Mapping game with no numerical element. This, in part, explains why the rules about the lines are so important in that game.

game is not especially limited. If the lines do not have to be straight but intersection is prohibited, the game is not appreciably limited. If the lines must be straight and there is no intersection, the game is limited and there are likely only a few solutions.

The Grouping Element

Mapping games are sometimes used to hide Grouping games. The Highways game discussed above appears to be a Mapping game, but closer analysis revealed that it is a Grouping game where the map has little meaning. As you analyze a game that appears to contain Mapping, ascertain if there are grouping elements (who can and cannot go with each other). If you discover Grouping is present, immediately attack that element and use the map only if necessary.

The last released LSAT Mapping game appeared in June 1995. That game is presented on the opposite page. Prior to June 1995, Mapping appeared five times on the modern LSAT. In Appendix One we have listed each Mapping game and also noted when the game contained strong grouping elements. At times, questions of classification can arise with Mapping since some games like the Highways game are really Grouping games.

The country of Zendu contains exactly four areas for radar detection: R, S, T, and U. Each detection area is circular and falls completely within Zendu. Part of R intersects T; part of S also intersects T; R does not intersect S. Area U is completely within R and also completely within T. At noon exactly four planes—J, K, L, M—are over Zendu, in a manner consistent with the following statements:

> Each plane is in at least one of the four areas.
> J is in area S.
> K is not in any detection area that J is in.
> L is not in any detection area that M is in.
> M is in exactly one of the areas.

7. Which one of the following could be a complete listing of the planes located in the four areas at noon, with each plane listed in every area in which it is located?

   (A) R: J, L;   S: J, M;   T: L;   U: L
   (B) R: J, L;   S: K;   T: M;   U: none
   (C) R: K;   S: J;   T: L;   U: M
   (D) R: K, M;   S: J, L;   T: J;   U: none
   (E) R: M;   S: J, K;   T: J, L;   U: none

8. If at noon K is within exactly two of the four areas, then which one of the following CANNOT be true at that time?

   (A) J is within area T.
   (B) K is within area R.
   (C) K is within area T.
   (D) L is within area R.
   (E) L is within area T.

9. Which one of the following is a complete and accurate list of those planes any one of which could be within area T at noon?

   (A) M
   (B) J, L
   (C) J, L, M
   (D) K, L, M
   (E) J, K, L, M

10. Which one of the following statements CANNOT be true at noon about the planes?

   (A) K is within area T.
   (B) K is within area U.
   (C) L is within area R.
   (D) M is within area R.
   (E) M is within area U.

11. It CANNOT be true that at noon there is at least one plane that is within both area

   (A) R and area T
   (B) R and area U
   (C) S and area T
   (D) S and area U
   (E) T and area U

12. If at noon M is within area T, then which one of the following statements CANNOT be true at that time?

   (A) J is within area T.
   (B) L is within area R.
   (C) L is within area S.
   (D) K is within exactly two areas.
   (E) L is within exactly two areas.

13. If at noon plane L is within exactly three of the areas, which one of the following could be true at that time?

   (A) J is within exactly two of the areas.
   (B) J is within exactly three of the areas.
   (C) K is within area S.
   (D) M is within area R.
   (E) M is within area T.

Analysis of Mapping Game #1: June 1995 Questions 7-13

On the surface this game appears to be a drawing exercise, and most students diagram the game as follows:

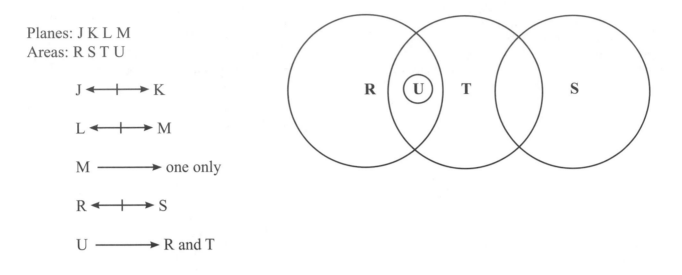

Planes: J K L M
Areas: R S T U

J ←—|—→ K

L ←—|—→ M

M ——→ one only

R ←—|—→ S

U ——→ R and T

However, much like the Islands game discussed previously, this is actually a Grouping game masquerading as a Mapping game. Especially indicative are the third and fourth rules, both of which are negative grouping rules. Since grouping is such an important principle on the LSAT, we felt it desirable to examine a game that has mapping elements but is controlled by grouping principles.

Although every student inevitably draws out the detection areas, it is probably easier to set this game up in a more linear fashion:

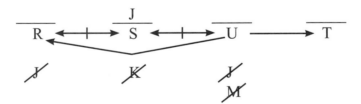

In this setup, we convert the air zones into a grouping relationship. For example, since U is inside of R and T, in our setup we show U with arrows heading towards R and T, meaning that any variable that is in U must also be in R and T. The game scenario indicates R and S do not overlap; our diagram puts a double not-arrow between R and S to indicate that any variable in one of R or S cannot be in the other. The same relationship holds for S and U.

Note that the grouping rules involving areas R, S, T, and U are easily displayed internally within this diagram. Also, since the detection areas are now represented linearly, it is easier to show the Not Laws that apply to each plane. The game is now diagrammed in a much more familiar format and should therefore be easier to attack.

Before moving on to the questions, let's take a moment to examine some of the Not Laws above. In considering these Not Laws, remember that the game is about where each plane is at exactly noon, and thus this is a snapshot at a given time.

Following the relationships above, we can begin to make inferences about the variables. For example, we are told that J is in S. From the relationships, we can deduce that J cannot be in R and U, and we make J Not Laws under R and U. We know that J and K cannot be in the same air zone. Hence, K cannot be in S and we can make a Not Law there. We also know that M can only be in one air zone, and thus M cannot be in U. Consequently, a corresponding M Not Law appears.

Remember, many games that would generally be classified as Mapping Games are actually Grouping games, and so often the best approach is to diagram the Grouping relationship as your primary diagram.

Question #7: Global, Could Be True, List. The correct answer choice is (D)

Answer choices (A) and (B) are eliminated since J cannot be in area R. Answer choice (C) is eliminated since M cannot be in area U. Answer choice (E) is eliminated since K cannot be in area S. It follows that answer choice (D) is correct.

Question #8: Local, Cannot Be True. The correct answer choice is (A)

If K is within exactly two areas, K cannot be in area U, since area U is also within areas R and T. Since K also cannot be in area S, K must be in areas R and T:

$$
\begin{array}{cccc}
\underline{\text{K}} & \underline{\text{J}} & \underline{} & \underline{\text{K}} \\
\text{R} & \text{S} & \text{U} & \text{T} \\
\cancel{\text{J}} & \cancel{\text{K}} & \cancel{\text{K}} & \cancel{\text{J}}
\end{array}
$$

Since K is in area T, J cannot be in area T, and answer choice (A) is correct.

Question #9: Global, Could Be True, List. The correct answer choice is (E)

A perfect situation to refer to earlier work. According to question #7, J can be in area T. Thus, answer choices (A) and (D)—which fail to include J—must be incorrect. According to question #8, K can be in area T, and thus answer choices (B) and (C)—which fail to include K—must be incorrect. Answer choice (E) is proven correct by process of elimination.

Question #10: Global, Cannot Be True. The correct answer choice is (E)

According to the Not Laws in our initial setup, M cannot be in area U, and thus answer choice (E) is correct.

Question #11: Global, Cannot Be True. The correct answer choice is (D)

Again, according to the relationships diagrammed in the initial setup, no individual plane can be within areas S and U at the same time, and thus answer choice (D) is correct.

Question #12: Local, Cannot Be True. The correct answer choice is (E)

The information in the "if" statement can be diagrammed as follows:

Note that the Not Law concerning plane L and area U occurs because L cannot be in area T (M and L cannot be in the same detection area). Any plane that cannot be in area T, area R, or both also cannot be in area U, and so L cannot be in area U. Furthermore, since no plane can be in both areas R and S, it follows that answer choice (E) is correct since L can be in only one detection area (R or S).

Remember, this is a Cannot Be True question, and thus the four incorrect answer choices could occur. For example, answer choice (D) could be true because K could be in both areas R and T.

Question #13: Local, Could Be True. The correct answer choice is (A)

If L is within exactly three areas, L cannot be in area S (if L were in S, then it could only be in S and T) and therefore L must be in areas R, U, and T:

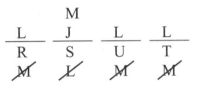

Since L and M cannot be in the same detection areas, M cannot be in areas R, U, and T, and therefore answer choices (D) and (E) are incorrect. Since M must be in at least one detection area, it follows that M must be in area S. According to the Not Laws in our initial setup, K can never be in area S, and therefore answer choice (C) is incorrect. In answer choice (B), it is impossible for J to be in three areas since any plane in area S cannot be in area R and U. Thus, J can only be in at most two areas. Since answer choice (B) is incorrect, answer choice (A) is proven correct by process of elimination.

When you begin a logic game, you should read through all of the rules *before* you begin diagramming. As you read, consider the true nature of the game. Law Services is often able to confuse test takers who fail to completely examine the nature of the rules and their interrelationships. This game provides a fine example of how a thorough and knowledgeable test taker can gain a significant advantage by recognizing the true nature of the rules.

CHAPTER EIGHT: ADVANCED FEATURES AND TECHNIQUES

Numerical Distributions

A Numerical Distribution allocates one set of variables among another set of variables. Since the distribution controls the placement of variables, the distribution is a basic, but critical, element in the game. Because of their importance, Numerical Distributions were naturally discussed in previous chapters. In Chapter Two the discussion of basic Linear games introduced the "one-to-one" distribution: the number of variables to be assigned matches the number of spaces to be filled. The following game scenario is an example:

> A tutor is planning a daily schedule of individual tutoring sessions for each of six students—S, T, W, X, Y, and Z. The tutor will meet with exactly one student at a time, for exactly one hour each session. The tutor will meet with students starting at 1 P. M., for six consecutive hours.

Recognizing distributions is critical to solid games performance.

The six students are each assigned to one of six hours, a Numerical Distribution of 1-1-1-1-1-1. At this level, the distribution is so basic as to appear obvious. As the discussion in Chapter Two progressed, the distributions became more complex, as in one of the games discussed:

> An apartment building has five floors. Each floor has either one or two apartments. There are exactly eight apartments in the building.

These two examples produce one distribution each. Some game scenarios produce multiple distributions.

The "eight apartments into five floors" scenario produces a 2-2-2-1-1 distribution. This distribution requires more attention than the 1-1-1-1-1-1 distribution since there is variation in the number: some floors have one apartment and others have two apartments. That imbalance is an element that must be tracked throughout the game.

Let us take a moment to examine the composition of the distributions above. In the 1-1-1-1-1-1 example, there are six hours and thus there are six separate numbers. There are also six students assigned to those six hours and so the numbers add up to six. In the 2-2-2-1-1 example, there are five floors and so there are five separate numbers. There are eight apartments assigned to those five floors, and so the numbers add up to eight. Therefore, each separate number represents apartments on a floor. Three floors have two apartments, and two floors have one apartment. Numerical Distributions follow this rule: the numbers add up to an amount equal to the total number of variables in the set being allocated; the number of separate numbers is equal to the number of elements "receiving" the allocated set.

Distributions occur with any two sets of variables; one of the sets is allocated among the other set. The set being allocated will have an equal or greater number of variables than the receiving set, as in the following examples:

Numerical
Distributions
appear within
a variety of
game types, as
illustrated by the
two examples
to the right: the
first distribution
example is from a
Linear game,
the second
distribution
example is from a
Grouping game.

1. The variable sets are of equal size.

   Six drivers will be assigned to six cars numbered consecutively 1 through 6. Exactly one driver is assigned to each car.

   The six drivers are distributed among six cars. Since there are six drivers and six cars, the distribution is 1-1-1-1-1-1.

2. One variable set is larger than the other variable set.

   Six chefs will cook four dishes. Each chef cooks exactly one dish, and each dish is cooked by at least one of the six chefs.

   The six chefs are distributed among the four dishes. Since each chef cooks one dish and there are four dishes to cook, there will be four separate numbers that add up to six. Since there are more chefs than dishes, at least one dish must be cooked by two or more chefs. This scenario creates two distributions: 2-2-1-1 and 3-1-1-1. In the first distribution two dishes are cooked by two chefs, and two dishes are cooked by one chef each. In the second distribution one dish is cooked by three chefs, and the other three dishes are each cooked by one chef each.

Creating Distributions Systematically

Because some games have three or more distributions, you must use a systematic approach to find every distribution. To find all the distributions in a game, follow these steps:

An extreme
distribution has
the greatest
variance in the
numbers, such as
5-1-1.

An average
or "middle"
distribution is
the one closest
to the center,
with the least
variance in
numbers, such as
3-2-2.

1. Satisfy the minimum requirements for the receiver set.

2. Examine the remaining or "extra" variables in the allocated set and count the number of ways the remaining variables can be distributed.

3. Create a distribution for each configuration in Step 2 by adding the minimum requirements to each configuration. Work from the extreme to the "middle."

Consider the following example:

   Five students are assigned to three separate groups. Each group must be assigned at least one student.

Since there are three groups, there will be three separate numbers, and since there are five students, the numbers will add up to five. The minimum requirements are:

	Group	Group	Group	
Minimums:	1	1	1	= 3

Note that the groups have not been numbered since the groups are not ordered. Since each group must be assigned at least one student, the minimum requirements claim three of the five students. This leaves just two "extra" students to consider. The two students can be distributed in only two ways: both can be assigned to the same group or they can be assigned to different groups.

	Group	Group	Group	
Minimums:	1	1	1	= 3
Distribution 1: (both students assigned to same group—the extreme)	3	1	1	= 5
Distribution 2: (the two students assigned to different groups—the middle)	2	2	1	= 5

Terminologically, "Numerical Distribution" refers to both single distributions and multiple distributions within a game.

Since the two "extra" students can be configured only two ways (together or separate), there are exactly two distributions. In Distribution 1 the two students are added to the minimum requirements to create a 3-1-1 distribution. In Distribution 2 the two students are separated and then added to the minimum requirements to create a 2-2-1 distribution. These two distributions represent the only two ways that the students can be assigned to the three groups when at least one student must be assigned to each group.

Please note that you cannot determine that there are two distributions just because there are two "extra" variables beyond the minimum requirements. Consider another example:

> Seven assignments are given to two workers. Each worker must be given at least two assignments.

There is no rule that allows you to immediately determine the number of distributions. Cases must be examined on an individual basis.

The seven assignments are distributed between two workers, so there will be two separate numbers that add up to seven. The minimum requirements claim four of the seven assignments:

Minimums:	Worker 2	Worker 2	= 4

There are just three "extra" assignments to consider. The three assignments can be distributed in only two ways: all three can be assigned to the same worker or two can be assigned to one worker and one can be assigned to the other worker:

	Worker 2	Worker 2	= 4
Minimums:			
Distribution 1: (all three assignments to one worker)	5	2	= 7
Distribution 2: (two assignments to one worker and one assignment to the other worker)	4	3	= 7

The most extreme distribution is usually the easiest to identify. Thereafter you work inwards to the most "average" distribution.

Generally, when you create distributions, it is easier to start by examining extremes. First establish the minimum requirements and then assign the extra variables in maximum-sized groups. In the example immediately above, the first distribution allocates all three extra assignments to one worker, and then divides the three assignments into smaller groups for the second distribution.

Fixed versus Unfixed Distributions

Numerical Distributions are either *fixed* or *unfixed*; that is, the allocated set may or may not be attached to a specific variable in the receiver set. In this chapter each distribution has so far been unfixed. In the last example the 5-2 distribution contains two possibilities: worker 1 is given five assignments and worker 2 is given two assignments; or worker 1 is given two assignments and worker 2 is given five. Since writing out every variation of a complex distribution would waste an incredible amount of time, distributions that can move around are called unfixed. Thus a 5-2 unfixed distribution immediately implies that the "5" and "2" are not assigned to any particular worker (and so the distribution could actually be 5-2 or 2-5). The same is true for the 4-3 distribution above. Either worker could be given the four assignments. The unfixed designation is useful because it delivers a great amount of information in a compact form and saves time in doing so.

In a 5-2, 4-3 unfixed distribution, there are really four fixed distributions: 5-2, 2-5, 4-3, and 3-4. The order of presentation is irrelevant.

Numerical Distributions can also be fixed, but there must be at least one rule that specifies a relationship among specific variables. Consider the previous example about students and groups:

> Five students are assigned to three separate groups. Each group must be assigned at least one student.

Now add a rule that states:

> Group 1 must be assigned exactly twice as many students as Group 2.

The rule connects two of the variables in the receiver set and as such it will fix the distribution in place:

In games with fixed distributions, it is often best to identify the Templates. This strategy will be discussed at the end of this chapter.

	Group 1	Group 2	Group 3	
Minimums:	1	1	1	= 3
Distribution 1: (Group 1 with twice as many students as Group 2)	2	1	2	= 5

If Group 2 has one student, then Group 1 must have two students, and the remaining two students are assigned to Group 3. If Group 2 has two students, then Group 1 would have four students, but Group 1 cannot have four students since that adds up to six students and there are only five total. Thus, only the 2-1-2 fixed distribution exists. The *fixed* designation signifies that the 2-1-2 student distribution is assigned to Groups 1, 2, and 3, respectively.

Numerical Distribution Identification and Use

Numerical Distributions occur in almost every game. Often the distribution is so clearly stated that no analysis is necessary. Games that contain a one-to-one distribution are a good example. Other games, however, demand that you recognize and understand the distributions present. To recognize Numerical Distributions other than one-to-one relationships, look for:

Always be on the lookout for Numerical Distributions!

1. A greater number of variables being distributed over a fewer number of variables. Examples include pets to cages, players to teams, and college students to dorm rooms.

2. Rules that include numbers. Since distributions are numerical in nature, it is necessary that the rules establish those relationships. Look for phrases such as "at least," "exactly," and "at most," as in the following examples:

At least one adult must be on each committee.

Each referee must work exactly one game.

At most five movies are shown.

File 1 has twice as many documents as File 2.

Rules that specify exact relationships in the receiver set, such as the file/document rule example above, almost always yield fixed distributions.

Note that when rules fail to establish minimums, the number of distributions increases dramatically. For example, consider this game scenario:

> A television executive is deciding the scheduling for five advertisements to be aired during one week, from Monday through Friday. The schedule must accord with the following:
> Exactly one advertisement is scheduled to air each day.
> No advertisement can air more than two days per week.

To many students, this appears to be a standard 1-1-1-1-1 distribution. But, nowhere in the rules does it state that each advertisement must be aired, and so some advertisements can air more than once and other advertisements do not have to air at all. This creates three distributions of days to advertisements:

Distribution #1:   2-2-1-0-0
(two advertisements air twice, one advertisement airs once, and two advertisements do not air)

Distribution #2:   2-1-1-1-0
(one advertisement airs twice, three advertisements air once, and one advertisement does not air)

Distribution #3:   1-1-1-1-1
(each advertisement airs once)

Recognizing the three possible distributions is critical; otherwise you will make faulty inferences about the use and placement of the advertisements on the Monday-though-Friday linear base.

Numerical Distributions are important because they fundamentally define all the variations a game can assume. As such, the distributions are a powerful and ultimately controlling force. Always check the distribution in a Logic Game, even if it is a basic one. The more complex the distribution, the more likely that you will be directly tested on your ability to identify the distribution.

Power™, first discussed in Chapter Five, modified now to include a numerical aspect:

Numbers

↓

Grouping

↓

Linearity
(including elements such as Sequencing)

Mapping Games, which are non-numerical, fall outside the Hierarchy.

The diagram above indicates that the higher terms dominate the lower terms. When you set up a game, always consider the dominant terms first. Thus, first consider the numerical aspect of the game, then the grouping aspect, and finally the linear aspect. Let us also revisit the example used in Chapter Five, again modified to include the consideration of numbers:

> Suppose you are offered free Super Bowl tickets. Your first reaction wouldn't be to start putting people in the first seat, or sixth seat, etc. Instead you would first establish how many free tickets you are being given. Then you would select the group of people to attend the game, and finally, once at the game, you would consider how to line up the individuals in seats.

The PowerScore LSAT Logic Games Ultimate Setups Guide contains setups for more than 100 LSAT games. If you would like more help with creating optimal setups, the book is an invaluable resource.

Operationally, the Hierarchy provides a logical order of analysis for any Logic Game. By examining the most potent areas first, you increase your chances of identifying the key inferences of the game and thus improving your performance.

Numerical Distribution Identification Drill

Each of the following game scenarios contain rules that lead to one or more numerical distributions. For each problem identify each of the possible fixed or unfixed numerical distributions created by the rules. *Answers on Page 336*

1. Six speakers must participate in a speech contest. Each speaker participates exactly once, and no two speakers speak at the same time.

2. Seven dog biscuits are given to three dogs—a Dalmatian, a Doberman, and a Great Dane. Each dog must be given at least one biscuit, and the Great Dane is given exactly twice as many biscuits as the Dalmatian.

3. Eight drinks are given to two bar patrons. Each patron is given at least three drinks and no more than five drinks.

4. Seven animals are placed into cages containing anywhere from one to three animals. At most one of the cages contains three animals. At least one of the cages contains exactly two animals. At most two of the cages contain exactly one animal each.

5. Eight students are assigned to five different floors in a dormitory. At least one student is assigned to each floor, and at most three students are assigned to a floor.

THE POWERSCORE LSAT LOGIC GAMES BIBLE

Numerical Distribution Identification Drill

6. Fourteen vitamin pills are placed into six bottles. At least two vitamin pills are placed in each bottle.

7. Ten cars are assigned to five different mechanics—mechanics A, B, C, D, and E. Each mechanic is assigned at least one car. Mechanic B is assigned two cars. Mechanic C is assigned more cars than Mechanic D. Mechanic B is assigned more cars than Mechanic A. Mechanic E is assigned the same number of cars as Mechanic D.

8. An unknown number of toys are given to four charities. Charity 1 is given three times as many toys as Charity 2. Charity 3 is given one more toy than Charity 4. Charity 2 is given at least one toy. Charity 3 is always given more toys than Charity 2. Charity 4 is given at most two toys.

Numerical Distribution Identification Drill Answer Key

1. Six speakers distributed into six time slots.
   Fixed: 1-1-1-1-1-1 (All one-to-one distributions are automatically fixed.)

2. Seven dog biscuits distributed to three dogs.
   Fixed: 1-4-2, 2-1-4
   (This distribution has appeared in several different games.)

3. Eight drinks distributed to two bar patrons.
   Unfixed: 5-3, 4-4

4. Seven animals distributed into an unknown number of cages.
   Unfixed: 3-2-2, 3-2-1-1, 2-2-2-1

5. Eight students distributed to five floors.
   Unfixed: 3-2-1-1-1, 2-2-2-1-1

6. Fourteen vitamin pills distributed into six bottles.
   Unfixed: 4-2-2-2-2-2, 3-3-2-2-2-2
   (This distribution appeared on the third game of the October 1991 LSAT, and also on a game in the 1980s.)

7. Ten cars distributed to five mechanics.
   Fixed: 1-2-5-1-1, 1-2-3-2-2

8. An unknown number of toys distributed to four charities.
   Fixed: 3-1-2-1, 3-1-3-2, 6-2-3-2

Note in items #4 and #8 the number in the allocated set or the receiver set is unknown; in spite of this, each item contains enough other information to allow distributions to be identified.

A reporter is trying to uncover the workings of a secret committee. The committee has six members—French, Ghauri, Hsia, Irving, Magnus, and Pinsky—each of whom serves on at least one subcommittee. There are three subcommittees, each having three members, about which the following is known:

> One of the committee members serves on all three subcommittees.
> French does not serve on any subcommittee with Ghauri.
> Hsia does not serve on any subcommittee with Irving.

17. If French does not serve on any subcommittee with Magnus, which one of the following must be true?

    (A) French serves on a subcommittee with Hsia.
    (B) French serves on a subcommittee with Irving.
    (C) Irving serves on a subcommittee with Pinsky.
    (D) Magnus serves on a subcommittee with Ghauri.
    (E) Magnus serves on a subcommittee with Irving.

18. If Pinsky serves on every subcommittee on which French serves and every subcommittee on which Ghauri serves, then which one of the following could be true?

    (A) Magnus serves on every subcommittee on which French serves and every subcommittee on which Ghauri serves.
    (B) Magnus serves on every subcommittee on which Hsia serves and every subcommittee on which Irving serves.
    (C) Hsia serves on every subcommittee on which French serves and every subcommittee on which Ghauri serves.
    (D) French serves on every subcommittee on which Pinsky serves.
    (E) Hsia serves on every subcommittee on which Pinsky serves.

19. If Irving serves on every subcommittee on which Magnus serves, which one of the following could be true?

    (A) Magnus serves on all of the subcommittees.
    (B) Irving serves on more than one subcommittee.
    (C) Irving serves on every subcommittee on which Pinsky serves.
    (D) French serves on a subcommittee with Magnus.
    (E) Ghauri serves on a subcommittee with Magnus.

20. Which one of the following could be true?

    (A) French serves on all three subcommittees.
    (B) Hsia serves on all three subcommittees.
    (C) Ghauri serves on every subcommittee on which Magnus serves and every subcommittee on which Pinsky serves.
    (D) Pinsky serves on every subcommittee on which Irving serves and every subcommittee on which Magnus serves.
    (E) Magnus serves on every subcommittee on which Pinsky serves, and Pinsky serves on every subcommittee on which Magnus serves.

21. Which one of the following must be true?

    (A) Ghauri serves on at least two subcommittees.
    (B) Irving serves on only one subcommittee.
    (C) French serves on a subcommittee with Hsia.
    (D) Ghauri serves on a subcommittee with Irving.
    (E) Magnus serves on a subcommittee with Pinsky.

22. Which one of the following must be true?

    (A) Every subcommittee has either French or Ghauri as a member.
    (B) Every subcommittee has either Hsia or Irving as a member.
    (C) No subcommittee consists of French, Magnus, and Pinsky.
    (D) Some committee member serves on exactly two subcommittees.
    (E) Either Magnus or Pinsky serves on only one subcommittee.

Analysis of Numerical Distribution Game #1: June 2005 Questions 17-22

This game was widely considered the most difficult of the June 2005 exam. After three linear-based games, the test makers saved a Grouping game for last.

At first, this game appears to be a straightforward Grouping game: six committee members serving on three subcommittees. However, the game scenario and rules indicate that there are nine subcommittee spaces, and that some committee members serve on multiple subcommittees. If each member served on only one subcommittee, the game would be considerably easier because the assignment of a member to a subcommittee would eliminate that member from further consideration. Thus, the Underfunded aspect of this game gave test takers more to consider as they looked at the composition of each subcommittee.

Note that since the committees do not have formal names, we have labeled as "SC."

The game scenario provides us with the following basic setup:

F G H I M P [6]

____	____	____
____	____	____
____	____	____
SC	SC	SC

Now, let us examine each rule.

Rule #1. With six committee members filling in nine spaces, and with the game scenario stating that each member serves on at least one subcommittee, you should be on the lookout for rules that reveal a specific Numerical Distribution. The first rule is just such a rule.

Because one of the committee members serves on all three subcommittees, the remaining five members must fill the remaining six subcommittee spaces. Since every member must serve on at least one subcommittee, the five members automatically fill five of the six spaces. The remaining subcommittee space can be assigned to any one of the committee members (aside from the one member serving on all three committees, of course). Thus, the game is controlled by a 3-2-1-1-1-1 distribution of spaces to committee members.

Rules #2 and #3. These two rules establish the following not-blocks:

While these not-blocks may appear standard, when combined with the 3-2-1-1-1-1 numerical distribution there is an important implication. First, because F, G, H and I are involved in the not-blocks, none of those four members can serve on all three subcommittees (otherwise there would be an overlap that would conflict with the not-block). Thus, only M or P can be the member who serves on all three subcommittees.

With the information on the previous page, the complete game diagram is:

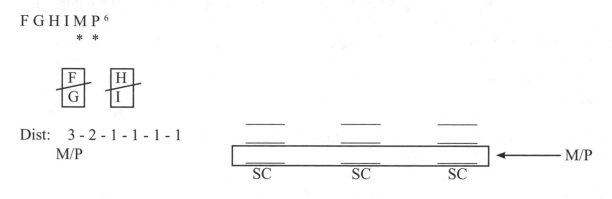

Question #17: Local, Must Be True. The correct answer choice is (C)

The condition in the question stem affects the Numerical Distribution discussed in the setup analysis. If F and M cannot serve on the same subcommittee, then M cannot be the member who serves on all three subcommittees, and P must serve on all three subcommittees:

Because P serves on all three subcommittees, every other member serves with P, and answer choice (C) is correct.

Question #18: Local, Could Be True. The correct answer choice is (C)

This is the most difficult question of the game. The wording of the conditions in the question stem is quite tricky, and you must carefully consider the meaning of each statement. The phrase, "P serves on every subcommittee on which F serves," means that when F serves on a subcommittee, then P also serves on that subcommittee. This relationship is diagrammed as:

$$F \longrightarrow P$$

The second condition is worded in a similar fashion, and can be diagrammed as:

$$G \longrightarrow P$$

Consequently, since F and G must serve on at least one subcommittee each, we know the following:

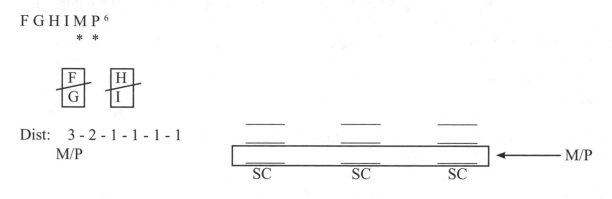

Answer choice (A): This answer is incorrect because if M serves on the same subcommittees as F and G, then H and I would be forced to serve on the same subcommittee, a violation of the third rule.

Answer choice (B): This answer is incorrect because there is not enough room for M to serve with both H and I (M can serve on one subcommittee with either H or I, but the other two subcommittees already have P and F, or P and G, and hence there is not space for two more members on those subcommittees.).

Answer choice (C): This is the correct answer. H could be the member who serves on two committees.

Answer choice (D): This answer is incorrect because if P serves on all three subcommittees then F would have to serve on three subcommittees, a violation of the numerical distribution; if P serves on two subcommittees, then F would have to serve on two subcommittees, and M would have to serve on all three subcommittees, creating a 3-2-2-1-1 distribution, which also violates the previously established numerical distribution.

Answer choice (E): This answer is incorrect for the same reasoning used to disprove answer choice (D).

Question #19: Local, Could Be True. The correct answer choice is (B)

Like question #18, the wording of the condition in the question stem is quite tricky, and you must carefully consider the meaning of the statement. The phrase, "I serves on every subcommittee on which M serves," means that when M serves on a subcommittee, then I also serves on that subcommittee. This relationship is diagrammed as:

$$M \longrightarrow I$$

This condition means that M cannot serve on all three subcommittees (if M did serve on all three, then I would have to serve on all three also, a violation of the numerical distribution). Consequently, we can deduce that P must serve on all three subcommittees. We can also infer that M will not serve on two subcommittees (again, I would serve on two as well, a violation of the distribution) and that M serves on only one subcommittee:

I		
M		
P	P	P
SC	SC	SC

Because F and G are in a not-block, we know that F and G must serve on different subcommittees:

I		
M	F	G
P	P	P
SC	SC	SC

The only remaining uncertainty is the placement of H, and whether H or I is doubled:

I	H/I	I/H
M	F	G
P	P	P
SC	SC	SC

Answer choice (A): As discussed in the question analysis, M cannot serve on all three subcommittees, and this answer choice is incorrect.

Answer choice (B): This is the correct answer because I could be the member who serves on two subcommittees.

Answer choice (C): This answer choice is incorrect because I cannot serve on all three subcommittees.

Answer choice (D): This answer choice is incorrect because, as shown above, F and M cannot serve on the same subcommittee.

Answer choice (E): This answer choice is incorrect because, as shown above, G and M cannot serve on the same subcommittee.

Question #20: Global, Could Be True. The correct answer choice is (D)

Answer choices (A) and (B): As established in the game analysis, either M or P must be the sole member who serves on all three subcommittees. If either F or H served on all three, there would be a violation of one of the last two rules. Consequently, both of these answer choices are incorrect.

Answer choice (C): If G serves on every subcommittee that M and P serve on, and we know that one of M and P serves on all three subcommittees, then G must serve on all three subcommittees as well. This scenario violates the numerical distribution, and is therefore incorrect.

Answer choice (D): This is the correct answer.

Answer choice (E): This answer choice creates a scenario where M and P serve on exactly the same subcommittees. Since only one of M and P serves on all three subcommittees, and the other serves on fewer subcommittees, this answer choice is incorrect.

Question #21: Global, Must Be True. The correct answer choice is (E)

This question trades on the M/P inference produced by the combination of the Numerical Distribution and the last two rules. As established in the discussion of the rules, either M or P must serve on all three subcommittees. Since one of the two must be on all three subcommittees, there must be an overlap between M and P, and consequently answer choice (E) is correct.

Question #22: Global, Must Be True. The correct answer choice is (D)

Again, we can use the distribution to quickly and easily destroy this question. As we have previously established, the game contains a 3-2-1-1-1-1 distribution, and exactly one of the committee members serves on two subcommittees. Hence, (D) is the correct answer choice.

Exactly seven film buffs—Ginnie, Ian, Lianna, Marcos, Reveka, Viktor, and Yow—attend a showing of classic films. Three films are shown, one directed by Fellini, one by Hitchcock, and one by Kurosawa. Each of the film buffs sees exactly one of the three films. The films are shown only once, one film at a time. The following restrictions must apply:

> Exactly twice as many of the film buffs see the Hitchcock film as see the Fellini film.
> Ginnie and Reveka do not see the same film as each other.
> Ian and Marcos do not see the same film as each other.
> Viktor and Yow see the same film as each other.
> Lianna sees the Hitchcock film.
> Ginnie sees either the Fellini film or the Kurosawa film.

13. Which one of the following could be an accurate matching of film buffs to films?

    (A) Ginnie: the Hitchcock film; Ian: the Kurosawa film; Marcos: the Hitchcock film
    (B) Ginnie: the Kurosawa film; Ian: the Fellini film; Viktor: the Fellini film
    (C) Ian: the Hitchcock film; Reveka: the Kurosawa film; Viktor: the Fellini film
    (D) Marcos: the Kurosawa film; Reveka: the Kurosawa film; Viktor: the Kurosawa film
    (E) Marcos: the Hitchcock film; Reveka: the Hitchcock film; Yow: the Hitchcock film

14. Each of the following must be false EXCEPT:

    (A) Reveka is the only film buff to see the Fellini film.
    (B) Reveka is the only film buff to see the Hitchcock film.
    (C) Yow is the only film buff to see the Kurosawa film.
    (D) Exactly two film buffs see the Kurosawa film.
    (E) Exactly three film buffs see the Hitchcock film.

15. Which one of the following could be a complete and accurate list of the film buffs who do NOT see the Hitchcock film?

    (A) Ginnie, Marcos
    (B) Ginnie, Reveka
    (C) Ginnie, Ian, Reveka
    (D) Ginnie, Marcos, Yow
    (E) Ginnie, Viktor, Yow

16. If exactly one film buff sees the Kurosawa film, then which one of the following must be true?

    (A) Viktor sees the Hitchcock film.
    (B) Ginnie sees the Fellini film.
    (C) Marcos sees the Fellini film.
    (D) Ian sees the Fellini film.
    (E) Reveka sees the Hitchcock film.

17. Which one of the following must be true?

    (A) Ginnie sees a different film than Ian does.
    (B) Ian sees a different film than Lianna does.
    (C) Ian sees a different film than Viktor does.
    (D) Ian, Lianna, and Viktor do not all see the same film.
    (E) Ginnie, Lianna, and Marcos do not all see the same film.

18. If Viktor sees the same film as Ginnie does, then which one of the following could be true?

    (A) Ginnie sees the Fellini film.
    (B) Ian sees the Hitchcock film.
    (C) Reveka sees the Kurosawa film.
    (D) Viktor sees the Hitchcock film.
    (E) Yow sees the Fellini film.

19. Each of the following could be a complete and accurate list of the film buffs who see the Fellini film EXCEPT:

    (A) Ginnie, Ian
    (B) Ginnie, Marcos
    (C) Ian, Reveka
    (D) Marcos, Reveka
    (E) Viktor, Yow

This a Defined-Moving, Balanced Grouping game. It has been chosen for this section since it features two Numerical Distributions that control the placement of film buffs to films. Although virtually all games contain a Numerical Distribution, the distribution becomes a significant element if there are multiple distributions, or if the single distribution is unusual. This game is one of the former.

The information in the game scenario establishes that there are seven film buffs attending a showing of three movies. Each film buff sees exactly one film. The first rule establishes two fixed distributions:

	Fellini	Hitchcock	Kurosawa
Fixed Distribution #1:	1	2	4
Fixed Distribution #2:	2	4	1

The two fixed distributions create two distinctly different scenarios. And since each scenario requires a different analysis, the best strategy is to create two templates, one for the 1-2-4 distribution, and another for the 2-4-1 distribution:

```
   1    2    4                    2    4    1

             ___                       ___
             ___                       ___
        ___  ___                  ___  ___
   ___  ___  ___                  ___  ___  ___
    F    H    K                    F    H    K
```

The rules can now be considered:

G I L M R V Y [7]

Of course, the rules impact each template:

```
   1    2    4                    2    4    1

             I/M
             R/G                       Y
             Y                         V
        L    V                    G/   L    /G
   G/   H    K                    F    H    K
   F        (∅)                       (∅)
```

Let us analyze the two diagrams. The fifth rule states that L sees the Hitchcock film. In the 1-2-4 this leaves one open space at Fellini, one open space at Hitchcock, and four open spaces at Kurosawa. But the third rule states that V and Y see the same film as each other, so in the 1-2-4 it can be inferred that V and Y see the Kurosawa film. In the 2-4-1 we can infer that V and Y see either the Fellini film or the Hitchcock film, but at the moment it is uncertain which one. G cannot see the Hitchcock film, and so Not Laws are drawn on both templates, and G split-options are placed on Fellini and Kurosawa.

The two negative grouping rules help fill in both templates. In the 1-2-4, there are four remaining spaces for G, R, I, and M: one space at Fellini, one space at Hitchcock, and two spaces at Kurosawa. Since G and R, as well as I and M, cannot see the same film, it can be inferred that one of G and R must see the Kurosawa film, and one of I and M must see the Kurosawa film.

In the 2-4-1 there are still six open spaces: two at Fellini, three at Hitchcock, and one at Kurosawa. Of the six remaining variables, two—V and Y—must see the same film. If V and Y see the Fellini film, then there would be three open spaces at Hitchcock and one open space at Kurosawa. Since G and R cannot see the same film, one must see Hitchcock and the other must see Kurosawa. That leaves two spaces at Hitchcock for I and M. But wait, I and M cannot see the same film, and so this scenario causes a violation of the rules. Essentially, when V and Y see the Fellini film, there are not enough remaining spaces to properly separate G, R, I, and M. It can therefore be inferred that in the 2-4-1 distribution V and Y see the Hitchcock film.

In both templates there are still several possible solutions, and in the next section we will discuss Identifying the Templates further. For now, it will be important to be aware of G, R, I, and M since they are the only variables still in play.

Question #13: Global, Could Be True, List. The correct answer choice is (D)

Answer choice (A) is incorrect because G cannot see the Hitchcock film. Answer choices (B) and (C) are incorrect because V can never see the Fellini film. Answer choice (E) is incorrect because M and R could never see the Hitchcock film at the same time. Answer choice (D) is therefore correct. Overall a much more difficult List question than usual, but easy if you have used the distributions to identify the two templates!

Question #14: Global, Could Be True. The correct answer choice is (A)

Remember, convert false into true when you analyze the question stem. Answer choices (D) and (E) are eliminated by applying the distributions. Answer choice (C) is eliminated by applying the templates, and answer choice (B) is eliminated by the fifth rule that states that L sees the Hitchcock film. Answer choice (A) is correct.

Question #15: Global, Could Be True, List. The correct answer choice is (C)

The first step is to apply the VY block rule because, if one does not see Hitchcock, it is certain the other will not see Hitchcock either. Answer choice (D) contains Y, but not V, and is incorrect.

The second step is to consider the Numerical Distributions. In the 1-2-4 distribution, two film buffs see the Hitchcock film, and five film buffs do not see the Hitchcock film. In the 2-4-1 distribution, four film buffs see the Hitchcock film, and three film buffs do not see the Hitchcock film. Thus, since this question stem asks for a complete and accurate list of the film buffs who do NOT see the Hitchcock film, the correct answer choice must contain either three or five film buffs. Since answer choices (A) and (B) contain only two film buffs, they can both be rejected without further analysis.

Since answer choices (C), (D), and (E) each contain three film buffs, it is apparent that they are each generated by the 2-4-1 distribution. In the 2-4-1 distribution we have already ascertained that L, V, and Y each see the Hitchcock film, and so any answer choice that contains L, V, or Y will be incorrect. This eliminates answer choice (D) and again eliminates answer choice (E). Answer choice (C) is therefore correct.

Question #16: Local, Must Be True. The correct answer choice is (A)

According to the information in the question stem, the film buffs are in the 2-4-1 fixed distribution. Accordingly, answer choice (A) is correct. Again, note the usefulness of the distributions and templates.

Question #17: Global, Must Be True. The correct answer choice is (E)

This question can be solved by either referring to the templates or by using the rules.

If the rules are used, the final two rules indicate that G and L must see different films. Consequently, answer choice (E) is proven correct.

If the templates are used, nothing in either template suggests that answer choice (A), (B), or (C) is correct. In answer choice (D), I, L, and V could all see the Hitchcock film under the 2-4-1. The templates ultimately show that answer choice (E) must be true.

Question #18: Local, Could Be True. The correct answer choice is (B)

V and G can only see the same film under the 1-2-4 template:

$$
\begin{array}{ccc}
1 & 2 & 4 \\
 & & \text{I/M} \\
 & & \text{G} \\
 & & \text{Y} \\
 & \text{L} & \text{V} \\
\text{F} & \text{H} & \text{K}
\end{array}
$$

The final two spaces are filled by R and the remainder of I/M. Accordingly, answer choice (B) is correct.

Question #19: Global, Cannot Be True, List. The correct answer choice is (E)

Since each answer choice contains two film buffs, the 2-4-1 fixed distribution applies. Under that distribution we have already inferred that L, V, and Y each see the Hitchcock film, and so any answer choice that contains L, V, or Y would be correct (remember, this is an Except question). Answer choice (E) contains V and Y and is therefore correct.

This game provides an excellent example of how the test makers use Numerical Distributions. Many of the questions force you to examine the templates created by each distribution and then attack the answer choices. The distributions are central to understanding this game: if you do not identify the distributions, the questions in this game cannot be answered correctly.

Limited Solution Set Games

Certain Logic Games are so restricted that only a limited number of solutions conform to the rules. In these games the best approach is to diagram each possibility before attacking the questions. With all of the possibilities in hand, the questions are easy.

Pure Sequencing games and Pattern games depend on a lack of certainty regarding variable placement. It is therefore not surprising that they rarely have a limited number of solutions.

Limited Solution Sets are a feature that appears in many different game types, including Grouping and Linear games, but there is no specific type of game that *always* uses this feature. Typically, the number of possibilities is constrained by some type of restriction or limitation that leads to just a few solutions.

Each year, there are usually several LSAT games that contain a limited number of solutions, and students who learn the best approach have a significant advantage. Because of their importance, games with limited solutions have already been previewed several times in this book. For example, in Chapter Two several of the problems in the Linear Setup Practice Drill have a reduced number of possible solutions. In this chapter, the Numerical Distribution game features two basic templates based on two distributions. When you attack Limited Solution Set Games, use one of the following two approaches: Identify the Templates™ or Identify the Possibilities™. Although similar, each leads to a different diagram and requires different decisions.

Identify the Templates™

Identify the Templates and Identify the Possibilities are not game types; rather, they are techniques for attacking certain games.

When a game is attacked by Identifying the Templates, the major possibility templates are diagrammed, but the exact possibilities within each template are not fully displayed. This approach is excellent for games where two or three major directions appear. In the Fellini/Hitchcock/Kurosawa game on page 343, two templates were generated by two fixed Numerical Distributions, 1-2-4 and 2-4-1. Since these distributions created two separate scenarios in the game, it made sense to create basic diagrams for each option. And because these basic diagrams provided a considerable amount of information, there was no need to show every single possibility. The templates were sufficient. Consider one of the templates from that game:

$$
\begin{array}{ccc}
 & \underline{\text{Y}} & \\
 & \underline{\text{V}} & \\
\underline{\text{G/}} & \underline{\text{L}} & \underline{\text{/G}} \\
\text{F} & \text{H} & \text{K}
\end{array}
$$

The diagram is considered a template because it does not show all of the information regarding the placement of the variables.

Identifying the Templates does not have to be connected to Numerical Distributions. For example, assume a rule states, "Marshall drives on either Wednesday or Thursday." If there are several other limiting rules, it might be wise to diagram the two possible templates: one where Marshall drives Wednesday and another where Marshall drives Thursday. The decision to show the templates is normally made when the rules that suggest a major component of the game is limited to just two or three options. This major component could be a variable, a powerful block, a numerical distribution, or some other element.

Focus on identifying limiting elements!

Identify the Possibilities™

Identify the Possibilities is an extension of Identify the Templates. Instead of creating basic templates to capture the general direction of the game, each possibility is written out. This usually takes more time during the setup, but since it results in perfect information the questions can be answered incredibly fast.

The difference between showing templates and possibilities is one of degree. Identifying the Templates exposes the major directions of the game; Identifying the Possibilities explores those directions in detail. Because Identifying the Templates is less detailed, it tends to take less time to apply. On the contrary, Identifying the Possibilities takes longer because it is more detailed.

When showing the possibilities, you should use some of the diagramming shortcuts discussed in earlier chapters. Dual-options are a great example. The following diagram uses dual-options to efficiently display two possibilities:

$$\begin{array}{cc} \underline{E/F} & \underline{F/E} \\ \underline{C} & \underline{D} \\ \underline{A} & \underline{B} \\ 1 & 2 \end{array}$$

The example to the right would be called a template that contains two possibilities.

The two possibilities are based on whether E or F is in group 1 or 2. It would be a waste of time to draw each possibility separately when the dual-option can perfectly capture the same idea.

How to Identify Limited Solution Set Games

There is no single type of rule or game that invariably produces a limited number of solutions. Instead, it is a combination of factors that leads to limited solutions and thus the decision to Identify the Templates or Possibilities. Typically, the number of solutions is constrained by a large number of disparate rules, some limiting principle in the game (such as a numerical distribution), or variable configurations such as unwieldy blocks

It can be quite difficult to identify Limited Solution Set games because there is no obvious feature that always leads to just a few possibilities. And thus it can be difficult to know when to Identify the Templates or Identify the Possibilities.

that have reduced placement possibilities. In part, an understanding of the restrictions comes from examining different games that are limited. In each instance there will be a controlling rule or set of rules that affects certain areas of the game in such a way as to suggest that only a few options are presented. You must examine each Limited Solution Set game to better understand why it is limited.

The Dangers of Misapplication

Identifying the Possibilities is a very seductive technique. Since it shows all the solutions to a game and makes the questions easy, some students try to apply it to every single game. That will be fatal over the course of a Games section because some of the games will have too many possibilities. Imagine trying to show all the possibilities in a game with 50 solutions. Remember, Identify the Possibilities cannot be applied to every game!

Identifying the Possibilities is a dangerous weapon: when it is used at the right time, it will result in absolute success; when it is used on the wrong game (one that has too many possibilities) it can waste time. Keep in mind that identifying all of the possibilities forces you to spend extra time during the setup, but that lost time is then regained during your swift demolition of the questions. Remember, though, this technique should be applied only to games with eight or fewer possibilities.

With Identifying the Templates the risk seems to be less: even if you decide that showing all the templates is not feasible, usually the process of looking at the various options increases your game knowledge. Identify the Templates should be used only in games with four or fewer major directions.

Since it can be difficult to determine which approach is best, you can always show the basic templates and then make the decision to explore each possibility. In this way you protect yourself against losing too much time by making an error in judgment.

Final Pregame Note

There are four games in this section. Two use Identify the Templates and two use Identify the Possibilities. Three of the games feature Numerical Distributions. The explanation for each game will illuminate the reasons for choosing the appropriate technique. Good luck!

During a single week, from Monday through Friday, tours will be conducted of a company's three divisions—Operations, Production, Sales. Exactly five tours will be conducted that week, one each day. The schedule of tours for the week must conform to the following restrictions:

Each division is toured at least once.

The Operations division is not toured on Monday.

The Production division is not toured on Wednesday.

The Sales division is toured on two consecutive days, and on no other days.

If the Operations division is toured on Thursday, then the Production division is toured on Friday.

14. Which one of the following CANNOT be true of the week's tour schedule?

   (A)   The division that is toured on Monday is also toured on Tuesday.

   (B)   The division that is toured on Monday is also toured on Friday.

   (C)   The division that is toured on Tuesday is also toured on Thursday.

   (D)   The division that is toured on Wednesday is also toured on Friday.

   (E)   The division that is toured on Thursday is also toured on Friday.

15. If in addition to the Sales division one other division is toured on two consecutive days, then it could be true of the week's tour schedule both that the

   (A)   Production division is toured on Monday and that the Operations division is toured on Thursday

   (B)   Production division is toured on Tuesday and that the Sales division is toured on Wednesday

   (C)   Operations division is toured on Tuesday and that the Production division is toured on Friday

   (D)   Sales division is toured on Monday and that the Operations division is toured on Friday

   (E)   Sales division is toured on Wednesday and that the Production division is toured on Friday

16. If in the week's tour schedule the division that is toured on Tuesday is also toured on Friday, then for which one of the following days must a tour of the Production division be scheduled?

   (A)   Monday

   (B)   Tuesday

   (C)   Wednesday

   (D)   Thursday

   (E)   Friday

17. If in the week's tour schedule the division that is toured on Monday is not the division that is toured on Tuesday then which one of the following could be true of the week's schedule?

   (A)   A tour of the Sales division is scheduled for some day earlier in the week than is any tour of the Production division.

   (B)   A tour of the Operations division is scheduled for some day earlier in the week than is any tour of the Production division.

   (C)   The Sales division is toured on Monday.

   (D)   The Production division is toured on Tuesday.

   (E)   The Operations division is toured on Wednesday.

18. If in the week's tour schedule the division that is toured on Tuesday is also toured on Wednesday, then which one of the following must be true of the week's tour schedule?

   (A)   The Production division is toured on Monday.

   (B)   The Operations division is toured on Tuesday.

   (C)   The Sales division is toured on Wednesday.

   (D)   The Sales division is toured on Thursday.

   (E)   The Production division is toured on Friday.

Analysis of Limited Solution Set Game #1: June 2000 Questions 14-18

This is a Defined, Unbalanced: Underfunded Linear game. The game is Underfunded because three division tours—O, P, and S—must be toured five times (3 into 5). The Underfunded aspect leads to a Numerical Distribution:

> Because S is toured exactly twice and each division is toured at least once, the five tours are distributed among the three divisions in a 2-2-1 partially fixed distribution. The distribution is partially fixed since S is toured twice, but the remaining three tours are assigned to P or O in a 2-1 unfixed distribution:

Partially	2	2	1
Fixed	S	O/P	P/O
Distribution			

> One of the challenges of the game is to keep track of the distribution of O and P.

Initially, most students diagram the game as follows:

O P S [3]

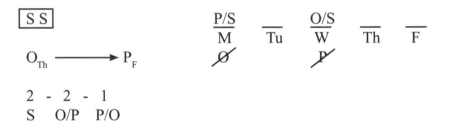

Because S is toured twice and the tours are consecutive, the placement options of the SS block are limited to four positions: Monday-Tuesday, Tuesday-Wednesday, Wednesday-Thursday, and Thursday-Friday. These four options split the game in four directions and are the basis for Identifying the Templates:

	M	Tu	W	Th	F
1. SS on Mon-Tue:	S	S	O	O/P	O/P
2. SS on Tue-Wed:	P	S	S	O/P	P/O
3. SS on Wed-Thu:	P	O/P	S	S	O/P
4. SS on Thu-Fri:	P	O/P	O	S	S

Although it is not necessary to number each template during the game, we do so here for purposes of the discussion to follow. Let us examine each template in greater detail:

1. SS on Mon-Tue: Since P cannot be toured on Wednesday, and the two tours of S are already scheduled, it can be inferred that O is toured on Wednesday. The only uncertain days are Thursday and Friday. Since neither can be S, O/P options have been placed on each. Note, however, that there are several possibilities for Thursday and Friday, such as O-P, P-O, and P-P. O-O is impossible because of the last rule.

2. SS on Tue-Wed: Since O cannot be toured on Monday, and the two tours of S are already scheduled, it can be inferred that P is toured on Monday. The only uncertain days are Thursday and Friday. Since neither can be S, dual O/P options have been placed on each. There are only two possibilities for Thursday and Friday, O-P and P-O. O-O is impossible because of the last rule, and P-P is impossible since O must be toured at least once during the five days.

3. SS on Wed-Thu: Since O cannot be toured on Monday, and the two tours of S are already scheduled, it can be inferred that P is toured on Monday. The only uncertain days are Tuesday and Friday. Since neither can be S, O/P options have been placed on each. There are three possibilities for Tuesday and Friday, O-P, P-O, and O-O. P-P is impossible since O must be toured at least once during the five days.

4. SS on Thu-Fri: Since O cannot be toured on Monday, and the two tours of S are already scheduled, it can be inferred that P is toured on Monday. Since P cannot be toured on Wednesday, it can be inferred that O is toured on Wednesday. The only uncertain day is Tuesday, which has either tour O or P.

This setup highlights the difference between Identify the Templates and Identify the Possibilities: The templates capture the four major directions of the game but do not map out every single possibility. With the templates in hand, there is sufficient information to attack the questions effectively.

When using the templates, you simply need to scan each to find the correct information. The questions will naturally direct you towards using some templates and away from using others.

Question #14: Global, Cannot Be True. The correct answer choice is (C)

Template #1 eliminates answer choice (A). Template #2 or #3 can be used to eliminate answer choice (B). Checking all four templates proves that answer choice (C) is correct. Template #1 eliminates answer choice (D). Template #4 (and less resoundingly, template #2) eliminates answer choice (E).

Question #15: Local, Could Be True. The correct answer choice is (B)

The conditions in the question stem eliminate template #2 from consideration. Since there are still three templates in consideration and thus a considerable number of possibilities, it is best to consider each answer choice against all remaining templates. For answer choice (A) only templates #3 and #4 have P toured on Monday; but neither have O on Thursday, and so answer choice (A) is incorrect. For answer choice (B) only templates #3 and #4 could have P toured on Tuesday, and template #3 allows S to be toured on Wednesday, so answer choice (B) is correct. For answer choice (C) only templates #3 and #4 have O toured on Tuesday. Template #4 does not have P toured on

Friday, and so it does not apply; template #3 could have P toured on Friday, but to do so would violate the condition in the question stem requiring one other division beside S to be toured twice. Consequently, answer choice (C) is incorrect. For answer choice (D), only template #1 applies, and if O were toured on Friday again, the condition in the question stem requiring one other division beside S to be toured twice would be violated. So answer choice (D) is incorrect. Finally, for answer choice (E) only template #3 applies, but if P were toured on Friday, the condition in the question stem requiring one other division beside S to be toured twice would be violated. So answer choices (C), (D), and (E) each can be eliminated by the condition in the questions stem. In this question it is easier to find the correct answer than it is to eliminate the incorrect answers.

Question #16: Local, Must Be True. The correct answer choice is (A)

Only template #3 allows the tours on Tuesday and Friday to be identical (O on both days). Therefore answer choice (A) is correct.

Question #17: Local, Could Be True. The correct answer choice is (E)

Template #1 is eliminated from consideration by the condition in the question stem, and for templates #3 and #4 to apply, O must be toured on Tuesday. If necessary, write out the three templates in consideration:

2. SS on Tue-Wed:	P	S	S	O/P	P/O
3. SS on Wed-Thu:	P	O	S	S	O/P
4. SS on Thu-Fri:	P	O	O	S	S

The first four answer choices can each be rejected by scanning the three remaining templates. Template #4 proves answer choice (E) correct.

Question #18: Local, Must Be True. The correct answer choice is (A)

Only templates #2 and #4 meet the condition in the question stem. Consequently answer choice (A) is correct.

The decision to diagram the four templates results in large part from the SS block, but it is also important to consider the impact of the O, S, and P trio. When the LSAT supplies only three options for a space the situation is inherently limited. If just one of the options were removed, then a dual-option would result automatically, making the situation easier to handle.

In this game the benefit of Identifying the Templates is obvious. And spending a bit more time during the setup simplifies the process of answering the questions.

Morrisville's town council has exactly three members: Fu, Gianola, and Herstein. During one week, the council members vote on exactly three bills: a recreation bill, a school bill, and a tax bill. Each council member votes either for or against each bill. The following is known:

  Each member of the council votes for at least one of the bills and against at least one of the bills.

  Exactly two members of the council vote for the recreation bill.

  Exactly one member of the council votes for the school bill.

  Exactly one member of the council votes for the tax bill.

  Fu votes for the recreation bill and against the school bill.

  Gianola votes against the recreation bill.

  Herstein votes against the tax bill.

19. Which one of the following statements could be true?

(A) Fu and Gianola vote the same way on the tax bill.
(B) Gianola and Herstein vote the same way on the recreation bill.
(C) Gianola and Herstein vote the same way on the school bill.
(D) Fu votes for one of the bills and Gianola votes for two of the bills.
(E) Fu votes for two of the bills and Gianola votes for two of the bills.

20. If the set of members of the council who vote against the school bill is the same set of members who vote against the tax bill, then which one of the following statements must be true?

(A) Fu votes for the tax bill.
(B) Gianola votes for the recreation bill.
(C) Gianola votes against the school bill.
(D) Herstein votes against the recreation bill.
(E) Herstein votes against the school bill.

21. If Gianola votes for the tax bill, then which one of the following statements could be true?

(A) Fu and Gianola each vote for exactly one bill.
(B) Gianola and Herstein each vote for exactly one bill.
(C) Fu votes for exactly two bills.
(D) Gianola votes for the recreation bill.
(E) Herstein votes against the recreation bill.

22. If Gianola votes for exactly two of the three bills, which one of the following statements must be true?

(A) Fu votes for the tax bill.
(B) Gianola votes for the recreation bill.
(C) Gianola votes for the school bill.
(D) Gianola votes against the tax bill.
(E) Herstein votes for the school bill.

23. If one of the members of the council votes against exactly the same bills as does another member of the council, then which one of the following statements must be true?

(A) Fu votes for the tax bill.
(B) Gianola votes for the recreation bill.
(C) Gianola votes against the school bill.
(D) Gianola votes for exactly one bill.
(E) Herstein votes for exactly one bill.

This is an Advanced Linear game with four variables sets: the three bills, R, S, and T; the three votes of Fu; the three votes of Gianola; and the three votes of Herstein. Notably, either the three bills or the three voters could be chosen as the base. Operationally they will produce no difference. We have chosen to use the three bills as the base and create stacks for Fu, Gianola, and Herstein:

$$
\begin{array}{lccc}
\text{H:} & \underline{} & \underline{} & \underline{} \\
\text{G:} & \underline{} & \underline{} & \underline{} \\
\text{F:} & \underline{} & \underline{} & \underline{} \\
 & R & S & T
\end{array}
$$

The choice of voting for (F) or against (A) will fill each space. Applying the rules creates the following basic diagram:

$$
\begin{array}{lccc}
\text{H:} & \underline{} & \underline{} & \underline{A} & \text{(at lst 1F)} \\
\text{G:} & \underline{A} & \underline{} & \underline{} & \text{(at lst 1F)} \\
\text{F:} & \underline{F} & \underline{A} & \underline{} \\
 & R & S & T \\
 & (2F, & (1F, & (1F, \\
 & 1A) & 2A) & 2A)
\end{array}
$$

The rules provide a considerable amount of specific information: the number of "for" and "against" votes each bill receives; the minimum "for" and "against" votes by Fu, Gianola, and Herstein; and certain votes each voter casts. From the supplied information several inferences can be made. First, since there are two votes for the Recreation bill and one vote against the Recreation bill, and it has already been established that Fu votes for the bill and Gianola votes against the bill, it can be inferred that Herstein votes for the Recreation bill:

$$
\begin{array}{lccc}
\text{H:} & \underline{F} & \underline{} & \underline{A} \\
\text{G:} & \underline{A} & \underline{} & \underline{} \\
\text{F:} & \underline{F} & \underline{A} & \underline{} \\
 & R & S & T
\end{array}
$$

Furthermore, since only two voting options exist (F or A), dual-options can be placed on the remaining open spaces:

$$
\begin{array}{lccc}
\text{H:} & \underline{F} & \underline{F/A} & \underline{A} \\
\text{G:} & \underline{A} & \underline{F/A} & \underline{F/A} \\
\text{F:} & \underline{F} & \underline{A} & \underline{F/A} \\
 & R & S & T
\end{array}
$$

Of course, further information about some of the dual-options would affect the choices in other dual-options. Regardless, examining the diagram makes it apparent that the voting possibilities are limited. Since there are only four uncertain spaces and even those have restrictions, why not try to show every possibility? Although there are several ways to identify each possibility, the first step we will take is to look at the votes for the school bill. If Gianola votes against the school bill and

Herstein votes for the school bill, only one solution exists:

	F	F	A
H:	F	F	A
G:	A	A	F
F:	F	A	A
	R	S	T

Possibility #1

In the diagram above, Gianola must vote for the tax bill since each council member votes for at least one bill; since there must be two votes against the tax bill, it can then be inferred that Fu votes against the tax bill.

The other scenario with the school bill switches the votes of Gianola and Herstein:

	F	A	A
H:	F	A	A
G:	A	F	F/A
F:	F	A	F/A
	R	S	T

Unfortunately, this information does not completely determine the votes of Fu and Gianola on the tax bill. One must vote for the bill and the other must vote against. Since this produces only two scenarios, show each one:

H:	F	A	A
G:	A	F	A
F:	F	A	F
	R	S	T

Possibility #2

H:	F	A	A
G:	A	F	F
F:	F	A	A
	R	S	T

Possibility #3

Thus, since all the options for the school bill have been explored, it follows that all the options for the entire voting record have been explored. These three solutions comprise the final setup to the game:

H:	F	F	A
G:	A	A	F
F:	F	A	A
	R	S	T

Possibility #1

H:	F	A	A
G:	A	F	A
F:	F	A	F
	R	S	T

Possibility #2

H:	F	A	A
G:	A	F	F
F:	F	A	A
	R	S	T

Possibility #3

With all of the possibilities fully realized, the questions can be destroyed at light speed.

Question #19: Global, Could Be True. The correct answer choice is (D)

Possibility #3 proves that answer choice (D) could be true and is therefore correct.

Question #20: Local, Must Be True. The correct answer choice is (E)

Only Possibility #3 meets the criteria in the question stem. Possibility #3 confirms that answer choice (E) is correct.

Question #21: Local, Could Be True. The correct answer choice is (A)

Possibilities #1 and #3 meet the condition established in the question stem. Possibility #2 does not meet the condition and is not considered while attacking the question. Possibility #1 proves that answer choice (A) could be true and is therefore correct.

Question #22: Local, Must Be True. The correct answer choice is (C)

Only possibility #3 meets the condition in the question stem. Consequently, it can be determined that answer choice (C) is true.

Question #23: Local, Must Be True. The correct answer choice is (E)

As with question #22, only possibility #3 meets the condition in the question stem. Consequently, it can be determined that answer choice (E) is true.

The test makers build the game around the two-value system of the votes and then provide a considerable amount of information about the game. Since there are only four undetermined votes and each vote has only two options, it follows that there cannot be a large number of possibilities. This inherently restricted situation leads to the decision to Identify the Possibilities.

Game #3: December 2006 Questions 1-5

A clown will select a costume consisting of two pieces and no others: a jacket and overalls. One piece of the costume will be entirely one color, and the other piece will be plaid. Selection is subject to the following restrictions:

If the jacket is plaid, then there must be exactly three colors in it.

If the overalls are plaid, then there must be exactly two colors in them.

The jacket and overalls must have exactly one color in common.

Green, red, and violet are the only colors that can be in the jacket.

Red, violet, and yellow are the only colors that can be in the overalls.

1. Which one of the following could be a complete and accurate list of the colors in the costume?

	Jacket	Overalls
(A)	red	red
(B)	red	violet, yellow
(C)	violet	green, violet
(D)	violet	red, violet
(E)	violet	red, violet, yellow

2. If there are exactly two colors in the costume, then which one of the following must be false?

(A)   At least part of the jacket is green.
(B)   At least part of the jacket is red.
(C)   The overalls are red and violet.
(D)   The overalls are red and yellow.
(E)   The overalls are violet and yellow.

3. If at least part of the jacket is green, then which one of the following could be true?

(A)   The overalls are plaid.
(B)   No part of the jacket is red.
(C)   No part of the jacket is violet.
(D)   At least part of the overalls are yellow.
(E)   At least part of the overalls are violet.

4. Which one of the following must be false?

(A)   Both green and red are colors used in the costume.
(B)   Both green and violet are colors used in the costume.
(C)   Both green and yellow are colors used in the costume.
(D)   Both red and violet are colors used in the costume.
(E)   Both violet and yellow are colors used in the costume.

5. If there are exactly three colors in the costume, the overalls must be

(A)   entirely red or else red and violet plaid
(B)   entirely yellow or else violet and yellow plaid
(C)   entirely violet or else red and violet plaid
(D)   entirely red or else entirely yellow
(E)   entirely red or else entirely violet

This is a Grouping game, with colors assigned to two distinct groups, the jacket and the overalls. One of the initial steps in any grouping game is to attempt to establish, if possible, the number of elements in each group. In this instance, it takes a combination of the game scenario and rules to determine how many elements are in each group.

The second sentence of the game scenario establishes that one of the two items will always be entirely one color, and then the first two rules establish the number of colors in each costume piece if the piece is plaid. Each rule creates a separate fixed numerical distribution:

Distribution #1

> This distribution comes from the first rule, which states that "If the jacket is plaid, then there must be exactly three colors in it."

> The rules states that if the jacket is plaid, then it must have exactly three colors. From the second sentence in the game scenario, then, the overalls must be exactly one color. This creates a 3-1 fixed distribution:

_____
_____
_____   _____
Jacket   Overalls

Distribution #2

> This distribution comes from the second rule, which states that "If the overalls are plaid, then there must be exactly two colors in them."

> The rules states that if the overalls are plaid, then they must have exactly two colors. From the second sentence in the game scenario, then, the jacket must be exactly one color. This creates a 1-2 fixed distribution:

_____
_____   _____
Jacket   Overalls

Because all the possibilities are established when each costume piece is plaid (or, alternately, when each costume piece is entirely one color), these are the only two possible distributions in the game.

With all the numerical possibilities established, you must now focus on the contents of each grouping. In this case, the contents are the colors, and the last three rules of the game address the colors of each piece of the costume. Accordingly, we will examine each of the last three rules against the two numerical possibilities.

Rule #3

This rule states that "The jacket and overalls must have exactly one color in common." From a representational standpoint, an easy way to diagram this rule would be:

However, this diagram, while useful, is not the best possible representation. A better approach would be to use internal diagramming and represent this rule directly on the diagram of each numerical possibility:

The 3-1 distribution: The 1-2 distribution:

In examining rules #4 and #5, we will keep in mind the operating effects of this rule.

Rule #4

This rule specifies that the colors of the jacket can only be green, red, and violet. In the 1-2 distribution, there is not an immediate impact from this rule (there will be an impact when this rule is combined with the rules #3 and #5). In the 3-1 distribution, however, since the jacket is a total of three colors, all three slots are filled:

The 3-1 distribution: The 1-2 distribution:

Note that at this point we have not yet considered the effects of the last rule, but even so we are not going to fill in the remaining slots with options that will ultimately be impossible. For example, in the 3-1, from rule #3 and rule #4, one could assume that the overalls must be either green, red, or violet. While this is true from those two rules, rule #5 will alter those possibilities to only red or violet, and so we will refrain from diagramming further at this time in order to avoid confusion.

<u>Rule #5</u>

This rule specifies that the colors of the overalls can only be red, violet, and yellow. A comparison of the color sets of the jacket and overalls shows that they share only two colors: red and violet. Thus, in the 3-1 distribution, because the jacket has already been determined to be green, red, and violet, the effect of rule #3 is that the overalls can only be red or violet:

The 3-1 distribution:

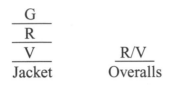

In the 1-2 distribution, the jacket must be red or violet (it cannot be green because it would not have a color in common with the overalls). Thus, one color selection for the overalls must be red or violet. The color selection for the overalls can be any color (other than the color the jacket and overalls have in common, of course):

The 1-2 distribution:

$$\underset{\text{Jacket}}{\underline{\text{R/V}}} \longleftrightarrow \underset{\text{Overalls}}{\overset{\text{R/V/Y}}{\underline{\text{R/V}}}}$$

This representation, while helpful, is not entirely satisfactory because it creates the possibility that an interpretation mistake could be made (for example, accidentally selecting the same color for both color selections for the overalls while visually scanning the arrangement). Since the jacket can only be two colors, a better approach is to create a template for each color option:

The 1-2 distribution, jacket is red:

The 1-2 distribution, jacket is violet:

Overall, there are three templates containing six solutions: two solutions in the 3-1 scenario, and four solutions in the 1-2 scenario (two solutions when red is the common color, two solutions when violet is the common color).

In reviewing the color contents of six templates, the controlling effect of the color sets and rule #3 becomes apparent: red and violet are featured prominently, whereas green and yellow do not appear as much. In fact, green and yellow cannot appear in the same costume together, an inference that is tested in question #4.

Combining all of the information above leads to the following optimal setup for the game:

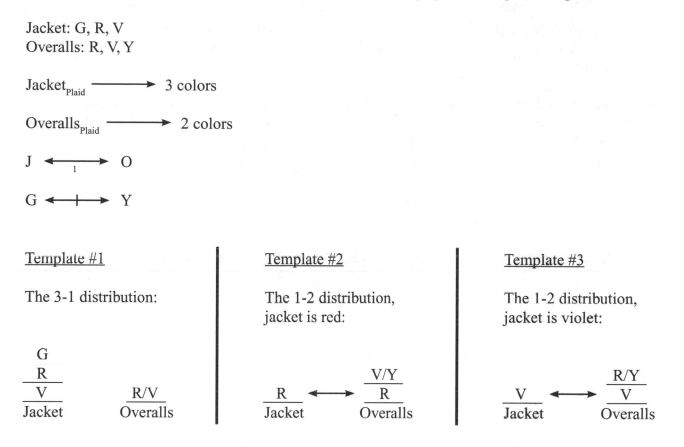

Jacket: G, R, V
Overalls: R, V, Y

At this point we are ready to attack the game with confidence since the setup elegantly captures all six solutions to the game.

Question #1: Global, Could Be True, List. The correct answer choice is (D)

As with any List question, simply apply the rules to the answer choices. In this game, the easiest approach is to apply the rules in the order given. Note that rule #1 does not eliminate any answer choices because none of the answers feature a plaid jacket.

Answer choice (A): This answer choice is eliminated by the rule in the game scenario that indicates that one of the pieces will be plaid (and thus contain multiple colors). Always remember that in a List question the game scenario might contain conditions that can eliminate answer choices.

Answer choice (B): This answer choice is eliminated by rule #3 because the pieces do not have a color in common.

Answer choice (C): This answer violates rule #5 because the overalls cannot be green.

Answer choice (D): This is the correct answer choice.

Answer choice (E): This answer violates rule #2 because when the overalls are plaid they only contain two colors.

Question #2: Local, Cannot Be True. The correct answer choice is (A)

The first item to attend to is converting the "false" statement in the question stem into terms of "true." "Must be false" is functionally equivalent to "cannot be true," and thus this is really a Cannot Be True question.

Proceeding, the condition in the question stem indicates there are only two colors in the costume. Thus, the only applicable scenarios feature the 1-2 fixed distribution (because the 3-1 distribution features three colors in the jacket). Before attacking the answers, quickly scan templates #2 and #3, which feature the 1-2 distribution, and then use those templates to attack the answer choices.

Answer choice (A): This is the correct answer choice. None of the solutions in templates #2 and #3 contain green as a color, and thus it cannot be true that green is a part of the jacket.

Answer choice (B): This answer choice is incorrect. Template #2 has a red jacket.

Answer choice (C): This answer choice is incorrect. Both templates #2 and #3 allow for red and violet overalls.

Answer choice (D): This answer choice is incorrect. Template #2 allows for red and yellow overalls.

Answer choice (E): This answer choice is incorrect. Template #3 allows for violet and yellow overalls.

Question #3: Local, Could Be True. The correct answer choice is (E)

The condition in the question stem establishes that part of the jacket is green, and that can only occur in the 3-1 fixed distribution. Accordingly, refer to template #1 to answer this question.

Answer choice (A): This answer choice is incorrect. In template #1, the jacket is plaid, not the overalls.

Answer choice (B): This answer choice is incorrect. In template #1, part of the jacket is red.

Answer choice (C): This answer choice is incorrect. In template #1, part of the jacket is violet.

Answer choice (D): This answer choice is incorrect. In template #1, the overalls must be red or violet.

Answer choice (E): This is the correct answer choice. In template #1, the overalls must be red or violet, and therefore it could be true that the overalls are violet.

Question #4: Global, Cannot Be True. The correct answer choice is (C)

This is the most difficult question of the game, and one that is not easy to answer from a quick glance at the rules.

First, convert the "false" statement into terms of "true." "Must be false" is functionally equivalent to "cannot be true," and thus this is really a Cannot Be True question.

Second, because this is a Global question, refer to your inferences for any negative deductions. In this case, when discussing the effects of rule #3, rule #4, and rule #5, we arrived at the inference that green and yellow cannot appear in the same costume together:

$$G \longleftrightarrow Y$$

This inference is directly tested in the correct answer, answer choice (C).

However, consider for a moment the approach to take if you did not see that inference while creating the setup. In this game, that would involve two separate steps:

1. Refer to the templates and eliminate incorrect answer choices. Template #1 (the 3-1) quickly eliminates answer choices (A) and (B), template #2 eliminates answer choice (D), and template #3 eliminates answer choice (E). Thus, answer choice (C) is the only remaining answer choice and must be correct.

2. Refer to the hypotheticals created in other questions. This approach is often helpful in Global questions with no obvious answer, and the hypothetical in question #1 eliminates answer choice (D). This approach could be used if step 1 failed to eliminate all incorrect answer choices.

Answer choice (A): This answer choice is incorrect. Template #1 proves that both green and red can be used in the costume together.

Answer choice (B): This answer choice is incorrect. Template #1 proves that both green and violet can be used in the costume together.

Answer choice (C): This is the correct answer choice. As discussed in the game setup, green and yellow can never appear in the costume together.

Answer choice (D): This answer choice is incorrect. Template #2 proves that both red and violet can be used in the costume together.

Answer choice (E): This answer choice is incorrect. Template #3 proves that both violet and yellow can be used in the costume together.

Question #5: Local, Must Be True. The correct answer choice is (E)

The question stem states that there must be exactly three colors in the costume. Templates #2 and #3 feature exactly two colors, and therefore template #1 is the template that applies to this question. The question stem also references the overalls, and since in template #1 the overalls are either red or violet, the correct answer must indicate that the overalls are red or violet, or indicate that the overalls are *not* yellow.

Answer choice (A): This answer choice is incorrect. In template #1, the overalls cannot be plaid.

Answer choice (B): This answer choice is incorrect. In template #1, the overalls cannot be plaid (or yellow, for that matter).

Answer choice (C): This answer choice is incorrect. In template #1, the overalls cannot be plaid.

Answer choice (D): This answer choice is incorrect. In template #1, the overalls cannot be yellow.

Answer choice (E): This is the correct answer choice.

Overall, this game is relatively easy as long as you use the numerical distribution to produce templates, which should enable you to complete the game very quickly with perfect accuracy.

On a Tuesday, an accountant has exactly seven bills—numbered 1 through 7—to pay by Thursday of the same week. The accountant will pay each bill only once according to the following rules:

Either three or four of the seven bills must be paid on Wednesday, the rest on Thursday.
Bill 1 cannot be paid on the same day as bill 5.
Bill 2 must be paid on Thursday.
Bill 4 must be paid on the same day as bill 7.
If bill 6 is paid on Wednesday, bill 7 must be paid on Thursday.

1. If exactly four bills are paid on Wednesday, then those four bills could be

   (A) 1, 3, 4, and 6
   (B) 1, 3, 5, and 6
   (C) 2, 4, 5, and 7
   (D) 3, 4, 5, and 7
   (E) 3, 4, 6, and 7

2. Which one of the following is a complete and accurate list of the bills any one of which could be among the bills paid on Wednesday?

   (A) 3, 5, and 6
   (B) 1, 3, 4, 6, and 7
   (C) 1, 3, 4, 5, 6, and 7
   (D) 2, 3, 4, 5, 6, and 7
   (E) 1, 2, 3, 4, 5, 6, and 7

3. If bill 2 and bill 6 are paid on different days from each other, which one of the following must be true?

   (A) Exactly three bills are paid on Wednesday.
   (B) Exactly three bills are paid on Thursday.
   (C) Bill 1 is paid on the same day as bill 4.
   (D) Bill 2 is paid on the same day as bill 3.
   (E) Bill 5 is paid on the same day as bill 7.

4. If bill 6 is paid on Wednesday, which one of the following bills must also be paid on Wednesday?

   (A) 1
   (B) 3
   (C) 4
   (D) 5
   (E) 7

5. If bill 4 is paid on Thursday, which one of the following is a pair of bills that could also be paid on Thursday?

   (A) 1 and 5
   (B) 1 and 7
   (C) 3 and 5
   (D) 3 and 6
   (E) 6 and 7

6. Which one of the following statements must be true?

   (A) If bill 2 is paid on Thursday, bill 3 is paid on Wednesday.
   (B) If bill 4 is paid on Thursday, bill 1 is paid on Wednesday.
   (C) If bill 4 is paid on Thursday, bill 3 is paid on Wednesday.
   (D) If bill 6 is paid on Thursday, bill 3 is also paid on Thursday.
   (E) If bill 6 is paid on Thursday, bill 4 is also paid on Thursday.

Analysis of Limited Solution Set Game #4: October 1999 Questions 1-6

This is a Defined-Moving, Balanced Grouping game. Even though the bills appear to have a numerical order, it quickly becomes apparent that they can be paid in any order or configuration. More important are the groups of bills paid on the two days, and the key to the game is the Numerical Distribution of the bills to the days. There are seven bills that must be paid on Wednesday or Thursday, and the first rule establishes that three or four will be paid each day. This leads to two fixed distributions:

	Wednesday	Thursday
Fixed Numerical	3	4
Distributions	4	3

These two fixed distributions suggest Identifying the Templates. We will initially set the game up that way and then discuss the decision to Identify the Possibilities. Let us begin by creating a basic diagram:

1 2 3 4 5 6 7

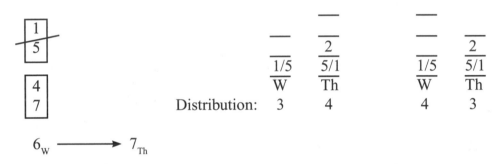

This game also contains a two-value system: all bills must be paid on Wednesday or Thursday. Since bill 1 and bill 5 cannot be paid on the same day, they must be paid on different days. But it is uncertain on which day each is paid, and so a 1/5 dual-option is placed on each day.

The two-value system also affects the last rule. The contrapositive of the last rule is:

Of course, if bill 7 is not paid on Thursday it must be paid on Wednesday, and if bill 6 is not paid on Wednesday, it must be paid on Thursday:

$$7_W \longrightarrow 6_{Th}$$

An examination of the final two rules suggests that the number of solutions is limited. Both rules contain bill 7, and especially important is the power of the 4-7 block. When the 4-7 block is applied to the 4-3 distribution, it has only one placement option; when the 4-7 is applied to the 3-4 distribution, it has only two placement options. On the basis of this limitation, a decision should be made to show all the possibilities of those three options. Each appears as follows:

Possibilities #1 and #2:

```
             3
    7        6
    4        2
   1/5      5/1
    W        Th
    3        4
   (4-7 on Wed.)
```

Possibilities #3 and #4:

```
             7
    3        4
    6        2
   1/5      5/1
    W        Th
    3        4
   (4-7 on Thu.)
```

Possibilities #5 and #6:

```
    3
    7        6
    4        2
   1/5      5/1
    W        Th
    4        3
   (4-7 on Wed.)
```

Each of the three templates includes two possibilities, each dependent on the placement of bill 1 and bill 5. Overall the game has only six solutions. Let us examine each of the three templates in more detail:

> Possibilities #1 and #2: 3-4 Numerical Distribution. When the 4-7 block is placed on Wednesday, no other bills can be paid on Wednesday, and they must all be paid on Thursday. The only remaining uncertainty involves bill 1 and bill 5. Since there are only two options for bill 1 and bill 5, this template contains two solutions.

> Possibilities #3 and #4: 3-4 Numerical Distribution. When the 4-7 block is placed on Thursday, no other bills can be paid on Thursday, and they must all be paid on Wednesday. The only remaining uncertainty involves bill 1 and bill 5. Since there are only two options for bill 1 and bill 5, this template contains two solutions.

> Possibilities #5 and #6: 4-3 Numerical Distribution. The 4-7 block must be placed on Wednesday since there is only one open space on Thursday. When 7 is paid on Wednesday, it can be inferred from the contrapositive of the last rule that bill 6 is paid on Thursday. Since three bills are now paid on Thursday, bill 3 must be paid on Wednesday. The only remaining uncertainty involves bill 1 and bill 5. Because there are only two options for bill 1 and bill 5, this template contains two solutions.

Note that the use of templates to show two possibilities reduces the amount of set up time required. The templates compactly display the uncertainty about bill 1 and bill 5, and there is no need to draw each of the six solutions out individually.

Question #1: Local, Could Be True, List. The correct answer choice is (D)

Possibility template #5 and #6 proves answer choice (D) correct. Using the templates for this question is actually somewhat difficult since the bills are listed in numerical order. Glancing at the 4-3 template, it is apparent that bills 3, 4, and 7 must be paid on Wednesday. Thus, any answer choice that does not contain bills 3, 4, and 7 can be eliminated. That leaves only answer choices (D) and (E). Since answer choice (D) contains bill 5, it is correct. Another approach is to realize that any answer choice that contains bill 2 or 6 must be incorrect. That eliminates every answer choice except answer choice (D).

Question #2: Global, Could Be True, List. The correct answer choice is (C)

The question requests a complete list of the bills that could ever be paid on Wednesday. From possibility template #1 and #2 it can be determined that bills 1, 4, 5, and 7 can be paid on Wednesday. Furthermore, from possibility template #3 and #4 it can be determined that bills 3 and 6 can be paid on Wednesday. Possibility template #5 and #6 does not add any insight. Thus, bills 1, 3, 4, 5, 6, and 7 can be paid on Wednesday and answer choice (C) is correct.

Question #3: Local, Must Be True. The correct answer choice is (A)

Only possibility template #3 and #4 meets the condition in the question stem. Accordingly answer choice (A) is correct. Answer choices (C) and (E) could be true, but they do not *have* to be true.

Question #4: Local, Must Be True. The correct answer choice is (B)

Only possibility template #3 and #4 meets the condition in the question stem. Accordingly answer choice (B) is correct. Answer choices (A) and (E) could be true, but they do not *have* to be true.

Question #5: Local, Could Be True. The correct answer choice is (B)

For the third question in a row, only possibility template #3 and #4 meets the condition in the question stem. Accordingly answer choice (B) is correct. Answer choice (A) could never occur since bill 1 and bill 5 cannot be paid on the same day.

Question #6: Global, Must Be True. The correct answer choice is (C)

This question requires checking all of the possibility templates. Answer choice (A) can be eliminated by possibility template #1 and #2. Answer choice (B) can be eliminated by possibility template #3 and #4. Answer choice (C) is proven correct since only possibility template #3 and #4 pays bill 4 on Thursday, and it is also the case that bill 3 is paid on Wednesday. Answer choice (D) can be eliminated by possibility template #5 and #6. Answer choice (E) can be eliminated by possibility template #1 and #2 and possibility template #5 and #6.

This game is a perfect display of the limiting power of Numerical Distributions. The two fixed distributions in combination with the grouping rules lead to the decision to Identify the Possibilities. And since this is the first game on the October 1999 LSAT, getting off to a good start is critical. Identifying the Possibilities in this game not only allows the smart test taker to answer the questions correctly, but, equally important, also allows the questions to be answered quickly.

It is also interesting to note that the Limited Solution Set games in this section featured one Basic Linear game, one Advanced Linear game, and one Grouping game. The advanced techniques of Identify the Templates and Identify the Possibilities can be used in a variety of games, and you should always examine the setup of a game to determine if the situation is limited.

CHAPTER NINE: SECTION STRATEGY AND MANAGEMENT

Approaching the Section Strategically

For many students, the Logic Games section is the most challenging section on the LSAT. How you approach the section depends in part on how good you are at Games. If Logic Games is your strength, and if anything less than completion of the section means failure to you, then much of what is contained in this chapter will not apply to you. On the other hand, if you are one of the many students who has difficulty with the Logic Games section, then the following advice is designed to assist you.

Time Management

Time management is critical to your success on this section. Each section of the LSAT is 35 minutes in length, and since there are always four games per section, you have exactly 8 minutes and 45 seconds to complete each game and transfer your answers. However, this assumes you will complete all four games. For many students that is not possible or advisable. Strong performance on the LSAT depends on two factors: speed and accuracy. If you rush to complete every question but miss most of them, you will not receive a high score. On the other hand, if, by slowing down, you increase your accuracy, you may be able to increase your score despite doing fewer questions. Consider the following comparison:

	Student #1	Student #2	Student #3
Questions completed in section	24	20	16
Accuracy Rate	50%	75%	100%
Total Correct Answers	12	15	16

Obviously, actual performance in a section depends on a variety of factors, and each student must assess their own strengths and weaknesses. Regardless, the message is the same: you might benefit from slowing down and attempting fewer games. The following table displays the amount of time that should be allotted to each game, depending on how many are attempted:

The Games section is often a bellwether of LSAT performance: the Games section tends to affect the rest of the test. If things go well on Games, most students feel as if the test has gone well.

Of course our preference is to have you complete each question and answer them all correctly. That should always be your goal. But as you practice with the techniques, you will naturally find a level of comfort. That may be doing all four games, or it may involve doing fewer games.

# Games Attempted	Time per Game Attempted
2	17 minutes and 30 seconds
3	11 minutes and 40 seconds
4	8 minutes and 45 seconds

The amount of time listed includes time for transferring answers. You cannot transfer your answers after the 35 minutes have expired.

If you rush through four games and only get 12 correct, then perhaps a better choice would be to attack only three games, spend more time on each game, and try for a higher accuracy rate. Practice will dictate which strategy is superior. Keep in mind though that there is a point of diminishing returns. Spending 35 minutes on one game and answering all six questions correctly does not lead to a very high LSAT score! Instead, you must seek the level that provides you with the best combination of speed and accuracy. We strongly believe that you should attempt at least three games unless there is a compelling reason to the contrary.

Doing Fewer Games

Prior to the test, if you decide to attempt three games or fewer, it would make sense to select the games according to your test-taking strengths. This requires two steps:

1. Know your personal strengths and weaknesses in the Games section. Assess which types of games you prefer, and be detailed in your assessment. For example, do you like Defined Grouping games but dislike Undefined Grouping games?

2. Choose the best games to work on when you begin the section. As the section begins, look for the game types you prefer. Usually a quick reading of the game scenario reveals the game type. Of course, to apply this, you must be intimately familiar with the various game types and corresponding rules.

At the beginning of each Logic Games section, quickly scan the scenario of the first game. If it looks like a game you would like to do or one that seems easy to do, start with that game. If, on the other hand, the first game appears hard or is of a type you dislike, move to the second game and scan the scenario. Complete the same analysis to decide if you want to do the game.

One factor to keep in mind when analyzing games is the number of questions in a game. Suppose two games appear equally attractive to you. In this case you should do the game with the greater number of questions, the theory being you get "more for your money" when there are more questions.

Your actions within each game are also important. As discussed in previous chapters, some questions are inherently more time-consuming than others, while certain questions tend to be more difficult. Perhaps

Apply this strategy after you have proven that you cannot complete four games with accuracy.

All else being equal, do the game with more questions.

the most time-consuming question is the one where each answer choice begins with the word "if." These "5 if" questions are like five questions in one since you typically have to create a new diagram for each answer choice. If you are particularly slow with Games, or if you are behind in a section, it makes sense to skip these questions. Also mentioned earlier, the last question in a game is often the most difficult question. The test makers do this for a variety of reasons. Many students arrive at the last question anxious to finish the question and complete the game. When the question proves difficult, they become unsettled and frustrated, and, as a result, often miss the question. Even worse, this frustration carries into the next game, and they begin the next game without the focus necessary to perform well. This in turn can lead to more missed questions. Keep this in mind whenever you approach the last question in a game. It is imperative that you keep your concentration, and if you do not see a clear path to solving the question, move on.

Avoid "5 if" questions if you are slow on Games.

Using a Timer

An excellent countdown practice timer can be purchased through our website at powerscore.com.

One of the most important tools for test success is a timer. Your timer should be a constant companion during your LSAT preparation. Although not all of your practice efforts should be timed, you should attempt to do as many questions as possible under timed conditions in order to acquaint yourself with the difficulties of the test. Time pressure is the top concern cited by test takers. After all, if the LSAT was a take-home test, no one would be too worried about it.

When using a timer, keep in mind the current Law Services test center regulations concerning time: "Supervisors will keep the official time. You may take an analog (nondigital) wristwatch to the test center. No other timepieces—including electronic timers—are allowed. This is a change from test center regulations of previous testing years" (from the LSAT & LSDAS Registration & Information Book).

Thus, your in-test timer must be a basic analog wristwatch. Although this rule is randomly enforced, you do not want to find yourself in a position of bringing only a digital timer and then having your timer taken away when you have come to depend on it. Second, the supervisors typically will call a warning with five minutes remaining. Since you have a watch this warning announcement should come as no surprise to you. As you progress through the section, check your watch every 4-5 minutes for tracking purposes. There is no need to check it every minute!

Practice doing as many games as possible with your timer so that you can develop a comfortable and familiar pace.

A timer is invaluable because it is an odometer for the section. With sufficient practice you will begin to establish a comfortable test-taking speed and the timer allows you to make sure you are maintaining this appropriate speed. If you go too quickly or too slowly you can then make adjustments during the test. Memorize the following time-markers:

# Games Attempted	Timer Marking Points (counting up from 0 to 35:00 minutes)
2	Move to game #2 at 17 minutes and 30 seconds
3	Move to game #2 at 11 minutes and 40 seconds; Move to game #3 at 23 minutes and 20 seconds;
4	Move to game #2 at 8 minutes and 45 seconds; Move to game #3 at 17 minutes and 30 seconds; Move to game #4 at 26 minutes and 15 seconds

Memorize these marking points!

The above table assumes that each game is done in exactly the allotted time. If you spend more time on one of the games, you must make up that time in another game to stay on pace. If you do one of the games more quickly, that gives you the luxury of spending more time on a later game.

Remember, the LSAT is what is known as a "speeded" test. The test makers presume that the average student cannot finish each section in the allotted time (e.g. that they are "speeded" up). So, most people do not finish all the questions in any of the sections. Increasing speed usually requires a lot of practice and analysis of your performance. The tools we use—Not Laws, knowledge of question and game types, diagrammatic representations, etc.—are designed to help you increase your speed once you are familiar with them. Yes, they take some time to adjust to at first, but this is true of any organized system. Keep practicing and work on becoming comfortable with the timed aspect of the test, and your LSAT score will improve.

The Answer Choices

Transferring your answers from the test booklet to your answer sheet is one of the most important tasks that you perform during the LSAT. Our research indicates that approximately 10% of all test takers make some type of transcription error during a typical five-section test. Since one question can translate into a difference of several percentile points, we strongly advise you to follow one of the two approaches discussed below. The method you choose is entirely dependent upon your personal preferences.

Once you have answered a question, it is critical you correctly transfer that answer choice selection.

1. <u>Logical Grouping</u>. This method involves transferring several answer choices at once, at logical break points throughout each section. For the Reading Comprehension and Logic Games sections, transfer answer choices after you complete the questions for each passage or game. For the Logical Reasoning section, transfer answer choices after you complete each two-page question group. This method generally allows for faster transferring of answers, but some students find they are more likely to make errors in their transcription.

2. <u>Question By Question</u>. As the name implies, this method involves filling in the answer ovals on your answer sheet after you complete each individual question. This method generally consumes more time than the Logical Grouping method, but it usually produces a higher transfer accuracy rate. If you use the Logical Grouping method and find yourself making errors, use this method instead.

Filling in the ovals

Although Law Services prints dire warnings against making stray marks on the answer sheet or incompletely filling in the ovals, these errors are not fatal to your LSAT score. If you believe that Law Services has incorrectly scored your test due to an answer sheet problem, you can have your answer sheet hand scored for an additional fee. Although rarely an issue, machine scoring errors can occur from stray marks, incompletely or improperly filled-in ovals, partially erased answers, or creases in your answer sheet. Remember, answers in your test booklet will not be scored, and two fully blackened answer choices to the same question will not be reviewed by hand scoring.

Three in a row?

Unlike the SAT, the LSAT often has three identical answer choices to consecutive questions (such as three D's), and on several occasions, four identical answer choices in a row have appeared. On the June 1996 LSAT, it even occurred that six of seven answer choices in one section were (C). The use of multiple answer choices in a row is one of the psychological weapons employed by the test makers to unnerve test takers. Any test taker seeing four (D)'s in a row on their answer sheet understandably thinks they have made some type of error, primarily because most tests avoid repetition in their answer choices. If you see three or four answer choices in a row, do not become alarmed, especially if you feel you have been performing well on the section. We are still waiting for the day that the LSAT has five identical correct answers in a row, but we will not be too surprised when it happens.

Guessing Strategy

Because the LSAT does not assess a scoring penalty for incorrect answer choices, you should always guess on every question that you cannot complete during the allotted time. However, because some answer choices are more likely to occur than others, you should not guess randomly. The following tables indicate the frequency of appearance of Logic Game answer choices over the years.

Never leave an answer blank on the LSAT! There is no penalty for wrong answers and so it is in your best interest to guess on any problem you cannot complete.

All Logic Game Answer Choices June 1991 - October 2010*

	A%	B%	C%	D%	E%
% appearance of each answer choice throughout the entire section	19.4	20.5	19.8	20.2	20.1

The table above documents the percentage each answer choice appeared as a percentage of all Logic Game answer choices between June 1991 and October 2010 inclusive. If history holds, when guessing on the LSAT Logic Games section, you would be best served by always guessing answer choice (B). Do not choose random answer choices; do not put in a pattern such as A-B-C-D-E etcetera. Although guessing answer choice (B) does not guarantee you will get the questions correct, if history is an indicator then guessing answer choice (B) gives you a better chance than guessing randomly. Consider the following comparison of students guessing on five consecutive answer choices:

We discuss guessing strategy and many other LSAT concepts in the Free LSAT Help Section of the powerscore.com website.

Correct Answer Choice	Student #1 Answer Choices (Pattern)	Student #2 Answer Choices (Random)	Student #3 Answer Choices (All B's)
B	A	D	B
D	B	C	B
E	C	A	B
A	D	E	B
C	E	B	B
# Correct =	0	0	1

Guessing randomly reduces each question to an independent event with a 1 in 5 chance of success.

Although one question may not seem significant, it adds up over four sections, and depending on where you are in the scoring scale, it can increase your score several points. And every point counts! By guessing answer choice (B), you increase your chances of getting an answer correct.

The next table summarizes the percentage appearance of answer choices in just the last five answer choices of the Logic Games section.

Last Five Answer Choices Per Logic Games Section June 1991 - October 2010*

	A%	B%	C%	D%	E%
% appearance of each answer choice throughout last five answer choices of the Logic Games section	22.1	20.9	17.6	20.3	19.1

Within the last five questions, the guessing strategy changes to dictate that you should guess answer choice (A). Notice the significant statistical deviation of answer choice (C). Answer choice (C) is not a good answer choice to guess in the last five answer choices!

The next table summarizes the percentage appearance of the last answer choice in each game over the years.

Last Answer Choice per Game June 1991 - October 2010*

% appearance of each answer choice for the last question of each game per section	A%	B%	C%	D%	E%
Game #1:	13.6	15.2	27.3	28.8	15.2
Game #2:	13.6	28.8	21.2	15.2	21.2
Game #3:	13.6	24.2	21.2	22.7	18.2
Game #4:	21.2	19.7	24.2	19.7	15.2
Average	15.5	22.0	23.5	21.6	17.4

*These statistics do not include the unreleased February 1998, February 2001, February 2002, February 2003, February 2004, February 2005, February 2006, February 2007, February 2008, February 2009, and February 2010 LSAT administrations.

The statistics in this final table have a greater variation since the sample (just over 264 total questions) is smaller.

Please keep in mind that the above advice holds only for pure guessing. If you are attempting to choose between two answer choices, do not choose on the basis of statistics alone!

We have provided the statistics for the last answer choice in each game in the interest of public knowledge. We do not think it is in your best interest to memorize a separate guessing strategy for the final question of each game. Rather, it would probably be better to know that the overall statistics suggest answer choice (C) is the best choice for the last question in each game.

On a related note, if you are a strong test taker who correctly answers most questions but occasionally does not finish a section, quickly review the answer choices you have previously selected and use the answer that appears least as your guessing answer choice. For example, if you have completed twenty questions in a section, and your answers contain a majority of (A)'s, (C)'s, (D)'s, and (E)'s, guess answer choice (B) for all of the remaining questions.

Test Readiness

The day before the test

Be sure you have received your LSAT admission ticket from Law Services. Double-check the information on the admission ticket for accuracy.

If you are not familiar with your test center, drive by the test center and examine the testing room and parking situation. This will alleviate any anxiety or confusion on the day of the test.

On the day before the LSAT, we recommend that you study very little, if at all. The best approach for most students is to simply relax as much as possible. Read a book, go see a movie, or play a round of golf. If you feel you must study, we recommend that you only briefly review each of the concepts covered in this book.

Eat only bland or neutral foods the night before the test and try to get the best sleep possible.

Do not study hard the day before the test. If you haven't learned the material by then, that final day won't make much difference.

The morning of the test

Attempt to follow your normal routine when you get up. For example, if you read the paper every morning, do so on the day of the test. If you do not regularly drink coffee, do not start on the morning of the LSAT. Constancy in your routine will allow you to focus on your primary objective: performing well on the test.

Dress in layers, so you will be warm if the test center is cold, but also able to shed clothes if the test center is hot.

Take along a clear plastic bag with all your pencils, sharpeners, highlighters, etc. Your bag, according to Law Services, can only be a maximum of one gallon and must be stored under your chair.

For the September/October, December, and February LSAT administrations, all students must arrive at the test center no later than 8:30 AM. For the June LSAT administration, all students must arrive at the test center no later than 12:30 PM.

Even though test regulations require you to be at the center at a certain hour, the test will not begin immediately. Bring the morning newspaper or other reading material so that you have something to do while waiting.

We strongly believe that performing well requires you to believe that you can perform well. As you prepare to leave for the test, run through the test in your head, visualizing an exceptional performance. Imagine how you'll react to each game, reading passage, and logical reasoning question. Many athletes use this same technique to achieve optimal performance.

At the test center

Yes, you read that correctly. You will be thumbprinted at the test center. This is done for test security purposes.

Upon check-in, test supervisors will ask you to present your admission ticket, one form of acceptable personal identification, and a thumbprint. Supervisors are instructed to deny admission to anyone who does not present a photo ID with signature.

The test supervisors will assign each examinee a seat. You are not permitted to choose your own seat.

Once you are seated, the test supervisors will read you the rules and regulations of the test, and have you write a certifying statement that attests that the person taking the test is the person whose name appears on the answer sheet and that you are taking the test for the sole purpose of admission to law school. Typically, the actual test will not begin until thirty to forty-five minutes after you are seated.

LSAC updates the test center regulations often, so be sure to check with LSAC prior to your test for any new policies.

You are allowed only the following items on your testing desk:

> Identification
> Wooden pencils
> Erasers
> A simple analog watch
> A highlighter
> A non-automatic pencil sharpener
> Tissues

The test supervisors keep the official time, but they are not obligated to use a digital timer. They should announce a five-minutes-remaining warning for each test section.

Be sure to ask the test supervisors how they will keep time. There have been many problems with sections being mis-timed.

You may work only on the assigned section. Testing supervisors may circulate throughout the testing room to ensure that all examinees are working in the appropriate section. Blackening of answer spaces on your answer sheet must be done before time is called for any given section. You will not be permitted time after the test to clean up your answer sheet or transfer answers from your test book to your answer sheet.

If you find it necessary to leave the room during the test, you must obtain permission from the supervisor. You will not be permitted to make up any missed time.

All test materials, including test books and answer sheets, are the property of Law Services and must be returned to Law Services by test supervisors after every administration. Legal action may be taken against an examinee who removes a test book and/or reproduces it.

If you engage in any misconduct or irregularity during the test, you may be dismissed from the test center and may be subject to other penalties for misconduct or irregularity. Actions that could warrant such consequences are creating a disturbance; giving or receiving help; working on or reading the test during a time not authorized by the supervisor; removing test materials or notes from the testing room; taking part in an act of impersonation or other forms of cheating; or using books, calculators, ear plugs, headsets, rulers, papers of any kind, or other aids. The penalties for misconduct are high: you may be precluded from attending law school and becoming a lawyer.

If you encounter a problem with the test supervision or test center itself, report it to a test supervisor. Reportable problems include: power outages, mis-timing of test sections, and any unusual disturbances caused by an individual.

If you feel anxious or panicked for any reason before or during the test, close your eyes for a few seconds and relax. Think of other situations where you performed with confidence and skill.

After the test

Test results will be available online approximately three weeks after the test, and a hard copy of your score will arrive approximately five weeks after the test.

The Logic Games section has a very abstract relationship to the practice of the law in the sense that the section does test the ability to juggle a large number of related facts as the circumstances around those facts change, just like a typical lawsuit. However, that said, the Games do not test a natural aptitude for law because when you practice law and work on cases, you have a context for everything, and everything is placed in the real world. Logic Games, by contrast, are just made up scenarios that no one really cares about or relates to personally.

Final Note

We would like to take a moment to thank you for choosing to purchase the *PowerScore LSAT Logic Games Bible*. We hope you have found this book useful and enjoyable. If you have any questions, comments, or suggestions, please do not hesitate to email your comments to us at lgbible@powerscore.com. Study hard and best of luck on the LSAT!

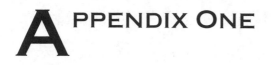

APPENDIX ONE

Comprehensive Game Classification

We recommend that you complete as many released LSATs as possible; working through more tests increases the opportunities you have to apply the techniques learned in this book. Released LSATs are tests created by Law Services, the producers of the LSAT. In general, we do not recommend that you study simulated LSATs. Released LSATs can be purchased from PowerScore through our website, http://www.powerscore.com, or from Law Services through their website, http://www.lsat.com. We recommend obtaining as many as possible.

In the list below we have identified every released LSAT from the modern era (June 1991 to the present) and listed the Law Services publication identifier. Not all tests are available for purchase at this time. Each game is classified according to the PowerScore system. The classification can be used to confirm that your analysis of each game is correct or alternately as a guide to finding more games of each type.

<u>Game</u>   **<u>Game Type</u>**

June 1991 (LSAT PrepTest 1)

Game #1:   Circular Linearity: Balanced   (This game is presented in Chapter Seven.)
Game #2:   Advanced Linear: Unbalanced: Underfunded
Game #3:   Pure Sequencing
Game #4:   Advanced Linear: Unbalanced: Underfunded

October 1991 (LSAT PrepTest 2, LSAT TriplePrep, Volume 1)

Game #1:   Pure Sequencing
Game #2:   Basic Linear: Unbalanced: Overloaded   (This game is presented in Chapter Two.)
Game #3:   Grouping: Defined-Moving, Balanced, Numerical Distribution
Game #4:   Advanced Linear: Balanced

December 1991 (LSAT PrepTest 3; LSAT TriplePrep, Volume 2)

Game #1:   Advanced Linear: Balanced
Game #2:   Basic Linear: Balanced
Game #3:   Advanced Linear: Balanced
Game #4:   Grouping: Partially Defined

February 1992 (LSAT PrepTest 4; LSAT TriplePrep, Volume 1)

Game #1:   Pure Sequencing
Game #2:   Grouping: Defined-Fixed, Unbalanced: Underfunded
Game #3:   Advanced Linear: Unbalanced: Underfunded
Game #4:   Mapping-Supplied Diagram, Identify the Possibilities

June 1992 (LSAT PrepTest 5; LSAT TriplePrep, Volume 1)

Game #1: Basic Linear: Undefined
Game #2: Grouping: Defined-Fixed, Unbalanced: Overloaded
Game #3: Grouping: Defined-Fixed, Unbalanced: Overloaded
Game #4: Advanced Linear: Balanced

October 1992 (LSAT PrepTest 6; LSAT TriplePrep, Volume 2)

Game #1: Grouping: Defined-Moving, Balanced, Numerical Distribution
Game #2: Pure Sequencing
Game #3: Mapping-Supplied Diagram, Directional
Game #4: Mapping-Spatial Relations (This could classified as a Grouping game: the map has little impact since the bridges are not straight.)

December 1992 (LSAT PrepTest 18; 10 Actual, Official LSAT PrepTests)

Game #1: Grouping: Defined-Fixed, Balanced
Game #2: Basic Linear: Balanced, Identify the Templates
Game #3: Mapping- Spatial Relations
Game #4: Grouping: Partially Defined

February 1993 (LSAT PrepTest 7; LSAT TriplePrep, Volume 2; 10 Actual, Official LSAT PrepTests)

Game #1: Basic Linear: Balanced
Game #2: Advanced Linear: Balanced   (This game is presented in Chapter Three.)
Game #3: Grouping: Defined-Moving, Balanced, Numerical Distribution
Game #4: Advanced Linear: Balanced, Identify the Templates

June 1993 (LSAT PrepTest 8; LSAT TriplePrep, Volume 3)

Game #1: Basic Linear: Unbalanced: Overloaded
Game #2: Circular Linearity: Identify the Possibilities
Game #3: Advanced Linear: Balanced
Game #4: Grouping: Partially Defined

October 1993 (LSAT PrepTest 9; LSAT TriplePrep, Volume 3; 10 Actual, Official LSAT PrepTests)

Game #1: Grouping: Defined-Fixed, Unbalanced: Underfunded, Numerical Distribution
Game #2: Grouping: Defined-Fixed, Unbalanced: Overloaded
Game #3: Pattern   (This game is presented in Chapter Seven.)
Game #4: Mapping-Supplied Diagram (Like many Mapping games this one has strong grouping elements.)

February 1994 (LSAT PrepTest 10; LSAT TriplePrep, Volume 3; 10 Actual, Official LSAT PrepTests)

Game #1: Pure Sequencing
Game #2: Basic Linear: Unbalanced: Overloaded, Numerical Distribution, Identify the Possibilities
Game #3: Pattern
Game #4: Grouping/Linear Combination   (This game is presented in Chapter Five.)

June 1994 (LSAT PrepTest 11; LSAT TriplePrep Plus with Explanations; 10 Actual, Official LSAT PrepTests)

Game #1: Grouping: Defined-Moving, Balanced
Game #2: Basic Linear: Balanced, Numerical Distribution
Game #3: Grouping: Defined-Moving, Unbalanced: Overloaded
Game #4: Pattern: Identify the Possibilities

October 1994 (LSAT PrepTest 12; LSAT TriplePrep Plus with Explanations; 10 Actual, Official LSAT PrepTests)

Game #1: Basic Linear: Balanced, Identify the Possibilities
Game #2: Grouping: Defined-Fixed, Balanced
Game #3: Grouping: Partially Defined
Game #4: Pattern: Identify the Possibilities

December 1994 (LSAT PrepTest 13; LSAT TriplePrep Plus with Explanations; 10 Actual, Official LSAT PrepTests)

Game #1: Grouping: Defined-Fixed, Balanced
Game #2: Basic Linear: Balanced
Game #3: Grouping/Linear Combination   (This game is presented in Chapter Five.)
Game #4: Pattern

February 1995 (LSAT PrepTest 14; 10 Actual, Official LSAT PrepTests)

Game #1: Grouping: Defined-Moving, Balanced
Game #2: Advanced Linear: Balanced, Identify the Templates
Game #3: Grouping: Partially Defined
Game #4: Advanced Linear: Unbalanced: Overloaded

June 1995 (LSAT PrepTest 15; 10 Actual, Official LSAT PrepTests)

Game #1: Basic Linear: Balanced
Game #2: Mapping   (Again, one with strong grouping elements. This game is presented in Chapter Seven.)
Game #3: Basic Linear: Unbalanced: Underfunded, Numerical Distribution
Game #4: Grouping: Defined-Fixed, Unbalanced: Overloaded

September 1995 (LSAT PrepTest 16; 10 Actual, Official LSAT PrepTests)

Game #1: Grouping: Defined-Fixed, Balanced
Game #2: Advanced Linear: Balanced, Identify the Templates
Game #3: Advanced Linear: Unbalanced: Underfunded
Game #4: Pattern

December 1995 (LSAT PrepTest 17)

Game #1: Basic Linear: Balanced
Game #2: Grouping: Defined-Fixed, Unbalanced: Underfunded
Game #3: Advanced Linear: Unbalanced: Overloaded
Game #4: Advanced Linear: Balanced, Identify the Possibilities

February 1996 (LSAT SuperPrep Test A)

Game #1: Basic Linear: Balanced
Game #2: Advanced Linear: Balanced, Identify the Templates (2)
Game #3: Advanced Linear: Balanced
Game #4: Advanced Linear: Unbalanced: Overloaded, Identify the Templates

June 1996 (LSAT PrepTest 19; 10 More Actual, Official LSAT PrepTests)

Game #1: Basic Linear: Balanced   (This game is presented in Chapter Two.)
Game #2: Advanced Linear: Balanced, Numerical Distribution, Identify the Templates
Game #3: Grouping: Defined-Fixed, Balanced
Game #4: Grouping: Defined-Fixed, Balanced

October 1996 (PrepTest 20; 10 More Actual, Official LSAT PrepTests)

Game #1:   Advanced Linear: Unbalanced: Underfunded
Game #2:   Grouping: Defined-Fixed, Unbalanced: Overloaded   (This game is presented in Chapter Four.)
Game #3:   Pattern
Game #4:   Grouping/Linear Combination

December 1996 (LSAT PrepTest 21; 10 More Actual, Official LSAT PrepTests)

Game #1:   Grouping: Defined-Moving, Balanced, Numerical Distribution, Identify the Templates
Game #2:   Basic Linear: Unbalanced: Overloaded
Game #3:   Advanced Linear: Unbalanced: Underfunded
Game #4:   Advanced Linear: Unbalanced: Underfunded   (This game is presented in Chapter Two.)

February 1997 (The Official LSAT PrepTest with Explanations, Volume One)

Game #1:   Basic Linear: Unbalanced: Overloaded, Numerical Distribution
Game #2:   Grouping: Defined-Fixed, Balanced, Identify the Possibilities
Game #3:   Pattern
Game #4:   Advanced Linear: Balanced, Identify the Possibilities

June 1997 (LSAT PrepTest 22; 10 More Actual, Official LSAT PrepTests)

Game #1:   Grouping: Defined-Moving, Balanced   (This game is presented in Chapter Four.)
Game #2:   Advanced Linear: Balanced, Identify the Templates
Game #3:   Advanced Linear: Balanced
Game #4:   Grouping: Defined-Fixed, Unbalanced: Overloaded

October 1997 (LSAT PrepTest 23; 10 More Actual, Official LSAT PrepTests)

Game #1:   Basic Linear: Balanced
Game #2:   Grouping: Undefined
Game #3:   Grouping: Defined-Fixed, Unbalanced: Overloaded
Game #4:   Pattern   (This game is presented in Chapter Seven.)

December 1997 (LSAT PrepTest 24; 10 More Actual, Official LSAT PrepTests)

Game #1:   Grouping: Defined-Moving, Balanced, Numerical Distribution, Identify the Possibilities
Game #2:   Basic Linear: Balanced
Game #3:   Advanced Linear: Balanced
Game #4:   Grouping: Defined-Fixed, Unbalanced: Overloaded

June 1998 (LSAT PrepTest 25; 10 More Actual, Official LSAT PrepTests)

Game #1:   Grouping: Partially Defined
Game #2:   Grouping: Defined-Moving, Balanced
Game #3:   Grouping: Defined-Moving, Balanced, Identify the Templates
Game #4:   Advanced Linear: Balanced

September 1998 (LSAT PrepTest 26; 10 More Actual, Official LSAT PrepTests)

Game #1:   Advanced Linear: Balanced   (This game is presented in Chapter Three.)
Game #2:   Basic Linear: Balanced   (This game is presented in Chapter Two.)
Game #3:   Grouping: Defined-Moving, Balanced, Numerical Distribution, Identify the Templates
Game #4:   Grouping: Defined-Fixed, Unbalanced: Overloaded, Identify the Possibilities

December 1998 (LSAT PrepTest 27; 10 More Actual, Official LSAT PrepTests)

Game #1: Basic Linear: Balanced
Game #2: Grouping/Linear Combination, Numerical Distribution, Identify the Templates
Game #3: Grouping: Defined-Moving, Balanced, Numerical Distribution, Identify the Templates (This game is presented in Chapter Eight.)
Game #4: Basic Linear: Balanced, Identify the Possibilities

February 1999 (LSAT SuperPrep Test B)

Game #1: Pure Sequencing
Game #2: Grouping: Partially Defined
Game #3: Circular Linearity
Game #4: Grouping: Defined-Fixed, Unbalanced: Overloaded

June 1999 (LSAT PrepTest 28; 10 More Actual, Official LSAT PrepTests)

Game #1: Basic Linear: Balanced, Identify the Templates
Game #2: Grouping: Defined-Fixed, Unbalanced: Underfunded   (This game is presented in Chapter Four.)
Game #3: Advanced Linear: Balanced
Game #4: Advanced Linear: Balanced, Identify the Possibilities   (This game is presented in Chapter Eight.)

October 1999 (LSAT PrepTest 29)

Game #1: Grouping: Defined-Moving, Balanced, Numerical Distribution, Identify the Possibilities   (This game is presented in Chapter Eight.)
Game #2: Grouping: Defined-Fixed, Unbalanced: Overloaded, Identify the Templates
Game #3: Basic Linear: Balanced
Game #4: Basic Linear: Unbalanced: Overloaded, Numerical Distribution

December 1999 (LSAT PrepTest 30)

Game #1: Grouping: Defined-Fixed, Unbalanced: Underfunded
Game #2: Grouping/Linear Combination, Numerical Distribution
Game #3: Advanced Linear: Balanced, Identify the Templates
Game #4: Basic Linear: Balanced

February 2000 (LSAT SuperPrep Test C)

Game #1: Grouping: Defined-Fixed, Balanced
Game #2: Pure Sequencing
      The rules produce two separate sequences that capture all possible orders in this game.
Game #3: Grouping: Partially Defined, Numerical Distribution
Game #4: Advanced Linear: Unbalanced: Overloaded, Numerical Distribution

June 2000 (LSAT PrepTest 31)

Game #1: Advanced Linear: Unbalanced: Overloaded, Numerical Distribution
Game #2: Grouping: Undefined
Game #3: Basic Linear: Unbalanced: Underfunded, Identify the Templates   (This game is presented in Chapter Eight.)
Game #4: Grouping/Linear Combination, Numerical Distribution

October 2000 (LSAT PrepTest 32)

Game #1: Grouping/Linear Combination
Game #2: Grouping: Partially Defined, Numerical Distribution
Game #3: Basic Linear: Balanced
Game #4: Advanced Linear: Unbalanced: Underfunded, Identify the Templates

December 2000 (LSAT PrepTest 33)

Game #1: Pure Sequencing   (This game is presented in Chapter Seven.)
Game #2: Grouping: Undefined   (This game is presented in Chapter Four.)
Game #3: Grouping: Defined-Moving, Unbalanced: Overloaded, Numerical Distribution
Game #4: Advanced Linear: Unbalanced: Underfunded

June 2001 (LSAT PrepTest 34)

Game #1: Basic Linear: Unbalanced: Underfunded, Identify the Templates
Game #2: Basic Linear: Unbalanced: Overloaded, Identify the Possibilities
Game #3: Basic Linear: Balanced, Identify the Templates
Game #4: Grouping: Defined-Moving, Balanced, Identify the Templates

October 2001 (LSAT PrepTest 35)

Game #1: Grouping: Defined-Fixed, Unbalanced: Overloaded (see the Profile Charting note on our website at
          http://www.powerscore.com/gamesbible)
Game #2: Grouping: Defined-Fixed, Unbalanced: Underfunded, single Fixed 1-2-2-3-1-2 Numerical Distribution
Game #3: Advanced Linear: Unbalanced: Underfunded
Game #4: Basic Linear: Balanced-Moving, single Unfixed 2-1-1-1-1-1-0 Numerical Distribution

December 2001 (LSAT PrepTest 36)

Game #1: Grouping: Undefined
Game #2: Advanced Linear: Balanced, Identify the Possibilities
Game #3: Advanced Linear: Balanced
Game #4: Advanced Linear: Balanced, Identify the Templates

June 2002 (LSAT PrepTest 37)

Game #1: Advanced Linear: Balanced
Game #2: Advanced Linear: Balanced
Game #3: Grouping: Defined-Fixed, Balanced, Identify the Templates
Game #4: Advanced Linear: Balanced, Identify the Templates

October 2002 (LSAT PrepTest 38)

Game #1: Pure Sequencing
Game #2: Advanced Linear: Balanced
Game #3: Grouping: Defined-Fixed, Balanced, Identify the Templates
Game #4: Advanced Linear: Balanced, Identify the Templates

December 2002 (LSAT PrepTest 39)

Game #1: Advanced Linear: Balanced
Game #2: Grouping: Partially Defined
Game #3: Advanced Linear: Unbalanced, Identify the Templates
Game #4: Grouping: Undefined

June 2003 (LSAT PrepTest 40)

Game #1: Basic Linear: Balanced   (This game is presented in Chapter Two.)
Game #2: Grouping/Linear Combination
Game #3: Grouping: Partially Defined
> Like many "Mapping" games, this game is really a Grouping game: the focus is on the connections, and they can best be displayed as grouping relationships.
Game #4: Grouping: Defined-Fixed, Unbalanced: Overloaded

September 2003 (LSAT PrepTest 41)

Game #1: Basic Linear: Balanced, Identify the Templates
Game #2: Advanced Linear: Balanced, Identify the Possibilities
Game #3: Grouping: Defined-Moving, Balanced, Numerical Distribution
Game #4: Circular Linearity

December 2003 (LSAT PrepTest 42)

Game #1: Grouping: Defined-Fixed, Unbalanced: Overloaded
Game #2: Basic Linear: Balanced
Game #3: Grouping/Linear Combination, Identify the Templates
Game #4: Grouping: Partially Defined, Numerical Distribution

June 2004 (LSAT PrepTest 43)

Game #1: Basic Linear: Balanced, Identify the Templates (4)
Game #2: Pure Sequencing   (This game is presented in Chapter Six.)
Game #3: Advanced Linear: Balanced
Game #4: Grouping: Partially Defined, Numerical Distribution

October 2004 (LSAT PrepTest 44)

Game #1: Basic Linear: Unbalanced: Underfunded, Numerical Distribution   (This game is presented in Chapter Two.)
Game #2: Grouping: Defined-Fixed, Balanced
> The Monday Tuesday Wednesday aspect of this game does not serve a linear purpose but is instead used for grouping purposes. Hence, this game is not a Grouping/Linear Combination game.
Game #3: Advanced Linear: Balanced   (This game is presented in Chapter Three.)
Game #4: Advanced Linear: Unbalanced: Underfunded, Numerical Distribution

December 2004 (LSAT PrepTest 45)

Game #1: Basic Linear: Balanced
> The two sequences control the placement of all variables.
Game #2: Grouping/Linear Combination: Numerical Distribution, Identify the Templates (2)
Game #3: Grouping: Undefined   (This game is presented in Chapter Four.)
Game #4: Grouping: Defined-Fixed, Unbalanced: Underfunded, Numerical Distribution (This game is presented in Chapter Four.)

June 2005 (LSAT PrepTest 46)

Game #1: Basic Linear: Balanced
Game #2: Advanced Linear: Balanced
Game #3: Advanced Linear: Balanced, Identify the Templates (2)
Game #4: Grouping: Defined-Fixed, Unbalanced: Underfunded, Numerical Distribution (This game is presented in Chapter Eight.)

October 2005 (LSAT PrepTest 47)

Game #1:   Basic Linear: Balanced
Game #2:   Grouping: Partially Defined
Game #3:   Grouping: Partially Defined, Unbalanced: Underfunded, Numerical Distribution
Game #4:   Advanced Linear: Unbalanced: Underfunded

December 2005 (LSAT PrepTest 48)

Game #1:   Grouping: Undefined
Game #2:   Pure Sequencing
Game #3:   Grouping: Partially Defined, Unbalanced: Underfunded, Numerical Distribution
Game #4:   Grouping/Linear Combination: Identify the Templates (4)

June 2006 (LSAT PrepTest 49)

Game #1:   Basic Linear: Unbalanced: Overloaded
Game #2:   Grouping: Defined-Moving, Unbalanced: Overloaded, Numerical Distribution
Game #3:   Grouping: Undefined
Game #4:   Basic Linear: Balanced

September 2006 (LSAT PrepTest 50)

Game #1:   Basic Linear: Unbalanced: Underfunded, Identify the Templates (2)
Game #2:   Grouping: Defined-Fixed, Unbalanced: Overloaded, Numerical Distribution
Game #3:   Advanced Linear: Unbalanced: Underfunded
Game #4:   Pure Sequencing: Numerical Distribution, Identify the Templates (2)

December 2006 (LSAT PrepTest 51)

Game #1:   Grouping: Defined-Moving, Unbalanced: Overloaded, Numerical Distribution, Identify the Templates (2)
                    (This game is presented in Chapter Eight.)
Game #2:   Basic Linear: Balanced, Identify the Templates (2)
Game #3:   Advanced Linear: Balanced   (This game is presented in Chapter Three.)
Game #4:   Pure Sequencing

June 2007 (Released as a Free LSAT)

Game #1:   Basic Linear: Balanced, Identify the Possibilities (6)
Game #2:   Grouping: Partially Defined
Game #3:   Basic Linear: Unbalanced: Underfunded
Game #4:   Grouping: Partially Defined

September 2007 (LSAT PrepTest 52)

Game #1:   Pure Sequencing
Game #2:   Grouping: Defined-Fixed, Balanced
Game #3:   Grouping/Linear Combination: Defined-Fixed, Balanced
Game #4:   Pure Sequencing

December 2007 (LSAT PrepTest 53)

Game #1: Grouping: Defined-Moving, Balanced, Identify the Templates (2)
Game #2: Pure Sequencing
Game #3: Advanced Linear: Balanced
Game #4: Advanced Linear: Balanced

June 2008 (LSAT PrepTest 54)

Game #1: Grouping: Undefined
Game #2: Advanced Linear: Unbalanced: Overloaded, Numerical Distribution
Game #3: Basic Linear: Balanced
Game #4: Basic Linear: Balanced, Identify the Templates (3)

October 2008 (LSAT PrepTest 55)

Game #1: Grouping: Defined-Fixed, Balanced
Game #2: Basic Linear: Partially Defined, Numerical Distribution, Identify the Templates (6)
Game #3: Pure Sequencing
Game #4: Advanced Linear: Balanced

December 2008 (LSAT PrepTest 56)

Game #1: Basic Linear: Balanced
Game #2: Grouping: Defined-Fixed, Unbalanced: Underfunded, Numerical Distribution
Game #3: Grouping: Defined-Fixed, Unbalanced: Underfunded, Numerical Distribution
Game #4: Advanced Linear: Balanced, Numerical Distribution

June 2009 (LSAT PrepTest 57)

Game #1: Basic Linear: Balanced
Game #2: Advanced Linear: Unbalanced: Overloaded, Numerical Distribution
Game #3: Grouping: Defined-Fixed, Unbalanced: Overloaded
Game #4: Advanced Linear: Unbalanced: Overloaded, Numerical Distribution

September 2009 (LSAT PrepTest 58)

Game #1: Basic Linear: Balanced
Game #2: Grouping: Undefined
Game #3: Advanced Linear: Balanced
Game #4: Grouping: Partially Defined

December 2009 (LSAT PrepTest 59)

Game #1: Advanced Linear: Unbalanced: Overloaded, Numerical Distribution, Identify the Templates (6)
Game #2: Basic Linear: Balanced
Game #3: Grouping: Defined-Fixed, Unbalanced: Overloaded
Game #4: Basic Linear: Balanced

June 2010 (LSAT PrepTest 60)

Game #1: Advanced Linear: Balanced
Game #2: Basic Linear: Balanced, Identify the Templates (2)
Game #3: Basic Linear: Balanced, Identify the Possibilities (7)
Game #4: Advanced Linear: Balanced

October 2010 (LSAT PrepTest 61)

Game #1: Grouping: Defined-Moving, Balanced, Numerical Distribution
Game #2: Pure Sequencing
Game #3: Grouping/Linear Combination
Game #4: Basic Linear: Balanced

LSAT Classification Notes:

1. The December 1993 LSAT was nondisclosed. It was later administered as the September 1995 LSAT and then released as PrepTest 16.

2. Starting in 1996, the February LSATs have been nondisclosed. In April 2000, the February 1997 LSAT was released as the Official LSAT PrepTest with Explanations, Volume One. In May 2004, the February 1996, February 1999, and February 2000 LSATs were released in The Official LSAT SuperPrep.

3. The classification for any test released after the publication of this book can be found on the book website at:

www.powerscore.com/gamesbible

APPENDIX TWO

Consolidated Answer Key

The *PowerScore LSAT Logic Games Bible* contains 30 games, each of which appeared on a previously released LSAT, and the answers to every LSAT game used in this book are found in the game explanations. The consolidated answer key in this section contains two parts: the first part provides a quick chapter-by-chapter answer key for students who need to find the answers quickly, and the second part provides a comprehensive listing of the source of all LSAT questions used in this book. The second part is especially helpful for students who are taking practice LSATs and want to know ahead of time which questions we have used in this book. They can then skip those questions ahead of taking the test, or avoid taking certain tests until later.

Chapter-by-Chapter Answer Key

The chapter-by-chapter answer key lists every game in this book in the presented order and proves the correct answer for each question in each game. You can use this answer key as a quick reference when you are solving problems. Each problem is explained in more detail in the text of the chapter.

Chapter Two: Linear Games

Game #1: June 1996 Questions 1-7
    1. B   2. E   3. C   4. E   5. D   6. D   7. C

Game #2: September 1998 Questions 8-12
    8. C   9. E   10. A   11. C   12. A

Game #3: June 2003 Questions 1-5   73
    1. D   2. C   3. A   4. C   5. D

Game #4: October 2004 Questions 1-6
    1. C   2. D   3. E   4. E   5. D   6. A

Game #5: October 1991 Questions 6-12
    6. D   7. E   8. A   9. E   10. C   11. B   12. C

Game #6: December 1996 Questions 18-24
    18. B   19. C   20. B   21. A   22. E   23. D   24. E

Chapter-by-Chapter Answer Key

Chapter Three: Advanced Linear Games

Game #1: September 1998 Questions 1-7
    1. C   2. B   3. A   4. D   5. E   6. A   7. D

Game #2: October 2004 Questions 13-17
    13. E   14. C   15. A   16. E   17. D

Game #3: December 2006 Questions 11-15
    11. D   12. E   13. D   14. D   15. E

Game #4: February 1993 Questions 8-12
    8. B   9. C   10. E   11. E   12. E

Chapter Four: Grouping Games

Game #1: October 1996 Questions 6-12
    6. A   7. E   8. B   9. A   10. A   11. C   12. E

Game #2: June 1997 Questions 1-7
    1. D   2. C   3. E   4. B   5. E   6. B   7. B

Game #3: December 2004 Questions 13-17
    13. B   14. E   15. D   16. B   17. A

Game #4: June 1999 Questions 6-12
    6. D   7. B   8. C   9. B   10. A   11. B   12. D

Game #5: December 2000 Questions 6-12
    6. D   7. E   8. D   9. C   10. A   11. A   12. B

Game #6: December 2004 Questions 18-22
    18. A   19. A   20. E   21. C   22. C

Chapter Five: Grouping/Linear Combination Games

Game #1: February 1994 Questions 19-24
    19. B   20. C   21. E   22. B   23. D   24. A

Game #2: December 1994 Questions 12-17
    12. B   13. A   14. E   15. D   16. B   17. E

Chapter-by-Chapter Answer Key

Chapter Six: Pure Sequencing Games

Game #1: December 2000 Questions 1-5
1. C   2. A   3. E   4. D   5. B

Game #2: June 2004 Questions 6-12
6. C   7. E   8. E   9. A   10. D   11. A   12. C

Chapter Seven: The Forgotten Few

Pattern Game #1: October 1997 Questions 19-24
19. D   20. D   21. B   22. E   23. C   24. A

Pattern Game #2: October 1993 Questions 14-18
14. D   15. B   16. B   17. C   18. D

Circular Linearity Game #1: June 1991 Questions 1-7
1. B   2. A   3. B   4. E   5. E   6. C   7. E

Mapping Game #1: June 1995 Questions 7-13
7. D   8. A   9. E   10. E   11. D   12. E   13. A

Chapter Eight: Advanced Features and Techniques

Numerical Distribution Game #1: June 2005 Questions 17-22
17. C   18. C   19. B   20. D   21. E   22. D

Numerical Distribution Game #2: December 1998 Questions 13-19
13. D   14. A   15. C   16. A   17. E   18. B   19. E

Limited Solution Set Game #1: June 2000 Questions 14-18
14. C   15. B   16. A   17. E   18. A

Limited Solution Set Game #2: June 1999 Questions 19-23
19. D   20. E   21. A   22. C   23. E

Limited Solution Set Game #3: December 2006 Questions 1-5
1. D   2. A   3. E   4. C   5. E

Limited Solution Set Game #4: October 1999 Questions 1-6
1. D   2. C   3. A   4. B   5. B   6. C

This section contains a reverse lookup that cross references each game according to the source LSAT. The tests are listed in order of the PrepTest number (if any). The date of administration is also listed to make the process easier. If a test is not listed, then no questions from that exam were used in this book.

Games listed under each test begin by listing the *Logic Games Bible* chapter the game appears in, the game date, and then the question numbers.

For information on obtaining the publications that contain the LSATs listed below, please visit our Free LSAT Help area at www.powerscore.com/lsat/help/pub_ident.htm

PrepTest 1—June 1991 LSAT

> Chapter 7, Circular Linearity Game #1: June 1991 Questions 1-7

PrepTest 2—October 1991 LSAT

> Chapter 2, Game #5: October 1991 Questions 6-12

PrepTest 7—February 1993 LSAT

> Chapter 3, Game #4: February 1993 Questions 8-12

PrepTest 9—October 1993 LSAT

> Chapter 7, Pattern Game #2: October 1993 Questions 14-18

PrepTest 10—February 1994 LSAT

> Chapter 5, Game #1: February 1994 Questions 19-24

PrepTest 13—December 1994 LSAT

> Chapter 5, Game #2: December 1994 Questions 12-17

PrepTest 15—June 1995 LSAT

> Chapter 7, Mapping Game #1: June 1995 Questions 7-13

PrepTest 19—June 1996 LSAT

> Chapter 2, Game #1: June 1996 Questions 1-7

Test-by-Test Game Use Tracker

PrepTest 20—October 1996 LSAT

    Chapter 4, Game #1: October 1996 Questions 6-12

PrepTest 21—December 1996 LSAT

    Chapter 2, Game #6: December 1996 Questions 18-24

PrepTest 22—June 1997 LSAT

    Chapter 4, Game #2: June 1997 Questions 1-7

PrepTest 23—October 1997 LSAT

    Chapter 7, Pattern Game #1: October 1997 Questions 19-24

PrepTest 26—September 1998 LSAT

    Chapter 3, Game #1: September 1998 Questions 1-7
    Chapter 2, Game #2: September 1998 Questions 8-12

PrepTest 27—December 1998 LSAT

    Chapter 8, Numerical Distribution Game #2: December 1998 Questions 13-19

PrepTest 28—June 1999 LSAT

    Chapter 4, Game #4: June 1999 Questions 6-12
    Chapter 8, Limited Solution Set Game #2: June 1999 Questions 19-23

PrepTest 29—October 1999 LSAT

    Chapter 8, Limited Solution Set Game #4: October 1999 Questions 1-6

PrepTest 31—June 2000 LSAT

    Chapter 8, Limited Solution Set Game #1: June 2000 Questions 14-18

PrepTest 33—December 2000 LSAT

    Chapter 6, Game #1: December 2000 Questions 1-5
    Chapter 4, Game #5: December 2000 Questions 6-12

Test-by-Test Game Use Tracker

PrepTest 40—June 2003 LSAT

Chapter 2, Game #3: June 2003 Questions 1-5

PrepTest 43—June 2004 LSAT

Chapter 6, Game #2: June 2004 Questions 6-12

PrepTest 44—October 2004 LSAT

Chapter 2, Game #4: October 2004 Questions 1-6
Chapter 3, Game #2: October 2004 Questions 13-17

PrepTest 45—December 2004 LSAT

Chapter 4, Game #3: December 2004 Questions 13-17
Chapter 4, Game #6: December 2004 Questions 18-22

PrepTest 46—June 2005 LSAT

Chapter 8, Numerical Distribution Game #1: June 2005 Questions 17-22

PrepTest 51—December 2006 LSAT

Chapter 8, Limited Solution Set Game #3: December 2006 Questions 1-5
Chapter 3, Game #3: December 2006 Questions 11-15

Flawed Setups: Checks, X's, and O's

Consider the setup from the first game presented in Chapter One, on page 9:

L M N O P S T[7]

For this same game, there are some preparation companies who recommend a setup similar to the following:

	1	2	3	4	5	6	7
T	X	X	X				
S							
P	O	X	X	X	X	X	O
O					X		
N	X						
M	X	X	O	X	O	X	X
L							X

In the setup, the possibilities are often shown as checks, crosses, and zeros, as indicated by the legend below:

    X = impossible
    O = possible
    ✓ = must be

The second setup is certainly more complex and confusing than the first setup and that will obviously have a negative effect when doing the questions. It will also be much more difficult to use the second diagram when answering individual questions because the grid takes time to reproduce.

In addition, this type of setup forces you to take an extra step when working with each variable and space. For instance, when you look at the first space to consider what is possible, there are three X's present and one

O. Seeing this, you must then translate the information to realize that the three X's represent M, N, and T, while the O represents P. This extra step has the effect of adding a layer of abstraction to your thinking. And on the LSAT, the more abstract things are, the more difficult they tend to be. In contrast, consider the first setup: when you look at the first space you can immediately see that P could possibly appear there and that M, N, and T cannot be placed in the space. There is no layer of abstraction present and this will allow you to work more quickly and accurately.

When working with games, avoid the use of X's, O's, and ✓'s which add abstraction. And should you use any preparation material that contain setups such as these, immediately discard that preparation material. It will lower your score!

MORE INFORMATION

Additional PowerScore Resources

We believe that the *PowerScore LSAT Logic Games Bible* is the single best written resource for attacking the Logic Games section of the LSAT.

Because new LSATs appear every several months, and access to accurate and up-to-date information is critical, we have devoted a section of our website to *Logic Games Bible* students. This online resource area offers updates on recent LSAT Game sections, discussions of additional Logic Game concepts, and general information. The *LSAT Logic Games Bible* online area can be accessed at:

www.powerscore.com/gamesbible

If you would like to comment on the *Logic Games Bible*, or make suggestions for additional sections, please send us a message at lgbible@powerscore.com. We thank you for purchasing this book, and we look forward to hearing from you!

CONTACTING POWERSCORE

POWERSCORE INTERNATIONAL HEADQUARTERS:

PowerScore Incorporated
57 Hasell Street
Charleston, SC 29401

Toll-free information: (800) 545-1750
Website: www.powerscore.com
Email: lsat@powerscore.com

POWERSCORE LSAT PUBLICATIONS INFORMATION:

For information on the *LSAT Logic Games Bible, LSAT Logic Games Bible Workbook, LSAT Logical Reasoning Bible, LSAT Reading Comprehension Bible, LSAT Deconstructed Series* or *LSAT Logic Games Ultimate Setups Guide*.

Website: www.powerscore.com/pubs.htm

POWERSCORE FULL-LENGTH LSAT COURSE INFORMATION:

Complete preparation for the LSAT. Classes available nationwide.

Website: www.powerscore.com/lsat/lsat.htm
Request Information: www.powerscore.com/contact.htm

POWERSCORE VIRTUAL LSAT COURSE INFORMATION:

Complete online preparation for the LSAT. Classes available worldwide.

Website: www.powerscore.com/lsat/virtual.htm
Request Information: www.powerscore.com/contact.htm

POWERSCORE WEEKEND LSAT COURSE INFORMATION:

Fast and effective LSAT preparation: 16 hour courses, 99th percentile instructors, and real LSAT questions.

Website: www.powerscore.com/lsat/weekend.htm
Request Information: www.powerscore.com/contact.htm

POWERSCORE LSAT TUTORING INFORMATION:

One-on-one meetings with a PowerScore LSAT expert.

Website: www.powerscore.com/lsat/tutoring.htm
Request Information: www.powerscore.com/contact.htm

POWERSCORE LAW SCHOOL ADMISSIONS COUNSELING INFORMATION:

Personalized application and admission assistance.

Website: www.powerscore.com/lsat/admissions.htm
Request Information: www.powerscore.com/contact.htm